THE BUILD-IT BOOK OF
CABINETS &
BUILT-INS

Other TAB books by the author:

No. 1002
$14.95

THE BUILD-IT BOOK OF
CABINETS &
BUILT–INS

BY S. BLACKWELL DUNCAN

 TAB BOOKS Inc.
BLUE RIDGE SUMMIT, PA. 17214

FIRST EDITION

FIRST PRINTING—JANUARY 1979
SECOND PRINTING—APRIL 1981

Library of Congress Cataloging in Publication Data

Duncan, S Blackwell.
    The build-it book of cabinets and built-ins.

    Includes index.
    1. Cabinet-work. 2. Built-in furniture. I. Title.
TT197.D85   684.1'6   78-11248
ISBN 0-8306-9854-X
ISBN 0-8306-1002-2 pbk.

Cover photo courtesy of *The Family Handyman* ® magazine.

The Family Handyman® is a trademark of The Webb Company,
trademark registered in U.S. Patent and Trademark Office.

Contents

Introduction

This book is based upon two particular premises. The first premise is that the skills, materials, tools, and above all, the essential principles of cabinetmaking, are the same for all cabinetry, built-in projects and general woodworking. The details differ, but the broad outline remains. Once you begin to understand what cabinetmaking is all about, you are capable of building a simple cabinet. And if you can build one cabinet, you can build any cabinet. Not with equal ease, of course, and not without some practice and experience, but that's the idea, anyway.

The second premise, unsubstantiated but reasonable, is that almost anyone can learn the cabinetmaking trade and attain a respectable degree of expertise.

Once you have the fundamentals of cabinetmaking well fixed in your mind, and with reference materials available for specifics if, as, and when necessary, then you are ready. You are equipped, at least mentally, to proceed with the construction of cabinets and built-ins to your heart's content. Pleasure and eventual satisfaction are assured. Furthermore, with the development of both skills and workshop, you can even advance to the making of fine furniture, should you desire. But that's another book.

This book is set up in three sections, though not actually designated so. The first chapter is a pep talk of sorts. It voices the thought that cabinets and built-ins can help the reader-homeowner to achieve a gratifying style of gracious and trouble-free living. The author points out that the reader can design cabinetry which he (or she) can then proceed to build, and that no prior experience is needed.

The next six chapters deal (sometimes literally) with the nuts and bolts of cabinetmaking. Here you will find discussions of the tools, equipment, materials and hardware pertinent to—often, peculiar to—the cabinetmaking craft. These chapters are a primer on joinery, the essence of fine cabinetmaking.

The remainder of the book is a mix of procedures, methods, operations, ideas, and actual projects. The projects are discussed not for their own sake, but rather to exemplify certain simple aspects of cabinetmaking. The projects are not to be slavishly imitated; they are intended to inspire you to design and construct projects which will fulfill your own needs.

In using this book, the author suggests that you first read through the entire volume, in order to get a broad overview of cabinetmaking, and then relate the contents to your own views and needs. Go back for further study to those parts which you find most relevant to your situation. You will find that specific information and details are spread throughout the volume, and that everything relating to, say, table saws, or dadoes, or sandpapering, is not necessarily clustered in one place. Details were inserted wherever they seemed most appropriate.

You should realize, too, that this book is not the last word in cabinetmaking. Nor, for that mater, is any other book. Cabinetmaking is a large and complex field, and it overlaps into areas of expertise. No single volume could contain all of the related material. You may well come up with some questions or problems which are not answered here. You may need some information on practices or procedures which are not covered. So be it. Further research at the local library will probably satisfy your requirements.

The author claims to be neither an expert in the field nor a master cabinetmaker. There are very few experts, and most of them are apparently self-appointed. So you may find some statements that are arguable, or some procedures that could be handled differently, or some methods which might be modified. Very well. That's the point, you see—the cabinetmaking craft has many aspects, and nobody has all the answers or a corner on all the ideas.

Much depends upon specific circumstances, materials, equipment, conditions, designs, personal preferences and judgments, desired end results, and a host of other odds and ends. All of this makes it difficult to pin down matters with neat, flat statements. So where does that leave us?

That leaves us with a lot of cabinets and built-ins to be put together, that's where, and it's time to get about it. Once you set your feet on the trail, you'll find your way all right. Just watch for the markers along the route.

S. Blackwell Duncan

Chapter 1
The Case for Cabinetry

The mention of cabinets immediately brings to mind a particular room in the house—the kitchen. That's understandable, because every house, no matter how small, has at least a few feet of base cabinets fitted with counter tops, above which are mounted a few linear feet of wall and overhead cabinets. The mention of built-ins usually conjures up an image of the same room, since we normally equate built-in cabinetry with such built-in appliances as drop-in ranges, trash compactors, and stove-top units. And it is indeed true that in many (perhaps in a majority of) homes, the use of cabinets and built-ins is confined wholly to the kitchen, if you choose to exclude closets from your definition. Cabinets and built-ins are often found in no other rooms of the house, with the possible exception of the bathrooms, where provision is made for a minimal amount of storage space.

Nor are most cabinets and so-called built-ins (sometimes it is difficult to distinguish between the two) built on the job nowadays. Instead, they are mass-produced at a factory, shipped to the job site, assembled to whatever degree is necessary, set into place, and trimmed out to form a part of the finished structure. The principal reason for installing factory-built units and components is a simple one—cost. Since expert finish carpenters are both expensive and difficult to locate, the contractor finds his life much easier if he just orders stock factory units from a wholesaler and fits them into place with a minimum of labor.

This system often has a lot of drawbacks for the homeowner, however. In the first place, merchandise lines of stock cabinets are designed primarily with the kitchen in mind. Cabinets from a stock line used in other areas of the house must usually be altered or redecorated in some fashion to suit the need at hand. In the second place, the homeowner, unless he is particularly lucky and finds exactly what he wants, is greatly restricted in his choices. The cabinetry offered may not be of a style, finish or shape to his liking. There is little opportunity for substitution and only a few standard models are available for combining and juggling about to make up a complete cabinet installation that will fulfill the needs.

As far as the true built-ins are concerned, they are not purchasable from any factory or sales room. Built-ins are exactly what the name implies. They must be constructed on the job to answer a particular requirement and to conform to a certain series of dimensions. All of this means that the only reasonable way to attain a satisfactory complement of cabinetry and built-ins is to design them yourself and either have them built by someone else or construct them yourself.

Why bother? Other than in the kitchen and baths, do you really need cabinets and built-ins around the house? Perhaps not. Much depends on how simple your life-style is, and what you are disposed to gather about you in the way of chattels and possessions. If you can pack everything you own into two suitcases, and home is merely a place to hang your hat until you move on to the next spot, then cabinets and built-ins probably won't do much for you. On the other hand, if your home is your castle, and you are like most other folks, cabinets and built-ins can contribute importantly to making your life easier and more enjoyable. And, of course, if you happen to be an inveterate do-it-yourselfer, the challenge of constructing your own cabinetry and built-ins is difficult to ignore.

Consider these two facts. The first is that we are all collectors, or perhaps a better term would be accumulators. This can be readily verified by consulting various consumer-product sales reports. The second fact is that most homes are woefully deficient in storage and display space. A quick analysis of these facts suggests that if most of us have a lot of goodies and most of us don't have a place to put those goodies, then most of us *need* a place to put those goodies. And that in turn clearly spells out cabinetry and built-ins. Cabinets and built-ins of all sorts can be designed into a new house during the planning stages with a minimum of effort, and cabinets and built-ins can be installed in virtually any older house without any undue amount of time or trouble.

There isn't a room in the house that can't use some storage space, especially if there is little or none to begin with. Even the kitchen, which presumably already has cabinets, deserves a hard look. The cabinets are there, but are they efficient and effective, doing the kind of job that you need done? There are many ways that stock kitchen cabinetry can be improved upon. In the case of a new kitchen, the cabinetry can be designed ahead of time to fulfull all manner of special needs. A library or den can be fitted out with various kinds of book shelving and perhaps cabinets and drawer space as well. The same can be done in a living room. A dining room or dining area needs storage space for linens, tableware, crockery, and table accessories. A pantry consists of an entire room full of shelves and cabinets, and perhaps counter space as well. All bathrooms should have a certain amount of built-in storage compartments and the master bathroom should be equipped with a substantial amount of space for toweling, linens, sick-room equipment, medicines and such.

Bedrooms, sadly enough, are seldom fitted out with anything beyond a small closet. How much better if the closet is large and equipped with stacks of drawers, separate compartments for shirts, trousers and other wearing apparel, racks for shoes and hats, and other special stowaway spots. Children's rooms are much more livable and convenient for all concerned if they contain built-in storage areas for toys, desks for school work, and shelves for books and all the paraphernalia that children like to have by them. Workshops and recreations rooms cry out for cabinets and built-ins of all kinds. Persons with a penchant for collecting things, like silver or china or glassware or old firearms, recognize the need for adequate storage and display space. After all, how much enjoyment can you get from a fine collection of Hummel figurines if they are wrapped in newspaper and stuffed under a bed? Yes, the list of uses for cabinets and built-ins is almost endless.

The cost of custom-made cabinetry and built-ins constructed on the job site by a professional finish carpenter is high. The price tag is comprised almost entirely of labor charges. Materials, however, constitute a relatively minor item in the schedule of charges, since most cabinets and built-ins don't require very much in the way of material. Time is the deciding factor. The assembly of a small amount of material into a fine piece of cabinetwork demands a considerable number of manhours. It follows then that, if *you* provide the labor instead of hiring a professional, several thousand dollars' worth of cabinets and built-ins can be put together for a cost of a few hundred dollars. Furthermore, the results will be exactly what you wanted. Very well, then, what is needed to prepare you for achieving your cabinetry goals?

The prerequisites are few, and all readily within reach. First, you need motivation—an incentive—to undertake the work. You could undertake the work as a hobby, as an enjoyable pastime, or as a response to a creative urge to put something together of your own design and with your own two hands. Or, you could undertake the work to answer a sudden need for some sort of cabinetry, and you had been unable to locate anyone to do the job for you. You may feel that you could do a better job than anyone else anyway. Or, your financial state could be the motivating factor; you have the time and the aptitude, but not the cash to attain your cabinetry goal.

Specific developed skills are not necessary at the outset. Admittedly, you'll eventually need a certain amount of mechanical aptitude and manual dexterity, but these can be developed in due time. Even those who constantly complain that they have five thumbs on each hand will find that with a little practice they can do a respectable job, and that they possess more mechanical know-how than they gave themselves credit for having. Motivation, plus a willingness to learn, will nearly always overcome that initial barrier of fumbling around, and you will find that you can do a much better job than you thought possible. In any event, there is no such thing as an instant cabinetmaker. Learning, knowledge, experimentation, and experience gained by doing are the principal ingredients of good craftsmanship.

You will also need patience. An abundance of it. Cabinetmaking is not a slap-dash operation like building a sandbox for junior or knocking together a shelter for your pet goat. The phrase, care and patience, cannot be repeated too many times where cabinetmaking is in question. This kind of work requires large chunks of time. Even small projects, especially if intricate or ornate, require hours and hours of labor. There is no way around this fact. Furthermore, cabinetmaking cannot be hurried, even by an expert. Each job will take a certain amount of time under the best of conditions and with the best of skills, and the old adage that haste makes waste is certainly valid in this field of endeavor.

Most cabinetmaking projects proceed in slow steps. Those steps involve careful planning, detailed layout and double-checking of dimensions, careful fitting of joints, elapsed-time periods for glue curing or finish drying, endless sandpapering and rubbing, and unhurried but intensive scrutiny throughout the entire course of the job. Before attempting any cabinetmaking work, adjust your mental attitude and tell yourself that you will not push the job and that you will do it correctly. That's the only way to achieve excellent results, and excellent results are what every true craftsman aims for. The finished actuality may turn out to be something different than the initial hope, but isn't that the normal course in most human activities?

Aside from the actual cabinetmaking skills involved, most of which are gained primarily through experience, one of your greatest assets will be knowledge. This entails learning as much as you can about any number of woodworking particulars. You'll need to find out what sorts of materials are available to you, what their different characteristics are, and which ones will be best for your purposes. You must have some idea of the potentialities of the hardware and fasteners which will help you to do the job. You'll need to know something about surface preparation, finishes, and finishing procedures. You'll require some concept of the various types of joints used in cabinetmaking, and of the details of joinery. You'll need an acquaintance with the various hand tools and power tools, some of them specialized and some not, which are used in cabinetmaking; and you'll have to understand how to use them most effectively. You'll have to learn how various types of cabinetry are assembled, and the many procedures used to assemble them, not only so that you can execute the procedures, but also so that you can use this knowledge to design your own projects. All in all, the more information you have at your fingertips concerning the entire field of cabinetmaking and woodworking, the easier your tasks will be, and the more successful the results.

And lastly, even for the most rudimentary projects you must have a certain amount of equipment. A large and exotically equipped workshop is not necessary for cabinetmaking, although of course that would be nice. In fact, you really don't need even a small workshop, just so long as you have some corner where you can park a workbench or a pair of sawhorses covered with planks so that you can work. In the case of built-in projects, this may actually be the job site itself. You can undertake the plain and simple projects with only the most basic of hand tools. As the projects become more complex, however, you'll probably find that you'll both need and want additional equipment. Often the purchase of this equipment is easily justified, so you might just as well accustom yourself ahead of time to the fact that you'll be laying out cash for more equipment, and perhaps even for a formal workshop, before your cabinetmaking days are needed.

How do you go about cabinetmaking? It would be foolish to say that cabinetmaking is a simple thing, because really it isn't. Cabinetmaking is detailed and precise, even at the beginning stages, and there seems to be an incredible amount of knowledge to be acquired and skills to be learned before one can become a master cabinetmaker. On the other hand, there is nothing arcane about cabinetmaking, and anyone with sufficient interest can learn the craft in a reasonable period of time, at least to the degree that he can do a creditable job. The levels to which the cabinetmaking skills are carried depends entirely upon the individual.

To start you you'll need to identify the requirements, or desires, or maybe both, for cabinetry and/or built-ins in your home. Your first step will be to acquire the basic knowledge of the cabinetmaking craft, not only by reading the remainder of this book, but by absorbing additional material as well. Coupled with this learning should be some on-the-spot research at your local lumberyard and hardware stores to discover what is available to you in the way of tools, equipment, and materials. Once you have this preliminary information in hand, you can commence to design the cabinetry projects which will fulfill your needs.

You can learn just so much, however, through reading and research. And much of what you do pick up will eventually be lost unless you utilize that knowledge in practical application. In other words, there comes a time when you will learn and retain best by doing, and so you must commit yourself to starting a project. One intermediate step that is extremely helpful here, if you can make the necessary arrangements, is to observe a professional cabinetmaker or finish carpenter as he goes about his daily work. If you can garner some personal instruction at the same time, so much the better. Even the briefest of lessions learned from a professional wood-worker is highly valuable, especially when you are starting out as a rank beginner in the woodworking field.

Whether or not this course is possible for you, you must eventually pick up the tools youself and start to work. In the early stages, you should proceed slowly and carefully, referring to instructional materials whenever you feel the need. If you are not quite sure about how to do something, stop and look it up or ask questions. The folks who staff your hardware and lumber supply outlets are often most helpful with suggestions, directions, and general information. Many of them have had long experience in the field. As you go along building your own projects, you will gradually acquire confidence, skill, and solid knowledge of procedures and operations, and it probably will not be long before you are reasonably self-reliant. There will be problems, setbacks, and frustrations, to be sure. Expect them. But remember that thousands of people have traveled this route successfully before you, so don't become discouraged.

Chapter 2
Tools and Equipment

Certain cabinets and built-in projects can be accomplished with a bare minimum of tools, just the ordinary ones found in any home workshop. Most projects can be finished without recourse to any power tools whatsoever. However, as the projects become more complicated, the use of specialized and increasingly sophisticated tools and equipment will generally be necessary to make the task go easier and to insure that the results are satisfactory. Most of us, although we thoroughly enjoy the process of putting something together, like to see the finished results in a reasonable length of time, and tend to think in terms of hours, rather than days as the oldtime craftsmen did. As cabinets and built-ins take on the quality and appearance of fine furniture, the use of special tools and equipment common to the woodworking and cabinetmaking fields becomes essential.

The tools listed below are all basic woodworking tools. Some of them are available in hardware stores, while others must be purchased in specialty shops. There is some duplication of use among them, and the specific tool that you choose will depend largely upon which one you feel will do the best job for you. Don't be dismayed by the great number of items offered. It is unlikely that you would ever need them all. Nor would any given project be likely to call for the use of such an array of tools. The object of this exercise is simply to make you aware of what is available and what may prove of value to you in

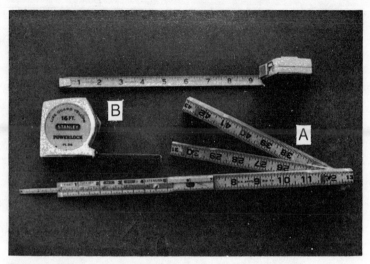

Fig. 2-1. (A) Carpenter's or zig-zag rule. (B) Flexible metal tapes.

your project. By knowing what tools are available and what their capabilities are, you can pick and choose to suit your needs and you won't have to acquire the implements until your project reaches the stage where they're required. There is little question that many of the specialty tools, even though used infrequently, do save a great deal of time and produce better results.

LAYOUT AND MEASURING TOOLS

The processes of layout and measurement are continuous throughout the life of any given project. Accurate and precise measurements are essential, and the quality of the tools used must be high in order to insure good results.

The bench rule is nothing more than a standard ruler much like the one you used in school. The bench rule's superiority owes to its precise manufacture and to its composition (normally stainless steel). Bench rules usually are one foot long and divided into sixtenths of an inch; they are used for making simple measurements and for adjusting dividers. The folding rule is similar to the bench rule but comes in a 36-inch length and collapses in the middle. Some bench and folding rules are graduated in tenths and twelfths of an inch. Metric rules are also available. The ordinary yardstick, manufactured from good quality hardwood, is a useful measuring device to have on hand. (Beware, though, of the shoddy giveaways of the hardware store.) None of these rules should be used as straightedges; they simply are not sufficiently accurate.

One of the most commonly used rules is variously called the zigzag, carpenter's rule, or extension rule. This rule is usually made of wood, and extends to 72 inches in 8-inch sections. The better models include an 8-inch brass slide for making inside measurements (Fig. 2-1A). Equally common and useful is the tape rule (Fig. 2-1B). This is the familiar long flexible metal tape which rolls back into a metal case. Available lengths vary with the brand, but common sizes are 6 feet, 8 feet, 10 feet, 12 feet, 16 feet, and 20 feet. To be sure of obtaining an accurate tape, always buy a quality brand name. Generally speaking, the extension rule and the tape rule are the ones you will use the most, and there are times when one will do the job while the other will not, and vice-versa.

The device used to square off a line or to mark an angle is called a square, and there are several different types. The try square (Fig. 2-2), available in assorted sizes, is used for making 90-degree angles and squaring the edges of boards; it can also be used to a limited degree in taking measurements. The try square is sometimes called a miter square and can be bought in a 45-degree configuration. As with any square, quality and precision milling are most important. The cheaper models frequently are not true. The combination square (Fig. 2-3) is similar to the try square, but with some added features. Marking and testing either 90-degree or 45-degree miters is possible; the blade will slide in the head, and there is a built-in level and scriber. The combination square also can be used for making limited measurements. It is generally available only in a 12-inch size.

Cabinetry projects frequently call for the measurement or marking of angles other than 45 or 90 degrees. In this case, a device

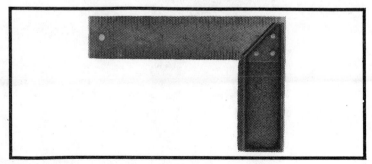

Fig. 2-2. Try square. Courtesy of Stanley Tools.

Fig. 2-3. Adjustable combination square. Courtesy of Stanley Tools.

known as the sliding T-bevel (Fig. 2-4) comes into use. The blade slides to a limited degree and is adjustable to any angle. In operation, the blade is set by a protractor or against a framing square and then locked into place. The framing square (Fig. 2-5) is commonly used in general carpentry, and is handy to have around for cabinetwork and built-ins. The 2-foot size is one of the most common, but larger sizes are readily available. The framing square is especially helpful in establishing accurate 90-degree angles, and can be used to lay out other angles as well. The Squangle (Fig. 2-6) is an interesting tool which is handy in numerous ways. It can be used as a T-square, try square, protractor, straightedge, or in layout work. It has a built-in level.

A constant chore in building cabinets and built-ins is checking to make sure that everything is level, true and plumb. The first essential tool for this work is a level (Fig. 2-7). You will probably want two,

Fig. 2-4. Sliding T-bevel. Courtesy of Stanley Tools.

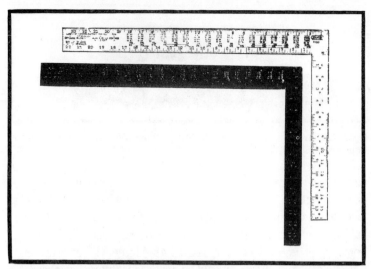

Fig. 2-5. This type of square is variously known as a rafter, flat, or carpenter's square, depending upon its markings. Courtesy of Stanley Tools.

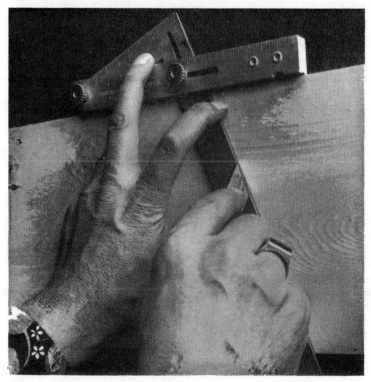

Fig. 2-6. A Squangle in use. Ducan Photos.

23

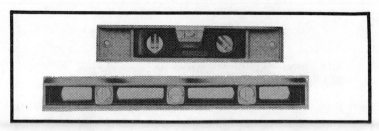

Fig. 2-7. Above, small torpedo level. Below, longer utility or carpenter's level. Courtesy of Stanley Tools.

and perhaps more. One could be small, maybe 6 or 8 inches in length, while the other should be about 2 feet long. A good spirit or bubble level has accurately milled edges and is absolutely straight. The bubble arrangements should allow top reading and side reading. Some spirit levels include a preset 45-degree vial as well. For reasons of safety all vials should be covered in unbreakable glass.

Determining whether an edge or a surface is level is very difficult if the line is not true. The best way to insure trueness is with the use of a straightedge. In a pinch a good level can itself be used as a straightedge. A good framing or flat square can be turned to the same purpose. However, the most useful types of straightedges seem to be 4, 6, and 8 feet long. Though you can buy them, you can also make your own. You can construct one containing a degree of accuracy that will be sufficient for all but the very finest of work. A long piece of electroplated strap steel might do the job, or you could trim a piece from a sheet of particle board or hardboard and use the straight mill edge of the material with excellent results.

If a surface or an edge is exactly vertical, then it is plumb. One way to determine this is with a level. However, there is another device which in some instances is more convenient. The device is a plumb bob, and it consists of nothing more than a pointed weight attached to a length of string (Fig. 2-8A). By securing one end of the string and letting the bob fall free, you can quickly see whether the line is indeed plumb. The plumb bob is also a handy device for transferring a point from one surface to another one directly below. A convenient tool often used in combination with the plumb bob is a chalk line (Fig. 2-8B). In operation, the chalk line is covered with colored chalk dust. The line is stretched between two points, lifted from the surface and allowed to snap down hard, leaving a line of chalk dust. The chalk line is used primarily for rough measurements

Fig. 2-8. (A) Plumb bob and reel line. (B) Chalk line and case, or "chalk box." Duncan Photos.

and for guidelines, since the line it leaves is broad and measurements taken from it are likely to be inexact.

Sometimes it is necessary to work with odd and difficult shapes, as when scribing a piece of material tight against an irregular surface. In this case the device to use is called a template former (Fig. 2-9). This tool consists of a series of adjustable needles or pins set in a frame clip retainer. By lining up all the needles against a straightedge, and then pushing them against the surface to be patterned, the proper outline is formed. The outline can be transferred to a pattern or to the workpiece itself.

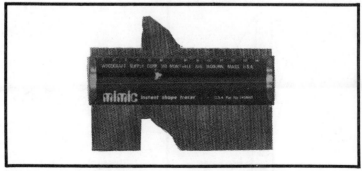

Fig. 2-9. Template former. Courtesy of Woodcraft Supply Corp.

Fig. 2-10. Adjustable protractor with opposite 180° graduations. Duncan Photos.

Working with various angles requires the use of two other instruments. The first is a protractor, but it is not like the protractor used in high school mathematics classes. Instead, it is made of stainless steel, and consists of an oblong plate etched with accurate graduations from 0 to 180 degrees. Attached to the plate is a movable protractor arm (Fig. 2-10). The other instrument is an angle divider (Fig. 2-11). This tool is helpful in laying out angles of all kinds, in making miters, and in laying out multisided figures.

Making layouts, or transferring measurements and dimensions from layout to workpiece or from point to point in the project itself, can often be made easier with the use of three particular instru-

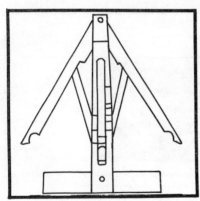

Fig. 2-11. Angle divider. Courtesy of Woodcraft Supply Corp.

ments. One is an inside caliper, the second is an outside caliper, and the third is a flatleg divider or just plain divider (Fig. 2-12). As the name implies, inside calipers are designed to take inside measurements, and they are available in a number of sizes. Outside calipers are used to measure outside dimensions. The flatleg dividers can be used for scribing arcs and circles, drawing parallel lines, and duplicating the line of an irregular surface upon a new piece of material which is to be butted up to it.

Good working or cabinetmaking calls for accurate dimensions and closely fitted joints. Because of this, the pencil is not the best instrument to use in marking the workpiece. A pencil line has a certain definite width, and that width may vary over the course of a long line. The use of a scratch awl (Fig. 2-13) will eliminate this problem. The sharp point makes a very thin and uniform line on a workpiece of any composition. The line is difficult to see, but can be readily identified if referenced by a series of arrows penciled along its length. All cutting and positioning will be done according to the scribed lines. Two other somewhat similar tools widely used by cabinetmakers will accomplish the same purpose. One is a striking knife, and it has a scribe at one end and a blade at the other. The second is a marking knife, and it contains only the marking blade (Fig. 2-14).

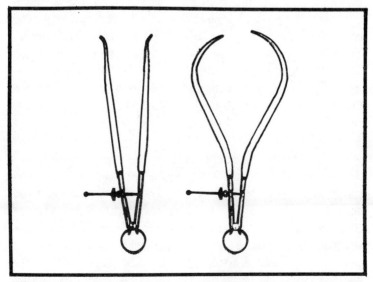

Fig. 2-12. Left, inside calipers. Right, outside calipers. Courtesy of Woodcraft Supply Corp.

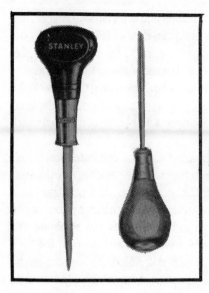

Fig. 2-13. Scratch awls. Courtesy of Stanley Tools.

The marking gauge (Fig. 2-15) is an adjustable measuring and scribing (scoring) tool commonly used in woodworking. Its primary purpose is to mark a line parallel to the grain of the wood by guiding the adjustable block along the edge of the workpiece or a straightedge. An almost identical tool used to mark across the grain with no tearing is a cutting gauge. Trammel heads (Fig. 2-16) are used for laying out or scribing circles, arcs, or wide-spaced parallel lines which are beyond the capacity of the other instruments. Trammel heads are made so that they can be attached to a wood beam of any length. Though they are seldom needed in most woodworking projects, when the occasion does arise, trammel heads are the only tool which will do the job adequately.

SAWS

The ordinary carpenter's handsaw has fallen somewhat into disfavor since the appearance of inexpensive power saws, but is still widely used and is the traditional method of cutting wood. If you don't happen to own a portable power saw, the handsaw will be one of the most important items in your tool box. Any ordinary handsaw will do the job, but those used for cabinetmaking are properly called panel saws. They range in length from 20 to 26 inches, and there are two basic types. The first is a crosscut, and the second, a rip. As the name implies, a crosscut blade is used to cut wood across the grain.

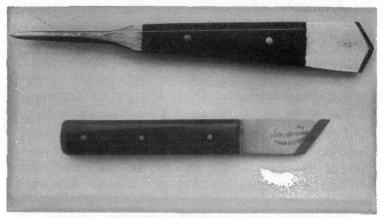

Fig. 2-14. Above, striking knife. Below, marking knife. Duncan Photos.

The rip saw is used to cut with the grain. Incidentally, the teeth on a saw blade are frequently referred to as points. The more points per inch of blade length, the finer the cut. In normal woodworking, 10 points is about right for general purpose work. A 10-point blade will cross-cut nicely, and with a little persuasion, can be made to rip adequately. A coarse crosscut has 7 points, while most rip saws have 4 to 4½ points. A 12-point crosscut can be used for fine work, while a 7-point crosscut leaves a comparatively rough edge. As far as length is concerned, 22 inches is an easy size to handle.

Using a panel saw successfully takes a bit of experience. It is important to realize that crosscut saws do about three-quarters of the cutting on the downstroke, and the rest on the upstroke. To start a cut, draw the saw upward several times to make a starting notch. Then gradually increase the downward pressure, while at the same time holding the saw with no sideways tilt. Keep your forearm lined up with the cut that you are making, your arm and elbow relaxed, and let the saw do the work. If you are cutting solid wood,

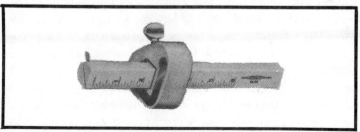

Fig. 2-15. Marking gauge. Courtesy of Stanley Tools.

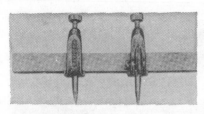

Fig. 2-16. Set of trammel points mounted on a beam. Courtesy of Stanley Tools.

hold the saw blade at an approximate 45-degree angle to the surface of the workpiece. If the material is plywood, particle board or hardboard, increase the cutting angle to about 60 degrees. With a little practice, you should be able to cut straight lines and square edges with satisfactory accuracy.

The backsaw is the cabinetmaker's best friend (Fig. 2-17A). Unlike panel saws, which are flexible and have hollow-ground points, the backsaw is absolutely true and rigid. The squared blade is fitted with a heavy steel or brass spine to keep it straight, and in many instances the points are not hollow-ground. Complete uniformity of cuts every time is insured. Many backsaws have 11 points to the inch, especially those used in miter boxes. The blades are adequate for most purposes. Where even finer cuts are needed, however, a 15- or 20-point blade will do a better job. If extremely fine cuts are needed, so smooth that virtually no finishing is required, then the bead saw (Fig. 2-17B) is used. Unlike the panel saw, a backsaw is used with the blade held parallel to the surface of the material being cut. A relaxed arm with the forearm again in line with the cut, a gentle, even pressure upon the blade, and short easy strokes will insure a good cut, whether the saw is being used in a miter frame or freehand.

The saw to use in awkward spots where nothing else seems to work, or where gentle inside or outside curves must be cut, is the compass or keyhole saw (Fig. 2-18A). Actually, these are two different types of saws, but with a similar appearance and an almost identical function. Many brands of keyhole saws are available with two or three interchangeable blades, a fine and a coarse for woodworking, and a hacksaw-type for metal. Some models also have adjustable handles so that the blade can be set at several angles to the handle for greater convenience. The pad saw (Fig. 2-18B) is a little brother to the keyhole saw. With its narrow 9-point blade and short overall length, it is handy for use in tight spots yet gives a good cut.

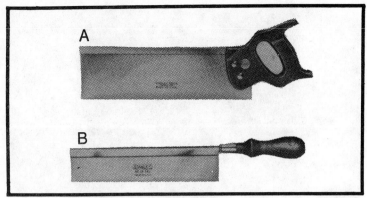

Fig. 2-17. Above (A), back, miter or tenon saw. Below (B), bead or dovetail saw. Courtesy of Stanley Tools.

Fret and coping saws (Fig. 2-19) look much alike and perform similar functions. The blades are very thin and delicate and can cut sharply curved lines with no trouble. Various types of these interchangeable blades are available with anywhere from 16 to 32 teeth per inch. Using these saws with a minimum of blade breakage requires a gentle and uniform touch. Always keep the blade straight up and down, and take care not to tilt the frame of the saw to one side or the other. A slight forward pressure and a slow, easy stroke will result in consistently good cuts.

If you will be working with veneers, there is one more specialty saw that might interest you (Fig. 2-20). The veneer saw is a compact and easy-to-use small tool with a double-edged blade. One side of the curved blade has straight-edged teeth, the other side tapered teeth. Not only is this saw excellent for veneer work, it is useful for other purposes as well.

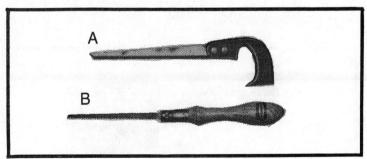

Fig. 2-18. Above (A), keyhole saw. Courtesy of Stanley Tools. Below (B), pad saw. Courtesy of Woodcraft Supply Corp.

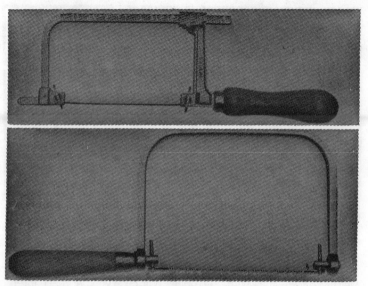

Fig. 2-19. Above, fret saw. Below, coping saw. Courtesy of Woodcraft Supply Corp.

This is as good a place as any to mention a device called a miter box (Fig. 2-21). A great many models are on the market today, ranging from an inexpensive hardwood box capable of cutting only four angles to a sophisticated precison-made machine with workpiece clamps, saw guides and accurately milled components. The purpose of the miter box is simply to allow the cutting of precise angles for making miter joints, and to assure smooth and accurate straight cuts in small workpieces. Though the more sophisticated miter boxes in the upper price ranges do make a dent in the wallet, these are the only ones really worth considering. The cheapies, especially those made of wood or plastic, lose whatever small amount of accuracy they had after only a short time in use. The more

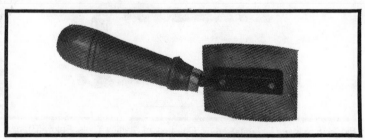

Fig. 2-20. Veneer saw. Courtesy of Woodcraft Supply Corp.

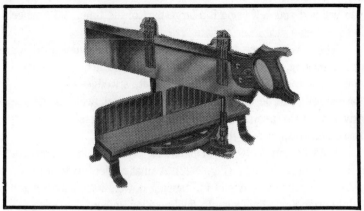

Fig. 2-21. Adjustable miter box with saw. Courtesy of Stanley Tools.

expensive miter boxes are much easier to use, will last a lifetime, and will produce uniformly excellent results, cut after cut.

HAMMERS

Strange though it might seem, a hammer isn't just a hammer. There are many varieties, each designed for a particular use. The most common is the one that you probably have in your own shop, the standard 16-ounce carpenter's claw hammer. This is indeed the most practical hammer for driving nails of 8-penny size and up. However, cabinetmaking frequently calls for smaller nails and brads. In this case, the most comfortable size is a 10-ounce claw hammer. Once you have gotten use to this lightweight outfit, chances are that

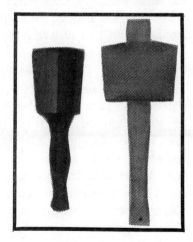

Fig. 2-22. Left, lignum vitae carver's mallet. Right, beechwood carpenter's mallet. Courtesy of Woodcraft Supply Corp.

33

you will find yourself using it a large part of the time. A 13-ounce head makes a nice intermediate size.

There is another type of hammer, especially designed for cabinetmaking, which serves a double purpose. The head weighs 10 ounces and the claw has been replaced with a wedge-shaped peen. Larger nails can be driven with the broad head, while brads are driven with the peen. Another style of hammer useful in driving brads and small nails is the tackhammer.

In addition to a selection of hammers, you may also have need of a small and a large mallet (Fig. 2-22). A small mallet, made of wood, plastic, or rubber, is useful for tapping dowels into place, or for lightly urging glued pieces into final position without damaging the surfaces. The larger size mallets are used with wood chisels fitted with wooden handles. These mallets have no metal striking caps on them.

SCREWDRIVERS

There is much more to the plain old screwdriver than meets the eye. Unfortunately, many of those foisted off upon us at the hardware store are not of good quality. Here again, a lot of time and frustration will be saved, and better results achieved, by using high quality, fitted screwdrivers. Good mechanic's screwdrivers made from forged alloy steel and fitted with comfortable hand grips can accomplish any appropriate task but shouldn't be expected to perform beyond their capacity. One of their greatest drawbacks is that the blade widths and thicknesses are not accurately sized to the screw slot sizes. Instead, the blades are manufactured in widths of fractions of an inch, such as ⅛ inch or ¼ inch.

High quality cabinetmaker's screwdrivers like those shown in Fig. 2-23 offer a great many advantages over standard mechanic's screwdrivers. In the first place, they are exceptionally well made, and thus a delight to anyone who enjoys owning fine tools. The blade tips are crossground to insure that they will not jack out of the screw slots. Further, the tips are sized for specific screw slot dimensions. One screwdriver fits a number 2 screw, another fits a number 8, 9, or 10, and so forth. The tool-steel blades are flattened at the upper end of the shank so that a wrench can be applied for more torque. The cylindrical wooden handles are partially flatted into a oval to allow a better grip with less fatigue. One of their drawbacks is that

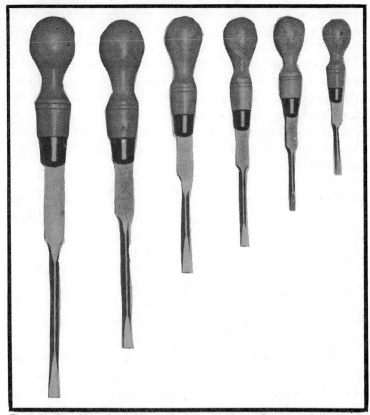

Fig. 2-23. Set of Marples cabinetmaker's screwdrivers. Courtesy of Woodcraft Supply Corp.

you can't beat upon them with a hammer as you can a plastic-handled mechanic's screwdriver. On the other hand, you shouldn't be doing that anyway.

Another type of screwdriver which comes in handy for occasional and miscellaneous work is the ratchet screwdriver. Several sizes and brands are available. The best known type is probably the Yankee. Most Yankee screwdrivers come equipped with at least three different sizes of alloy steel screwdriver bits, which are securely set into a collet chuck at the tip of the screwdriver. These screwdrivers can be locked in a closed position for standard operation, or unlocked to use the spiral ratcheting return mechanism for fast and easy screw driving or removal.

Another type of tool which uses interchangeable screwdriver bits is the same bit brace that is used for boring holes. Several sizes of bits are available, and the use of a bit brace as a screwdriver has two great advantages. One is that tremendous pressure can be brought to bear upon the screw head: an immense amount of torque can be applied because of the leverage of the bit brace handle. The second advantage is, when a great number of screws are to be driven, a bit brace causes far less wear and tear on the hands and arms than does a standard screwdriver. The bit brace can also work faster than the standard screwdriver, but you have to take great care that the bit does not jump out of the screw slot and gouge the workpiece.

CHISELS

The number of times that you will reach for a wood chisel during the course of an extensive cabinetmaking project is truly surprising. Generally it is not necessary to have a great array of them, but you will need at least two or three different sizes. One type of chisel that is nice to have is an aged wood chisel which has seen better days. You can use it for prying, wedging, scraping glue, and making rough gouge cuts. Good chisels, however, should be treated with great care.

Several different types of chisels and a myriad of sizes are available. Most types have special uses, and complete sets of all the different types could easily cost in excess of a thousand dollars. Chances are, though, that you can get by with one or two individuals or a small set of butt chisels. The butt chisel is a general purpose type, fitted with a steel impact cap at the end of the handle for protection and for centering the hammer blow. For heavy-duty use, socket chisels are the best bet. These too are available with leather-capped or steel-ringed handle tips for use with a heavy mallet. Deep-mortise chisels are specifically made for mortising work, and are used only with the hand or with a light mallet. The cabinetmaker's firmer chisels are somewhat similar, but have a slightly different blade configuration. These are excellent for general work but are made to be used by hand only, or with a light mallet. You will probably find that the most useful sizes are the standard ¼-inch, ½-inch, and ¾-inch blade widths.

PLANES

In earlier cabinetmaking eras, a broad selection of planes was one of the most important assets to the shop. A variety of special

Fig. 2-24. Bench plane, jack model. Courtesy of Stanley Tools.

planes—in many shapes and sizes—was used for cutting all of the moldings, ploughs, rabbets, and other forms, and for carrying out most smoothing operations. However, unless you plan to wander off into the building of fine furniture, the chances are that you will need only two or, at most, three different planes.

A bench plane (Fig. 2-24) is essential. There are several types, including the smooth, jack, fore, and jointer. The two most generally useful types are the smooth and the jack. Both are general purpose planes, capable of making both heavy and light cuts. Both are used for smoothing edges *and* surfaces. About the only difference between the two is the size (length and width) of the blade. Smooth planes run approximately 7 to 10 inches in length and are ideal for general small work. Jack planes are 14 or 15 inches long, with blades about 2 inches wide; they work very well in smoothing long edges or extensive flat surfaces. Fore planes and jointer planes are longer yet, approaching two feet overall; they are used primarily in large work.

Another useful type of plane is the block plane (Fig. 2-25). It is normally about six inches long, has a low blade angle, and fits comfortably in the grasp for one-handed use. It works exceptionally well for beveling edges and for making small fine cuts, and can be used on edge grains as well as surfaces. Similar in design but much

Fig. 2-25. Block plane. Courtesy of Stanley Tools.

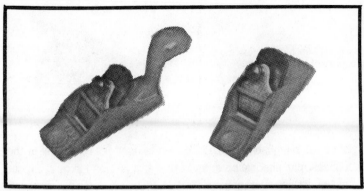

Fig. 2-26. Two types of palm planes. Courtesy of Woodcraft Supply Corp.

smaller is the palm plane (Fig. 2-26). Fitting comfortably in the palm of the hand, these little critters are ideal for edge beveling or for getting into cramped, tight quarters.

For persons interested in the direct on-project cutting of decorative patterns, such as beading or tonguing or various plough and dado cuts, the multiplane (Fig. 2-27) may be the answer. Though expensive, a well-made multiplane is a lifetime investment; it is

Fig. 2-27. Multiplane and assorted irons (blades). Courtesy of Woodcraft Supply Corp.

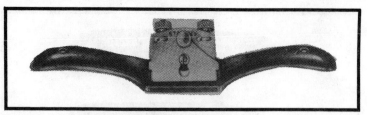

Fig. 2-28. Spokeshave. Courtesy of Stanley Tools.

capable of doing a wide variety of fine work whose finished appearance can be gained in no other way.

Another bladed tool with a long and illustrious history, and still useful at times to the cabinetmaker, is the spokeshave (Fig. 2-28). While the plane, because of its shape, cuts only on flat surfaces, the spokeshave can be used to trim or bevel edges or even narrow surfaces of irregularly shaped material. Its first-cousin, the drawknife, can be used for similar purposes, but must be handled with painstaking care and skill. Though a drawknife can perform intricate wonders when guided by an artist, its principal use is to remove large chunks of material from the workpiece in a short time.

Edgetrimmers are blood relatives of the plane. Several brands and types are available, and they are used in two principal applications. When working with veneers, a veneer edgetrimmer is the quickest and most effective way to accurately trim the workpiece edges. Other edgetrimmers, frequently equipped with carbide cutting blades (Fig. 2-29), are used in a similar fashion to trim the edges of Formica and other plastic laminates. When assorted adjustments

Fig. 2-29. Veneer and laminate trimmer. Courtesy of Woodcraft Supply Corp.

39

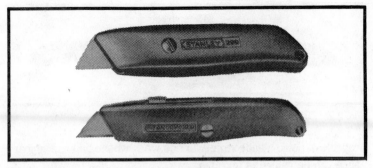

Fig. 2-30. Above, utility knife. Below, utility knife with adjustable blade. Courtesy of Stanley Tools.

are made to it, the edge trimmer can be used to produce accurate beveled edges. It is handy for trimming panels and drawer bottoms as well.

KNIVES

Even though your tool kit contains many other types of bladed instruments, you will frequently have need for a knife with a fine sharp blade. The most familiar knife is the inexpensive utility knife (Fig. 2-30) found in almost any hardware store. The retractable, adjustable, replaceable blade is flexible and capable of making precise, clean cuts. This knife is an excellent adjunct to any tool box. A quality cabinetmaker's adjustable knife is another tool which will prove its worth time and again. This knife has an adjustable blade which retracts into a brass frame fitted with rosewood grips. The body of the knife is big enough to allow a good grip, and the replaceable blade is tough and sharp (Fig. 2-31).

The bench knife (Fig. 2-32) is somewhat smaller and lighter than the cabinetmaker's knife. It is primarily a carving or whittling tool, but has many uses. The small, sharp nonreplaceable blade is stiff and strong and tapered to a fine point. Another knife which is primarily found in the woodcarver's shop is the carver's hook (Fig. 2-33). With a blunt-ended, slightly curving blade whose cutting edge

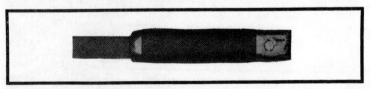

Fig. 2-31. Cabinetmaker's knife with rosewood handle and adjustable blade. Courtesy of Woodcraft Supply Corp.

Fig. 2-32. This type of chip carving knife makes an excellent general purpose bench knife. Courtesy of Woodcraft Supply Corp.

is meant to be pushed, the carver's hook is very useful for trimming in awkward spots.

In addition to the above assortment, many other knives are available for various purposes. Both handles and blades come in a spectrum of sizes and shapes for many specific purposes and for utilitarian use as well. Among the better known knives are the sloyd knives, various types of chip carving knives, all-purpose knives with blades designed to be reground to various contours, and the ever-popular X-Acto knives.

Depending upon the type of work you plan to do, you may find some of the various special purpose knives to be of considerable value. For instance, the filling of small dents in a wood surface can be accomplished by the application of solid shellac. To do this you will need a burn-in knife (Fig. 2-34). This knife has a flexible round-tipped blade with no edge. The tip of the knife is heated and used like a putty knife to work the solid shellac into the dents. An artist's palette knife is quite similar in design and will do the same job. The cutting of acrylic, polystyrene and similar types of pressure-sensitive sheet plastic can be done with a saw. However, it is much easier to use a plastic cutter designed for the purpose (Fig. 2-35). This knife heavily scores the workpiece, which then can be cleanly broken along the scored line, much in the way that glass is cut. Another knife, quite similar in design, uses a carbide-tipped blade for scoring laminated plastics like Formica.

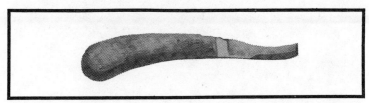

Fig. 2-33. Carver's hook, with reverse curved blade. Courtesy of Woodcraft Supply Corp.

Fig. 2-34. Burn-in knife. Courtesy of Woodcraft Supply Corp.

DRILLS

Though we tend to think in terms of drilling holes with a power drill, there are times when this is either impractical or simply improper. Hand drills have a definite place in any woodworking shop. Holes with a diameter of ¼ inch and larger are drilled with a bit brace (Fig. 2-36). The better models of bit braces have ballbearing top grips and chucks, and have a ratcheting feature which allows them to be used locked in a full 360-degree swing, or to be operated in fractional arcs in either direction. Smaller holes are drilled with a hand drill (Fig. 2-37), sometimes called an eggbeater drill. Most of these drills have a chuck capacity of 1/16 to 5/16 inch. The breast drill (Fig. 2-38), a somewhat larger version of the hand drill, is meant for heavy-duty use and has a chuck capacity of up to ½ inch.

The push drill (Fig. 2-39), often referred to as a Yankee drill or a Yankee screwdriver, is an excellent tool for making pilot holes, starter holes and the like. It can be easily used with one hand, and comes equipped with a set of collet-chuck bits. Another device of ancient lineage but not much used today is the gimlet (Fig. 2-40). Gimlets are used for making pilot holes or screw-setting holes of

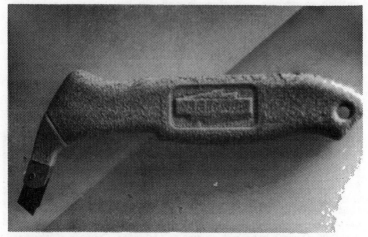

Fig. 2-35. Heavy duty laminate and sheet plastic cutter. Duncan Photos.

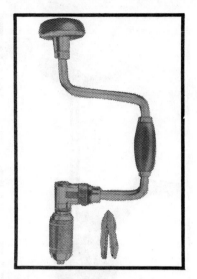

Fig. 2-36. Bit brace, or bitstock.
Courtesy of Stanley Tools.

various sizes ranging from ⅛ to ¼ inch. The bits are not inter-changeable and a full set is required to cover the range. Drilling small holes for tiny brads or screws can be something of a chore with a full-size drill. One answer to the problem is a set of brad awls. The specially formed point of the brad awl (Fig. 2-41) will make a clean hole with a minimum of effort. A brad pusher or brad driver with a magnetic tip will drive and set a brad, either with or without a pilot hole (depending upon the type of material), in one easy motion and without the use of a hammer. If you have to drill tiny holes, use the

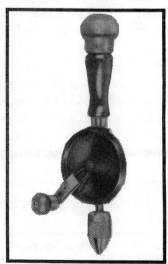

Fig. 2-37. Hand drill. Courtesy of
Stanley Tools.

43

Fig. 2-38. Breast drill. Courtesy of Woodcraft Supply Corp.

pin vise (Fig. 2-42), a tool familiar to most model makers. This tiny handheld chuck will grip a variety of small drill bits or burrs, and is operated simply by twirling the tool between thumb and forefinger.

DRILL BITS

There are a great many special types of drill bits for use with hand operated drills, but only a few of them will be of interest to you. Auger bits are used with a bit brace (bitstock) and are available in a range of sizes from ¼ inch to 1¼ inches in single-twist or double-twist configuration (Fig. 2-43). Either type will do a good job, but the

Fig. 2-39. Yankee Handyman push drill, also used as a screwdriver. Courtesy of Stanley Tools.

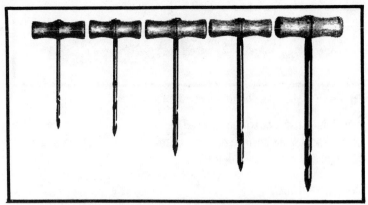

Fig. 2-40. Set of gimlets. Courtesy of Woodcraft Supply Corp.

single-twist bores deep holes better while the double-twist bores cleaner, truer holes and clears away chips faster. When larger holes must be drilled, use an expansive bit (Fig. 2-44). Several variations of these are available, but all operate in essentially the same way. The cutting blade is adjustable from about 1 inch to 3 inches, or there may be two blades for a double range of hole sizes. For boring a hole of limited depth with a flat bottom, the bit to use is a Forstner bit (Fig. 2-45). Some types of twist bits are made for use with bitstocks, and others are made expressly for use with power drills. Some of the power drill twist bits can be chucked in hand or breast drills. Push drills come equipped with their own sets of specially made small bits.

When setting flathead wood screws, it is necessary to countersink each hole. Countersink bits (Fig. 2-46) are available in a number of sizes and head shapes for use with either bitbraces or hand drills. Another useful woodworking accessory is the bit depth gauge (Fig. 2-47). There are two or three different types, but the purpose is the same. The gauge is clamped to the shank of the auger bit and the

Fig. 2-41. Set of brad awls. Courtesy of Woodcraft Supply Corp.

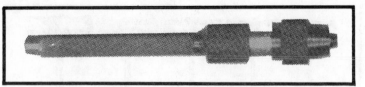

Fig. 2-42. Pin vise. Courtesy of Woodcraft Supply Corp.

adjustable shaft set to the desired height. When the surface of the shaft reaches the surface of the workpiece, the tip of the auger bit has reached the proper depth.

DOWELING TOOLS

Doweling is a common process in cabinetmaking and furniture building—more about that later—and requires some special equipment. Dowel centers, which commonly come in sets of eight, are used to line up dowel holes in two workpieces. After drilling the holes in one workpiece, the appropriate dowel centers are inserted in the holes. Then the workpiece is postioned next to the adjoining workpiece and the two sections are tapped together, registering an

Fig. 2-43. Boxed set of Jennings type double twist auger bits. Courtesy of Woodcraft Supply Corp.

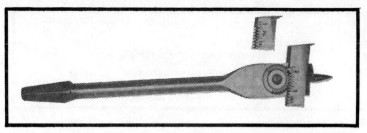

Fig. 2-44. Micor-Dial expansive bit. Courtesy of Woodcraft Supply Corp.

accurate position mark to guide the drilling of the second set of holes. The four most common dowel sizes are usually sufficient for home shop use (Fig. 2-48).

Another and more accurate method of positioning dowels is carried out with the use of a doweling jig (Fig. 2-49). By setting the

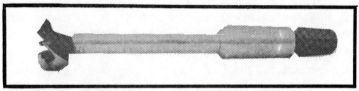

Fig. 2-45. Forstner bit. Courtesy of Woodcraft Supply Corp.

jib on the workpiece, you can quickly locate the dowel hole sites and then drill accurately through the bushed apertures provided for the purpose. The jig has great flexibility, and can be used with wide or odd-shaped workpieces. There are other varieties of doweling jigs, some complicated and some not. But no matter which variety is employed, the process of drilling dowel holes is simplified.

Dowel holes can be drilled by hand with a bit brace and a special dowel bit which looks very much like an ordinary single-twist auger

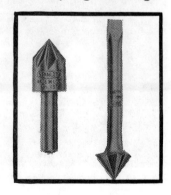

Fig. 2-46. Countersink bits, one for a bit brace and the other for an electric drill. Courtesy of Stanley Tools.

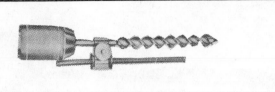

Fig. 2-47. Bit depth gauge. Courtesy of Stanley Tools.

bit. There are also special precision brad point dowel bits for use with power drills. These bits cut rapidly, freely and accurately. Most other types of drill bits are not recommended, because they seldom cut a crisp, true hole, an essential bit of business if the dowels are to line up properly.

You can even make your own dowels, using a special dowel-making tool in combination with a lathe, drillpress, or electric hand drill. However, the most practical approach is to buy ready-made dowel stock. This can produce some peculiar problems at times, if the quality control department at the mill was lax. Dowels often are not true to size, but a tool called a dowel sizer (Fig. 2-50) will take care of the problem. By simply running it through the appropriate hole, the dowel can be reshaped and resized. Another problem with

Fig. 2-48. Set of dowel centers. Duncan Photos.

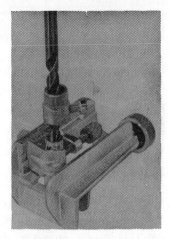

Fig. 2-49. Doweling jig. Courtesy of Stanley Tools.

dowels sometimes arises when you try to insert a perfectly square-ended dowel into a tight dowel hole. A quick way to eliminate this difficulty is to use a dowel pointer (Fig. 2-51). This is a specially made adjustable cutting tool which is run over the end of the dowel and turned a few times to produce a tapered edge for easier insertion.

CLAMPS

You are unlikely to proceed very far in woodworking before finding a need for clamps of one sort or another. You'll have a broad variety of clamps from which to choose, and among the most useful will be the C-clamps (Fig. 2-52). These are available in assorted depths, with jaw capacities ranging from ½ inch to a foot or more. Deep-throated C-clamps are like other C-clamps except that they have a much greater depth from the jaws to the back of the frame. One variation of the C-clamp is the two-way or three-way edging clamp (Fig. 2-53), and it allows the application of clamping pressure from two or three directions. Because all clamps of this type have

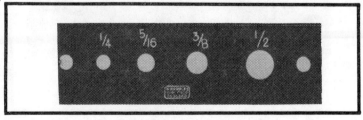

Fig. 2-50. Dowel sizer. Courtesy of Woodcraft Supply Corp.

Fig. 2-51. Dowel pointer. Courtesy of Woodcraft Supply Corp.

metal jaws, you must be careful if you are to avoid crushing or marring the surface of the workpiece. The usual method is to use small blocks of wood or scraps of cardboard between each jaw and the workpiece.

Many cabinetmakers prefer another type of clamp known as the hand screw (Fig. 2-54). Hand screws too are available in many different sizes. Most models are made with heavy hardwood jaws which won't harm the surface of the workpiece. Some models, however, have felt-covered jaw facings. The double steel screw spindles allow the jaws to grip nonparallel surfaces.

Pipe clamps (Fig. 2-55) are also handy to have around. The two jaws of the clamp are discrete pieces and are sold separately. The purchaser attaches them to a piece of ½-inch or ¾-inch pipe in whatever length he desires. One jaw slips along the pipe and can be set at any desired point. The second jaw, or head, is adjustable by means of a threaded shaft. Pipe clamps have two advantages over other types of clamps. The first advantage is that they can be used over a wide span, as when you are laminating wide workpieces from

Fig. 2-52. C-clamps. Courtesy of Woodcraft Supply Corp.

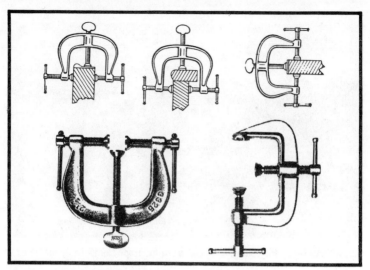

Fig. 2-53. Above, three-way edging clamp. Below, two-way edging clamp. Courtesy of Woodcraft Supply Corp.

several smaller edge-to-edge sections, or when you are applying pressure to two widely separated workpieces. The second advantage is that the heads can be turned around to apply reverse or pushing pressure. Another somewhat similar clamp, which performs virtually the same function and comes as a unit, is the deep engagement clamp. Rather than pipe, a special rail is used and only one head is adjustable. The jaws of these clamps can be fitted with polyethylene jaw pads to prevent flawing of workpiece surfaces.

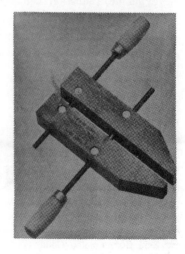

Fig. 2-54. Cabinetmaker's hand screw with pivoting spindles. Courtesy of Woodcraft Supply Corp.

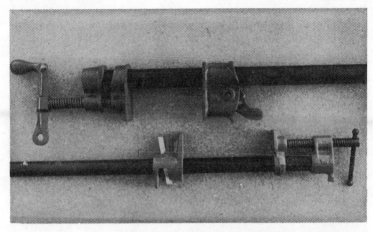

Fig. 2-55. Above, ½-inch pipe clamp. Below, ¾-inch pipe clamp. Duncan Photos.

One type of clamp which is almost essential for making up cabinet frames, paneled door frames and similar pieces is the corner clamp (Fig. 2-56). Good corner clamps are expensive, but they are carefully made and precision ground to insure that miter joints will be accurately joined. The use of several of these clamps will make glueing and nailing of miter joints and squared corners a simple process, and you will have the assurance that the finished product will be accurate and square, with no racking.

One further type of clamp that deserves mention is a device called the flexible clamp or band clamp (Fig. 2-57). Perhaps you will never get into a situation requiring the use of such a clamp, but if you do, you will realize at once that no other clamp will do quite the same job. Flexible clamps usually come in standard sizes with capacities of

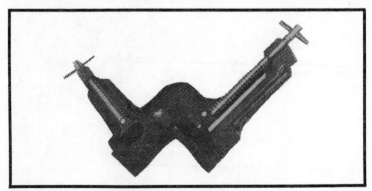

Fig. 2-56. Corner clamp. Courtesy of Woodcraft Supply Corp.

Fig. 2-57. Band clamp—20-foot size capable of pressures up to 2800 pounds per square foot. Courtesy of Woodcraft Supply Corp.

from 4 to 8 feet, but they are also available in 15-foot, 20-foot and even larger sizes. The shape of the workpiece or pieces to be glued is immaterial, since the band is simply wrapped around the work object in whatever fashion is most suitable. Pressure is then applied by turning the screw handle. With a little ingenuity and perhaps the help of some additional angle brackets, blocks, and supports, you can apply uniform pressure to practically any kind of workpiece.

FORMING AND FINISHING TOOLS

The kind of forming and finishing tools that you will add to your tool box depends on a great extent on the type of cabinetwork that you are doing. However, of the great number of individual implements available, you will sooner or later probably want to acquire most of the following items.

One of the quickest, most accurate, and readily controllable ways to remove wood from the workpiece is with the use of a file.

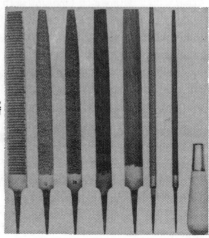

Fig. 2-58. Cabinet files and rasps, with universal handle. Courtesy of Woodcraft Supply Corp.

53

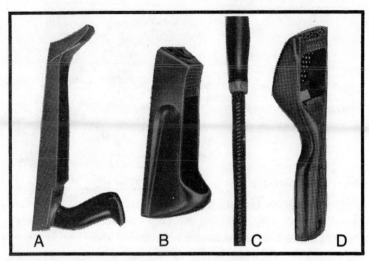

Fig. 2-59. Plane type Surform (A); pocket plane type Surform (B); Surform round file (C); surform shaver (D). Courtesy of Stanley Tools.

Cabinet rasps (Fig. 2-58) will cut evenly and leave a relatively smooth finish. They can be purchased according to length and to coarseness of the abrading surface. While the rasp is used to cut the wood, a file is used to smooth the wood, and thus it is designed to remove far less material per stroke. Wood or cabinet files are available in several sizes and abrading patterns and in flat, half-round, or round (rattail) cross sections. Most hardware stores have a reasonable selection of both rasps and files; a selection of three or four will probably fulfill your needs. Be sure to purchase a file card (file brush) as an adjunct. One side of this tool is set with semiflexible fine wires, while the other side is a stiff fiber bristle brush. A file card is the only practical way to keep the teeth of a file or rasp clear of imbedded material without damaging the cutting edges.

Surform is the trademark for a patented type of cutting configuration on a series of shaping tools. These tools are used both for roughing and for the last forming and contouring prior to the final finish of sanding or scraping. Surforms (Fig. 2-59) are offered in several different styles. There are round and square files, and a broad flat file with an offset handle. Other Surforms resemble planes in block and jack sizes; one has an adjustable handle. The blades are replaceable in some models.

Though seldom used any more, shave hooks (Fig. 2-60) do a marvelous job of smoothing wood surfaces, especially hardwoods.

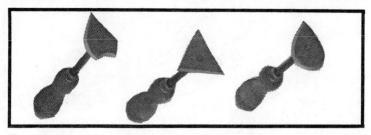

Fig. 2-60. Shavehooks. Courtesy of Woodcraft Supply Corp.

The various blade shapes are designed for use in tight quarters, or on flat, convex, or concave surfaces. A little practice with shave hooks will enable you to achieve a finish smoothness that is almost glassy. For larger surfaces, especially those that are uneven or rough, the similar but larger scrapers will do the job.

When it comes to final finishing, sandpapering is usually the best method. You can simply wrap sandpaper around a scrap block of wood, but there is an easier way. A handsanding block made of rubber (Fig. 2-61) will secure the sheet of sandpaper solidly, provide a resilient base for the paper, and reduce the strain on your fingers and arm. A different approach, both practical and effective, is embodied in the tools known as sanding planes (Fig. 2-62). These planes are light in weight and ruggedly made of hardwood with aluminum bases. They have sponge rubber cushioned soles and are highly maneuverable. The sandpaper locks in tightly on this type of plane. Convex, half-round, and flat models of sanding planes are available.

SHARPENING EQUIPMENT

One of the most important facts to remember about woodworking tools is that all cutting edges must be kept sharp. There simply is

Fig. 2-61. Rubber sanding block.
Courtesy of Woodcraft Supply Corp.

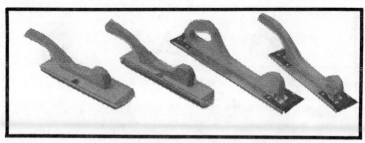

Fig. 2-62. Sanding planes. Courtesy of Woodcraft Supply Corp.

no way to do a good job with tools that are dull or nicked or out of true. Yet, unfortunately, an amazing array of shabby blades seems to be common to every workshop, and the owner seems to have little idea of how to go about correcting the situation. Dull blades are not only a nuisance and a source of constant irritation, but are dangerous in the bargain. There are a number of sharpening techniques, the specifics of which vary according to the design of the blade. In general, however, there are two phases to the sharpening process. The first is grinding, and the second is honing. Grinding is usually required only when the blade has worn untrue or become badly nicked. Normally, all that is necessary to keep a blade in good shape is periodic honing.

Hand grinding an edge can be done with a hand grinder mounted on the edge of a workbench. The bench grindstone, bit brother to the hand grinder, will also do the job. A third possibility for grinding a blade is a large, handheld, coarse utility stone. Generally, however, grinding of this sort is done with a power bench grinder, a tool which will be treated in the next chapter.

Honing must be done by hand for best results. The most commonly used tool for sharpening or honing flat blades is the bench stone (Fig. 2-63). There are numerous types of bench stones in several sizes, sometimes cased in wood boxes and sometimes uncased. They are composed of any of several sorts of material, with soft Arkansas, hard black Arkansas, and Washita being among the most common. Bench stones are also made from several grades of crystalon, fine India, and other artificial stones. Differences between the various types of stones lie in the characteristics of hardness and coarseness, and in the kind of edge produced.

Whatever the type of stone, the sharpening procedure begins with a relatively coarse grade, then advances to a finer grade as the edge becomes keener. If an extremely acute edge is desired, the final honing should be done on a special honing stone, or upon a pair of leather strops, the first moderately coarse and the second fine. Use a sharpening oil with all stones to preserve the integrity of the stone and to aid the sharpening process. Great care should be taken not to gouge or deform the surface of the stone in any way. If the stone does not remain perfectly flat, you will be unable to do a decent sharpening job.

Obviously not all blades are flat, and so those that are not require the use of special stones, natural and artificial, of many sizes and shapes. The special stones are known as slipstones (Fig. 2-64), and are designated as round-edge slipstones, knife-edge slipstones, half-round gouge stones, tapers, rounds, points and auger bit stones. With enough searching you can find a slipstone of the size and shape to fit virtually any blade known to man. As with the bench stones, sharpening oil must be used.

Often the specific angle of the cutting edge is of great importance. Since the human hand and human judgment are notoriously fallible, a variety of jigs has been devised over the years to hold each type of blade in its proper position. You can purchase adjustable jigs for sharpening plane and chisel blades at the correct angles. The jigs can be used with both bench stones and grinders. Drill sharpening jigs are used with twist drills, and there are numerous devices to assist in sharpening all kinds of saw blades. Auger bits, spokeshaves, drawknives, screwdriver tips and similar tools, however, must be done by hand and with the aid of whatever tool rests or jigs you can fashion yourself.

Fig. 2-63. Cased bench stone—Washita. Courtesy of Woodcraft Supply Corp.

The sharpening of saw blades, whether they be panel saws, back saws, or circular saws, is a tedious chore. On the other hand, saws and saw blades are expensive, and must be kept sharp. Having saw blades sharpened by a professional is costly. With this in mind, you might decide to do your own. If that's the case, one or two of the jigs mentioned above will aid in the sharpening process and also set the teeth at a proper angle. These jigs and a few of the proper files will put you in business. Your choice of files will depend to some extent upon the type of blades you will be sharpening. A single-cut tapered saw file can be used on almost any kind of blade and is available in several sizes. A bastard-cut mill file with single-cut edges is also a utilitarian type, and can be used for sharpening drill bits of all kinds.

The actual methods and procedures for sharpening the various kinds of blades are somewhat complicated and do require some practice. On the other hand, there is nothing mysterious about the process, and skill in blade sharpening will stand you in good stead and be well worth the learning. Consult the reference desk at your library; there should be at least one book on the market dealing solely with sharpening procedures.

MISCELLANEOUS

The miscellaneous category of tools covers just about everything else that you can think of that hasn't already been mentioned. At one time or another, you will probably have use for most of the other tools that are lying around your shop, as well as the specialized woodworking tools. There is one other item that is unique to woodworking, but which does not fit into any of the previous categories; it

Fig. 2-64. Slipstones. Left, assorted India rounds, points and tapers. Right, Arkansas round edges. Courtesy of Woodcraft Supply Corps.

Fig. 2-65. Nail sets. Duncan Photos.

is the nail set. Nail sets usually come in four sizes, designated 1/32, 2/32, 3/32, and 4/32. This refers to the diameter in inches of the tip. The use is exactly as the name implies: to drive or set the head of nail slightly below the surface of the workpiece without damaging the material (Fig. 2-65).

The remaining miscellaneous items could consist of nearly anything. For instance, you will probably need wrenches of one sort or another for changing saw blades, adjusting power tools, or doing repair work. For these and similar tasks, you may also need such tools as water pump pliers, Visegrips, Stillson wrenches, crescent wrenches, flat nosed pliers, cold chisel, hacksaw, and perhaps even socket wrenches. Constructing cabinets and built-ins often involves areas other than pure woodworking, and this may demand the use of tools peculiar to other crafts. Don't be surprised if you find yourself setting glass, working with sheet metal, forming sheet plastics, laying laminated plastics, perhaps even shaping metal pipes and iron bars. Some types of built-ins include lighting fixtures, which means getting into some electrical work. Always use the proper tool for the job if you possibly can. Buying a new tool or two is always less expensive than hiring something done, and using the right tools for the job inevitably results in a better end product.

Chapter 3
Power Tools

If you don't happen to own any power tools, don't be discouraged. That is no reason not to tackle cabinetry or built-in projects. The hand tools mentioned in the previous chapter are perfectly adequate to enable you to turn out fine finished products. All you need is a little time and patience, and sufficient interest and enthusiasm to become adept at the various woodworking skills. The proof that it can be done is all around you. For instance, the country is full of beautiful old homes built entirely by hand, replete with carved paneling, formed moldings, intricate trimming, balustrades, parquetry and even marquetry. The fine pieces of early period furniture which are so lovely to look at and demand such high prices in today's antique marketplace were all produced wholly by hand. To say that you can't build yourself a set of bookshelves simply because you do not have a workshop stocked with an imposing array of motorized equipment is ridiculous. From that standpoint, one could say that power tools, like so many of the appliances and gadgets that we surround ourselves with, are little more than a crutch.

On the other hand, crutch or no, power tools are highly useful, and have a number of advantages. To be sure, there are skills to be learned in the use of power tools, just as there are with hand tools. But for anyone with a reasonable degree of manual dexterity and mechanical aptitude, these skills can be much more rapidly acquired than many of the traditional woodcrafting skills. There is little question that power tools save a considerable amount of human energy, though the time factor in some operations is not too much different than with hand tools. This is simply because the process of setting up or readying the equipment for a particular job often takes considerably longer than the job itself. Perhaps the greatest advantage in using power tools lies in the fact that clean, precise results can be attained on a repetitive basis. Once the proper procedures for setting up are learned, you can expect square cuts, trim and true edges, tight and well-formed joints, accurate dimensioning, and smooth surfaces every time. From the standpoint of overall elapsed time for any given project, you can expect to turn out a completed article in a matter of hours, rather than a matter of days as in times of yore. Furthermore, you can tackle some complex woodworking projects which you might not otherwise feel capable of attempting, with reasonable assurance that you will end up with a unit that is both functional and good-looking.

Power equipment is indeed expensive. If the fact puts you off, don't despair; you may be able to justify, or at least rationalize, the expense. Suppose, for instance, that you need a substantial amount of bookshelf space. A visit to the local furniture store will quickly show you that even cheap bookcases are expensive. With the price of commercial book shelves looming before you, sit down and calculate the cost of the materials needed to produce the same result in built-in shelves. You will find a whale of a cost differential, and that differential will probably allow you to purchase some power equipment. Then you can set about building your own shelves, and you will likely end up with a more satisfactory arrangement of shelving to boot.

Suppose that you would like to renovate your large kitchen and fit it out with a full set of base and overhead cabinets. Calculating with representative labor and materials costs, you can estimate that a contractor would charge you $2,000 to build a full set of custom cabinets. Purchasing readymade cabinets and having them installed might run to $1,500. On the other hand, the cost of all the materials needed for you to build the cabinets might come to only $200 or $300. If you can afford the time, then you can build your own cabinets at a considerable savings, purchase some power equipment to help you out, and end up with a full set of cabinets built exactly to your liking, plus some power tools which should last you a lifetime and be available for many more projects.

Most modern power tools designed for the home workshop are versatile. Though basically intended for one or two principal operations, they can be modified through the use of accessories and jigs to perform a number of functions. Sometimes the functions of one machine will overlap those of another, but in most cases there is one machine that is the best for one or two particular functions. The fundamental operating procedures for any given type of power tool are usually quite easy to learn but as more demands are placed upon the tool and a project becomes more complex, so do the procedures. There are literally dozens of ideas, methods, hints, kinds, and techniques involved in the more advanced stages of power tool operation. In fact, many books have been written which can give you a complete course in the subject. The following material is necessarily basic in scope, but will allow you to pick and choose among the various power tools with an eye toward selecting what might be best for your own workshop.

POWER HAND SAW

A power hand saw (Fig. 3-1), also variously known as a Skilsaw, a circular saw, or a portable saw, is a common power tool in many home workshops. Though not usually considered in conjuction with cabinetmaking, the power hand saw does indeed have its place. Available are many brands and models, ranging in cost from dirt cheap to very expensive. Neither extreme is the one to consider for the home workshop. Instead, choose something in the middle price

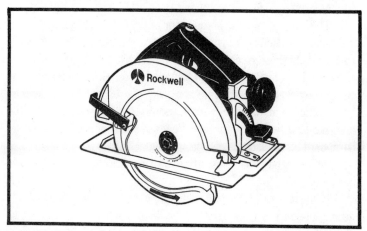

Fig. 3-1. Hand power saw, or circular saw. Courtesy of Rockwell International.

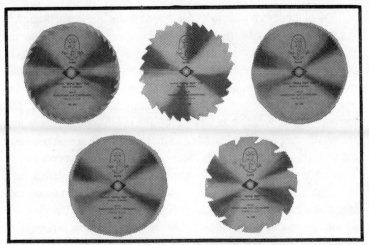

Fig. 3-2. Some of the more popular types of circular saw blade patterns. Top, left to right: rip, chisel combination, extra-fine crosscut. Bottom left: standard crosscut, standard combination. Courtesy of Woodcraft Supply Corp.

range. A saw with helical gear drive, rather than worm drive, is perfectly adequate. A blade size of 7¼-inch or 7½-inch diamter works best, and a motor size of 2 horsepower is ample. Look for ball and roller bearing construction throughout.

The blades are interchangeable, and a variety of different types is available (Fig. 3-2). Follow the manufacturer's information for using each type of blade, and match the blade as closely as possible to the type of work you are doing. By and large, the finer the teeth on the blade, the finer the cut. Also, certain types of blades work well in some materials, but not in others.

This type of saw can be used for both crosscutting and ripping; it can also be used for bevel cuts. Aside from portability, the saw's chief contributions to cabinetmaking derive from its abilities to serve as a cut off saw and to cut large sheets of material. For instance, you can quickly chop off a small piece from a long board, which can then be trimmed and trued by other methods. Or, you can use the portable saw to rip out sizable pieces from sheets of plywood or hardboard for shelf stock and cabinet sides. This type of saw is also sometimes handy for trimcutting stock which has already been installed.

Using the portable saw is a simple chore, though it takes some getting used to. It is designed to be used freehand, but any cut so made should not be considered a finish cut. No matter how steady your hand, the line will not be exactly true. To make accurate rip cuts, clamp a rip guide to the workpiece, adjusted in such a fashion that the blade edge will follow the cutting line exactly. You can purchase a commercial straightedge for your rip guide, or you can use the factory edge of a strip cut from a sheet of plywood.

Crosscutting can also be done with a guide, but is usually done freehand unless the cut is exceptionally long. Since in cabinetwork the cut should be retrimmed on a table saw, allow some excess length for the additional trimcut. After marking the guide line, adjust the depth of the blade so that it extends below the lower surface of the workpiece by about ⅛ inch. This will give you the most effective cut, and is also the safest method. Guide the saw gently but firmly, and let the weight of the machine do the work. Always be ready for binds and kickups, which can jump the entire saw completely out of the cut. Note that the cutting action of the blade is from the bottom upward. This means that the bottom edge of the cut will be smooth while the upper edge will be ragged and splintered. For this reason, the good side of the material, especially plywood, should always be placed face down.

Few accessories are available for portable hand saws, primarily because their basic function is to cut, and this is the only job they do well. You can use a special set of dado blades with the portable saw, but dado cutting can be better done with other machines. One helpful accessory if you will be doing much angle cutting is a special adjustable guide which helps in making accurate angle cuts. Another interesting item is a miter arm which converts the saw to a sort of small radial saw and allows quick and easy angle, dado and rabbet cuts. However, this work also can be done easier and more effectively in other ways.

Another type of portable saw, sort of a smaller version of the standard portable saw, is the plywood saw. This tool is a great value if you are doing much work with heavy or light veneers or light wood panels. It is a small, easily maneuverable, lightweight unit which uses a 4-inch blade operating at high speed. The fine teeth produce accurate, smoothly trimmed cuts.

SABER SAW

The saber saw (Fig. 3-3), also known as a hand jigsaw or bayonet saw, is the best of the power saws for cutting internal and

Fig. 3-3. Sabre saw, or jig saw. Courtesy of Rockwell International.

external curves. Though the shop band saw can also cut these curves, the saber saw is the only one which can make these cuts on the project site. Many models are available, but the best buy almost surely will not be the cheapest one. A good saw has variable-speed capability, a motor of about ¼ horsepower, and is constructed with ball and sleeve bearings. A built-in sawdust blower to keep the cutting line clear and a tilt base are useful features.

Using the saber saw is simple, but can be tricky at first. Hold the saw firmly against the workpiece surface, and guide it slowly, keeping the blade cutting all the time. Use a rip guide for accurate lengthwise cuts, and tilt the base for bevel cuts. Curves and circles can be cut freehand, or you can devise a template to use as a guide. This is another type of saw which cuts with an upward motion, leaving a smooth edge at the bottom and a rougher one at the top. As with the portable saw, the good side of the workpiece should be faced down. Various kinds of blades (Fig. 3-4) are available for use with different materials.

The scroll saw is a similar tool, but a bit larger, heavier, and more expensive. This type of saw, however, is versatile and easy to use in making intricate scrolling cuts. Instead of turning the entire saw body, the blade alone is turned by rotating a knob at the top of the saw head. Better models feature a double-tilt base which allows bevel cutting to both the right and left.

TABLE SAW

If you are able to buy only one piece of motorized equipment for your workshop, you could do no better than to choose a table saw

(Fig. 3-5). Also known as a circular, variety, or bench saw, the table saw is versatile, accurate, easy to use, and almost indispensable for either the beginning or the advanced cabinetmaker. On any project, a larger part of the basic cutting, as well as much of the finish cutting and specialized work like tenons or coves, can be done on the table saw. In fact, when it is fitted out with sundry attachments, accessories, and jigs, the table saw can accomplish just about anything.

The basic table saw consists of a heavy steel box frame (usually set upon a stand), a precision-ground table top, and an arbor. The arbor is attached to an electric motor, either by means of belts and pulleys or in a direct-drive arrangement. The cutting blade is fitted to the arbor, and protrudes through the top of the table. The arbor on most table saws will tilt to a 45-degree angle in one direction, and can be raised or lowered to adjust the height of the saw blade above the table. Most saws come equipped with a certain number of accessory

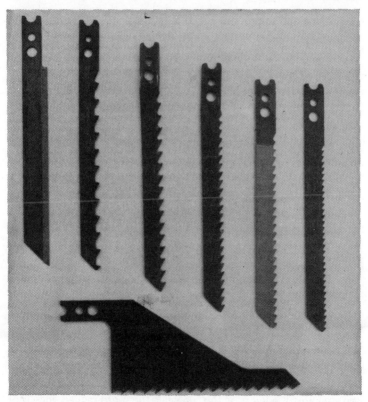

Fig. 3-4. Various sabre saw blade configurations. Many others are available for specific cutting chores. Duncan Photos.

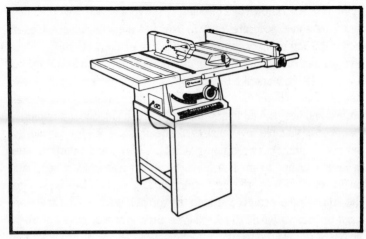

Fig. 3-5. Table or bench saw, with two table extensions. Courtesy of Rockwell International.

items. One and sometimes two table extensions are provided. The adjustable rip fence against which the workpiece is guided during ripping cuts is a standard accessory, as is the miter gauge. The miter gauge is adjustable through an arc of 180 degrees, rides in premilled slots on the table top, and is used for making crosscuts and miter cuts. The saw blade is equipped with a guard, splitter, and antikickback device.

The best way to buy a table saw is to go out and shop for one. A number of brands, sizes, and models are manufactured, and only by comparing the specifications of the various units can you make a reasonable judgment as to which saw best suits your requirements. In general, a 8-inch, 9-inch, or 10-inch size (the reference is to the diameter of the saw blade) is about right for the home shop. The 10-inch size is perhaps a bit more useful than the others. One or two horsepower is perfectly adequate, depending upon the size of the saw. Look for easy-to-turn tilt and height controls and rip fence locking mechanisms.

The types of blades used with the table saw are similar to those used in the portable hand saw (Fig. 3-1), and the selection is made in about the same manner. Note, however, that the cutting action of the table saw blade is exactly opposite to that of the portable hand saw. The cutting action of the table saw blade is downward, so that the smooth cut edge is on the top while the more ragged edge is at the bottom. This means that layout work can be done on the good side of the workpiece and is a somewhat easier process than layout work with the portable hand saw.

Making straight cuts on a table saw is a simple matter. First, check to make sure that the saw blade stands exactly perpendicular to the table top. Use a square that you know to be accurate. When the blade is positioned correctly, the pointer on the tilt scale or angle indicator should read exactly zero, or rest against its stop. If something is awry, make the necessary adjustments. Check the adjustments frequently, as vibration may knock them out of whack occasionally.

With everything lined up properly, set the miter gauge in one of the two milled slots in the table top. Make sure the miter gauge too is accurately adjusted so that the face of the gauge will be precisely at right angles to the saw blade when the indicator is set at 90 degrees. Set the height of the blade to protrude about one-eighth on an inch above the workpiece. Mark the necessary guide lines on the workpiece, and position it on the table ahead of the miter gauge. Turn on the saw and allow the blade to reach full speed. Slowly push the workpiece, securely butted to the miter gauge, against the saw blade.

Making rip cuts is equally easy. First, verify the accuracy of the pointer on the fence with the markings on the graduated guide bar upon which the fence rides. Make adjustments as necessary; the setting will vary slightly with saw blades of different thicknesses. Set the rip fence in place at the desired width of cut, and lock it down tight. Make sure the miter gauge and other odds and ends are removed from the saw table. Then line the workpiece up against the rip fence and slowly push it past the saw blade.

Bevel cuts are made simply by tilting the saw blade to the desired angle. If the cut is a crosscut, use the miter gauge. For longer cuts guide the workpiece along the rip fence. When making bevel cuts several precautions must be taken. Make sure the blade does not rub the table, or touch the blade guard or rip fence. When the workpieces are small, various jigs, hold-downs, fingers, or other holding devices have to be used, and these too have to be kept clear of the blade.

The table saw, if improperly used, can be lethal. Safety in its operation is of paramount importance. Keep the following points in mind. Use the blade guard whenever possible. When the standard guard cannot be used, substitute other types of guards to provide

Fig. 3-6. A table saw accident just waiting to happen, and a lesson in how not to run a saw (or any other power tool). For instance: insufficient working space; stock propped up against table; tools and stock on table; table not clear of sawdust and chips; blade far too high; no blade guard; no splitter; no antikickback fingers; operator's hands far too close to blade; no jig or hold-down on workpiece; operator holding pencil; operator wearing bulky ring; loose cuffs on operator's shirt; operator not wearing goggles or face shield; cigarette smoke curling up into operator's eyes and hot ashes about to drop onto his fingers; operator standing right in front of blades. The whole setup is a dangerous mess. Duncan Photos.

more work space. At the very least, use additional safety devices. For instance, the workpiece should always be pushed past the saw blade with a push stick and not the fingers. Don't lean over the table to remove stock from the blade at the rear. Retrieve stock by walking around the saw, or let a helper on the other side of the saw perform the operation. Clear away scraps near the blade with a long stick. Take the precaution of wearing safety goggles while working.

The smart operator never stands in line with the cutting plane of the blade. Making freehand cuts is asking for trouble, and allowing your fingers to come anywhere near the blade is just plain idiocy. Table saws have a dangerous propensity known as "kickback," whereby the saw blade first seizes the workpiece then flings it violently, usually in the direction of the operator. Because of this, never try to hold small or awkward pieces with your fingers; use hold-downs, clamps, or fastening jigs whenever possible. When sawing long or wide stock, get someone to help you support the material. If no helper is available, place roller supports under the stock or use a piece of plywood clamped vertically to a sawhorse. Above all, concentrate on what you are doing. Pay attention; you cannot be too careful. Figure 3-6 shows several poor but commonplace practices in using a table saw. Any of these practices could lead to a serious accident.

Fig. 3-7. Adjustable dado blade. Duncan Photos.

Fig. 3-8. Table saw hold-downs in use during grooving operation. Duncan Photos.

By adding accessories you can make the table saw perform a great variety of tasks. One of the most useful accessories is a dado set (Fig. 3-7). A dado blade is designed to make wide cuts or grooves, and may consist of a single adjustable-width blade or several thin blades used in combination to achieve the desired width of cut. Dado blades can be used either across, or with, or diagonally to, the grain of the wood. The possible widths of cuts range from ⅛ inch to nearly 1 inch. You will use the dado blade for making grooved, ploughs, various kinds of joints, decorative cuts, tenons, and rabbets, as well as a variety of other cuts.

In making fancy cuts and working with odd-shaped stock, you will have to improvise devices for holding the workpiece in place on the saw table. One such device is a hold-down like the one shown in Fig. 3-8. The spring steel fingers attached to the fence apply constant pressure to the workpiece throughout the length of the cut. This helps to prevent chattering and jumping, and allows you to keep your fingers well away from the blade area. A universal jig (Fig. 3-9) is another device which with a little ingenuity can be used to hold the workpiece for all manner of saw operations. The clamping miter gauge shown in Fig. 3-10 performs a similar function, though with less versatility. Mounted on this miter gauge is another accessory, called a stop rod. The stop rod is used for repetitive cutting when several pieces of the same dimensions are needed.

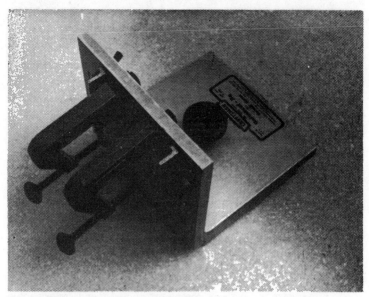

Fig. 3-9. Adjustable universal jig for table saw use. Duncan Photos.

Square cuts are easy enough to line up with the miter gauge or rip fence, and angle cuts are readily made with the miter gauge or mitering jig. Taper cuts, however, are something else again. Not only is an accurate tape very difficult to achieve, it is a difficult

Fig. 3-10. Clamping miter gauge for table saw use. Duncan Photos.

Fig. 3-11. Taper jig, here set out from rip fence for clarity. Duncan Photos.

operation to attempt without some sort of guide, and never should be attempted freehand. The answer to the problem is a device called a taper jig (Fig. 3-11). This jig is completely adjustable from zero degrees to about 15 degrees, provides a good solid guide for the workpiece, and will allow the cutting of gentle tapers even in long workpieces. The capability of making taper cuts of this sort can be invaluable when cabinetry must be fitted against a wall or other surface which is out of level or plumb.

Another useful accessory for the table saw is a molding head (Fig. 3-12). Of the several types available, the best is the cylindrical type which holds three blades locked tightly in place. The cutters are entirely interchangeable, and can be obtained in about 40 configurations. When the molding head has been set in place and properly adjusted, you can cut edge molding configurations into large stock or directly into the workpiece, or you can cut small and thin moldings for later application. In addition, you can make numerous decorative cuttings into the workpiece surface. The use of various jigs, clamps, hold downs, and guides is necessary when working with a molding head. The great advantage of this accessory is that you need not depend upon the limited supplies of mill-made moldings available at your local lumberyard. Instead, with materials of your own choice you can create decorative combinations whose possibilities are restricted only by your own imagination.

One more accessory is worthy of mention: the sanding wheel. Sanding wheels are available in 8-inch and 10-inch sizes, and consist of a cast steel or aluminum disc onto which standard sanding discs are glued. Some types are flat on both sides and can be used with a different grit on each surface; other types are slightly tapered on one side and flat on the other. The sanding wheel is a most useful device for sanding operations of all kinds, and is particularly helpful in removing small amounts of material from surfaces which must remain square and true, such as joint faces.

RADIAL SAW

The argument over whether the table saw or the radial saw (Fig. 3-13) is best for all-round shop use bids fair to go on forever. Both machines can perform approximately the same functions, and a competent craftsman can turn out fine work on either type of saw. Each has some advantages, and each has some disadvantages. For instance, ripping large sheets of material is easier on the table saw, but crosscutting is easier with a radial saw. Various cuts can be made on the table saw by simply positioning the workpiece properly. With the radial saw, however, the workpiece remains stationary, but the

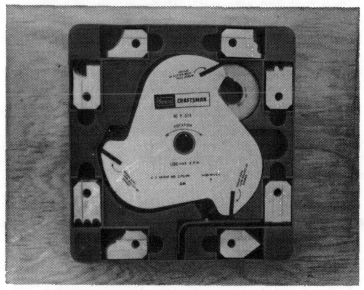

Fig. 3-12. Molding head for table or radial saw, with assorted cutter-bits. Duncan Photos.

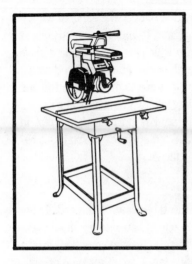

Fig. 3-13. Radial arm saw. Courtesy of Rockwell International.

saw head must constantly be adjusted. With the table saw, all the cutting action occurs beneath the workpiece, and the operator can't see what is happening. On the other hand, the radial saw cuts from above, and all layout lines and the action of the blade are clearly visible.

The radial saw, or radial arm saw, consists of only a few main parts. A heavy column is set upon a table, and an overarm and/or an arm track extends from the column. The motor unit and saw blade, together with the blade guards and various controls, slide back and forth on the arm track. Both blade and track are adjustable through a wide range of angles, allowing an almost infinite variety of cuts. The most common sizes for home shop use are the 10-inch and 12-inch saws, usually powered by a 2 or 2½ horsepower motor.

Because of the design and the fact that kickback is almost impossible during most sawing operations, the radial saw is perhaps the safest of the sawing machines. On the other hand, as with any motorized equipment, it must be treated with respect. In general, the safety rules which apply to table saws also apply to radial saws. You should keep in mind a few additional points. All of the clamps and locking handles must be kept tight, and the saw unit returned to the rear of the table after each cut. As with the table saw, extension tables, roller stands, and other supports must always be used when workpieces are too large for the table. Guards should be in place whenever possible, and antikickback fingers used during ripping operations. Never stand directly in line with the cutting plane of the saw blade. Keep the table clean of sawdust and free of chips and scraps, and never remove material from the table until the saw is in return position and stopped.

Crosscutting operations on a radial saw are no chore at all. They include straight cutting, miters, rabbets, dados, and bevels. The first step in crosscutting is to make sure the saw blade is exactly perpendicular to the table and exactly at right angles to the guard fence located at the rear of the table. Then adjust the depth of cut so the teeth of the saw blade stand about 1/16 inch below the table surface in a clearance groove. With the guards and antikickback fingers set in the proper positions and all the adjustments locked, slide the workpiece tight against the guide fence and align the layout lines correctly with the blade. Turn on the power and let the blade come to full speed. Draw the head along the arm track toward you, holding the workpiece firmly against the guide fence. Ease the saw slowly until the cut is complete. Return the saw to the rear of the table and turn it off. This process, along with whatever adjustments to blade and arm track are necessary, is used in the great percentage of all radial saw cutting operations. Jigs, hold-downs, clamps, and guides may be necessary, depending upon the specific operation.

Ripping can be done in two ways: in-ripping and out-ripping. In either case, the saw blade must rotate up and toward the operator, never in the opposite manner. Note that the cutting action of the blade is downward (place material good side up) during crosscutting, but upward (place material good side down) during ripping. Once the necessary settings have been accurately made and locked into place, and the saw head rotated so that the blade is parallel with the guide fence, then the guards and antikickback fingers can be moved into place. Place one edge of the workpiece against the guide fence, and switch on the saw. Allow the blade to come to full speed and feed the stock steadily into the blade, using a push stick and hold-down fingers as necessary. The out-rip position is used for wide stock and the in-rip position for narrower pieces. Bevel ripping is done in the same manner, with the blade tilted to the desired angle. The radial saw, just like the table saw, uses a jig to do taper cutting. Horizontal cutting, where the saw blade is parallel to the table top and usually housed in a special guard, can be readily accomplished. Both horizontal crosscutting and horizontal ripping are possible.

The radial saw, like the table saw, can be adapted for various purposes with the addition of accessories. Several dado sets are available, and making all manner of dado cuts on a radial saw is a pleasure, simply because you can always see exactly what you are doing. Blind grooving is a snap, and nearly all the basic cabinetmaking joints can be readily cut. Furthermore, the addition of simple jigs and setups will allow repetitive identical cuts.

The same molding head and cutters used with a table saw can be used with the radial saw. The saw head can be positioned either vertically or horizontally, depending upon the demands of the job. The guide fence (two of which may be necessary for some operations) is a different kind than that used for sawing. A replacement constructed from two pieces of wood can often be employed, but in some instances a special shaper-jointer fence must be used. Also, a special guard must be mounted upon the saw head. As in other operations, jigs and hold downs must frequently be set up.

A special planer blade and head can be adapted to the radial saw to allow either edge or surface planing. A sanding drum attachment can be used for edge sanding. In addition, some radial saws can be adapted to do a certain amount of routing, though for most purposes a standard power router is more utilitarian.

SANDERS

Perhaps the most laborious part of cabinetmaking is smoothing the completed articles preparatory to applying a finish. Power sanders, however, do much to ease the strain. Of the many types of sanding machines available, two are of particular interest to the cabinetmaker.

The first type is the belt sander (Fig. 3-14). The belt sander uses an easily replaceable continuous strip of sandpaper secured over two revolving drums to present a wide and continuously moving sanding surface. A 1 or 1½ horsepower unit with a sanding surface of 14 to 24 square inches is a good size for cabinetwork and general purpose usage. Automatic dust pickup is a valuable feature which prevents the operator from being continuously surrounded by a cloud of sawdust. Some types of sanders can be converted into a small finishing machine by attachment to a special stand. This adds a very handy tool to the shop.

The belt sander cuts rapidly, and is tricky to use until you get used to it. For best results, drape the cord over your shoulder, grip the machine tightly, and turn on the power. After the initial kick,

Fig. 3-14. Belt sander. Courtesy of Rockwell International.

lower the sander so that the rear drum section touches the workpiece first. Then lower the forward part, keeping the machine moving all the time. Never let the sander stop moving; the belt will immediately cut deep grooves in the workpiece. Move the sander forward and back in a straight line, using only light pressure. The acutal sanding process takes place during the back stroke; very little action occurs on the forward stroke. Make sure the sanding surface remains flat to the workpiece. Sanding is usually done parallel with the grain of the wood, but if the surface is uneven, or the wood is striated with a combination of hard and soft grains (such as a fir plywood), then cross-sanding may also be necessary.

The second type of sander is a finishing sander (Fig. 3-15). Actually, this type is seldom called by this name; it is normally referred to as a pad sander or, sometimes, an orbital sander. For medium duty use in the home shop, a sander of about ¼ horsepower with a capacity for one-third of a standard sheet of sandpaper is ideal. The larger sizes will do more work more rapidly, but are harder to use because of their bulk and weight. Here again an automatic dust pickup feature is nice to have. The primary function of this type of sander is not to remove large quantities of material, but to prepare the surface for the application of finish coats, or to sand the surface between finish coats.

Three different actions of the pad are available: orbital, straight line, and multimotion. Some sanders are dual-action; this means that flipping a lever you can change from orbital to straight-line or vice-versa, whichever is preferable. In woodworking, however, the

Fig. 3-15. Finishing sander. Courtesy of Rockwell International.

straight-line action is invariably the most effective one. Orbital and multimotion actions can easily cause crossgrain scratches or peculiar looking whorls in the finished surface. Unlike the belt sander, pad sanders are always used parallel with the grain of the wood.

A power pad sander is no harder to use than a sanding block. It is readily controllable; and not as likely to get away from you as a belt sander. After clipping the appropriate type of sandpaper to the pad, turn on the machine and lower it gently and flat onto the surface of the workpiece. Move the machine forward and back slowly in the direction of the wood grain with as little sideways motion as possible. Applying pressure is not necessary; the weight of the sander will do the work.

One type of pad sander is made especially for cabinetwork. It is a small, single-handled machine with a high-speed drive and a relatively small pad. It is quite light in weight. Its greatest advantage is that it can be controlled with one hand. It can be used in tight quarters and for overhead sanding with little fatigue. It works well on irregular and curved surfaces.

DRILLS

The familiar small hand-held electric drills (Fig. 3-16) are designated by the size of the largest bit shank that the chuck will accept: ¼ inch, ⅜ inch, and 1 inch. On most models the chuck is an in-line prolongation of the body of the drill, a design suited for straight-ahead drilling, but for use in cramped quarters models are available

80

with chucks set at 45- and 90-degree angles to the drill body. Some types of drills are reversible and some have two-speed and variable-speed capabilities. The chucks of most models are of the geared or Jacobs type. For all-round general shop and cabinetmaking work, a ⅜-inch drill of about ⅓ or ⅜ horsepower with reversing and variable-speed features is the best bet. Drills with a plastic (rather than metal) housing are safer because they are shock-proof.

The portable electric drill is a highly versatile tool. It can perform a lot of operations quickly and easily; the trick is in knowing just which accessories to use for the job at hand. The drill's principal function, of course, is to bore holes, and many types of bits are available for the purpose.

Spade or speed bits (Fig. 3-17) are generally used for fast boring, in soft and hard woods, plywood, and composition board. Because they cut a rough hole, these bits are not recommended for precision boring or doweling. Their diameters range from ¼ inch to 1½ inches in increments of 1/16 inch. Wood screw pilot bits (Fig. 3-18) look much like spade bits but are more specialized in use. They are sized to match the various sizes of wood screws, and are manufactured in several depths for each screw size. The lead part of the bit bores a pilot hole and the upper part of the blade cuts an accurate countersink.

You can obtain several types of brad point bits and drills (Fig. 3-19). The single-spur brad point is a fast boring bit which creates minimal friction and cuts cleanly. The double-spur bit with a spiral grind and polished edges cuts extremely accurate holes in all kinds of woods with a minimum of friction and heating, and virtually no travel. The precision type of brad point dowel bits is used especially for doweling. Also available are long-shanked, short-bit brad points, expressly designed for use with portable drills.

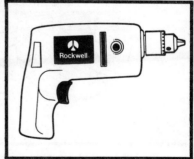

Fig. 3-16. Portable electric drill. Courtesy of Rockwell International.

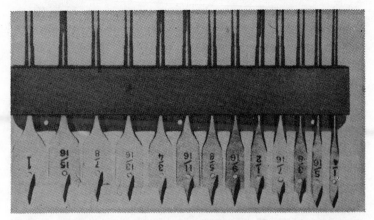

Fig. 3-17. Set of spade bits. Larger sizes are available. Courtesy of Woodcraft Supply Corp.

Twist drills (Fig. 3-20) are a familiar type of bit. Carbon-steel twist drills are used only with wood and similar soft materials, and are available in diameters ranging from 1/32 inch to ¾-inch in increments of 1/64 inch. High-steel drills can be used on wood, metal, and some plastics. They are sold in sets of three different sizes: fractional, numerical, and letter (Fig. 3-21). A standard set of fractional sizes is made in diameters ranging from 1/64 inch to ½ inch in increments of 1/64 inch. More sizes are available above ½ inch for use in large hand drills and drill presses; some have turned-down shanks for use in smaller drills. Though the fractional sizes are most commonly used in the woodworking shop, number and letter drills,

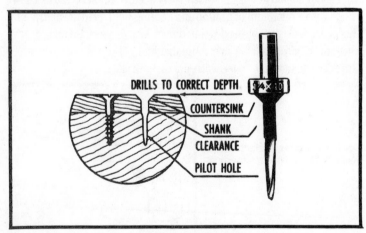

Fig. 3-18. Typical pilot bit. Courtesy of Stanley Tools.

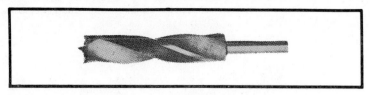

Fig. 3-19. Brad point bit. Courtesy of Woodcraft Supply Corp.

particularly the former, are essential to accurate thread tapping and through-drilling, especially in materials other than wood.

Tool manufacturers offer a number of specialized bits which can be of considerable value to cabinetmakers on certain occasions. Twist drills with carbide tips, for instance, are used to drill through highly abrasive materials like laminated plastics. Diamond-tipped drills are used for penetrating glass or ceramic tile. The multispur machine center bit, while primarily designed for use in a lathe, can be used in an electric hand drill for boring through veneered stock.

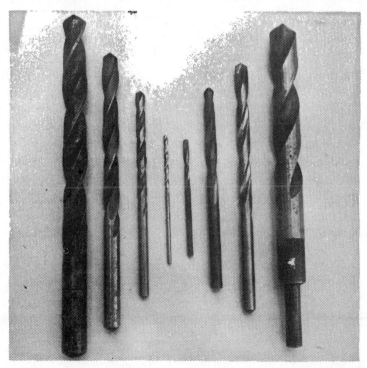

Fig. 3-20. Typical twist drill bits. From the left, the first four are standard bits. The next two are solid carbide. The seventh is carbide-tipped. The last is a standard bit, larger size, with a turned ¼-inch shank. Many other speciality variations are available. Duncan Photos.

NUMBER DRILLS

Size	Dia.	Size	Dia.
1	0.2280	41	0.0960
2	0.2210	42	0.0935
3	0.2130	43	0.0890
4	0.2090	44	0.0860
5	0.2055	45	0.0820
6	0.2040	46	0.0810
7	0.2010	47	0.0785
8	0.1990	48	0.0760
9	0.1960	49	0.0730
10	0.1935	50	0.0700
11	0.1910	51	0.0670
12	0.1890	52	0.0635
13	0.1850	53	0.0595
14	0.1820	54	0.0550
15	0.1800	55	0.0520
16	0.1770	56	0.0465
17	0.1730	57	0.0430
18	0.1695	58	0.0420
19	0.1660	59	0.0410
20	0.1610	60	0.0400
21	0.1590	61	0.0390
22	0.1570	62	0.0380
23	0.1540	63	0.0370
24	0.1520	64	0.0360
25	0.1495	65	0.0350
26	0.1470	66	0.0330
27	0.1440	67	0.0320
28	0.1405	68	0.0310
29	0.1360	69	0.0292
30	0.1285	70	0.0280
31	0.1200	71	0.0260
32	0.1160	72	0.0250
33	0.1130	73	0.0240
34	0.1110	74	0.0225
35	0.1100	75	0.0210
36	0.1065	76	0.0200
37	0.1040	77	0.0180
38	0.1015	78	0.0160
39	0.0995	79	0.0145
40	0.0980	80	0.0135

FRACTIONAL DRILLS		LETTER DRILLS	
Size	Dia.	Size	Dia.
1/64	0.0156	A	0.2340
1/32	0.0312	B	0.2380
3/64	0.0469	C	0.2420
1/16	0.0625	D	0.2460
5/64	0.0781	E	0.2500
3/32	0.0937	F	0.2570
7/64	0.1094	G	0.2610
1/8	0.1250	H	0.2660
9/64	0.1406	I	0.2720
5/32	0.1562	J	0.2770
11/64	0.1719	K	0.2810
3/16	0.1875	L	0.2900
13/64	0.2031	M	0.2950
7/32	0.2187	N	0.3020
15/64	0.2344	O	0.3160
1/4	0.2500	P	0.3230
17/64	0.2656	Q	0.3160
9/32	0.2812	R	0.3390
19/64	0.2969	S	0.3480
5/16	0.3125	T	0.3580
21/64	0.3281	U	0.3680
11/32	0.3437	V	0.3770
23/64	0.3594	W	0.3860
3/8	0.3750	X	0.3970
25/64	0.3906	Y	0.4040
13/32	0.4062	Z	0.4130
27/64	0.4219		
7/16	0.4375		
29/64	0.4531		
15/32	0.4687		
31/64	0.4844		
1/2	0.5000		

Fig. 3-21. Drill size chart.

Bellhanger's drills in lengths of up to two feet are available in several diameters for drill deep holes. Shell augers are used for a similar purpose and other types of auger bits, resembling those used with a bit brace, are used for general purpose boring at low speeds.

Tapered drills, with countersinks and stopcollars (Fig. 3-22), afford the best way to prepare fine work for woodscrews. They are

Fig. 3-22. Set of tapered drills with countersinks and stop-collars. Courtesy of Woodcraft Supply Corp.

designed primarily for use with hardwoods, and are machined to exactly match the various screw sizes. Drilling of pilot holes, countersink holes for screw heads, and counterbores for plugs can be accomplished in one operation with great accuracy. The Forstner bit, similar to the one used with a bit brace, is for cutting shallow and flat bottomed holes.

A number of special cutters are used with electric drills. Cutting large-sized holes requires the use of a hole saw (Fig. 3-23). Hole saws are available in various sizes from ¾ inch to 2½ inches and

Fig. 3-23. Two styles of interchangeable hole saws and mandrels. Duncan Photos.

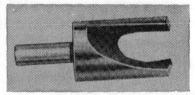

Fig. 3-24. Plug cutter. Courtesy of Stanley Tools.

larger. One type of hole saw has an integrated pilot drill and blade; another type has a single mandrel with interchangeable blades of different sizes. A plug cutter (Fig. 3-24), also available in several sizes, cuts smooth plugs with chamfered edges. The plugs are used to hide counterbored screw heads. A combination tool called a plug and dowel cutter (Fig. 3-25) is available in various sizes for creating cylinders with diameters of from ⅜ inch to 2 inches and lengths of up to 3 inches. A similar but more specialized tool, the tenon cutter (Fig. 3-26), is used for making dowel ends on spindles.

Fig. 3-25. Combination plug and dowel cutter. Courtesy of Woodcraft Supply Corp.

In addition to the board assortment of standard bits and cutters, a number of other accessories are handy to have around the shop. For instance, by securing your drill to a drill stand, you can make yourself an inexpensive drill press which will furnish the stability needed for precision drilling. Small grinding wheels can be adapted to your drill and so can sanding discs and sanding drums. Right-angle-drive gear boxes can be adapted for polishing, sanding, and buffing. Lamb's-wool buffing pads and polishing bonnets are drill accessories that can be used for finishing work. You can adapt buffing wheels and use various polishing compounds to shine and polish cabinet hardware. A drum file or rotary rasp fitted to your drill works well in removing large quantities of material from the workpiece. Certain types of routing are possible with a drill, as well as precision grinding. Available for general shop purposes are still other accessories, such as wire brushes and paint stirrers.

Fig. 3-26. Tenon cutter. Courtesy of Woodcraft Supply Corp.

Fig. 3-27. Router. Courtesy of Rockwell International.

ROUTER

The router (Fig. 3-27) is a particularly useful tool for the cabinetmaker. Several sizes and many brands are available, and any one of them will do a good job. Generally speaking, a model with a ¾ to 1 horsepower motor, quality construction, accurate adjustment controls, and the capability of accepting a wide variety of cutters and accessories, is your best bet. The machine should be fitted throughout with ballbearings.

A full set of router bits (Fig. 3-28) can accomplish a great variety of cuts. Standard steel bits are for use with wood; certain carbide-tipped bits are for use with abrasive materials like laminated plastics. In addition to employing the router to create a number of decorative cuts and molding effects, you can use it to make many of the standard cabinetmaking joints.

The adaptation of various accessories to the router increases its capabilities considerably. For instance, a dovetail joint fixture will allow you to make the necessary cuts for either flush or rabbeted dovetail joints easily and quickly. Special trammel points are useful for making accurate circular grooves. Butt-hinge templates make short work of mortising your door hinges, and letter templates simplify sign making. By inverting the router and mounting it to the bottom of a specially built table, you can convert it to a junior-size shaper for making edge moldings at the workbench. Top-of-the-line tables come equipped with rip fence, blade guard, and miter gauge. Another device converts the router to an outside-edge-cutting precision lathe for making intricate spindle cuts.

The router is a tricky tool to use because it operates at extremely high speeds and must be closely and carefully controlled. At first it is heavy and awkward to handle, but with time and experience the task becomes simpler. Whenever possible the router should be guided along a straightedge or some sort of edge guide. Bits with pilot ends will automatically control a part of the cut, usually the depth. Templates (patterns) are used as guides for special work. Freehand routing is fully possible, but the quality of the finished work is entirely dependent upon the skill of the operator, since no guides or templates are used. A large amount of practice is necessary.

It should be noted that a route can be an extremely dangerous tool, since it can make a cut before you realize what has happened. Furthermore, it strays chips and sawdust in abundance. Always use bits that are sharp and make sure than no air vents on the machine are plugged. Check the bits frequently to make sure they are tight. Switch the motor on before lowering the router to the workpiece; switch the motor off before removing the router from the workpiece. You will find that wearing safety goggles or a face shield is a necessary precaution.

POWER PLANE

The power plane, or planer, (Fig. 3-29) makes a uniform surface cut by means of two or three cutter blades set in a rapidly revolving drum. The tool has three especially valuable capabilities. One, it can plane a 3½-inch-wide swath (which makes it practical for use when large surface areas have to be smoothed). Two, it can cut bevels at various angles with uniform results. Three, when adjusted for the assignment, it can make certain types of rabbet cuts. Because of the planer's high blade speed, even tough end grains can be precisely trimmed.

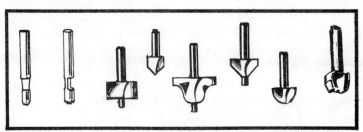

Fig. 3-28. A few of the many available router bit configurations. Courtesy of Stanley Tools.

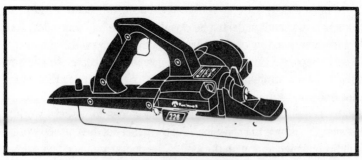

Fig. 3-29. Power planer. Courtesy of Rockwell International.

The greatest advantage of this tool is that it can be transported easily to the work site and used for various planing operations with decent results. However, because it is a hand-held tool, it isn't likely to produce perfect results. In most cases, it it better to bring the workpiece to a stationary power tool instead. The application of the power plane in cabinetmaking is somewhat limited, especially if there are other tools available which can duplicate the planer's functions. However, it can be of considerable help when edges have to be trimmed from already installed pieces that, for whatever the reason, did not come out quite true.

JOINTER

One problem commonly encountered in cabinetmaking is that the lumberyard never seems to have exactly the width or thickness of stock you want. Another problem frequently arises from the fact that the stock the lumberyard does have is warped, or rough, or cut shy. The answer to these problems is the jointer (Fig. 3-30), an extensive and bulky piece of equipment which is otherwise of rather limited use. The jointer is mainly used to square up stock and to reduce it to the desired thickness.

Facing or surfacing will remove cup or mild twist warp from the stock. Edge jointing will remove lengthwise bows from the stock. With the proper procedures, all four sides of the stock, as well as the end grains, can be made absolutely rectangular and true.

The jointer can also be used in rabbeting, beveling, and chamfering. Furthermore, with the right setup and a little practice, you can cut long tapers, short tapers, and stop tapers.

Probably the most common size of jointer for the home workshop is the 6-inch-width machine. Somewhat larger jointers are manufactured, but are intended for commercial use. Where greater capacity for surfacing is needed, the machine to use is the planer. However, because of their large size and great expense, planers are seldom found in home shops. If you have wide stock which needs to be surfaced, your best bet is to have a mill or commercial woodworking shop do the job for you.

SHAPER

The high speed shaper (Fig. 3-31) is essentially an overgrown inverted router set in a table. Its principal function is approximately the same as that of the molding heads and cutters mentioned earlier for use with the table or radial saw. Because of size and expense, the shaper is of dubious practical value in the average shop, especially since its function can be duplicated by other tools at less expense and with more convenience.

GRINDER

The bench grinder (Fig. 3-32), while not directly used in cabinetmaking, nonetheless is a valuable asset to the shop. As

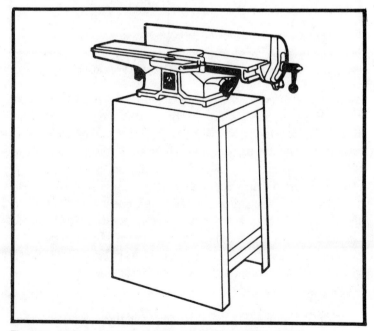

Fig. 3-30. Jointer and stand. Courtesy of Rockwell International.

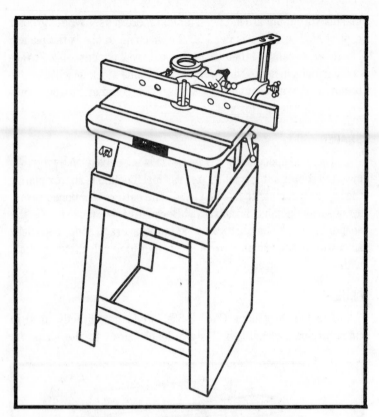

Fig. 3-31. Shaper and stand. Courtesy of Rockwell International.

mentioned previously, the cutting edges of all woodworking tools must be kept absolutely sharp, and the bench grinder is a help in this respect. In most cases, a large elaborate machine is unnecessary. A small unit of about ½ horsepower with to 6-inch wheels, a pair of eye shields, and a pair of adjustable tool rests should be sufficient. By all means, choose a unit which runs entirely on ballbearings.

Various tool holders and grinding attachments can be added to the bench grinder to aid in sharpening different kinds of blades. Grinding wheels are available in any of several grades of grit. For polishing, the grinding wheels are replaced by buffing wheels. Some grinders will also accept a disc sander attachment.

DRILL PRESS

The drill press (Fig. 3-33) is another of those expensive shop tools which are awfully nice to have on hand, but certainly not

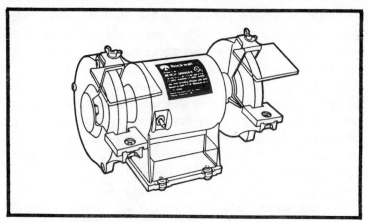

Fig. 3-32. Bench grinder. Courtesy of Rockwell International.

essential. They are available in either bench top or freestanding floor models. Some drill presses have heads which can be rotated, tilted, and raised. However, most units are equipped only with a swing head and adjustable table. The multiple- or variable-speed feature is almost essential, since different jobs require different drilling speeds.

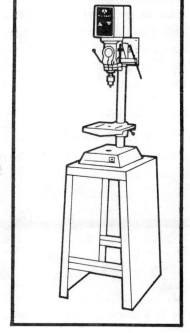

Fig. 3-33. Drill press and stand. Courtesy of Rockwell International.

While the primary purpose of a drill press is accurate hole boring, the addition of accessories can extend the range of its usefulness. For instance, a rotary planer can be chucked to plane surfaces or dress wood stock. The addition of a shaper fence, plus the appropriate cutter, will allow you to make moldings and decorative cuts, though this can also be done with a molding head on other tools. Various sanding attachments are also available, and so are rotary rasps, files, and circle cutters (devices which accomplish the same purpose as a hole saw). With a set of hollow square mortise chisels and bits, you can quickly and easily make mortises for mortise-and-tenon joints (Fig. 3-34). Another possibility is to add a dovetail attachment which, in combination with the proper type of router bit, will enable you to cut accurate dovetail joints.

MITER BOX

The motorized miter box (Fig. 3-35) is a relative newcomer to the home workshop. Its purpose is exactly the same as that of the manual miter box discussed earlier, but there are some additional advantages. Most obvious is the fact that virtually no elbow grease is required. Also, once adjusted, this device has a high degree of accuracy. Cuts will be true and uniform every time. The stock can be firmly set in place on the table, and there is little opportunity for it to shift or for the cut to get out of line, as can sometimes happen with a manual miter box. The greatest drawback is the price, which can be justified only by the cutting of a great many miters or by the fact that the prospective owner simply likes to collect power tools.

ODDS AND ENDS

The power tools mentioned above are by no means the only ones. Several have gone without mention, primarily because they

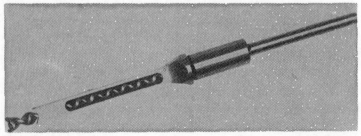

Fig. 3-34. Hollow square mortise chisel and bit. Courtesy of Woodcraft Supply Corp.

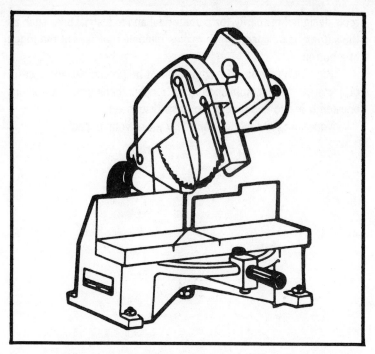

Fig. 3-35. Motorized or power miter box. Courtesy of Rockwell International.

are not particularly oriented to the construction of cabinets and built-ins. This is not to say that some of them cannot be useful, or substitute when no other tools are available. For instance, the reciprocating saw can in certain circumstances be used in place of a scroll saw or portable electric hand saw. The high speed rotary disc sander, similar to the grinders used in auto body shops, can be used for quick removal of stock, or for grinding off unwanted nail heads or points. A small rotary grinder might be used for one thing or another, but is primarily a hobbyist's or modelmaker's tool. An electric stapler might be of use in applying hardboard backings to some types of cabinetry.

A bench-mounted combination belt-disc sander would be nice for extensive sanding and shaping operations, but is not essential. The bench-mounted scroll saw lies in the same category. A woodworking lathe, of course, is a marvelous adjunct to any home workshop, but its use in cabinetry is limited; it is more attuned to furniture making. A band saw likewise would be a lovely tool to own, but is limited in use for this type of work. Then there are the various power tools designed primarily for commercial and industrial use, such as the automatic mortiser which makes multiple mortises at the touch of a button.

But, let's face it; the great bulk of home cabinet and built-in projects can be accomplished quite nicely, thank you, with about one-tenth of the equipment we have discussed.

You pays your money, and you picks your peanuts.

Chapter 4
Materials

Not many decades ago, 99 percent of the materials which went into the building of cabinets and furniture was raw, solid wood. Today, the solid woods account for only a small percentage of the materials used in cabinets and built-ins. Today, in addition to the solid woods, we have a variety of manufactured wood-base products, several lines of standard and stock synthetic components which are available from numerous sources, and an assortment of manmade nonwood materials for sundry purposes. To a degree, your success in constructing cabinetry and built-ins will depend upon your knowledge of all of these materials. With such a diverse array from which to choose, the more information about them you have at your command, the easier your task will be, and the better the finished results.

WOOD

Of all the materials available to use, wood is undoubtedly the most remarkable. Although it may appear to be simple enough, it actually is incredibly complicated and amazingly versatile. The wood itself consists of millions upon millions of tiny cellular structures, all bonded together by a substance called lignin. The walls of the cells form the supportive structure of the tree in life, and after death comprise the solid material with which we work.

Composition

Looking at a cross section of a tree trunk (Fig. 4-1), you will see several distinct layers, circles within circles. Furthest from the center is the outer bark, a protective covering. Only the thin inside layer of the bark, called phloem or bast, is alive. This is where the sap travels. The cambium layer is extremely thin, sandwiched between the bark and the wood, and is responsible for the entire outward growth of the tree. Each year, a tiny amount of bark grows on the outside of the cambium, while a considerable amount of growth takes place on the wood or inside segment. These yearly circles of growth, which are obvious in most species, are called annular because of the ring shape.

When the tree is cut for use as lumber, all of the outside layers are peeled away. What remains is the wood itself. This part of the tree is classified into two components, the sapwood and the heartwood. The sapwood is the lighter-colored, outer portion; the heartwood is the darker, inner portion. The heartwood has long since ceased to grow. In some species, distinguishing between sapwood and heartwood is difficult.

Each yearly growth ring is composed of a broader, brighter band called the springwood and a narrower, darker band called the summerwood. Differentiating between springwood and summerwood is not always easy; in some species it may be impossible. In those species where the growth rings are clearly defined, you can determine the age of the tree simply by counting the rings.

Characteristics

No two species of trees, and there are more than 100,000 species in the world, are quite alike. Each exhibits its own characteristics, of which the most important is density. The cell walls of trees are approximately the same in composition, but the open spaces within the cells vary greatly. The density of a wood is determined by measuring its specific gravity. The process involves comparing a certain volume of the wood in question with an identical volume of water at 4°C. The specific gravity of maple, for instance, is approximately 0.49, or about half that of water, an important point if you need to build a hardwood cabinet that will float easily. More important, however, is the simple fact that the specific gravity of a wood is an excellent indicator of its relative strength and hardness.

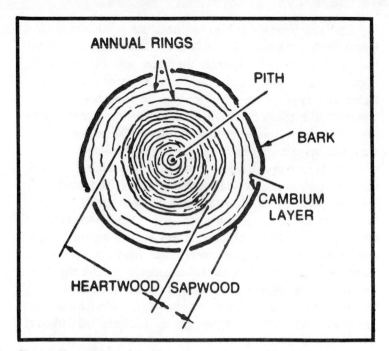

Fig. 4-1. The structure of a tree.

The higher the specific gravity, the stronger the wood, as a general rule. In some cabinetmaking and most furniture building, specific gravity is an important concern.

Another significant characteristic of any wood is its grain. The cellular structure of wood extends predominantly parallel to the tree trunk. When the wood is cut, in whatever direction, certain portions of the cell walls are exposed, and the visible arrangement of cell walls is what we call grain. When the cell walls are all relatively parallel to the center of the tree and run in approximately straight lines, the result is called straight grain. Growth problems (knots, foreign bodies, etc.) in the tree can cause peculiar growth patterns, and this results in irregular grain. Sometimes, instead of growing straight, the cells will grow in a spiral fashion, and this is called a spiral grain. Curly grain occurs when a series of distorted and whorled patterns appear throughout the wood. If the growth pattern spirals in opposite direction, the cellular structure twisting as it grows, the grain is called interlocked. Whatever the original configuration of the grain, additional visible effects are produced according to the manner in which the log is sawed.

99

Each kind of wood also has its own texture, which is dependent upon a number of factors. Primarily, the smaller the wood cell, the finer the texture, and the larger the wood cell, the coarser the texture. Texture may be influenced by the apparent grain, and also by the fibrosity of the wood. You will hear the terms open grain and tight grain; these refer to still other cellular structure characteristics that affect the texture. Open-grained wood, like oak, exhibits a surface distinguished by numerous pores and openings (empty cell cavities that have been exposed to view). Birch, on the other hand, has a non-porous texture and is called a tight-grained wood.

The color of wood varies not only between species, but also between individual trees of a given species, and even between various parts of one tree. Most of the species used in cabinetmaking and furniture building exhibit characteristic individual colorations. Wood color is caused by pigments imbedded in the cell structure, and since these pigments are likely to be more plentiful in the heartwood, this portion of the tree is often darker than the sapwood. Nearly all woods, because of the pigment oxidation, will darken in color when exposed to the air.

Another characteristic common to all woods is known as figure. In some woods, or sections of a given species of wood, figure is a prominent feature, while in others it is unnoticeable or singularly unimpressive. Figure is an indeterminant patterning of the wood which can be caused by one or a combination of growth factors. Irregularities in grain, or color, or even staining, all play a part. Growth rings are sometimes much in evidence, and in some species the rays, which radiate outward laterally from the center of the tree at right angles to the grain, are also distinctive. Knots and other defects may also add to figure, becoming assets instead of liabilities. Distinctive and unusual figure is often highly important and widely sought after for use in the building of fine cabinetry or furniture.

This is probably as good a time as any to clear up the confusion about whether a wood is hard or soft, and whether it is consequently a hardwood or a softwood. As mentioned earlier, hardness has to do with density, and is a measure of the resistance of a species of wood to denting and scratching. If the specific gravity of a wood is 0.25, it is quite soft. If the specific gravity of a wood is 0.75, it is extremely hard.

The terms hardwood and softwood have nothing to do with specific gravity; they are botanical terms. Softwood trees belong to the conifer category of trees. The category comprises mostly evergreens. Hardwood trees, on the other hand, are members of the deciduous or broadleaf category. Deciduous trees lose their leaves at some point each year. All pines, firs, and larches are conifers. All maples, birches, and fruitwoods are broad-leafs.

The fact is, some softwoods are hard wood, while some hardwoods are soft woods. This is the case with aspen or poplar, which has a low specific gravity but is a broad-leaf. On the other hand, western larch a conifer with a specific gravity of about 0.51, can be classed as moderately hard.

The worker of woods soon discovers that the various species of woods have additional characteristics which are best learned through working with them. For instance, some woods are excellent for certain purposes, and terrible for others. The western larch just mentioned makes good rough-dimension construction material, but does not lend itself to cabinetwork. White pine may be used successfully for either purposes. Beech is excellent for food containers, since it transfers no odor or flavor to the contents. Redwood and cedar both have high resistance to rot and insect damage. Walnut has always been a popular wood for cabinetwork and furniture with a transparent finish because of the inherent beauty of the wood. The same can be said for numerous other woods such as maple, oak, mahogany, and zebrawood.

Also important to the woodworker is the manner in which the wood will act and react under the assault of assorted woodworking tools. For instance, sugar maple can be turned easily on a lathe. White pine is soft and tight-grained, and works nicely with either hand or power tools. Yellow poplar will machine adequately, holds paint and stain well, and seldom will split when nailed. Red oak does not take kindly to shaping. Lauan mahogany can be rip-sawed without blade waver, and leaves an edge so smooth that only minor touch-up with sandpaper is needed. Cottonwood, on the other hand, leaves a ragged or feathery edge. And so the list goes on. With a bit of research, you can tailor the type of wood exactly to your needs and specifications. The only problem then is in finding a source for the materials that you want, and this can sometimes be something of a chore.

Seasoning

Green lumber, right off the stump, contains an incredible amount of moisture. At this point, all of the cells which make up the structure of the wood are chock full of water and nutrients. The wood is rough-sawed into lumber and allowed to air-dry. After a certain period of time, the free moisture within the cell cavities evaporates, and until then no shrinkage in the wood takes place. But when the moisture content reaches 30 percent, the liquid begins to leave the cell walls and shrinkage starts.

Proper air-drying is seldom carried out anymore. The old rule of thumb was that a piece of lumber should air-dry for one year for every inch of thickness of the stock. Today, however, that time span has been reduced to something on the order of two to three months. The lumber is then wheeled into huge kilns and force-dried under controlled conditions. The shrinkage continues, but not equally in all directions. The kiln-drying process continues until the moisture content is brought down to somewhere around 20 percent. By industry terms, the wood is then "dry."

There are some common misconceptions about this so-called dry wood. One is that kiln-dried wood is somehow better than air-dried wood, but such is not the case. Wood which comes out of the kiln is no better than the wood that goes into the kiln, and there is no difference whatsoever between air-dried and kiln-dried wood as far as quality is concerned. Nor does age have any bearing. A twenty-year-old piece of wood is not necessarily any drier than a similar piece one year old. In fact, depending upon how the old wood was stored, it may be wetter than the newer wood. Nor does "dry" wood remain dry. All woods, regardless of species, are continually "working." This means that they continually absorb and expel moisture, depending upon conditions of humidity, temperature, and ventilation. This action never ceases, and in fact you may even notice some small differences occurring during the course of putting a cabinetmaking project together, as the wood shrinks and swells with the weather. Nor can you stop the process by applying paints or stains. Indeed, in certain cases these applications can do more harm than good.

This constant working is also a constant problem, and one which has meaning for you as a cabinetmaker. Since no way has yet been devised to stop this action, you must live with it, and exercise the best craftsmanship you can under the circumstances. This means that joints must be accurate and tight, measurements must be precise, fastenings must be secure, and the general workmanship must be as good as you can make it. In some cases, allowances must be built in to compensate for expansion and contraction.

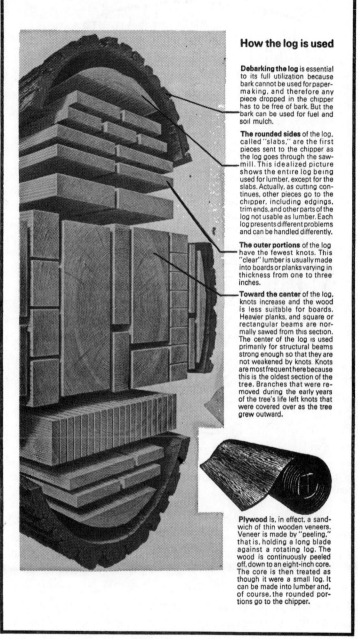

How the log is used

Debarking the log is essential to its full utilization because bark cannot be used for paper-making, and therefore any piece dropped in the chipper has to be free of bark. But the bark can be used for fuel and soil mulch.

The rounded sides of the log, called "slabs," are the first pieces sent to the chipper as the log goes through the saw-mill. This idealized picture shows the entire log being used for lumber, except for the slabs. Actually, as cutting continues, other pieces go to the chipper, including edgings, trim ends, and other parts of the log not usable as lumber. Each log presents different problems and can be handled differently.

The outer portions of the log have the fewest knots. This "clear" lumber is usually made into boards or planks varying in thickness from one to three inches.

Toward the center of the log, knots increase and the wood is less suitable for boards. Heavier planks, and square or rectangular beams are normally sawed from this section. The center of the log is used primarily for structural beams strong enough so that they are not weakened by knots. Knots are most frequent here because this is the oldest section of the tree. Branches that were removed during the early years of the tree's life left knots that were covered over as the tree grew outward.

Plywood is, in effect, a sandwich of thin wooden veneers. Veneer is made by "peeling," that is, holding a long blade against a rotating log. The wood is continuously peeled off, down to an eight-inch core. The core is then treated as though it were a small log. It can be made into lumber and, of course, the rounded portions go to the chipper.

Fig. 4-2. A complex log cut, yielding several kinds of stock. Courtesy of St. Regis Paper Co.

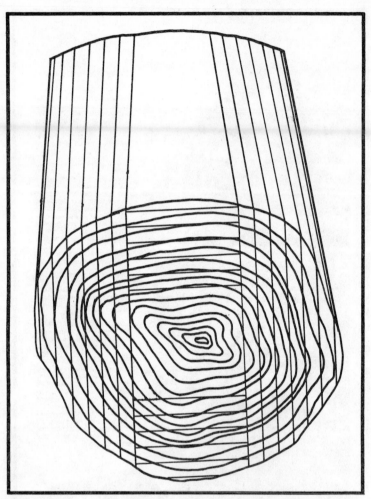

Fig. 4-3. Slash-sawing is a common and inexpensive method of reducing logs to boards and dimension stock.

Another helpful move that you can easily make is to "season" your own lumber. This means simply allowing the stock that you plan to use a liberal period of adjustment time. The material that you buy for your projects will probably be stored in outdoor bins or racks, or in unheated and/or unventilated warehouses. The atmospheric conditions will be totally unlike those in your own home. Purchase the materials well ahead of time, and store them, well stacked so that air can reach all surfaces, in your home. Don't stuff the stock in the garage or under the house, but rack it up indoors where it can remain for a period of three weeks or a month or more, so that it can adjust to the same conditions it will have when converted to a completed project. You will find that you will have far fewer problems.

Cuts

You can use any of several methods when you cut up a log. The specific number and manner of cuts often are dependent upon the size and type of log, the purpose for which the resulting lumber is intended, and the general procedures of individual mills. Some of these cutting patterns can be rather complicated (Fig. 4-2). Two cuts in particular are of interst to the woodworker.

The simplest method of sawing up a log consists merely of slicing off the outer slabs, partially squaring the log, then slash-sawing what is left. The log may be simply run back and forth, a piece being sliced off on each excursion until nothing remains. Or, several pieces may be removed from one side, several more from the opposite side, and the remainder rotated 90 degrees and the process repeated, along the pattern of the sketch in Fig. 4-3. The resulting boards are called flat-grained if the material is a softwood, or plain-sawed if a hardwood. The growth rings are tangentially sliced and form free-flowing patterns across the surface, often at various angles to the lie of the grain (Fig. 4-4).

Fig. 4-4. A section of slash-sawed softwood, called flat-grained. Similarly cut hardwood is called plain-sawed. Duncan Photos.

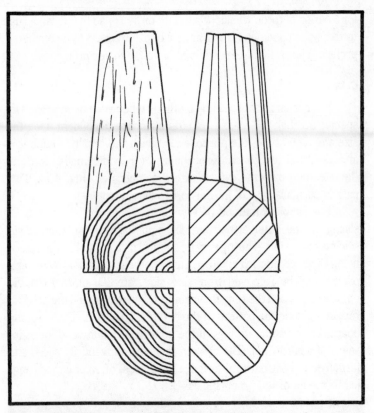

Fig. 4-5. Pattern of quarter-sawing a log.

Another method of sawing is to slice the log down the middle, then to slice the two halves down their middles. The boards are then cut from each quarter in the manner shown in Fig. 4-5. Here, the cut across the growth rings is not tangential, but varies from about 60 degrees to 90 degrees. The ring lines run with the grain, and appear as roughly parallel lines along the surface (Fig. 4-6). The rays appear as small flakes along the board edges. Wood cut in this manner is called edge-grained or vertical-grained if the material is softwood, and quartersawed if hardwood.

The first method is the cheapest way to saw wood; the second requires more labor and produces more waste, and is consequently more expensive. This is reflected in the purchase price of the two types of cuts. There are other considerations important to the cabinetmaker as well. For instance, plain-sawed or flat-grained planks will shrink a fair amount in the width, but very little in thickness. Quartersawed or edge-grained planks, on the other hand, shrink less in width than plain-sawed or flat-grained and also have less of a tendency to warp. Depending upon the species involved, edge-grained or quartersawed wood may be worked to a smooth finish more easily than plain-sawed or flat-grained wood. The strength characteristics are also somewhat different.

Defects

Seldom will you find a piece of wood without defects of one sort or another, and there are a great many to watch out for. Some defects are detriments, while others may be assets, depending upon the use to which the material will be put. Because certain defects may be permissible in your projected use, you may be able to buy your material at a reduced price. Other defects, even though minor, may render that particular piece completely unusable. Request permission to select your own stock at the lumberyard, and examine the available material carefully. This is the only way you will get exactly what you want and what you need.

The most obvious defect in lumber of any species is warp. This may be caused by uneven drying and ventilation, or by other defects and grain irregularities in the wood itself. The former type of warp

Fig. 4-6. The surface of this section of softwood exhibits a grain pattern called edge grain. In a hardwood, it would be called quarter-sawed. Duncan Photos.

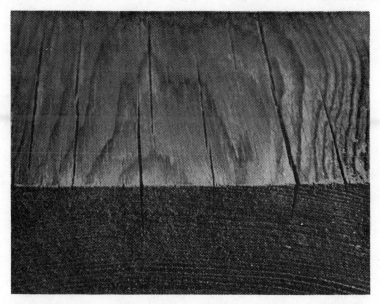

Fig. 4-7. The surface cracks in this piece of dimension stock are called checks. Duncan Photos.

may straighten out with time, but the latter never will. When a board curves up at one or both ends and will no longer lie flat, the condition is called bow. When the longitudinal edges of a board curl so that the center of the board is lower than the edges, the condition is called dish or cup. This most often occurs with plain-sawed or flat-grained wood, and the curl is usually away from the heart side. A twist is just that; the board takes a longitudinal zag which you may or may not be able to straighten under pressure. Crook occurs when one edge of a board contracts more than the opposite edge, giving the effect of a rocker. In addition, stock can warp in ways which defy description, rendering a piece totally worthless.

Knots are common lumber defects which may or may not be bothersome, depending upon the type of wood and the use to which it is put. In fact, knots are frequently an asset, as in the familiar knotty pine panelling. There are knots, and there are knots; the wide assortment of classifications is unimportant to us. All you really have to note is whether the knot is a sound knot, which has no decay and presents a solid surface, or if the knot is an unsound and contains some rot. A tight knot is a solid part of the wood, and will retain its position. A not-firm knot is fairly solid, but may be movable. A loose knot cannot be relied upon, and indeed, may consist only of a knothole by the time you see the wood.

Rot speaks for itself; dote means the same thing. Pecky wood has areas of pits and pockets in an otherwise sound piece of stock; strength is usually unaffected, though the surface finish will be. In some cases, however, as with pecky cypress panelling, this may be an asset. Pith or punk is somewhat similar to rot. All of these conditions are obvious and easily distinguishable, and in some instances the affected part can be cut out.

Stain is any discoloration, natural or otherwise, which is not in keeping with the characteristic pigmentation of the wood. If there is bark on the edges or corners of the piece, the condition is known as wane. If the bark is found wholly enclosed in the wood, this is a bark pocket. Wormholes, which may be caused by worms or beetles, are usually obvious. Often these are not bothersome because they can simply be filled prior to final finish, or the wormy sections can be cut from the stock.

There are four natural defects in wood which commonly cause problems primarily because they often go unnoticed until work begins on the piece or until the stock is subjected to climate variations. Check (Fig. 4-7) is a fissure, which extends only partway into the material but may be of considerable length. If the check goes completely through the stock, then it is a split (Fig. 4-8). Pitch, a

Fig. 4-8. A split is a common natural defect of wood. The surface roughness of this board is a mechanical defect; it was caused by the surfacer and is called torn grain. Duncan Photos.

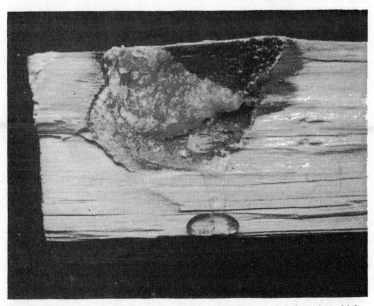

Fig. 4-9. This piece of stock was split open to reveal a massive pitch pocket which could drain through a surface pinhole for months (photo half size). Duncan Photos.

resinous substance common to the conifers, is most annoying and can raise hob with finished cabinetwork. Massed pitch is usually obvious, but pitch pockets (Fig. 4-9) may not be. Pitch pockets are graded in numerous sizes, but all sizes have the same problem. The pocket itself is an opening in the wood fibers. If there is no pitch within, the pocket may still be difficult to fill. If the pitch remains, you can be sure that one day it will leak out. When it does, the finish will be ruined and the repair job difficult.

Wood also has some mechanically caused defects as well. Some of them can be troublesome. A shy cut may occur along the edge of a piece of stock close to the end, where the straight edge is not maintained, but curves inward. The result is that the piece is not of full width. Unfortunately, this condition is often not discovered until the piece is cut and fitted into place on a project. Another problem is called roller check. This pecularity is caused when a piece of cupped lumber passes through the feed rollers of a dressing machine, with interesting results to the surface. Skip happens when the planer blades miss the surface of the stock. Machine burn is a dark and sometimes cupped area caused when the planer blades stick and overheat. A tear is caused when a machine blade catches on the workpiece and rips out a series of small chunks, leaving a roughened and cratered surface. A rock roll (Fig. 4-10) is not music at all, but a wandering gouge, usually deep and cross grained, caused by a sharp-edged pebble being caught between two pieces of stock and rolled around as the material is handled. These marks can be filled if the surface is to receive an opaque finish, but cannot be satisfactorily sanded out for a transparent finish.

Grading

All commercially available lumber stock is graded. This has to do with quality, not size, and the process is a highly complex and confusing one. Much of the confusion stems from the fact that different standards, designations, and terminology are used for hardwoods and softwoods, and that a whole slew of organizations and associations, including the United States Government, are involved in the grading process. Even so, there are some reasonably uniform general standards. There is little point in going into this subject in depth, but a brief look may be of some assistance.

With respect to softwoods, the top of the line is called "1 and 2 Clear" or "B or Better." This is the best quality, and costs the most.

Fig. 4-10. The wandering gouge is an annoying defect caused by the excursions between pieces of stock of grit and pebbles introduced by careless handling and storage. The smaller defects are pinholes made by worms or beetles. Duncan Photos.

The stock is free from defects of all kinds, but deserves careful inspection nonetheless. "C Select" is just a bit lower in quality, with only minor defects. You may find a few small problem areas in "D Select." Below these catagories are the commons. "1 Common" has some noticeable defects, usually knots, and "2 Common" has yet a few more. By the time you arrive at "5 Common," you have material that is only of marginal utility even for apple crates and hog-pen fencing. These are by no means the only categories, and you will find numerous variants throughout the country.

The hardwood grading is even more complex and variable. The top of the line is generally referred to as FAS, which means "Firsts and Seconds." Below this is a grade called "Selects," usually the lowest grade used for furniture and cabinetmaking. The lower categories contain a variety of commons, including classifications with such curious names as "Sound Wormy."

You should keep in mind certain points in regard to grading. The first point is that the price of the material is dependent upon the grade. The lower the grade, the lower the price. Therefore, the lower the grade that you can successfully put to work, the lower will be your cost.

The second point is that the grade classification of a given piece of stock may bear little relation to the project you have in mind. If you order some hardwood for cabinet doors, for instance, you will most likely automatically get FAS. The stock will be prime, and so will the price. On the other hand, perhaps you could do something imaginative (and cheap) with "Sound Wormy."

Remember, too, a grade is given to each side of a piece of stock. Softwoods are most often graded the same on each side, but this is not the case with hardwoods. A piece of hardwood lumber could be FAS on one side, and "Common 3B" on the other. If one face of the stock will be invisible in your project, then there is no need to pay the added price for two top-grade faces. One will do.

The last point about grading to remember is that each piece of stock is appraised according to the characteristics of the entire length and width of the faces of the piece. Thus, because of some serious defects over a total of perhaps 3 feet in a 10-foot length of stock, the entire piece may be graded low. The remainder, however, may well be top-notch material. You can buy the piece for a low price, use the good section, and throw the rest in the fireplace. Or, it may be that your project consists of many small elements. In this case, you may be better off to buy a low grade at a low price, use the good parts where they will show and the bad ones as supports or glue blocks or wherever they will be out of sight.

What this boils down to is that you should thoroughly inspect all stock that you contemplate purchasing; don't simply order it by a certain grade over the counter. Make up your own grading system according to the needs of your project and the thickness of your wallet, and be guided by that.

Sizing

There is almost no standard sizing of hardwood stock. You can buy hardwood stock rough-cut (unplaned or undressed) in almost any thickness and width and length, within reason. Widths are likely to be in increments of 2 inches, starting at 4 inches and increasing from there. Lengths are most often random, and may be as short as 2 feet or as long as 20. Planed stock is available in a similar wide assortment of sizes. In addition, you can buy small pieces of stock which may be exceptionally thin, short, or narrow, for special work.

Nominal	Actual
1 x 2	$3/4$ x $1\frac{1}{2}$
1 x 4	$3/4$ x $3\frac{1}{2}$
1 x 6	$3/4$ x $5\frac{1}{2}$
1 x 8	$3/4$ x $7\frac{1}{4}$
1 x 10	$3/4$ x $9\frac{1}{4}$
1 x 12	$3/4$ x $11\frac{1}{4}$
2 x 2	$1\frac{1}{2}$ x $1\frac{1}{2}$*
2 x 4	$1\frac{1}{2}$ x $3\frac{1}{2}$
2 x 6	$1\frac{1}{2}$ x $5\frac{1}{2}$
2 x 8	$1\frac{1}{2}$ x $7\frac{1}{4}$
2 x 10	$1\frac{1}{2}$ x $9\frac{1}{4}$
2 x 12	$1\frac{1}{2}$ x $11\frac{1}{4}$
4 x 4	$3\frac{1}{2}$ x $3\frac{1}{2}$
4 x 6	$3\frac{1}{2}$ x $5\frac{1}{2}$

*In actuality, more often $1\frac{1}{2}$ x 1 5/8.

Fig. 4-11. Standard dimensions of finished softwood lumber.

Fig. 4-12. This is the result of inadvertently using stock of slightly different finished thicknesses. The problem is difficult to correct after the piece is completed. Duncan Photos.

This is especially true of many of the exotic woods used for inlay and small work. Hardwood may be sold by the lineal foot, by the board foot, by the pound, or even the the piece.

The situation with softwoods is entirely different. The chart in Fig. 4-11 shows you the standard dimensions of finished softwood lumber. The rounded-off sizes by which the stock is designated are called the nominal sizes. Once the rough-cut lumber has passed through the planers, those dimensions are no longer accurate. The actual sizes are considerably smaller. Rough-cut lumber is seldom available anymore, unless you buy it directly from a mill. If you desire a rough surface, request resawn material, which is saw-textured on one surface. Otherwise, the stock is planed on all four sides, with the exception of some general construction material. Most softwood stock is sold by the nominal board foot.

Even though established by industry standards, the actual size of wood stock is seldom a constant. The chances are that you will find slight fractional variations in all dimensions from piece to piece, even from the same mill-run of stock. Much of the discrepancy is due to shrinkage, though some mills plane their stock a bit thinner than others. Where stock dimensions are critical to a project, be sure to measure them accurately before buying the piece. Of particular importance is thickness. Good hardwood stock, for instance, is frequently cut to exactly ¾-inch thickness, but occasionally some pieces will run a bit more or a bit less. Sometimes this can create major problems, as in the cabinet face-frame shown in Fig. 4-12. The center piece in this middle-rail butt joint was milled a bit thinner than the other two pieces, and the difference went unnoticed until the piece was in place. Unfortunately, uneven surfaces in joints are horribly obvious, and rectifying the discordance is not easy.

A piece of stock which is nominally 4 inches or more wide and 1 inch thick is referred to as a board. If the piece of stock has a thickness between the nominal dimensions of 2 and 4 inches, it is designated dimension stock. When the piece of stock has measurements exceeding 4 inches, it is called a beam. All beams are rectangular in cross section.

Stock smaller than that mentioned above is classified as molding. Some moldings are rectangular or square in cross section; others are round or partly round. The majority, however, have configurations of various sorts, each with its own name (Fig. 4-13). Some of these names vary from place to place; cover molding may sometimes be referred to as scotia, for instance. While many varieties of moldings are commercially milled, most yards do not stock

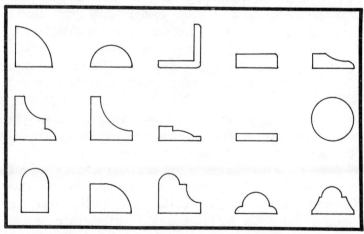

Fig. 4-13. Cross sections of a few of the more common types of moldings. Top, left to right: quarter round, half round, corner bead, stop, stop. Middle, left to right: cover, cove, stop, lattice, full round. Bottom, left to right: screen, base shoe, nose, screen, astragal.

more than a dozen or so popular types. Moldings are generally available in both softwood (ponderosa pine, white pine, and sometimes fir) and hardwood (commonly oak and mahogany).

With all of these various woods on the market and with all of their assorted characteristics, the question is often raised as to which are best for cabinetwork. Probably the first consideration should be to investigate what is available locally. If you can make choices between the materials which are readily obtainable, based upon your estimation of quality, appearance, usability, and workability, your task will be easier and less expensive. If you must order anyway, then you have a wide-open field from which to choose. Insofar as the finished result is concerned, practically all of the commercially processed hardwoods and softwoods can be, and have been, used in cabinetmaking with great success. Your choice of wood will depend on the desired finished appearance, cost to you at the job site, and personal preference. Virtually no species of wood is unusable.

VENEERS

A veneer is nothing more than a sheet of extremely thin solid wood. In today's veneer manufacturing process, a full-size log—often 8 feet to 10 feet in diameter—is chucked in a giant lathe and spun at high speed. A gouging wheel strips away the entire outer surface of the log and smooths the wood to a huge round. Then a sharp cutting blade peels a continuous strip of wood from the log until the bolt is too small to work any further. This method is responsible for producing about 80 percent of the veneer in this country today. Most of this production is softwood and is used in the manufacture of plywood.

A different procedure is used in the manufacture of face veneers. These veneers are usually cut from hardwood stock, and ultimately end up with a transparent finish on a piece of fine furniture or cabinetry. In this process, a large block of previously steamed stock is secured firmly and forced against a razor-like blade. Since the sheets come off the block like slices from a loaf of bread, the sheets are carefully handled in sequence so that they can be matched later.

The art of veneering by the individual home craftsman is now almost a lost one. Nearly all veneer production is allocated to the manufacture of plywood, and certainly it is much easier to handle and work in this fashion. On the other hand, veneer sheets of fine woods are still available from wood speciality houses for veneering by the old-time methods. Veneering is still the most practical, and, in some cases, the only method for some kinds of projects. If the project is a small one, it can be constructed of inexpensive or imperfect grades of wood, utility plywoods, or particle board, and then covered with veneer to present a handsome finished product. Veneering also lends itself nicely to covering rounded edges and convex and concave surfaces, and is the only material suitable for many types of wood inlay work.

PLYWOOD

As far as cabinetmaking and built-ins are concerned, plywood is the most popular material with the home craftsman. It is extremely versatile, easy to work, available in large sheets, and comparatively economical. In addition, plywood offers a wide variety of different woods for selection. Many of the varieties are of multipurpose utility. As with solid woods, knowing which veneers to use and when to use them is important.

Construction

Plywood is a sandwich made up of three or more layers of wood, all bonded together with special glues. There are two general types of construction. One is veneer-core, the composition of which consists of three, five, seven or nine sheets of veneer of varying thicknesses all glued together at right angles to one another. Lumber-core plywood uses the same construction principle, but few layers. The core of the sheet is a matrix of small sticks of lumber, slightly thicker than veneers and edge-glued together. Upon this core the exterior veneer layers are glued. As with the solid woods, plywoods are separated into the two categories of hardwood and softwood. Softwood plywoods are most commonly manufactured by the veneer-core method, hardwood plywoods by the lumber-core method.

The overall construction of plywood is well balanced. The process begins with either a veneer core or a lumber core. A second and third layer are added to the top and the bottom of the core in such a way that their grains are at right angles to the core again. In some cases, these may be the only layers, and the resulting sheet is called three-ply. Thicker sheets require the application of more veneers. Again, one layer is added to the top and another to the bottom, making a five-ply sheet. The top and best quality sheet of material is called the face veneer. The bottom sheet is called the back veneer, and is usually of poorer quality. The two sheets between the face and back veneers and the core are called crossbands. If more thickness is desired, more veneers are added. With most lumber-core plywoods, the process stops at five plies, while veneer-core plywoods frequently employ more. After the desired number of sheets has been laid up and the glue applied, the whole sandwich is set in a hot press. Here the glue is transformed under high temperature and high pressure into a sheet whose bonds are frequently stronger than the wood.

General Characteristics

Plywood will exhibit the visual characteristics and texture of whatever wood has been applied as a face veneer or back veneer. However, a good many variations can be introduced by mechanical means, and frequently are. For instance, the face veneer on a panel may be made up from several smaller sections of veneer, all of which are edge-matched to produce combinations of grain patterns, figures, colors, and other features never found in nature. Or, the finish surface may be sandblasted to produce a rippled or weathered effect, grooved to present the appearance of multiple random-width boards, resawn for a rough finish, or cut to produce striations. These features are only superficial, and have little bearing on the strength of plywood as a structural material.

One of the great advantages of plywood is that it comes in large sheets, whereas lumber does not. Just as important is the fact that a sheet of plywood is relatively stable. Because of the manner in which it is constructed, the dimensions of a sheet are unlikely to change to any great degree in any direction. And since atmospheric moisture has so little effect, plywood seldom will warp noticeably.

Plywood is a strong, stiff and tough material. While solid wood is strong in the direction of the grain but weaker across the grain, plywood has an equal strength, often greater than that of the wood from which it is made across the sheet and lengthwise of the sheet. It should be noted, however, that the strength and rigidity of plywood vary according to the type of plywood and are not necessarily equal in both directions.

Some plywoods are made with special properties. Fiberply, for instance, is a product which contains two more plies per standard thicknesses than normal plywood. The surfaces are impregnated with a resin which forms an exceptionally smooth base upon which a paint finish can be applied without using a primer coat. Another specialty item is hardwood paneling which is treated with a permanent factory finish that requires no further finishing. Though designed primarily for walls, this stock can easily be used for all kinds of cabinetwork. Also available are materials which consist of a layer of wood veneer applied to a cardboard backing. Another variation is flexwood, a thin wood veneer applied to a cloth backing. The advantage of flexible veneers is that they can be applied to curved backings or frames.

Grading

As with solid woods, plywoods are graded differently in the hardwood and softwood categories. There are six hardwood plywood grades. Premium grade is the top of the line. Good grade is nearly as prime as premium but edge matching is not done quite as carefully. Either grade is acceptable for use with a transparent finish. Sound grade is not matched for grain or color, and while there will be no irregularities in the surface, there may be streaks and stains. This grade is usually given an opaque finish. The utility grade is for general use, and may have numerous imperfections of various kinds. The backing grade is not very pretty, and may have an abundance of imperfections. None of the defects will impair the strength of the sheet, but the backing is normally used where it is out of sight. Specialty grade covers those plywoods which are made-to-order architectural materials, and special veneers. These are not commonly found in lumber shops.

Softwood plywoods are made in many combinations, and are graded in two ways. The grading systems are used concurrently. First, the plywoods are set up into four groups. Almost all of the softwood plywood currently being manufactured makes use of Douglas fir, with the remainder being made up of some 35 or 40 additional species. The species are categorized according to strength and stiffness of the finished product. Group 1 includes the strongest and stiffest types, of which the Douglas fir is one. Most of the softwood plywood that you will buy will be in this group.

The other grading system which you will encounter on a regular basis is shown in Fig. 4-14. This is based upon the use of the letters "N," "A" through "D," and sometimes "X." The "N" is used to indicate a well-nigh perfect face suitable for cabinetwork and natural finish. "A" plywood is almost as good, but not quite. There will be no open defects, but some neat repair work is allowable if the resulting surface will take a good finish. A "B" surface may have patches and solid knots up to an inch in diameter. The "C" and "D" surfaces are usually unsatisfactory for cabinetwork, except as backers for other surfacing materials, or as unseen structural pieces. The "X," though not shown as such in Fig. 4-14, is a common designation for exterior types of plywood made with waterproof glue.

Sizing

By far the most common size in plywood sheets is 4 feet by 8 feet. There are a few varieties of softwood plywoods which can also be bought in a 3-foot width. Once in a great while, special sizes will turn up, and you can sometimes purchase half- or quarter-sheets at lumber shops. These, and other odd sizes as well, are usually cut from full sheets which have been damaged in shipping.

The most commonly available thicknesses of softwood plywood, irrespective of the number of plies, are ¼ inch, ⅜ inch, ½ inch, ⅝ inch, and ¾ inch. Also made, but more difficult to obtain, are the 3/16-inch and 5/16-inch sizes. The same thicknesses are available in hardwood plywoods, with the additional size of ⅛ inch. The hardwood 3/16-inch size, unlike its softwood counterpart, is a common size. You also may be able to locate some 1-inch stock, with a bit of looking.

Working with Plywood

Working with plywood is much the same as working with solid woods, insofar as tools and equipment are concerned. Most of the standard procedures and practices used with solid woods apply equally well. There are, however, a few additional points to bear in mind.

The face or back veneers of plywoods will splinter readily when cut with a saw. Always use a blade of at least 10 points to the inch, regardless of the type of saw. If a fine-tooth blade is not available, a sharp combination blade on a power saw will do nearly as well. Always check the cutting action of the blade, and set the good surface of the workpiece in the appropriate position. With a handsaw the good face should be up, and the same is true of a table or radial saw. If you use a power hand saw or a scroll saw, the good face must be down.

The edge treatment of plywood is different and a bit more difficult than the edge treatment of solid wood. Planing is no great problem, but strokes should always begin at the ends and move toward the middle, rather than the other way around. If operated in the wrong direction, the plane blade will tear pieces from the interior plies as it reaches the corner of the workpiece. The same problem occurs even with smaller tools like files. Edge cutting must be done with short, shallow cuts executed by an extremely sharp blade. The rule of thumb is: a little bit at a time and take it easy.

Plywood joinery, or the making of the joints, also requires some special attention, again because of the fact that the interior plies may cause problems. Butt joints work fairly well as long as the stock is ½ inch or greater in thickness. Thinner stock should be first applied to a framework if a butt joint is to be used. The greatest problem here may be that one plywood edge is revealed. The ordinary rabbet joint, which is easy to make, is a good plywood joint. The various types of miter joints are perhaps the most useful and the best. Locking joints are the strongest.

The common fasteners, like nails and screws, don't hold well along the edges or at the corners of plywood workpieces. Where you can, eliminate as much raw-edge fastening as possible. Where you cannot, use thin nails or brads which are approximately three times as long as the thickness dimension of the stock. Wood screws should be approximately 2½ times as long as the thickness of the stock. Number 8 screws should be used for ⅝-inch and ¾-inch plywood, number 6 for ⅜-inch and ½-inch, and number 4 for ¼-inch. When working near the edges, drill pilot holes for both nails and screws. When there is plenty of stock surrounding the fastener location, pilot holes need not be drilled for nails, but should be for screws. Careful counterskinking for screws is necessary to prevent chips and splinters from lifting from the face veneer.

In some of the finer cutting operations like sawing and boring, the absence of any rough edges is desirable, but not always easy to

	Grade Designation (2)	Description and Most Common Uses	Typical Grade-trademarks	Veneer Grade Face	Veneer Grade Back	Veneer Grade Inner plies	Most Common Thicknesses (inch) (3)					
							1/4	5/16	3/8	1/2	5/8	3/4
Interior Type	N-N, N-A, N-B INT-APA	Cabinet quality. For natural finish furniture, cabinet doors, built-ins, etc. Special order items.	NN G1 INT APA PS1 74 / N-A G2 INT APA PS1 74	N	N.A. or B	C						3/4
	N-D-INT-APA	For natural finish paneling. Special order item.	N-D G3 INT APA PS1 74	N	D	D	1/4					
	A-A INT-APA	For applications with both sides on view. Built-ins, cabinets, furniture and partitions. Smooth face; suitable for painting.	AA G4 INT APA PS1 74	A	A	D	1/4		3/8	1/2	5/8	3/4
	A-B INT-APA	Use where appearance of one side is less important but two smooth solid surfaces are necessary.	AB G4 INT APA PS1 74	A	B	D	1/4		3/8	1/2	5/8	3/4
	A-D INT-APA	Use where appearance of only one side is important. Paneling, built-ins, shelving, partitions, and flow racks.	A-D GROUP 1 INTERIOR PS1-74 000	A	D	D	1/4		3/8	1/2	5/8	3/4
	B-B INT-APA	Utility panel with two smooth sides. Permits circular plugs.	BB G1 INT APA PS1 74	B	B	D	1/4		3/8	1/2	5/8	3/4
	B-D INT-APA	Utility panel with one smooth side. Good for backing, sides of built-ins. Industry: shelving, slip sheets, separator boards and bins.	B-D GROUP 3 INTERIOR PS1-74 000	B	D	D	1/4		3/8	1/2	5/8	3/4
	DECORATIVE PANELS—APA	Rough-sawn, brushed, grooved, or striated faces. For paneling, interior accent walls, built-ins, counter facing, displays, and exhibits.	DECORATIVE BD G1 INT APA PS1 74	C or btr.	D	D		5/16	3/8	1/2	5/8	
	PLYRON INT-APA	Hardboard face on both sides. For counter tops, shelving, cabinet doors, flooring. Faces tempered, untempered, smooth, or screened.	PLYRON INT APA PS1 74			C & D				1/2	5/8	3/4
	A-A EXT-APA	Use where appearance of both sides is important. Fences, built-ins, signs, boats, cabinets, commercial refrigerators, shipping containers, tote boxes, tanks, and ducts. (4)	AA G3 EXT APA PS1 74	A	A	C	1/4		3/8	1/2	5/8	3/4
	A-B EXT-APA	Use where the appearance of one side is less important. (4)	AB G1 EXT APA PS1 74	A	B	C	1/4		3/8	1/2	5/8	3/4

Fig. 4-14. Guide to appearance grades of softwood plywood.

	Description	Grade stamp	A	C	C	1/4	3/8	1/2	5/8	3/4
A-C EXT-APA	Use where the appearance of only one side is important. Soffits, fences, structural uses, boxcar and truck lining, farm buildings, Tanks, trays, commercial refrigerators. (4)	A-C GROUP 1 EXTERIOR APA PS 1-74 000 (BB) G1 EXT APA PS 1-74	B	C		1/4	3/8	1/2	5/8	3/4
B-B EXT-APA	Utility panel with solid faces. (4)		B			1/4	3/8	1/2	5/8	3/4
B-C EXT-APA	Utility panel for farm service and work buildings, boxcar and truck lining, containers, tanks, agricultural equipment. Also as base for exterior coatings for walls, roofs. (4)	B-C GROUP 2 EXTERIOR APA PS 1-74 000	B	C	C	1/4	3/8	1/2	5/8	3/4
HDO EXT-APA	High Density Overlay plywood. Has a hard, semi-opaque resin-fiber overlay both faces. Abrasion resistant. For concrete forms, cabinets, counter tops, signs and tanks. (4)	HDO·60·60 BB PLYFORM·I EXT APA PS 1-74	A or B	A or B	C or C plgd		3/8	1/2	5/8	3/4
MDO EXT-APA	Medium Density Overlay with smooth, opaque, resin-fiber overlay one or both panel faces. Highly recommended for siding and other outdoor applications, built-ins, signs, and displays. Ideal base for paint. (4)	MDO BB G4 EXT APA PS 1-74	B	B or C			3/8	1/2	5/8	3/4
303 SIDING EXT-APA	Proprietary plywood products for exterior siding, fencing, etc. Special surface treatment such as V-groove, channel groove, striated, brushed, rough-sawn. (6)	303 SIDING 16 oc GROUP 1 EXTERIOR APA PS 1-74 000	(5)	C	C		3/8		5/8	
T 1-11 EXT-APA	Special 303 panel having grooves 1/4" deep, 3/8" wide, spaced 4" or 8" o.c. Other spacing optional. Edges shiplapped. Available unsanded, textured, and MDO. (6)	303 SIDING 16 oc T 1-11 GROUP 1 EXTERIOR APA PS 1-74 000	C or btr.	C					5/8	
PLYRON EXT-APA	Hardboard faces both sides, tempered, smooth or screened.	PLYRON EXT APA PS 1-74		C				1/2	5/8	3/4
MARINE EXT-APA	Ideal for boat hulls. Made only with Douglas fir or western larch. Special solid jointed core construction. Subject to special limitations on core gaps and number of face repairs. Also available with HDO or MDO faces.	MARINE AA EXT APA PS 1-74	A or B	A or B	B	1/4	3/8	1/2	5/8	3/4

Exterior Type (7)

(1) Sanded both sides except where decorative or other surfaces specified.
(2) Available in Group 1, 2, 3, 4, or 5 unless otherwise noted.
(3) Standard 4x8 panel sizes, other sizes available.
(4) Also available in Structural I (all plies limited to Group 1 species) and Structural II (all plies limited to Group 1, 2, or 3 species).
(5) C or better for 5 plies; C Plugged or better for 3-ply panels.
(6) Stud spacing is shown on grade stamp.
(7) For finishing recommendations, see form V307.
(8) For strength properties of appearance grades, refer to "Plywood Design Specification," form Y510.

Fig. 4-14. Guide to appearance grades of softwood plywood. Courtesy of the American Plywood Association.

attain. In boring holes, the top surface will remain clean if you start the hole slowly and carefully, and if the drill bit is sharp. To minimize bottom splintering, you can remove the bit before it goes clear through, and then counterbore from the opposite side. Or, you can clamp the workpiece to a block of scrap wood and then bore through and into the scrap. When sawing, use the same trick; clamp the workpiece firmly to some scrap stock and adjust the saw blade to cut through the workpiece and into the scrap. Sometimes a strip of masking tape will accomplish a similar purpose.

The characteristic banded edge of plywood stock is not especially attractive and, even though carefully cut and sanded, may contain many defects. This means that the craftsman, when working with plywood, must constantly be thinking about how to cover up these edges. One possibility, and probably the best, is to make cuts and joints in your project in such a way that no raw edges are exposed. Sometimes, rather than making a full-fledged joint, you can sneak by with simply rabbeting away all the plies except for the face veneer. This small bit of exposed veneer then serves to cover the raw edge of the mating piece. The other method of hiding plywood edges is to add another surface as a cover or cap. This cover should be a stock solid wood molding, or a strip of edge-band veneer designed especially for the purpose. Such veneers are sold in rolls, like friction tape, and can be obtained either with or without an adhesive backing.

There is one more point which needs mention. Plywood as a material is tough and rugged. On the other hand, cabinet grades are easily damaged and should be handled with care. As explained before, the weakest portion of a sheet of plywood is the edge, and the corners are particularly susceptible. Also, the face and back veneers are thin, often as little as 1/28 of an inch. Extreme care must be taken to protect the face surfaces from mechanical harm. Scratches and gouges can render a piece of stock useless for a transparent finish, and must be carefully filled when an opaque finish is planned. Never attempt to sand out scratches or blemishes. More often than not you will go through to the lower ply. All sanding operations on plywood of any kind must be done with caution and a light touch, especially when using power sanders.

COMPOSITION BOARDS

There are many varieties of composition boards, most of which find their principal use in the field of general residential, commercial, and industrial construction. Some types, however, are particularly suited to cabinetry, built-ins, and even fine furniture. As a group, composition boards for these uses are economical, readily workable, and widely available; best of all, they are ecologically sound products. Though they also have some inherent problems, good workmanship and a knowledge of the materials will keep you out of trouble.

Particle Board

Particle board, sometimes referred to as chipboard, is a general term of confusingly broad application. Though to the untrained eye one sheet of particle board looks much like any other sheet, there are actually about two dozen distinct types. All of them are made in a similar fashion, with primary ingredients of sawdust, chips, flakes, and splinters of wood. The chief differences between the various types lie in the density, weight per cubic foot, and the way the ingredients are laid up.

Despite the multiplicity of types, your local lumberyard probably will handle only one or two, and may not know the difference between those two. Fortunately, this is not a problem, because you can successfully use any of the types for home projects. You will probably find that a sheet size of 4 feet by 8 feet is the only one available readily, though 5 feet by 8 feet is another stock size. Also available are widths of 2 or 3 feet, and lengths up to 16 feet. Thicknesses range from ¼ inch to 2 inches, but ⅜ inch, ½ inch, ⅝ inch and ¾ inch are the most common.

Particle board is worked essentially in the same manner and with the same tools as solid wood and plywood. However, when working with particle board, you should keep in mind a number of points. Particle board has no grain, and thus is not particularly strong over its long dimension. It will bend just so far, and then break completely. It should be used with as much edge support as possible, and the thinner sheets are not suited for long shelves. Edges and corners are susceptible to damage; under pressure they will crumble away. Setting nails or screws into edges or near corners can be a tricky business. Unless the nails are centered and driven straight, they may deflect and force a large chip out of the surface. Nails driven close to corners may cause the corners to split. In either case, the holding power of the nails is nil.

Though made from wood, particle board is highly abrasive. It will rise total hob with a saw blade in short order. Just a few passes with a power saw will practically ruin a good blade, and what the material will do to a fine panel shouldn't be told. You can get around this problem in several ways.

First, don't use a good handsaw. If you must make some cuts with a handsaw, use an old one, or be prepared to do some frequent sharpening. A fine-toothed blade with little set will bind quite easily, so you will have to use a relatively coarse blade. Cutting particle board is far easier with a power saw anyway. Here you have two alternatives. You can equip your saw, be it table, radial, or the hand power type, with throwaway blades. The best blade to use is a standard fine-tooth crosscut type. These cost only three or four dollars, and are good for a considerable number of 8-foot cuts before you have to pitch the blade in the trash. A combination blade will work, but will wear out faster. Blades with finer teeth will bind or wander.

If you anticipate doing a considerable amount of work with particle board, consider investing in a carbide-tipped blade. Though much more expensive, this type of blade will outlast a throwaway blade by probably 10-to-1, and can be easily resharpened. A coarse-tipped utility blade will cut particle board like butter, but removes large chips from one edge. To get a finer cut, use a blade with very fine teeth; be aware, though, that this kind of blade will cost more than a blade with larger teeth.

When cutting particle board, especially when making long rips, you will need to take some extra safety precautions. Chips and particles fly about at a great rate, and they are sharp and hard. When they hit, they hurt. When they get in your eyes, severe irritation is likely to result both from the particles and the resinous material used as a bonding agent. Always wear goggles or a face shield, preferably the former. In addition, the cutting process raises a great cloud of very fine dust, not unlike flour. The dust particles are so light that they hang in the air for a long time, and are altogether too easily inhaled. This can, in many cases, lead to coughing and hacking, respiratory infection, severe sinus trouble, and some degree of debilitation. Take no chances. If you are working indoors, allow plenty of cross ventilation, and wear a respirator. Ideally, particle board should be cut out of doors where the dust is quickly dispersed.

Particle board lends itself to some types of joinery and not to others. Butt joints are appropriate, and simple to make. Also appropriate, but much stronger, are spline, dowel, and dovetail corner joints. Glue as well as mechanical fasteners should be used. This material serves as an excellent core for a veneer or a plastic laminate surface. Application is easy enough, when contact cement is used. If you are going to apply a liquid finish, either transparent or opaque, a filler and sealer must be used to produce a smooth surface. Most factory surfaces are rather rough and pitted.

Hardboard

Hardboard is another manmade product which is readily available and useful in a number of cabinetmaking and built-in projects. There are various methods of manufacture, but basically all of the types are made from tiny wood fibers pushed together and compressed into a dense mat. The mat is then further compressed, heated, and chemically treated as necessary, until the completed product emerges in the familiar form of thin, hard sheets.

The three basic types of hardboard are standard, tempered, and service. The standard type is hardboard just as it emerges from the presses. Tempered hardboard receives further treatment to give it additional stiffness, hardness, and smoothness. The service hardboard is of somewhat lower quality then the standard, and is made specifically for general purpose work, such as flooring underlayment, where strength, hardness and surface properties are less of a consideration. The most commonly stocked types of hardboard have only one finished surface, with the back being screened or textured. However, a smooth finish on both sides is available.

The standard size of hardboard is the 4-foot by 8-foot sheet. You can also buy, although probably only by special order, 5-foot widths and lengths up to 16 feet. The most common thicknesses are ⅛ inch, 3/16 inch, and ¼ inch. The whole range, however, runs from 1/16 inch to ¾ inch.

Beside the standard dark brown types, there are several specialty hardboards. Perhaps the best know is perforated hardboard, also called pegboard. Some types of hardboard are embossed on one surface with patterns that simulate woodgrain, basketweave, and leather. Other types have one surface printed with the colors and textures of assorted woods and fabrics, and are intended for service as wall paneling. In addition, you will find a multitude of specially finished hardboards.

Hardboard can be used for dozens of purposes in home projects, and it works extremely well, provided that you stay within the capabilities of the material. For instance, it is excellent for drawer bottoms. Enclosed in wood frames, hardboard makes good center panels for cabinet doors. It is also appropriate for cabinet backs. It can be solidly applied over a base of low quality and otherwise marginally useful lumber of plywood and then finished or covered with veneer or plastic laminate. Incidentally, it also makes an inexpensive and easily replaceable topping for workbenches.

Hardboard is easily worked with either hand or power tools. For sawing, the blades should be kept as sharp as possible, and, if a great deal of cutting is to be done, carbide-tipped blades will do a better job with less wear. Again, make sure that you have the face of the workpiece in proper relationship to the cutting direction of the blade, as one edge or the other will inevitably be ragged. Hardboard can be planed or routed easily, but again, sharp blades and carbide tips are in order. Sanding is usually not needed unless the surface of the material has been broken. When sanding does become necessary, use a fine grit and a modicum of caution. Drilling is also no problem, so long as entry is from the good face and a support block of scrap wood placed underneath.

The usual methods of fastening can be used with hardboard. The material is so hard that pilot holes sometimes have to be drilled, especially for brads and fine nails. The 3-penny finish nail works about the best in thin stock, but the short-shank ring nail serves nearly as well. Pilot holes for wood screws should be through-drilled, so that the screw shank does not bind in the hole. Flat heads must be fully countersunk. Hardboard has excellent screw-holding capability. To attach hinges or similar hardware directly to hardboard, drill a tap-size hole and install sheet metal screws. Hardboard can also be stapled, but a power driven stapler is required.

PLASTICS

This is the age of plastics, and, not unexpectedly, plastics have entered the field of cabinets and built-ins. Of the endless array of plastic materials being marketed today, four general types deserve consideration.

Acrylics

Of all the plastics which can be worked and assembled in the home shop, the acrylics probably have the most virtues. Acrylics—one well-known brand name is Plexiglas—are easy to use, and for the most part can be worked with ordinary hand and power tools. Acrylics are available in a wide variety of sheets, as well as in rods, tubes, and blocks. Sheets come in opaque, semiopaque (translucent), and transparent colors, solar-control tints of gray and bronze, and crystal clear. The surfaces may be highly polished or impressed with a variety of decorative patterns.

Working with acrylics is simple if you remember two points. The first is that acrylic is a thermoplastic, and consequently is susceptible to the effects of heat generated by power cutting tools. The second point is that acrylic is a relatively soft material and is easily scratched.

Cutting can be done with handsaws or power saws, or you can score sheets with a cutter and then break them. When sawing, use only fine-toothed blades, leave the protective paper on the stock, and never force either the stock or the saw blade. Drilling is best done with a hand drill. Use a sharp twist drill bit, slow speed, and light pressure, with a block of scrap material beneath the hole. A power drill may also be used, but only with special drill bits designed for the purpose. Edge finishing is accomplished by filing first, then dry sanding or wet sanding, followed by buffing with a compound. Acrylic can be fastened with screws, can be drilled and tapped, or can be secured with special cements. It can also be easily heat-formed, will take paints and lacquers for a decorative finish, and can be etched or scribed.

In cabinetwork, the clear polished acrylics in sheet form make excellent doors, either hinged as complete units, set with door frames, or used as sliding panels. Clear or colored materials can be installed as sliding drawer tops to protect bulk staples within the drawer, as drawer bottoms, and as built-in complete bin or drawer units to store dry foodstuffs such as flour, rice, and macaroni. Applied over a wood base, acrylics can be used for cutting boards and pastry boards, and as protective sheets on counters and desktops. The semiopaques or colored transparents are useful as built-in light diffusers. Small pieces can be formed or built up to make attractive drawer handles and cabinet door knobs. Let your imagination run loose for a short time, and you'll be able to dream up another hundred uses for this versatile material.

Laminates

Plastic laminates, such as Formica and Micarta, are found in almost every modern home. These high-pressure plastics are made up of layers of thin kraft paper, phenolic resins and melamine resins, all bonded together through a complex industrial process. Plastic laminates, though somewhat difficult to work with, are long-lived, attractive, easily cleaned, and highly resistant to stains, soil, burns, and abrasion.

An array of different types of laminates is available. There are many, many colors, as well as several surface textures. The textures include glossy, matte, and linen finishes. Even embossed wood grain and simulated wood grain patterns are manufactured. Laminates are offered in a number of grades, with the most useful being the general purpose grade. This comes in a 1/16-inch thickness, and is the grade to use for general indoor home applications like countertops and desktops. The postforming grade is considerably thinner and is used in heat-forming applications or where the material must be applied to rolled edges. Where application is made upon a vertical surface, such as a cabinet door, the vertical grade is the one to use.

Sheet lengths and widths vary somewhat with the manufacturer, but a range of sizes are available without special order. Most common widths are 24 inches, 30 inches, 36 inches, 48 inches, and 60 inches. Stock lengths run from 5 feet to 12 feet. If you contemplate using laminates, first work out the exact sizes of the pieces that you will need. Next, determine which sheet sizes are readily obtainable in the pattern/color you want. Then make a scale layout to find out which sheet size will cover your needs, allowing for cuts, edge trimming, and a mistake or two.

Plastic laminates are designed to be applied to cores and subsurfaces. Subsurfaces must be solid and stable, and may be made from plywood, hardboard, or particle board. In most instances, a minumum ¾-inch thickness should be used. There are a number of bonding agents, but for home use contact cement is by far the best.

Plastic laminates are both brittle and thin, so great care must be taken in cutting them. The workpiece should be supported along the entire length of the cut. The stock can be scored along a line and then broken, just as glass is cut. Or you can use a power saw. A saber saw works well using a fine-tooth blade, or a table saw equipped with a fine-toothed carbide-tipped blade. A hand power saw using a guide and carbide-tipped blade will also do the job. The material is highly abrasive, hence the carbide cutting tools. As a last resort, you can use a handsaw of 12 points or more, keeping the blade edge almost flush against the face of the workpiece.

The easiest way to bore holes in plastic laminates is with a bitbrace and auger bits. If you opt for a power drill, use carbide-tipped bits. In any event, place a block of scrap wood beneath the hole. Removal of small amounts of material during a fitting process can be done in several ways. A file works well if carefully handled, and so does a sander or a sanding block. Small cuts can be made with a device known as a nibbler. A block plane or a Surform tool will work, too, but the material is tough on blades.

Plastic laminates are usually applied with a bit of extra material extending past the core along the lead edge. After the adhesive has set, this edge is trimmed flush with the core. For this job, you can use either a laminate edge trimmer or a router equipped with carbide-tipped blades made especially for this purpose.

Though we commonly think of plastic laminates as being useful only for countertops, nothing could be further from the truth. This material can be used for a broad variety of purposes. Not only can you surface countertops and edges, you can actually cover every face of the kitchen cabinetry, or, for that matter, any other type of cabinetry. Shelves, sides, dividers, rails, and even the flooring and undersurfaces of cabinets can be completely covered in laminate. You can apply it to the insides of drawers, to desks, dressing tables, and bartops. You can use it as a decorative inset in door frames, as a cover for built-in furniture, as a trim for window and door frames, or as a colorful inlay in ornamental work. Here again, the only limitation is your imagination and your energy.

Poured Plastic

There are several types of poured plastics that are designed primarily for floor covering, but which will work equally well in other applications. One is a polyester resin which is set in place as a base coat. Upon this material you can sprinkle colored quartz aggregate, mica flakes or some other accent material, and then apply a special finish coat. With the proper planning, you can provide yourself with a handsome seamless countertop, poured directly in place, and having excellent characteristics of toughness, stain resistance and durability.

Another possibility for countertopping, cabinet door panels, and similar surfaces is a high-gloss polymer coating. This is a transparent substance which can be flooded into place over a surface which has previously been decorated in any fashion you chose. You can even embed dried flowers, seeds, grains, sea shells, painting, documents, and any sort of decoupage.

Floor Covering

Floor coverings in cabinet work? You bet. Floor coverings used to be called linoleum, but the industry has gone far beyond that stage now. Today's floor coverings are made from sheet vinyl, an exceptionally tough and long-lasting material. Sheet vinyl is generally available in widths of 6 feet and 12 feet, bought by the running foot, and paid for by the square yard. A tremendous selection of patterns and colors is available through any decorating or housewares shop.

The sheets themselves consist of a vinyl surface of varying thickness (depending upon the type and the manufacturer) backed by a layer of foam plastic. Most surfaces are textured as well as patterned, and no waxing or polishing is necessary to maintain the finish.

Used with the proper edge treatment, floor covering also makes good counter covering where heat is not a problem, and it works particularly well as covering for cabinet and drawer bottom and shelf tops. One common practice is to order slightly more material than is necessary for covering a floor, and then to use the remaining pieces to cover the shelving in the same room. Application is simple. Merely cut the pieces to the proper size, either directly or by means of a pattern or template, and glue them down with the same adhesive and with the same techniques as used on the floor. Then install an edge molding or lipped cap to hide the raw edges of the shelf and vinyl.

GLASS

Glass is a commodity which finds a place in cabinets and built-ins more often than one would expect. The principal application is as glass doors, either set in frames or used as sliding panels. Glass is also commonly used for vanity and dressing table mirrors, for decorative colored mirror sections and tiles, and for accent mirrors placed at the rear of show and display cabinets. Another possibility, paralleling a popular hobby today, is for setting stained glass sections in doors and as decorative panels and divider screens.

Stained glass is available in a myriad of sizes, shapes, and colors at most hobby stores. Other types of glass, such as plain window glass, plate glass, smoked or bronze-tinted glass, and mirror stock can be bought from hardware stores and glass shops. Usually you can have the material cut to size at the shop. Failing this, you can cut the glass yourself without undue difficulty with a good glass cutter. Practice first on some scrap pieces, however.

Glass can be drilled with diamond tipped bits, or with a hardwood dowel in a drill press. (Dowel drilling will require liberal applications of automotive valve grinding compound.) Edge grinding is a somewhat more difficult chore and entails the use of special equipment. If necessary, have this sort of work done at a glass shop.

CERAMICS AND MASONRY

The principal use of ceramics in cabinets and built-ins is for countertopping. For the most part the materials take the form of various types of ceramic tile. These may be either the standard 4¼-inch by 4¼-inch tiles such as are found in bathrooms, or may be of the smaller mosaic type (Fig. 4-15). The handcrafted "Mexican" tiles are also popular in some areas of the country. In addition, you can use masonry items like thin pavers (a brick-like material made for floors), large 12-inch by 12-inch tiles (also used for flooring), and natural materials such as thin slate and marble. Some precast commercial materials simulate marble and other stones, and are used primarily for vanity tops.

With the exception of the precast materials, all of these items should be laid on a sturdy, stable base or core. Any of the normal countertop cores such as plywood and particle board can be used, but should be well supported. Working with these materials is not difficult once you get the hang of it, and the best bet is to follow to the letter the manufacturer's instructions for installation. Which type of adhesive or cement is used to secure the material to the core depends upon the nature of the material. Some kinds of tile are

Fig. 4-15. Four varieties of ceramic tile. Duncan Photos.

pregrouted, while others must be grouted after they are installed. The grouting is a special dry-mix material which is mixed with water and squeegeed into the cracks between the tiles to form an unbroken surface.

Ceramic tiles can be cut by scoring the backs, either with a special tool or with a glass cutter, and then breaking the tile along the score. Alternatively, you can borrow or rent a tile cutter or nipper from the tile supplier. When calculating the number of tiles you will need for a job, allow for several extras. Tiles do not always break accurately, and some will be wasted. Edging may be accomplished either with special tiles which provide a deep lip along the countertop core, or with wooden or metal moldings which act as a concealing trim.

Standard tiles are usually sold by the case, but can also be bought by the piece in some stores. Mosaic tiles generally are preset on a 12-inch by 12-inch backer, and are sold by the square foot or by the case. Pavers and floor tiles can usually be bought by the piece, as can slate and similar materials. The precast synthetics necessarily come in certain standard sizes, patterns and configurations, and you must determine exactly what you want and then build the cabinet to suit. This grouping as a whole seems to contain an endless array of patterns, colors, textures, and sizes from which to choose.

Chapter 5
Hardware

The array of hardware available to home craftsmen is truly bewildering. There must be ten million separate items parked on display and stock shelves in stores throughout the country. Somewhere, there seems to be a piece of hardware designed to suit any situation or to solve any problem that has ever existed in the woodcrafting field, and yet new pieces appear with astonishing regularity. Unfortunately, the pieces are not always accessible to the home craftsman because many of the items enjoy only regional distribution, many are not well advertised or well known, and, besides, the sheer number of items is so great that no store can possibly stock even a representative selection of what is available. It is regrettable that the home craftsman is frequently unaware of numerous hardware items which could simplify, improve, or enhance his work projects, and unfamiliar with many construction possibilities that the more esoteric sorts can allow.

On the following pages, we will briefly discuss several general categories of hardware to give you a reasonable overview of the field. Be aware that the smart craftsman will first investigate the hardware field as it applies to local stocks and conditions and to the needs and dictates of his projected work, and then design the project around the hardware available to him. In fact, to avoid difficulties and disappointments, his wisest course is to actually have the hardware in hand before beginning a project. With this fact in

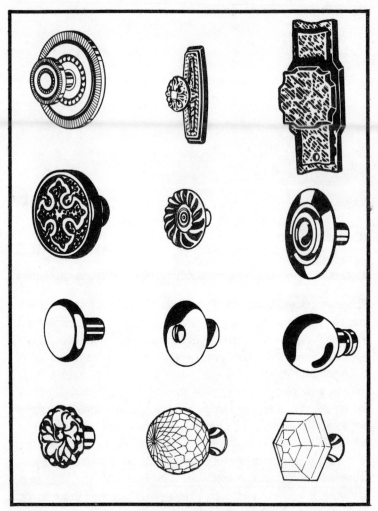

Fig. 5-1. A few of the hundreds of knobs available. Courtesy of Amerock Corp.

mind, then, once you have a fundamental knowledge of the world of hardware you can get down to specifics by doing your own research. This entails trips to hardware stores, poring through any and all hardware catalogs that you can get your hands on, and perhaps a visit to the library as well. Books in the cabinetmaking and furniture building fields may give you some ideas about using various hardware items. In addition, check the Thomas Register, a compendium of United States manufacturers, for various sorts of specialized hardware.

KNOBS

You already know about knobs (Fig. 5-1); you've been pulling on them for years. Really, not much need be said about them. There is a stupefying assortment from which you can choose of practically every style, color, configuration, pattern, material, and finish known to man. Sizes range in diameter from about ⅜ inch to 4 inches. Most knobs are attached by means of a machine screw or a wood screw inserted from the back of the material, but some are equipped with an embedded screw for attachment from the face side. Their use is obvious; they offer handholds for opening cabinet doors or drawers.

PULLS

Much of what was said about knobs can be said of pulls (Fig. 5-2). There are a thousand different kinds, often made to match a series of knobs. Two points of attachment are generally used, with the most common method being machine screws inserted from the rear. A few pulls, however, are attached from the front with wood screws. Though most pulls project beyond the surface upon which they are mounted, some are designed to be inset flush with the surface. The flush types require a cutout or a mortise in the face of the workpiece. A similar type, known as a finger pull, is a cupped, button-like disc which is pressed into a shallow bored hole.

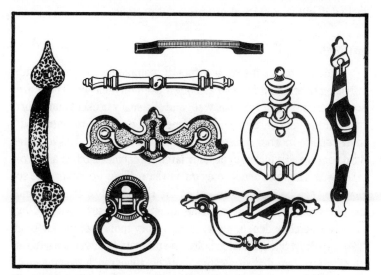

Fig. 5-2. Pulls can be found in dozens of either decorative or utilitarian styles. Courtesy of Amerock Corp.

CATCHES

Cabinet catches (Fig. 5-3), as you might expect, are used on cabinet doors. They can be broken down into two major groups; concealed, and visible. The concealed types are completely functional and are not fancy. The visible types range from the strictly funcitonal to the highly decorative.

Visible cabinet catches, which consist of a handle and operating mechanism on the outside of the door and a catch assembly mounted on the inside, are called latch-bolt catches. There are three types of concealed catches. Friction catches depend upon spring clips for the closure operation. The roll catch consists either of a spring-load ball which snaps into a mating cup opposite or a spring-loaded rubber roller which engages a mating clip or ramp. The magnetic type of catch employs a small permanent magnet on one half of the assembly and a matching steel plate on the other. Since there is no handle integral with any of these catches, a knob or pull must be added. The only exception is a special catch called a finger release, or push catch. Once this type of concealed catch is properly adjusted, all that is needed is a slight push on the cabinet door and the catch will release and pop the door open. No pull or knob is necessary, and the face of the door remains empty of any hardware. With a little ingenuity, most catches, whether concealed or visible, can be attached in either a vertical or horizontal position.

LATCHES

Latches or latch-sets are mostly commonly associated with full-sized doors, and as such are often used on built-ins. There are smaller cabinet door types as well, and all usually present some sort of decorative effect. Some are designed to be surface mounted, but most require mortising into the door frame and jamb. Unlike standard passageway locksets or door latches, cabinet latches are provided with a knob or handle only on one side. They are reversible so that they can be installed on either the right-hand or the left-hand margin of a cabinet drawer. While most catches are operated by pressure, latches depend upon some rotary motion of the knob or handle to draw back the latch bolt. The ultimate funciton of a latch is no different than that of a catch, but the appearance is somewhat different, the cost is usually higher, and the installation is more difficult.

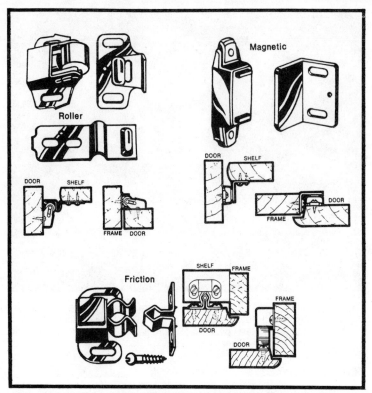

Fig. 5-3. These three types of cabinet catches are among the most readily available and widely used. Courtesy of Amerock Corp.

LOCKS

Locks (Fig. 5-4) which are especially made for cabinets and furniture are frequently used in such applications as desk drawers, bureau drawers, gun cabinets, china cabinet doors, and chest lids. Often the reasons are as much for decoration and appearance as for security.

As with other types of hardware, there is a great variety of finishes, sizes, and styles of locks. Among them are such items as chest locks, wardrobe locks, and drawer locks, all of which have a somewhat different appearance and are somewhat differently installed. Some are designed to be mounted upon the surface, while others require full mortising, or may be mounted on the inside with the tumbler assembly protruding through a bored hole. The operation of the lock assemblies themselves may be by a sophisticated series of tumblers or by a simple skeleton key.

Fig. 5-4. Cabinet locks are more useful for decoration and to deter the curious than for security. Left, ratchet lock for sliding glass cabinet doors. Center, ornamental brass hasp with padlock. Right, pin tumbler door or drawer lock cylinder and mount plate. Duncan Photos.

HINGES

Hinges can be puzzling because there are so many of them. Not only do they run the full gamut of sizes, colors, patterns, and finishes, but there are also a number of types which must be suited to the particular job. Decorative effects aside, you have a number of decisions to make concerning the visibility of the hinge, the way in which it will work, the method in which it is attached, and the serviceability and quality of the hinge itself.

The strap hinge (Fig. 5-5A) is a common type available in lengths from 2 to 20 inches. It is designed to be mounted fully upon the surface, has a nonremovable pin, and is available in either utility or decorative grades. The T-hinge (Fig. 5-5B) is a similar style.

Butt hinges (Fig. 5-6) are widely employed for general purpose, utility, and cabinetry types of work. Butt hinge is a generic term which covers many specific designs. Butt hinges are categorized in two different ways. The first has to do with the pin upon which the two leaves move. A loose-joint butt hinge is made in two halves with one half secured by a pin and the other half pivoting freely. The two leaves may be separated by lifting the loose leaf off the pin affixed to the other leaf. These hinges cannot be interchangeably used on left- and right-swinging doors, because, if a left-hand hinge is used on a right-hand door, the hinge will be upside down and the door will fall off.

The fast-pin butt hinge is interchangeable from left to right, because the pin is secured and not removable. The two leaves cannot be separated. The loose-pin butt hinge is constructed in such a way that the pin can be driven out of the barrel, separating the two leaves. The hinge is interchangeable from right to left by merely removing and reversing the pin so that the head is always upper-most. This means, too, that a door can be easily taken off by simply slipping the pins from the hinge barrels, separating the leaves with-out removing them from either door or cabinet frame.

The second set of butt hinge designations refers to the manner in which they are mounted. The full-surface type is designed to

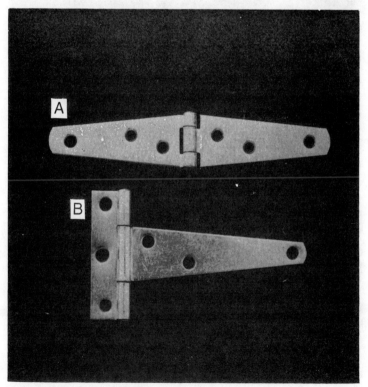

Fig. 5-5. Above (A), steel utility strap hinge, fixed pin. Below (B), steel utility T-hinge, fixed pin. Duncan Photos.

Fig. 5-6. Loose pin butt hinges. Duncan Photos.

mount with one leaf on the surface of the door and the other on the surface of the jamb (Fig. 5-7A). A full-mortised hinge (Fig. 5-7B) has both leaves inset into the jamb and the door, with only the pin portion of the hinge visible. A half-mortised butt hinge (Fig. 5-7C) is designed so that one leaf is mortised into the door edge, while the other mounts on the surface of the jamb. Similarly, the half-surface hinge (Fig. 5-7D) has one leaf surface-mounted on the cabinet door and the other leaf surface-mounted on the jamb. In all cases, if the hinge is secured with wood screws, it is called a nontemplate hinge. If the hinge is held in place with machine screws, as on a metal frame, the hinge type is a template hinge. Note too, that many hinges of a decorative nature and designated as cabinet hinges are actually butt hinges in disguise.

One of the most important types of hinge to the cabinetmaker is called the decorative surface hinge. Most of these are designed and styled especially for use on cabinets and furniture, though there are some larger and heavier types for general purpose work. Figure 5-8 shows a few of the abundant selection from which you can choose. Both loose-pin and fast-pin types are available. They are made in several variations to conform to the type of door which is to be hinged. The full-surface type (Fig. 5-9A) is used where the cabinet

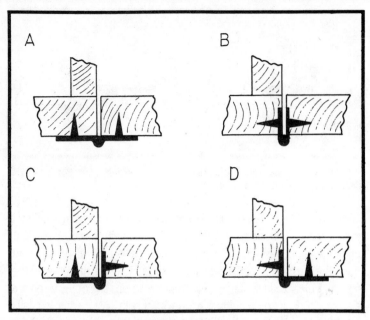

Fig. 5-7. The four principal butt hinge configurations. A, full surface. B, full mortise. C, half mortise. D, half surface.

door and the frame to which it will be hinged are flush across the surface. If the cabinet door is lipped, with part of the thickness of the door being within the cabinet and part extending past the outside surface of the face-frame, then the hinges must be offset to compensate for the thickness of the lip (Fig. 5-9B). Lipped cabinet doors may also be called offset doors, and the hinges referred to in the

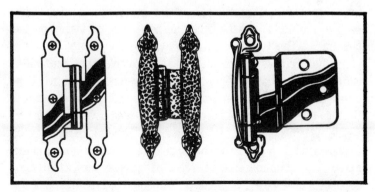

Fig. 5-8. Decorative surface hinges are widely used in cabinet applications. Note that the hinge on the right is a half-surface decorative hinge. Courtesy of Amerock Corp.

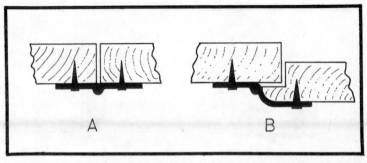

Fig. 5-9. A, full surface decorative hinge mounted on flush door. B, full surface decorative hinge mounted on lipped door.

same way. These hinges are designated by the amount of the offset they require. Thus, one leaf of a ⅜-inch offset hinge will mount flush upon the jamb, while the other will require a ⅜-inch offset to mount upon the surface of a door which protrudes ⅜ of an inch beyond the frame. This size is probably the most common, but other sizes are also made. Before making your doors, check to see what is easily available to you. Keep in mind, too, that hinges are made for both square-edged and curve-edged doors.

There are also several types of semiconcealed hinges for cabinet doors. In most cases, the only part of the hinge that can be seen is the barrel and pin. One such, called a loose-pin cabinet hinge, is shown in Fig. 5-10. This is the so-called wraparound style, and works well even with heavy doors. The removable pin allows the hinge to be used on either right or left sides. This particular design happens to be for ¾-inch flush doors, but other styles are available. Some are of the half-surface type, where one leaf is concealed on the back of the door, and the other surface-mounted visibly on the face-frame. This type is obtainable for lipped doors, too.

When it comes to concealed hinges, the choices become far less and the cost increases. Figure 5-11A shows one type of fully concealed hinge, available in numerous sizes and weight capacities. Actually most hinges which are called concealed have some portion visible. The most popular of the "concealed" hinges is the pivot type, as shown in Fig. 5-11B. The sort of pivot hinge which mounts at the extreme top or bottom edges of a cabinet door may show a thin edge, depending upon how it is installed. With another type the tip of the pivot-point is exposed in a small slot cut in the door as part of the mounting process. Pivot hinges are usually used on overlay doors.

144

Fig. 5-10. Pair of semiconcealed wraparound cabinet hinges, loose pin. Duncan Photos.

Fig. 5-11. Concealed hinges. Left (A), Soss hinge is mortised and wholly hidden. Right (B), pivot hinge shows only the tip of the pivot. Duncan Photos.

145

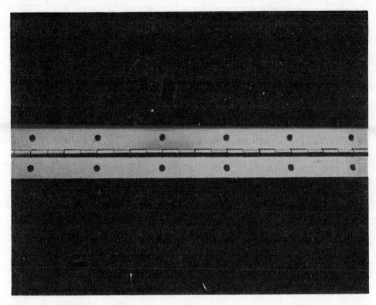

Fig. 5-12. Section of piano hinge, a continuous strip hinge available in several widths and lengths. Duncan Photos.

Where strength, good support, and evenly matched edges are necessary, as with a drop section in a counter or a fold-down writing surface, use a piano hinge (Fig. 5-12). This is a continuous strip hinge, available in lengths of from two to six feet, and in a plain steel or bright brass finish. Most are designed for installation by the full-surface method, but with a bit of finagling they can also be applied in half-surface, full-mortise, and half-mortise modes. A groove can be cut to accept the barrel of the hinge.

PLATES AND BRACES

Plates and braces often afford the most practical way to provide additional support or strength to joined members of a cabinet or built-in. Plates are just various-sized flat pieces of steel and brass with pre-drilled holes which have been modified to permit the countersinking of wood screws. The most common shapes of plates are straight, tee, and flat corner or ell. Braces or corner braces are straps which are bent at right angles, much like a shelf bracket. Miter corner braces have a center web, and are used to reinforce miter corners, such as on a cabinet door frame. Screen corner braces have a turned-down lip on the inside of the angle, so that they can be attached to both surfaces and edges of a corner. Typical plates and braces are shown in Fig. 5-13.

STANDARDS AND BRACKETS

Standard, or shelf standard, is the name given to a special type of steel strip used to hold shelf brackets in place. Two principal types are widely available. One has a continuous series of horizontal rectangular slots, the other a continuous series of vertical rectangular slots. Each type is predrilled for mounting screws, and can be set directly upon the surface or recessed for a flush installation. The first type uses small clips as shelf supports (Fig. 5-14A), while the second accepts a special full-sized shelf bracket (Fig. 5-14B). Clip-type standards are usually arranged so that there are two at each end of the shelving section, and if the shelves are long, another standard is placed at the rear halfway mark. The standards using full brackets are positioned at the rear of the shelving, with the spacing between standards being dictated by the length of the shelves and the load that will be placed upon them.

Brackets, in both decorative and utility styles, are available in any number of sizes. Some are made for wood shelving, and are predrilled for both mounting and shelf securing. Others are equipped

Fig. 5-13. Corner plate, angle braces, T-plate, and straight mending plate. Duncan Photos.

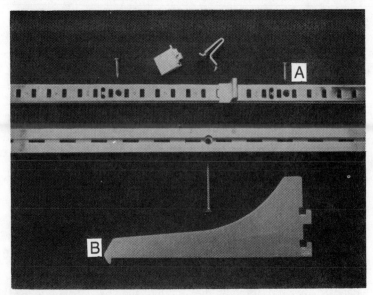

Fig. 5-14. Above (A), standard and clips. Below (B), standard and bracket. Duncan Photos.

with spring clips to receive glass shelves, and a few styles are designed so that they will swing to either side or fold up against themselves.

Pin brackets are handy little devices which are really nothing more than glorified pegs. They are made in many sizes, with either plain or fluted shanks, and have flat surfaced heads upon which the shelves rest. Installation is accomplished by boring a series of the proper sized holes, and tapping the pin brackets into place.

SLIDES

You can install a drawer in a number of ways so that it will slide in and out freely and easily. Many of these methods require no hardware whatsoever, and consequently little or no expense. However, of all the methods employed, ballbearing drawer slides are among the most effective, provided that cost is not a consideration. There are several types and styles of drawer slides, one of which is shown in Fig. 5-15. This particular system consists of four elements, and the operation is similar to that used in the better grades of file cabinets. A guide track is fixed to each side of the cabinet frame and a mating slide section is mounted, properly positioned, on each side of the drawer. A stop block is provided so that the drawer cannot be pulled completely out. When the drawer is fully closed, the rollers drop into a slight depression so that the drawer cannot slide open of its own volition if the back of the drawer is slightly higher than the front.

Another system employs only one guide track, mounted either above or below the drawer along the center axis. One roller is attached to the rear bottom of the drawer to run in the track and two more are attached as guide rollers to the front supporting rail of the cabinet. Still another system uses double tracks and rollers which mount beneath the drawer.

Also available are various types of slides and guides, usually made entirely of plastic, which can be attached to the drawer sides, bottom outside edges, or to the bottom center. Some of these systems consist only of tracks and formed runners which lock onto them, while other systems use small plastic rollers. In either case, the drawer action is smooth and even, but without the advantage of full-open drawer suspension

TRACKS

Cabinets and built-ins often are equipped with doors which slide rather than swing. This requires the use of tracks and track

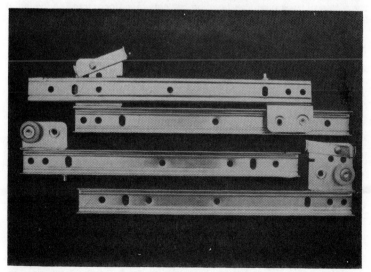

Fig. 5-15. Roller drawer slides. Above, mated pair. Below, separated set. Duncan Photos.

Fig. 5-16. Utility cabinet sliding doors set in surface-mounted plastic track. The same type of track protrudes from the cabinet; deep upper track on the left, shallow lower track on the right. Duncan Photos.

hardware. Several varieties are available and the buyer usually chooses a type appropriate to the size and weight of the door.

Double track, shown in Fig. 5-16, is perhaps the simplest and least expensive. This type of track is installed on the surface at the top and bottom of the door opening, or, for a flush installation, it may be recessed into a groove or encased in molding. The track lengths come in different sizes to accommodate different panel thicknesses, with ¼ inch, ½ inch and ¾ inch all being standard sizes. The track used at the top of the door is deeper than the one at the bottom. With the door cut to the proper height, it can be lifted upward to clear the bottom track for easy removal. Aside from fasteners to secure the track and knobs and pulls on the panel doors, no further hardware is needed. Tracks of this type are generally made of plastic, aluminum, or plated steel. The door panels can be made of any material of suitable thickness, including glass.

Another simple type of track for double sliding doors that is easy to use actually looks like a miniature railroad track. Two tiny rails protrude from a base in an integral molded unit. The track is surface-mounted with screw holes provided for the purpose. All that is necessary then is to cut matching grooves in the top and bottom edges of the door panels and slip them into place.

Large and/or heavy doors have to be hung with somewhat different equipment. The usual method employs a support track in the overhead position, with rollers attached to the top of the door and fitted onto the track. The entire door assembly is suspended, and may or may not run in a guide track along the bottom of the door. The top rollers are usually adjustable to a certain degree to insure that the door will hang straight. This is the type of mechanism to use for wide and full-length sliding doors which cover an entire storage or shelving section.

A number of slides are made for special purposes and unusual applications. There are curved or curvable tracks for use with tambour doors (like the sliding top on a rolltop desk) or flexible closures. One type makes use of a series of ballbearings in a track, upon which a heavy plate glass door will slide freely and smoothly. Pass tracks are used for exceptionally thick panels, and are designed in such a way that one panel first pulls out and then slides across, in order to clear the other panel.

FITTINGS

The general term, fittings, covers a vast area of hardware and accessories designed for particular purposes. The largest group is composed of kitchen cabinet fittings, with closet fittings and bath fittings running close behind. Kitchen cabinet fittings include such prosaic items as wastebasket shelves which slide out for easy access when you open the cabinet door, spice or knife racks which are designed to be built in, and pullout pastry boards. There are steel rod slideout towel racks, stands or racks designed especially for hanging cups, stacking plates and racking up cans of vegetables or pop. There are various types of containers made for storing staples, grains, and similar foodstuffs which are intended to be installed beneath overhead cabinets or within the cabinet structure. And so the list goes on and on; most of these items are designed to maximize the available space in or on cabinets and built-ins.

The situation is much the same with closet fittings and bath fittings. There are a thousand items on the market, some useful and some not. You will find closet rods, shoe racks, small drawer sections which can be installed in closets, necktie racks, and so on. A similar line of space-savers and utility items is available for baths, laundries, dining rooms, and of course workshops.

Much of this material comes from small manufacturers and is available in different forms locally. Every hardware or houseware shop carries a certain number of items; mail order catalogs are full of them; and there are always a myriad of pertinent advertisements to be found in periodicals dealing with household affairs. The entire field seems to be about equally divided between useful things and gimcracks. Make your own determination as to what you want and can use, and then purchase the items before building cabinetry especially to suit them. The reason for this is that much of this equipment is here today and gone tomorrow.

SPECIALTY HARDWARE

The broad assortment of specialty hardware offered by manufacturers can take all manner of peculiar forms. Whatever your ideas or problems with regard to a specific project, somewhere there is a piece of hardware which will help you do the job. For instance, one way to gain extra space at a serving counter is to provide a pullout, popup, extension leaf. Special leaf slides are made for this purpose. Tambour doors are difficult to build in the shop, but you can buy them ready-made in a variety of sizes, complete with fitted slides. To support a lift-up opening in a countertop, you will need a special type of hinged bracket known as a stay support. Double swivel plates, joined with a ring of loose ballbearings, are manufactured specifically for use in lazy susans. This makes the task for constructing a multiple-shelf lazy susan in a corner cabinet much easier. Popup extension hinges are used when you want to make a platform for a food mixer or similar appliance which will pop up out of a cabinet when you open a door. Elbow hinges are made for similar purposes. You can buy slides and dividers for making adjustable compartmented drawers or drawers within a drawer. If you want to install a built-in electric clock in a cabinet face, there are kits for that purpose. A fold-down (or up) service counter may require the use of a folding leg assembly. Decorative chain can be used to support a fold-down writing surface or counter section. You can use various sorts of decorative metal grillwork or fabric covers over cabinet openings. There is a whole group of hardware items designed to aid in the installation of built-in sound systems. The list could go on forever; the chore of finding exactly what you need has to be yours alone.

Chapter 6
Fasteners and Glues

The process of putting together a cabinet or built-in presupposes that you will begin with a bunch of small pieces and eventually assemble them into one completed article. This in turn means that you will need various devices and bonding agents to hold the small pieces together, both during and after assembly.

FASTENERS

The devices used for joining and securing the individual elements of a cabinet or built-in are called fasteners, and of the hundreds of separate items in this field, several are of paramount importance to the cabinetmaker. One of the most important aspects of successful cabinetmaking is a thorough knowledge of the applicable fasteners, their characteristics, their functions, and their advantages and disadvantages for a given task. Using the right fastener in the right place makes the job easy and trouble free. Using the wrong one, or using the right one improperly, can lead to all manner of frustration.

The following information is not incontrovertible; after all, we all do cut corners occasionally, and get away with it. On the other hand, the material is based upon long field experience in cabinetmaking and woodworking by thousands of craftsmen, as well as on laboratory testing in such areas as shear strength, holding power, compression pressures, and similar abstruse details.

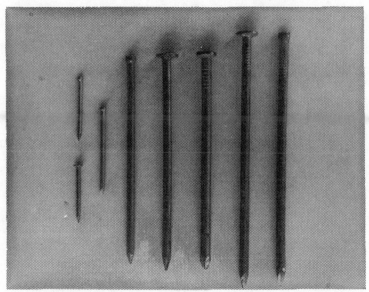

Fig. 6-1. The six most widely used kinds of nails in general woodworking. Left above, brad; below, wire nail. Then, from left to right: 3d finish; 10d finish; 10d box; 10d common; 16d box (for comparison); 16d casing. Duncan Photos.

NAILS

The first consideration in choosing a nail for a given task is to pick the right kind. Six types in particular are of interest to the cabinetmaker and woodworker (Fig. 6-1). The common nail has the largest head diameter and the largest shank diameter, in any given size, of all six types. The head is also of greater thickness. Common nails are used primarily in heavy work, and always where the heads will be concealed, or where their appearance makes no difference. The box nail is similar to the common nail, but has a thinner, smaller head, and a slightly thinner shank. Casing nails are used for finish work. The head diameter is not much greater than the shank diameter, and the shank diameters of casing nails are equal to those of box nails for a given size. The gently tapered underside of the casing nail head allows them to be easily set flush or countersunk. Usually, the head is countersunk and then concealed with filler. Finishing nails are somewhat similar, but are thinner and have a small, somewhat rounded head. These nails too are used in decorative woodwork, where the heads are to be concealed. Finishing nails and casing nails are often used interchangeably, although casing nails have somewhat greater holding power in most work. Wire nails are junior-sized

156

box nails, with short, slender shanks and flat, thin heads. They are used for securing small pieces of material where strength is not a factor, and where the appearance of the exposed heads makes no difference. Brads are simply tiny finish nails, used for securing small moldings, thin workpieces, and the like.

The next consideration in choosing the proper nail is length. Common, box, casing, and finish nails are not classified in inch-

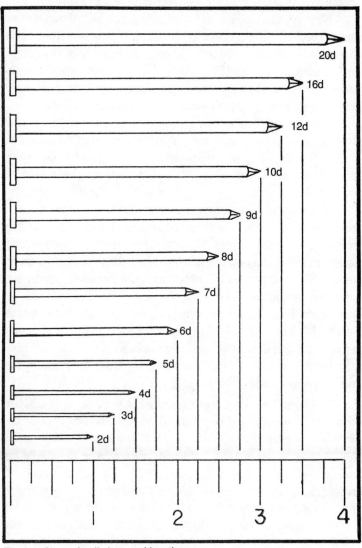

Fig. 6-2. Chart of nail sizes and lengths.

lengths, but rather by means of the penny system. The penny-length then refers back to the length in inches. Awkward, but that's the system and you will soon get used to it. The symbol for penny is written as d. Thus, an 8-penny nail is symbolized as 8d or 8-d, and is 2½ inches long. The chart in Fig. 6-2 shows the size breakdown. In cabinetwork, the most commonly used sizes are 3d, 4d, 6d, and 8d. Occasionally you may also have use for 10d and perhaps 12d. Not all of the four types of nails are available in all sizes (Fig. 6-3).

Nails are also made in certain specific diameters, designated as gauge numbers. The gauge refers to the size of the wire from which the nail was formed. An 8d common nail, for instance, is 10¼ gauge, and a 3d finish nail is 15½ gauge. With the four types of nails discussed above, the gauge number is almost never of any consequence, and generally doesn't even appear on the carton label.

The situation is different, however, with wire nails and brads. Both of these types of classified first by their actual length in inches, and then by the gauge number of the shank. Lengths for both types run from ½ inch to 2 inches, and they are available in gauges from 16 through 19.

There are also various types of specialized nails, some of which you may need at one time or another. Ring nails, which have thin shanks lined with a series of sharp concentric rings, are helpful where extra holding power is needed. Masonry nails, which come in many styles and have either ribbed or spiral-threaded shanks, are designed specifically for driving into masonry. These might be necessary when you have to secure mounting cleats to a concrete block wall. There are various types of tacks, for general purpose, upholstery, and decorative work. Escutcheon pins, which are usually made from brass or stainless steel, are also used primarily for decorative purposes.

The techniques of nailing are neither difficult nor involved, but there are a few tricks of the trade which can give you a better job with less trouble. First, make sure that you have the right type, length, and diameter nail for the task at hand. The nail should be neither too large nor too small. If you are working with hardwood, or nailing close to an edge or at a sharp angle where the material might have a tendency to split, first drill a pilot hole. The hole should be slightly smaller in diameter than the shank of the nail, should pass entirely through the top workpiece, but on into the second piece only

158

Nail	2	3	4	5	6	7	8	9	10	12	16	20
Common	847	543	294		167		101		66	61	47	29
Box		588	453	389	255	200	136		90		69	50
Finish		880	630		288		196		124			
Casing			489		244		147		96		73	

Fig. 6-3. The various nail size/type combinations that are readily available. The figures indicate the number of nails per pound.

to a total depth which is somewhat less than the overall length of the nail. Depending upon the nature of the second piece, often it is just as well not to drill a pilot hole there at all. But as a general rule, the total depth of the hole should be about ⅔ of the length of the nail. Also, size the hammer to the nails you are using; there is an old saying about the efficacy of driving a tack with a sledgehammer.

There are two ways of nailing; straight nailing, and toenailing. Straight nailing is used most of the time, and simply involves driving a nail straight down through one surface into the second. The term is a bit misleading, because for best results, the nail should actually be tilted to a slight angle for better holding power. Be careful that you don't tilt the nail so that it will come out through the side of the second piece. In some materials, the nail must be tilted so that it does not deflect against a tough growth ring, bend, and unexpectedly pop through the surface of the second workpiece. And never try to nail through a knot. That just doesn't work at all. Also, where you have sufficient room, do not drive a series of nails in a straight line. Stagger them slightly for greater overall joining strength. It is also a good idea not to drive two or more nails close together along the same grain line; the workpiece is very likely to split, and, even if it does not, the material could be seriously weakened.

Even the seemingly simple process of driving the nail has its own little techniques. For instance, the smaller the nail, the lighter the hammer tap, and the smaller and lighter the hammer head. Nails from 6d on down in size have to be treated gently, because they bend quite readily. Hold the nail between your thumb and forefinger, and, even if you have drilled a pilot hole, give it two or three gentle taps until it stands free. Then get your thumb out of the way, and drive the nail home with firm taps. As the nail goes in, keep your eye on it to make sure that it remains properly aligned. The last blast of the hammer is the one you should not apply. That's the one that puts a dent in the finish surface. As the nailhead approaches the work surface, restrain yourself. Let the nailhead stick up a bit, and finish the driving process with a nail set.

As you drive the nail, use mostly wrist action and keep your forearm and elbow relaxed. As the nail size becomes larger, or the workpiece tougher, you can begin to use more and more arm and shoulder action. Perhaps the most obvious point of all is the one that seems to cause the most difficulty. You have to hit the nail—another old saying with merit—square on the head. Now, you may feel that all this palaver about driving a nail is a bit silly. And if we were talking about building a raft, or rough-framing a house, you'd be right. In such circumstances a few dings and dents and bent-over nails don't matter much. Good cabinetmaking, however, rests to a large degree upon the skill, patience, and care that the cabinetmaker exercises.

One more point. Sometimes, despite all your efforts, a nail doesn't drive correctly and has to be removed. There are techniques for this too. There are two considerations: (1) protect the surface of the workpiece from damage and marring as you draw the nail, and (2) prevent the nail from pulling out a chunk of material as it leaves the workpiece. If the nail is only partly driven, you can slip the claw of the hammer over the nail, and then slide a block of scrap wood beneath

Fig. 6-4. Removing nail with diagonal cutters. Duncan Photos.

the hammerhead. This will provide protection for the workpiece surface, and give you added leverage in drawing out the nail. If the nail sticks up only a small amount, substitute a piece of thin cardboard for the scrap wood. If you can't work the claw of the hammer into position, use a flat-bar nail puller, with a piece of wood or hardboard underneath for protection. In either case, as the point of the nail nears the surface, ease off on the pulling strain, and work the nail free of the hole gently. This will prevent splinters and chunks from popping free of the workpiece surface around the hole. If you can't purchase on the nailhead with either a hammer or a nail puller, you may be able to work the jaws of a pair of electrician's diagonal cutters under the head (Fig. 6-4). Use a thin piece of flat steel under the cutters as a fulcrum. Take a firm grip on the nail and work it up in short bites. If the nail is bedded so tight that the pulling process may destory or weaken the assembly, carefully clip or saw the nailhead off, drive the remains below the surface with a nail set, and patch up the hole.

SCREWS

Though nails are the most commonly used fasteners, screws run a close second. Freestanding cabinetry and furniture of the better grades is put together with screws rather than nails, and quality cabinets and built-ins also employ screws. The reason for this is that, despite the extra difficulty and time involved, the finished product is considerably stronger, longer-lived, and less susceptible to racking, loosening up, and similar problems. In addition, unlike nails without glue, screws without glue can later be demounted, thus permitting the disassembly of an article.

How do you know when to use screws instead of nails? Simple, use screws in any of the following four situations. First, whenever you need maximum holding power, use wood screws, There could be several reasons to do this, such as to bear a hefty weight or load, to insure complete stability, or to minimize the possibility of an assembly working loose from repeated strain or vibration. Second, whenever the fastener must be left exposed, or you want exposed fasteners for some decorative effect, use screws. Screws can be obtained in various head configurations and finishes, and used with special finishing washers to provide this decorative effect. In any case, they look better than exposed nailheads. Third, whenever you

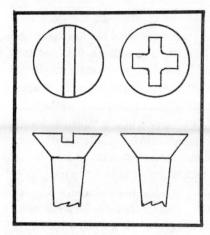

Fig. 6-5. Left, standard straight slot. Right, Phillips or recessed slot.

are working in cramped quarters where driving nails would be awkward and there is a possibility of damaging the workpiece surface, use screws. Often you can predrill and drive a screw faster and easier than you can drive a nail. And fourth, whenever there is any chance that the work will be taken apart at some later date, always use screws and no glue.

There is also one more occasion when screws are helpful. Sometimes a panel will warp out of place, or a joint will spring apart, after the assembly is complete or even during construction. The remedy may well be to drive the panel or joint back into place under pressure, but nails seldom have the necessary holding power to do the job. However, one or two judiciously placed screws probably will accomplish what the nails can't.

As with nails, you have to pick the right sort of screw for the job, and there is quite a selection from which to choose. Of them all, wood screws are the most important to cabinets and built-ins, and for general woodworking as well. Wood screws are made in two slot configurations, the straight slot, or the Phillips (recessed) head (Fig. 6-5). The Phillips is primarily used in factory production work, because it lends itself more readily to mass assembly techniques. For home shop purposes, however, the straight slot is easiest to use and equally effective, unless you prefer the different appearance of the Phillips. The straight slot comes in a wider range and is usually more readily available than the Phillips.

Wood screws have sharp, spiraled threads. The thread starts at a gimlet point, tapers for about the first one-third of the screw shank, and ends at about two-thirds of the overall length. There are five principal head shapes (Fig. 6-6), each used in a somewhat different manner. The flat-head, often abbreviated F.H., is designed so that the top of the screwhead sits flush with the surface of the workpiece. Flat-head screws may also be deeply countersunk and then covered with putty or filler, or counterbored to a greater depth and concealed with a wood plug. The round-head, abbreviated R.H., is set so that the bottom side of the head lies flush with the workpiece surface and the rounded top protrudes. The oval-head screw has a head tapered underneath and rounded on top. This type of screw is countersunk into the workpiece to the depth of the head taper, leaving the rounded top above the surface. It may also be used with a special finish or cup washer for a decorative effect. The oval-head is also frequently used for mounting hardware such as drawer pulls, and is available in chrome and other decorative finishes. The fillister-head screw has a flat underside, a slight shoulder, and a rounded top. The screw has a somewhat better appearance than a standard round-head, and the slot is elevated above the surface of the workpiece to minimize any possibilities of damage to a finished surface. The lag screw has a thick head which may be either square or hexagonal. Lag screws are found only in the larger sizes, and are principally a structural fastener. However, you may find use for them when securing heavy cabinets in place.

Wood screws are referred to by a three-part designation: (1) length, (2) shank or gauge number, and (3) head style (Fig. 6-7). The

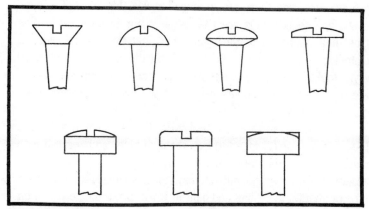

Fig. 6-6. The most common screw head configurations. Top, left to right: flat head; round head; oval head; truss head. Bottom, left to right: fillister head; pan head; lag.

length of a flat-head screw is measured from the tip of the point to the top surface of the head. Lag-, round-, and fillister-head screws are measured from the tip to the underneath surface of the head. Oval-head screws are measured from tip to the point where the taper of the head stops and the rounded top begins. The gauge or shank number refers to the diameter of the shank. The smaller the number, the smaller the diameter. Lengths range from ¼ inch to 4 inches, and gauges from 0 to 24. However, most suppliers will stock only the middle range of sizes, which are the most frequently used.

Ranking next in importance to wood screws are the sheet-metal screws. These also have excellent holding power, and while originally designed for use in sheet metal assembly, they work nicely for other applications as well. They are ideal for securing sheet metal, metal strips, and metal fixtures to wood. They also work well in materials such as hardboard and particle board.

The threads on sheet-metal screws look somewhat similar to those on wood screws, but are cut somewhat differently and extend from tip to head. They are called self-tapping screws, because of their ability to cut a matching thread in the receiving material as they are driven. Several specific types are available, but only two are of use in woodworking. Type A is the most common and most familiar. The type F screw is made with an off-center chip-clearing slot at the tip, and is called a self-drilling sheet-metal screw. No pilot hole is needed with this type, since the slot also acts as a drill, and the screw drills its own hole as it is driven. Both Phillips and straight-slot heads are available, and there are five head styles (Fig. 6-6). The flat-, oval-, and round-heads are the same as for wood screws. The truss-head is similar to the round-head, but thinner and wider in diameter. The pan-head, which is probably the most commonly used style, looks somewhat like a thin fillister-head. Lengths and gauges are the same as for wood screws, but the overall selection is not quite as extensive.

Machine screws are designed to be (1) threaded into drilled and tapped holes, or (2) inserted into through-holes and secured with matching nuts. For the most part, these screws are used for the assembly of metal parts, but you may run into a need for them at one time or another in cabinet and built-in work. Since they can be a bit confusing, a quick look at their characteristics may be of some future help.

Screw #	1/4	3/8	1/2	5/8	3/4	7/8	1	1 1/4	1 1/2	1 3/4	2	2 1/4	2 1/2	2 3/4	3	3 1/2	4	Dia.
1	X																	0.073
2	X	X	X															0.086
3	X	X	X	X														0.099
4		X	X	X	X	X	X											0.112
5		X	X	X	X	X	X											0.125
6		X	X	X	X	X	X		X									0.138
7		X	X	X	X	X	X	X	X									0.151
8			X	X	X	X	X	X	X	X	X		X		X			0.164
9				X	X	X	X	X	X	X	X	X	X					0.177
10				X	X	X	X	X	X	X	X	X	X			X		0.190
11					X	X	X	X	X	X	X	X	X		X			0.203
12						X	X	X	X	X	X	X	X			X		0.216
14								X	X	X	X	X	X	X	X	X	X	0.242
16								X	X	X	X	X	X	X	X	X	X	0.268
18									X	X	X	X	X	X	X	X	X	0.294
20										X	X	X	X	X	X	X	X	0.320

Lengths

Fig. 6-7. The most readily available screw gauge/length combinations and screw gauge diameters.

To begin with, both straight and Phillips slots are available. The head styles are flat, oval, round, fillister, and pan. They are classified according to length in inches, gauge size (which is not quite the same as with wood or sheetmetal screws), and thread.

The guage of a machine screw refers to a specific diameter of shank expressed in decimal fractions of an inch. Unlike the diameter of other types of screws, this diameter is important for reasons which we will go into shortly. A machine screw has a flat tip and thread which extends the entire length of the shank in most types. Lengths are measured in the same manner as wood screws. The gauge numbers are 2, 3, 4, 5, 6, 8, 10, and 12, and then the designation jumps to fractions: ¼ inch, 5/16 inch, ⅜ inch, and ½ inch. The threads are classified in two ways, National Coarse and National Fine. The abbreviations are usually used: NC and NF. The classifications differ in thread pitch and number of threads per inch of shank. The specific thread is referred to by a number, which stands for the number of threads per running inch. Thus, a (gauge) number 6 machine screw may have 32 threads per inch (NC) or 40 threads per inch (NF). A complete screw designation would be #6-32 × ¾ F.H. or #6-40 × 1½ O.H. Translation: gauge number 6, 32 threads per inch in a National Coarse configuration, ¾-inch length, flat head; gauge number 6, 40 threads per inch in National Fine configuration, 1½-inch length, oval head. Following this, there may also be a designation as to the type of material (nickel, brass, steel) or the finish (cadmium, galvanized, zinc).

The specific size of a machine screw is important when it comes to drilling a hole to receive the screw. The hole must be accurately sized, and reference should be made to a tap drill chart (Fig. 6-8) to find the right combination. For any given machine screw diameter/ thread combination, one drill size is used for a through-hole, and another for a tapping hole of approximately 75 percent thread height. The nature of the material, or a somewhat different thread height requirement, may indicate the use of a slightly larger or smaller drill size.

The techniques of driving screws are simple enough, so much so that they are often ignored. However, the only way to attain excellent results is to follow the rules. Most importantly, always drill a pilot hole, even though the material may be soft, before driving a screw. There are two different diameters on wood screws, the

Screw Size	Screw Dia.	Clear Drill	Tap Drill
1-64	0.073	49	53
1-72	0.073	49	53
2-56	0.086	44	50
2-64	0.086	44	49
3-48	0.099	39	46
3-56	0.099	39	44
4-40	0.112	33	43
4-48	0.112	33	42
5-40	0.125	1/8	38
5-44	0.125	1/8	37
6-32	0.138	28	33
6-40	0.138	28	32
8-32	0.164	19	29
8-36	0.164	19	29
10-24	0.190	11	25
10-32	0.190	11	21
12-24	0.216	7/32	16
12-28	0.216	7/32	14
1/4-20	0.250	1/4	7
1/4-28	0.250	1/4	7/32
5/16-18	0.3125	5/16	F
5/16-24	0.3125	5/16	I
3/8-16	0.375	3/8	5/16
3/8-24	0.375	3/8	R

Fig. 6-8. Clear and tap drill chart for machine screws.

shank diameter and the full-thread diameter. With flat-head or oval-head screws, the diameter of the head must also be considered. Before driving the screw, first drill a shank hole to clear the non-threaded portion of the screw shank. The depth of this hole should be just slightly more than the screw shank length. Then, center a smaller bit at the bottom of the shank hole and drill a pilot hole to accommodate the threaded section. The diameter of the pilot hole should be somewhat smaller than that of the full thread. With oval-head or flat-head wood screws, the next step is to countersink, or if the screw head is to be covered with a plug, counterbore. Use an 82-degree countersink for this purpose, and check the diameter of the countersink hole frequently. When its diameter is just slightly less (in softwood) or exactly the same (in hardwood) as the diameter of the screw head, stop countersinking. The rest of the operation is done with the appropriate sizes of bits. Or, to save time and increase accuracy, you can use the specially made pilot drills which perform all three operations consecutively with one bit.

The size and depth of the holes naturally will vary. The shank hole should be equal to, or a few thousandths of an inch larger than, the shank diameter of the screw. Pilot hole sizes vary according to thread diameter and to the density of the material. The chart in Fig. 6-9 will give you the necessary figures. The shank hole should never be deeper than the shank length of the screw. The pilot hole should be approximately one-half as deep as the length of the screw thread in soft woods. In extremely hard woods such as oak or birch, the pilot hole should be full depth.

Once in a while you will see some misguided soul drive a screw with a hammer, along with the statement that the slot is only for removing the screw. Don't make that mistake. This action destroys the wood fibers within the hole, and practically eliminates the holding power of the screw. Sometimes, too, even with a properly drilled pilot hole, a screw will bind in the wood and become very difficult to drive. Don't force it. This is especially true when using screws made from soft materials like brass or aluminum; the heads twist off with startling ease. Instead, remove the screw and rebore the pilot hole to a slightly larger diameter, and try again. Another old trick is to wipe soap onto the threads to make the screw go in more easily. Don't do that, either. Soap causes a chemical reaction with the wood fibers, and after a time the screw becomes literally cemented into

Screw #	1	2	3	4	5	6	7	8	9	10	11	12	14	16	18	20
Clear hole – Frac. drill	$\frac{5}{64}$	$\frac{3}{32}$	$\frac{7}{64}$	$\frac{7}{64}$	$\frac{1}{8}$	$\frac{9}{64}$	$\frac{5}{32}$	$\frac{11}{64}$	$\frac{3}{16}$	$\frac{3}{16}$	$\frac{13}{64}$	$\frac{7}{32}$	$\frac{1}{4}$	$\frac{17}{64}$	$\frac{19}{64}$	$\frac{21}{64}$
Clear hole – # drill	49	44	39	33	30	28	24	19	16	11	6	2	–	–	–	–
Pilot hole – Soft wood – Frac. drill	$\frac{1}{32}$	$\frac{1}{32}$	$\frac{3}{64}$	$\frac{3}{64}$	$\frac{1}{16}$	$\frac{1}{16}$	$\frac{1}{16}$	$\frac{5}{64}$	$\frac{5}{64}$	$\frac{3}{32}$	$\frac{3}{32}$	$\frac{7}{64}$	$\frac{7}{64}$	$\frac{9}{64}$	$\frac{9}{64}$	$\frac{11}{64}$
Pilot hole – Soft wood – # drill	68	68	56	56	52	52	52	47	47	42	42	35	35	28	28	17
Pilot hole – Hard wood – Frac. drill	$\frac{1}{32}$	$\frac{3}{64}$	$\frac{1}{16}$	$\frac{1}{16}$	$\frac{5}{64}$	$\frac{5}{64}$	$\frac{3}{32}$	$\frac{3}{32}$	$\frac{7}{64}$	$\frac{7}{64}$	$\frac{1}{8}$	$\frac{1}{8}$	$\frac{9}{64}$	$\frac{5}{32}$	$\frac{3}{16}$	$\frac{13}{64}$
Pilot hole – Hard wood – # drill	68	56	52	52	47	47	42	42	35	35	30	30	28	22	12	6

Fig. 6-9. Chart of clear (shank) and pilot hole drill sizes.

the hole. But you can use powered graphite or paraffin wax, and this is often a good idea when driving screws made of soft metals into hard woods. Incidentally, always use brass screws when working with oak, especially if the finish will be transparent. Steel screws react with oak to form an obvious stain after a time.

You may, at one time or another, inadvertently twist a screw off in its hole. This is not nearly as difficult as it sounds, even with a mild-steel screw. If this should happen, you have three alternatives. One is simply to forget the whole thing, and hide the broken screw with filler. If the screw must be removed, there are two methods. The first, a tricky one, is to exactly center a drill on the broken shank of the screw. Bore dead center down through the entire length of the screw, and then pick out the few remaining particles. Most likely you will have to make a replacement with the next screw size up. The other method is to drill a small, shallow hole of an appropriate size in the center of the broken screw shank. Then use a special tool called a screw extractor (also called an easy-out) to remove the screw by backing it out on its threads.

Many of the problems that arise in using screws derive directly from using the wrong size. The rule of thumb is simple: the entire length of the threaded portion should be embedded in the second workpiece, the member to which the surface workpiece is to be attached. With heavy or thick pieces, use the heavier screws. Thin workpieces require smaller-gauge screws. When driving through a surface workpiece and into an edge grain, use a relatively small gauge. Joining plywood has its own requirements (Fig. 6-10).

Screws driven into an edge grain lose much of their potential holding power, and the joint will be a weak one. Increasing the length of the screw substantially beyond normal will help to some degree. A smaller than usual pilot hole will also help, but this practice incurs the risk of splitting the wood. Perhaps the best way to counteract this problem is to bore a transverse hole through the workpiece from edge to edge, back a short way from the edge-grain surface. Plug the hole with a hardwood dowel glued in place. Then predrill the screw holes as usual. When the screws are driven fully into place, a portion of the threads will bite solidly into crossgrain hardwood, instead of edge grain alone. If the workpiece is too wide to bore satisfactorily, you can mark the screw locations and then bore the same number of holes from surface to bottom, just back from the edge-grain surface.

Plywood size	Screw size	Screw length *
1"	10	2"
3/4"	8	1 1/2"
5/8"	8	1 1/4"
1/2"	6	1 1/4"
3/8"	6	1"
1/4"	4	3/4"

Fig. 6-10. Proper wood screw size/length combinations for plywood.

Plug these holes with dowels, flush on each workpiece surface, and proceed as before. In both cases, use screws long enough to extend through the dowels.

As was mentioned earlier, always use a quality screwdriver with a fitted blade, in a size which accurately fits and fills the screw slot. This is important even though the screw head may later be covered. A sloppy screwdriver bit can jack out of the slot and drive into the workpiece surface. With screws made of soft materials, and screws whose heads will not be concealed, using the right screwdriver is literally mandatory, as is exercising care and caution.

Bolts

Bolts of one sort or another are sometimes used in cabinetmaking, and there are three types with which you should be familiar. These are called stove, machine, and carriage bolts (Fig. 6-11). Note that lag screws are frequently called lag bolts, although they are really not bolts at all. Also, note that most sizes of machine screws, when equipped with nuts, can also be used as bolts.

Stove bolts look much the same as machine screws, though the sizes are different. Stove bolts range in diameter from 5/32 inch to ½ inch, and in length from ⅜ inch to 6 inches. The slot configurations and head shapes are the same as those of machine screws. Stove

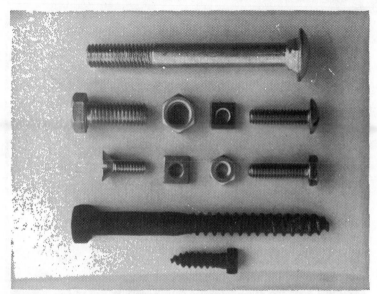

Fig. 6-11. Assorted bolt types. Top, carriage bolt. Second row left, hex head machine bolt with hex nut; right, square nut and truss head machine bolt. Third line left, stove bolt and square nut; right, hex nut and hex head machine bolt. Bottom, lag bolts or screws. Duncan Photos.

bolts may be used with either square or hexagonal nuts, but are usually supplied with the former. In most cases, the thread extends the entire length of the bolt shank.

Machine bolts are heavier and sturdier than stove bolts, have square or hexagonal heads, and are available in diameters of ¼ inch to 1 inch and more. Lengths vary from ¾ inch to 2 feet or more. Either square or hexagonal nuts can be used with them. A carriage bolt has a round head, underneath which is a square shoulder a bit larger than the shank size. This type of bolt was originally designed for use in wood—in the carriage-making trade, in fact—so that the squared shoulder would seat firmly into the workpiece when the nut was drawn up. Carriage bolts come in diameters of from 3/16 inch to ¾ inch, and in lengths of from ¾ inch up to about a foot. Again, either square or hexagonal nuts can be used.

Washers

Washers of various sorts and in different combinations are usually used with nuts and bolts. There are several types (Fig 6-12), and the one you use depends upon the task at hand. Flat washers,

172

sometimes called punched hole washers, are used to provide additional support below the bolt head or below the nut face, so that extra pressure can be applied, and so that the nut (or bolt head, or both) can be turned without digging into the workpiece surface. If there is any possibility that the nut might work loose, set a lock washer between the nut and the flat washer. The nut can be easily run down into place, but the lock washer will prevent it from loosening except under the force of a wrench. Shakeproof washers, sometimes called star washers, are used for a similar purpose but are available in small sizes that can be used with machine screws. Two styles are available: inside-toothed, and outside-toothed. Fender washers are extra wide in relation to the hole size, and will work effectively when the bolt load must be spread over a wider area, or when the material is soft. Burrs look the same as common flat washers, but are tiny. Though intended for use with rivets, they work equally well with machine screws.

Anchors

Anchors (Fig. 6-13) are separated into two general groups: masonry, and hollow wall. Sometimes the nomenclature can be a bit

Fig. 6-12. Different types of washers. The large one is a fender washer. Flanking to the right: above, cup or finish washer; below, flat or punched washer. Bottom, left to right: lock; shakeproof internal; shakeproof external, or star. Duncan Photos.

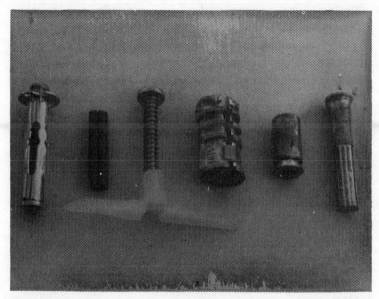

Fig. 6-13. Various kinds of anchors and shields. Left to right: molly bolt, plastic plug anchor, drywall anchor, lag shield, machine bolt anchor, rawl plug. Duncan Photos.

confusing, since different terms are used in different parts of the country. There are several hollow-wall anchors, known variously as toggle bolts, spring-head toggle bolts, molly bolts, and expansion bolts. A hollow-wall anchor protrudes into the cavity of a hollow wall, expands, and locks into place as the bolt is tightened. This is the fastener to use in securing cabinets, shelves, and similar items to any hollow-wall surface. Always follow the manufacturer's instructions in installing them, and make sure that the weight upon them does not exceed the load rating of the fastener. Various lengths are available to accommodate different wall thicknesses.

Masonry wall anchors include machine-bolt shields, nail anchors, machine-screw anchors, lag-screw shields, lead screw anchors, and assorted nylon, neoprene and plastic expansion-plug anchors. There is a wide assortment of lengths and diameters, and they are usually designed to fit specific sizes and types of bolts and screws. They are installed by first drilling an appropriate hole with a carbide-tipped masonry drill, and then inserting the anchor. When the screw or bolt is driven into the anchor, the anchor expands and grips the wall surfaces of the hole. Again, follow the manufacturer's instructions to the letter, taking careful note of holding power and loading characertistics. Some of these anchors can also be used in plasterboard, wood paneling, or similar materials.

Miscellaneous

Miscellaneous hardware covers a tremendous quantity of items, and there is no possible way to list everything available. However, there are a few items which enjoy considerable popularity and are found in many home shops (Fig. 6-14). An acquaintance with these items may be of value to you. Hanger bolts are made in two ways: (1) with a tapered wood screw on one end and a machine thread on the other, and (2) with both ends machine-threaded. You can screw or bolt them to one surface, then hang a cabinet or other fixture on the stud, securing the cabinet with washers and nuts for easy removal. Threaded rod is handy when you can't find a bolt of the right length. Just lop off a suitable portion of rod, and add washers and nuts to each end. One example of use: a thick counter or table top made of sticks of wood placed on edge can be through-bored and sandwiched together with threaded rod, with the nuts hidden in deep counterbores and covered by plugs. An alternative to using threaded rod is using sections of plain rod and then threading each end to suit.

Small staples are often used with a staple gun to secure cabinet backs, thin wood sheets, vinyl coverings, upholstery, and the like. The larger sizes are used for heavier work and driven in with a

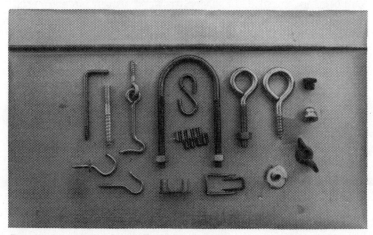

Fig. 6-14. Miscellaneous hardware. Top, threaded rod. Center, left to right:angle hook, hanger bolt, hook-and-eye, U-bolt, S-hook, corrugated fasteners, eye bolt, screweye, knurled nut, cap nut, wing nut. Bottom: cup hook, screw hook, joining staple, flat stales, and tee nut. Duncan Photos.

hammer. U-bolts are designed to secure a round member, such as a rod or pipe, to a flat surface. They also work well as a hanger device. Set in place of an eyebolt, the U-bolt provides twice the supportive strength because of the two threaded shanks. Screw eyes and screw hooks have a wood-screw thread, while eyebolts and hook bolts are machine-threaded, and are used with nuts. All four items are hanger fasteners. A considerable assortment of sizes and lengths is available.

Besides the common hex nut and flat square nut, there are some special types. The wing nut allows quick and easy tightening and removal by hand. Knurled nuts present a mildly decorative look, and are designed for finger tightening. Acorn nuts cap the ends of the bolts to provide a more attractive appearance. T-nuts are recessed into the wood and have stove bolt or machine screw threads.

Corrugated fasteners, also called wiggle nails or Scotch fasteners, are used as a aid in holding flat miter or butt joints together. They may be used parallel with, or at an angle to, the wood grain with little fear of the wood's splitting, and are driven flush with the workpiece surface. Generally they are applied only on reverse sides, out of sight.

You can make your own dowel pins, but you can buy ready-made dowel pins which are better. The best kind, available in several diameters and lengths, have fluted edges, specially cut spiral glue channels, and are made of quality hardwood, usually birch. You can also cut your own straight plugs, but it's easier to buy them. Commercially-made plugs are available in several sizes, usually are made of birch, and have slightly tapered sides to offer the best possible glue surface and to insure a tight fit. The disadvantage with this type of plug is that it probably will not match your workpiece surfaces, a practical consideration if the finish is transparent. A button plug looks a little like a small mushroom. These plugs come in several diameters and are made from a variety of hardwoods. The straight lower shank conceals the screw head, while the rounded top imparts a decorative effect.

GLUES

There are perhaps a dozen basic kinds of glue, with numerous variations on each. Every base has different characteristics and properties, and no one type will do every kind of gluing job. There are differences in setting times and in curing times, and there are differences in strength. Ambient temperatures have varying effects, moisture resistance differs, and gap-filling capabilities vary. To obtain good results from any given gluing task, you have to know which glue to use. The chart in Fig. 6-15 will give you quick reference to the major characteristics and properties of the most widely used glues.

Animal Glue

Animal glue, also called liquid hide glue, is a tried-and-true type which is still widely popular. It provides a tough and long-lived bond on wood-to-wood surfaces, and is an excellent choice for all sorts of cabinetmaking. It is not waterproof, however, and will weaken in high-moisture environments.

Animal glue is very strong, and will not become brittle. It is good for structural bonding or veneering, as well as for general cabinetwork. It has good gap-filling properties, and so can be used even on joints which are poorly fitted.

Animal glue works best if the room temperature is at least 70°F. Yet you can heat this glue and use it at lower temperatures if the cooling rate is not overly fast. The best method is to apply a thin coat to each surface, and wait until the glue is just tacky. Then mate the two surfaces and clamp the parts securely for about 3 hours.

Casein Glue

Casein glue is another of the natural glues, derived from milk, and is available only in powdered form. It must be mixed with water for each job, and only in small quantities, since the shelf life is relatively short. If the task is long, mix small quantities in paper cups and, as soon as the glue begins to thicken, throw it away and start afresh.

Casein glue is a very strong adhesive with fair resistance to moisture and good gap-filling properties. It can be used in any temperature above freezing, but the warmer the better. It will handle nearly all general cabinetmaking jobs, but should not be used outdoors. When applied to highly acid woods like oak or redwood, a stain will result. On the other hand, this is the glue to use with oily woods like yew, pitch pine and teak.

To mix casein, follow the directions on the package. Usually this involves mixing an equal amount of powder and water, stirring

Glue	Uses	Temp.	Clamp	Strength	Mois. Res.	Workability
Animal	Interior Furniture Cabinetry General	70°+	2-3 hrs.	Very high	Poor	Excellent Fills well
Casein	Interior Oily woods Laminating End joints General	32°+	2-3 hrs.	High	Fair	Good Fills well
Contact Cement	Bonding of veneers, laminates, etc. to wood	70°+	Instant bond	--	Exc.	--
Epoxy	Interior Exterior Wood to dis-similar material	Any	None	Very high	Water-proof	Machinable Excellent filler
Plastic Resin	Interior Protected exterior Veneering Cabinetry End joints General	70°+	16 hrs.	Very high	High	Good Fills poorly
Polyvinyl Resin	Interior Cabinetry Veneering Furniture General	60°+	1-2 hrs.	High	Fair	Good Fair filler
Resorcinol	Exterior General	70°+	16 hrs.	Very high	Water-proof	Good Fills well

throughly, waiting a few moments, and then stirring again. The length of time that casein is usable varies somewhat; in some cases the time span may be as much as eight hours. The best gluing method is to apply a thin coat to each surface, immediately mate the parts, and clamp for about 3 hours.

Contact Cement

Contact cement is a special kind of glue made from a base of synthetic rubber. Its principal use is in bonding veneers, plastics, and plastic laminates to wood. It will also bond particle board and hardboard, and can be used successfully to bond leather and some heavy fabrics. Contact cement has a deserved reputation for being a dangerous glue to use, because it is extremely explosive, and the fumes are highly toxic. When using the volatile type of contact cement, always, always, always make sure of plenty of ventilation, turn off all electrical power in the area, and make sure that all pilot lights are extinguished. Obviously, no smoking is the rule. In answer to this hazard, new types of contact cement which do not have these lethal characteristics have been developed. Though the bond is perhaps not quite as good, the advantages of using the nonvolatile cement in place of the old type far outweigh the disadvantages, especially for the amateur craftsman working in his home.

Contact cement is tricky to use because there is no turning back once the pieces are mated. The pieces are immobile. No clamping is necessary, but as soon as the pieces are joined, pressure should be applied to the top surface with a heavy roller or by gently tapping a block of wood moved from place to place.

Contact cement comes ready to use from the can. The usual application is made by brushing on a fairly thick coat, letting it dry for about half an hour, and then applying a second coat. Application is made to both surfaces. After a second drying period, test the surfaces with a piece of brown wrapping paper. If the paper does not stick to the surface, the glue is ready. Joining practices vary, but one method is to lay a sheet of wrapping paper completely over one surface. The veneer or laminate is then set exactly into place upon the wrapping paper, and held firm while the paper is slid from between the mating surfaces. Bonding is practically instantaneous. All work should be done at a room temperature of 70°F or better.

Aliphatic Resin

Aliphatic resin glue is a chemical glue of high strength. It is particularly good for edge-gluing, and is a good choice for all kinds of cabinetwork and casework, with good gap-filling properties, but low moisture resistance. It is relatively heat resistant, and sands and works easily. There may be some separation of glue and vehicle during storage, but they can be remixed.

Aliphatic resin can be used at any temperature above 45°F. Keep it well mixed, and spread it on in a moderate coat. Mate the workpiece surfaces immediately after gluing. Clamp at once. Normal clamping time is about 1½ hours.

EPOXY CEMENT

Epoxy cement is a synthetic glue known also as epoxy resin or simply epoxy glue. This is another synthetic glue which should be used with plenty of ventilation. Epoxies do not work well in gluing wood to wood, but are ideal for combination situations where ceramic tile, plastics, metal, glass, and foils must be bonded to wood. It will neither shrink nor swell during the curing process, and is completely waterproof and impervious to oils.

Epoxies must be mixed from two materials, the resin and the hardener, immediately prior to the gluing job. Shelf life is very short once the components are mixed. There are numerous procedures; follow the manufacturer's instructions explicitly. As soon as the material is completely mixed, apply to one or both mating surfaces with a brush or stick, mate the surfaces, and let them alone. Clamping is not necessary, and the curing time, though variable, can be shortened by the application of heat. Epoxy gluing can be done at any temperature. Epoxies, unlike other glues, can be machined, drilled, filled, and shaped. They can also be used to fill large holes. They take paints nicely, and sanding them is no problem.

Plastic Resin

Plastic resin glue, which comes in powdered form, is good for general woodworking purposes and for instances in which a reasonably high degree of moisture resistance is desired. It is a high-strength glue, but its gap-filling properties are poor. This means that it can only be used with closely fitted components and tight joints. Any looseness or gaps will not be taken up by the glue, and the joint will prove weak. Also, tight clamping is always necessary.

During application, the ambient temperature should be at least 70°F, and the glue will set better at higher temperatures, even up to 90°F. The useful life of the glue after mixing is from 3 to 4 hours, depending upon temperature and humidity. The glue should be applied in thin coats to both surfaces, and the parts mated immediately. Clamp the workpieces with plenty of pressure for about 16 hours at 70°F. The higher the temperature, the shorter the curing time.

Polyvinyl Resin

The name may not sound familiar to you, but the product probably is. It is the familiar and popular white glue found on the shelves of every hardware store, and its full name is polyvinyl white liquid resin glue. It is a synthetic glue which is fine for all-around shop and household use, and is a good, though not the best, choice for cabinetmaking and casework. It does work especially well for small assemblies, general repair work, hobby work of all sorts, and it even does a good job with paper and leather.

White glue forms a moderately strong bond, but is not nearly as tough as animal glue. It has poor moisture resistance, is water soluable, and will not fill gaps at all. It will also soften when subjected to heat and solvents. On the other hand, it is easy to use, nonstaining, quicksetting, and a help where clamping cannot be easily accomplished.

White glue can be used at temperatures above 60°F, but works better as the temperature rises. It sets quickly in low humidity situations, and all the workpieces to be joined should be ready to go with no wasted time. The glue can be spread on one or both surfaces, though one is usually sufficient, and then the pieces should be mated immediately. Set the clamps at once and allow the glue to dry for about 1½ hours.

Resorcinol Glue

This is the glue to use if you want to build a boat. Of course, it works equally well for cabinetry which will be exposed to the weather out on the patio, too. This is a resin type of glue of high strength which comes in powder form, and its most important characteristic is extremely high water resistance. (In effect, it's waterproof.) It is excellent for structural bonding of all kinds, and can be used for all manner of general purpose gluing. It works best on wood-to-wood bonds.

This glue also works very well with poor joints, since it has good gap-filling qualities. The ambient temperature must be at least 70°F, and preferably higher. Resorcinol is easy to mix and easy to work with. Apply a thin coat to each surface, mate the parts, and clamp for about 16 hours. The useful life of the glue after mixing is 6 to 8 hours.

Specialty Glues

There are numerous special types of glues for various applications. Most of them are not necessary to cabinetmaking, but you may have recourse to some at one time or another, especially in the installation of accessory items and decorative trim work.

The mastic adhesives are thick, tacky, fast-bonding pastes. They are available in small tubes or in cartridge tubes for caulking guns. Mastics are often used to apply wall panels to a backer. They can also be used to secure metal trim pieces, to set parquet tiles and ceramic tiles on countertops, and to set metal wall tiles for splashbacks and mirror tiles for decorative effect. They have medium strength characteristics, excellent water and moisture resistance, and will fill gaps satisfactorily. Most mastics do not dry hard, are attacked by solvents, and in general should not be used where a joint might be left exposed.

The silicone seals, sometimes known as silicone caulks, can also be used as bonding agents. They come in various types and colors, and their minor characteristics may differ somewhat. For the most part, however, they are alike, in that they cure in a short period of time into a tough, rubbery substance. They are excellent for bonding glass, porcelain, pottery, and metal. Silicone seals are quite utilitarian, are completely waterproof, and have medium strength. One common use for them is to set acrylic plastic sheets into wood or metal frames, where its flexibility allows expansion and contraction of the sheets with no harm.

There are a number of products of the Space Age Technology which are sometimes classed as superglues. There is quite an assortment of them, and they all have one thing in common; they will stick anything to anything forevermore, including your fingers. They can be used to glue practically any surface to any other surface just by following the directions. Application procedures and specific purposes vary greatly so you will have to seek out the best brand for the job you want to do, and then follow the instructions on the label to the letter. The superglues are generally best for small projects of a highly specialized nature, since they are available only in small quantities at considerable expense. Many of them have short shelf lives, and some even have to be refrigerated.

Gluing Techniques

As in just about any operation, there are certain techniques involved in working with glues. The first step, of course, is to choose the proper type. Beyond this, there are a few general points to bear in mind. Foremost is the fact that a good glue joint depends upon the mating pieces being properly aligned and fitted. Even a glue with good gap-filling properties cannot completely compensate for an assembly which is poorly fitted together. To effect an evenly bonded and properly fitted joint, glue should be applied to the surfaces as evenly as possible. When mating flat surfaces, spreading an excess amount of glue simply means that some will be squeezed out at the edges and will have to be wiped off or trimmed off later with a chisel. However, if you pour too much glue into a dowel-pin hole, and then drive the dowel in, the result will probably be a split workpiece, because the excess has no place to go.

The porosity of the surface upon which the glue is spread has an effect upon the glue joint. All woods are porous, some kinds more so than others. Gluing along edges uses the least amount of glue, face-to-face gluing requires a bit more glue, and gluing edge grains requires a significantly larger amount because the glue is absorbed into the end-grain openings. Remember to make allowances for this. On the other hand, gluing such tight materials as hardboard requires a thinner coat of an appropriate type of glue. Experience is the best teacher; after a while you'll develop a "feel" for proper glue coatings.

Glues must be applied to surfaces which are completely free of dust or particles. The dustier the surface, the weaker the joint will be. Most glues will not adhere to an oily surface, either. Drying rates vary considerably from type to type, as described previously, and the drying rate of each type can vary from day to day, depending upon weather conditions. The safest bet is always to have everything ready and close at hand so that you can position, apply, mate, clamp, and then drive fasteners in as short a time span as possible.

The integrity of a good glue joint also depends upon the moisture content of the material. While the effect is practically unnoticeable with relatively inert materials like hardboard, or normally stable and nonporous materials like metals, this is an important factor with wood. Ideally, the moisture content of the wood should be no more than 10 percent. If the moisture content is lower than that, so much the better. The problem is that the moisture within the wood will be drawn into the glue, thinning it and creating a weak joint. From a practical standpoint, this is a matter that is most difficult to judge, especially for the amateur cabinetmaker in his home workshop. About all you can do is to make sure that the stock you are using has been stored inside for several weeks, and that it was kiln dried or properly air cured for a long period of time previously. Chances are, in most cases the moisture content of the wood will be low enough so that no obvious problems will result. It is wise, too, to allow glue joints to dry for a lengthy period of time, perhaps as much as a couple of days, before attempting to surface the material. If you surface a glue joint before it is thoroughly dry, a sunken line will appear at the joint edges when the wood does dry completely.

When setting up for a gluing operation, first check the fit of all the pieces, and their order of assembly if necessary, to make sure everything is correct and that no more work need be done. Mark mating surfaces with a lumber crayon, and make light pencil marks so that you know which end goes where and which side or edge is supposed to be up or down, or whatever. If necessary, outline in pencil the area where glue should be applied, so that no glue will end up on an exposed surface where it does no good and may even cause some harm. When you apply the glue, don't lavish it on, but on the other hand, don't apply so little that the thin layer will dry before the joint is made up, or that there won't be enough to make a joint in the first place. There really is no way to tell you exactly how to go about this; again, it is a matter of experience, of "feel."

Once the glue is on, assemble the parts rapidly, and try to position them as accurately as possible on the first shot. Moving the pieces around after they are mated may weaken the joint, especially if the glue is setting up rapidly. Apply the clamps quickly, using blocks for surface protection and to spread the clamp pressure as necessary. Adjust the pressure of the clamps more or less equally, checking to see that none of them squidge apart as you do so.

Occasionally it may be necessary to knock a piece back into accurate position with a mallet. If you have applied the right amount of glue, you will have achieved the correct pressure on the clamps when a thin bead of glue appears at the edge of the joint. If you apply too much pressure, you may end up with what is known as a starved joint: not enough glue to do the job. All of it got squeezed out at the edges. Actually, this seldom happens, and the greater danger is in not applying enough pressure. Again, this is a matter of experience. and only after some practice will you begin to acquire that difficult-to-define feel which tells you when the glue is right, the pressure is right, and that the material will bond properly.

Once the clamps are in place, then you can set the fasteners— nails or screws. Note, however, that fasteners are not always used. And also, in some instances you may want to set the fasteners first, then clamp. This can be a tricky business, and the resulting glue joint is not always the best if the glue sets before the clamps are applied. In other instances you may want to follow a process of applying fasteners, then clamping, then applying more fasteners, and then clamping again, in a continuous series. In any case, before setting fasteners which will irrevocably position the workpieces, make a quick last check to insure that everything lines up properly and is in the right place. If you discover something awry, work fast. Yank the clamps off and pry the offending part away from the assembly before it is too late. If you have done a proper job, the glue joint will quickly become stronger than the material it is bonding.

Chapter 7
Joinery

Joinery is the process of constructing articles by joining pieces of wood together. This is the heart and soul of cabinetmaking and furniture building, and important to general woodworking as well. In a way, joinery is almost a craft unto itself, in that it involves a thorough working knowledge of the many methods and techniques of joining two or more pieces of wood together. A joiner must be able to select the proper joint for a given task, establish dimensions, and lay the work out properly. Then he has to make the necessary cuts with the appropriate type of equipment, fit the cut pieces together and trim or reshape as necessary, and assemble the joint. This is no small chore when you consider the wide assortment of woods available for use, the vast array of possible joint situations, and the fact that there are well over one hundred different types of basic joints.

While the home cabinetmaker need not by any stretch of the imagination develop himself into a master joiner, a certain amount of fundamental knowledge is essential. When working with cabinets and built-ins, no matter how simple, there is no way to avoid becoming involved in a certain amount of joinery. Like the weak link in a chain, a cabinet or piece of furniture is no better than its weakest joint. The quality of the cabinets and built-ins that you put together in your own home will depend to a great degree upon the quality of the joints you make.

The following pages deal with some of the basic woodworking joints, how they are made, and the purposes for which they are intended, as well as some of the general principles of joinery. The terminology can be a bit confusing, and some of it may be unfamiliar to you. To get on track, then, we will start with some definitions, in the hope of precluding derailments later on.

Edge—the side of a piece of stock, running parallel with the grain. Often, but not always, the long dimension.

Butt—the end of a piece of material which is pushed up against another piece of stock. Usually end grain, but may be edge grain.

Lap—a piece of stock, or part of a piece of stock, that extends over another piece of stock.

Splice—a joining of two pieces of stock, end to end.

Rabbet—an L-shaped channel or groove cut out of the edge or end of a piece of stock.

Dado—a rectangular groove cut into and across the surface of a piece of stock.

Miter—an angle cut. An oblique surface formed on a piece of stock as a result of an angle cut.

Mortise—a hole, groove, or slot in a piece of stock, into which another piece fits. Usually rectangular, but may be round or rounded. May be cut partially through or clear through the stock.

Tenon—the projecting portion of a piece of stock which inserts into a mortise.

Dovetail—a special type of tenon which is narrower at its base than at its head; in cross section, a triangle with the top lopped off.

Spline—a thin strip of wood, metal, or plastic, tightly fitted into matching grooves in two mating pieces of stock, for added strength. Also called a key, or feather, in some circumstances.

These are the basic terms used in the designation of the various types of cabinetmaking joints. They are joined with other definitive terms to denote specific types of joints within a general area. Once you sort out all the differences, joints are really not that difficult to understand. To wit:

EDGE JOINTS

Edge joints are about the simplest kind to make, and are widely used in all kinds of woodworking. The main idea is to build up larger surfaces from two or more smaller pieces, laid edge to edge in a series, with the grain running parallel. If the stock being used is plain-sawed (hardwood) or flat-grained (softwood), the first piece should be placed with the heart side up, the second piece with the heart side down, and so on. This way, the arc of the annual growth rings will curve in opposite directions and result in a workpiece which can be more easily surfaced and is more stable.

The simplest edge joint is known as a butt or plain edge joint (Fig. 7-1A). If the mating edges are smooth, as when sawed by a fine-toothed blade on a power saw, and if they are fully straight, no further surfacing is necessary. If the edges are a bit rough or not quite true, though, they should be surfaced. The butting edges are then covered with an appropriate glue, drawn together, and clamped securely, using holding blocks to make sure that the pieces do not buckle at the edges. Properly done, the resulting joints are stronger than the material.

The dowel edge joint (Fig. 7-1B) is similar, except that dowel pins are inserted for extra strength. The dowel holes must match accurately so that the mating edges of the successive pieces will be flush. A spline edge joint (Fig. 7-1C) is stronger yet. Cut a shallow groove the full length of each adjoining edge, fit a spline of plywood, hardboard, or solid hardwood, and sandwich the entire assembly together.

Figure 7-1D shows a tongue-and-groove joint, frequently abbreviated as t&g. Tongue-and-groove stock is often available as a standard item at the lumberyard. Don't fret if you are unable to obtain the proper stock; you can easily make your own t&g joints with a dado head or a molding head. A milled edge joint (Fig. 7-1E) is sometimes called a glue joint, and the specific shape of each edge is of little importance so long as a large mating surface is provided. The edge is cut with a molding head or on a shaper. However, not much additional strength is gained from the extra work involved. You can make a rabbet edge (Fig. 7-1F) by cutting matching rabbets on opposite sides of the pieces to be joined. The cutting can be done with a table saw, radial saw, power plane, or even a router or molding head. The joint is easy to make, and provides a strong bond.

BUTT JOINTS

Butt joints, also called plain joints, are probably the most widely used joints in woodworking. They are simplest to make, and are also

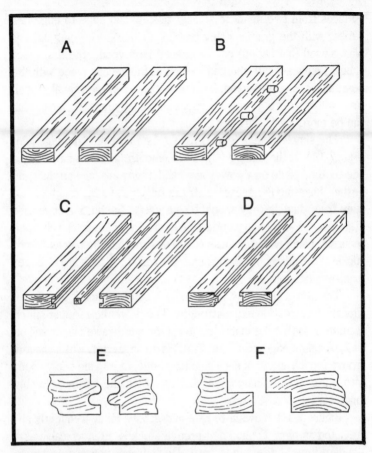

Fig. 7-1. Edge joints. (A) plain edge. (B) dowel edge. (C) spline edge. (D) tongue and groove. (E) milled edge. (F) rabbet edge.

the weakest. Butt joints invariably need something to reinforce them. Basic butt joints come in two modes. One is the flat butt, where an end is joined to an edge as in a picture frame, with the material lying flat. The other is the edge butt, where an end is joined to a surface as in a drawer or box, with the pieces standing on edge.

Figure 7-2A shows a flat butt joint with no reinforcing. The dowel flat butt joint in Fig. 7-2B is simple to make and much stronger. This is called a frame butt joint. The same type of joint on edge (Fig. 7-2C) is called a dowel corner butt joint. A middle-rail butt joint (Fig. 7-2D) can be of either the edge or flat variety, end to edge or end to surface, and to have reasonable strength should be made with dowel pins.

Because of the weakness of butt joints, other methods of reinforcing may be used instead of, or along with, dowel pins. One common method is to provide a glue block of one sort or another (Fig. 7-2E). You might also use mending plates, one of the various commercially made special metal corner blocks, or wood corner blocks screwed and glued into place. Some of these wood corner blocks can be installed with joints, for extra strength.

DADO JOINTS

Dado joints are easy to make, and constitute perhaps the most useful series of joints for home cabinetmaking and built-ins. They are

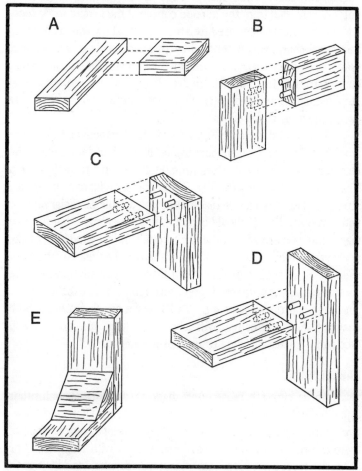

Fig. 7-2. Butt joints. (A) flat butt. (B) dowel or frame flat butt. (C) dowel corner butt. (D) dowel middle rail butt. (E) glue block corner butt.

used wherever edge support is needed, as in cabinet shelves or bookcases. The dado joint provides additional holding surface, and makes for a tight, solid piece of cabinetwork that is unlikely to rack or warp. The simple or plain dado joint (Fig. 7-3A) is the easiest to make. Simply cut a dado into one workpiece, and fit the butt end of the second workpiece into the groove, making sure that the fit is tight. The problem with a plain dado is that the joint is exposed at the edges, and, unless covered with trim molding, the appearance may be considered unattractive. A stop or blind dado (Fig. 7-3B) solves this problem. The dado groove, with a square end, stops about an inch or two short of the outside edge of the material. A matching notch is removed from the outside corner of the joining workpiece, and the two workpieces are fitted together to show what appears to be a simple butt joint. A cut made with a dado blade on a table saw, however, will leave a rounded end on the groove. You can match that curve in the notch removed from the joining workpiece for a rounded stop dado. The rounded notch should be carefully shaped to fit the dado groove as closely as possible.

The corner dado joint (Fig. 7-3C) is used to mount a transverse workpiece into an open support frame, like a shelf set between the legs of a table. For extra strength, add a dowel pin to each corner. The half-dovetail dado joint (Fig. 7-3D) is a lock joint of considerable strength. The cuts can be made either on a table or radial saw, or with a router. The fit should be snug, but not so tight that the two pieces must be driven together by force. This is a good joint to use where the weight on the shelf will be heavy. The full-dovetail joint (Fig. 7-3E) is similar. It requires a little more work and must be carefully fitted, but provides great strength and an excellent lock. The dado-and-rabbet joint (Fig. 7-3F), while not as strong, is both easy to make and effective. With a bit of ingenuity, you can make it in stop form, in resemblance to the normal stop dado.

RABBET JOINTS

Rabbet cuts are most often made in conjunction with other types of joints, because of the nature of the cut. There are, however, three simple rabbet joints which are useful at times. None of them are overly strong, so reinforcing them with glue blocks or backer plates is a good idea. One easy joint to make—and it's a good one to use for constructing cabinet frames or base frames—is the

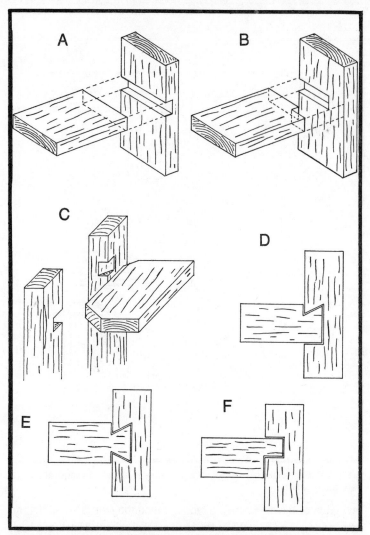

Fig. 7-3. Dado joints. (A) simple or plain dado. (B) stop or blind dado. (C) corner dado. (D) half dovetail dado. (E) full dovetail dado. (F) dado-rabbet.

simple rabbet joint (Fig. 7-4A). Essentially, the joint consists of nothing more than the removal of a notch from one workpiece to accommodate the full-thickness dimension of the second workpiece. Similar but stronger is the double rabbet (Fig. 7-4B). Here, two workpieces are notched to accommodate one another. The same process can be used to make edge joints for box and case construction (Fig. 7-4C). When making a cabinet case, it is desirable for the

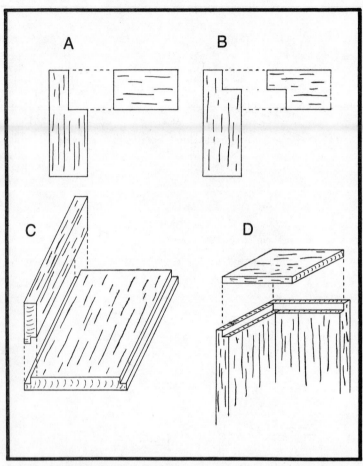

Fig. 7-4. Rabbet joints. (A) simple rabbet. (B) double rabbet. (C) edge rabbet. (D) back-panel rabbet.

end grain of the side panel to face the mounting surface, so that no end grains are visible. When the case must also have a back, the back can be installed after cutting what is called a back-panel rabbet joint (Fig. 7-4D).

Rabbets can be cut easily with a table saw, radial arm saw, or router. For single full rabbets, the depth of the cut should be about one-half of the thickness of the material, while the width of the cut should equal the thickness of the material. When cutting double rabbets you will have to equalize or adjust the cut depths and widths depending upon the thicknesses involved. Rabbet joints are usually secured with glue and screws or nails.

MITER JOINTS

Miter joints are made up of two workpieces cut at angles and joined so that the cut surfaces, whether end or edge, of both pieces are hidden. The joints may be flat or edge, with the adjoining pieces placed at any desired angle to one another. Miter joints are essentially quite weak, and need help. Compound miter joints are pieces joined at angles in two planes, and can become rather complex.

One way to strengthen a simple miter joint is to use dowels as shown in Fig. 7-5A. Figure 7-5B shows a keyed or feathered flat miter. The joint in Fig. 7-5C is called a splined flat miter. If the spline passes only partway through the material, and is visible only at one edge, it is called a blind spline miter joint. These joints are assembled with the use of glue, and often nails or screws as well. Fastening should be done with care so as not to dislodge a key or spline.

Compound miters can be cut in an almost infinite number of ways; the choice depends upon the job. Compound miters are made necessary when the article being constructed must have mitered corners, but consists of tapered component pieces. One familiar example is a square taper-sided box used as a planter. Another is a shadow box with slanted sides. Polygon miters are cut at angles of less than 45 degrees in the construction of multisided articles. One example is a vertical-sided hexagonal umbrella stand.

Where extra strength is needed in a miter joint, consider the offset miter (Fig. 7-5D). This is a strong joint, and a particularly useful one for plywood and end grains for three reasons: (1) it presents considerable surface area for gluing; (2) its configuration helps to hold the pieces straight and tight; and (3) it is readily amenable to fastening.

The lock miter (Fig. 7-5E) is one of the strongest of the miter joints. You can make this joint with a series of individual cuts on a table or radial saw, but you may run into some difficulty. Because of the configuration of the joint faces, the cuts must be made almost perfectly or the joint will not fit together. The best method is to use a matching set of lock-miter cutters on a shaper or router. This will insure a perfect match of the mating edges.

LAP JOINTS

Lap joints are strong, rugged, easy to make, and have many variations. Whenever one member of an assembly laps over

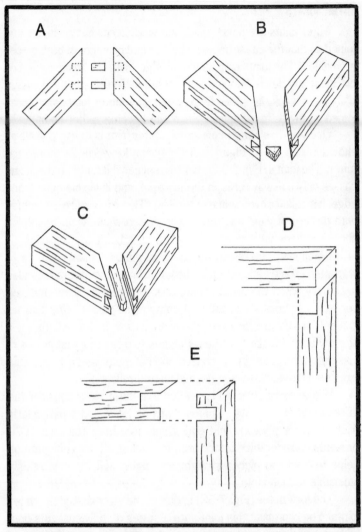

Fig. 7-5. Miter joints. (A) doweled flat miter. (B) keyed flat miter. (C) splined flat miter. (D) offset miter. (E) lock miter.

another, a lap joint is formed. A cross lap (Fig. 7-6A) is made when two members lap over one another with their surfaces flush. The edge crossed lap (Fig. 7-6B) is a similar joint in which the edges of the two workpieces are flush. To make either joint it's only necessary to cut matching notches from each workpiece so that their surfaces or edges line up flush. In a T lap joint (Fig. 7-6C), instead of cutting a dado in each workpiece, one receives a dado cut and the other a rabbet cut. This is also called a half or middle lap, and it is frequently used in frame building or casework. It can easily be turned into a locking joint by simply modifying the cuts into the shape of a dovetail. The resulting joint is called a dovetail lap (Fig. 7-6D). Where the T lap is cut at the end of the workpiece, as in Fig. 7-6E, it becomes an end lap. By cutting an appropriate rabbet in each workpiece, you produce a joint of strength and rigidity. Note that the simple rabbet of Fig. 7-4A is also known as a stop lap joint. A half lap (Fig. 7-6F) is used as a splice to joint two pieces together, end to end. Figure 7-6G shows a squared splice, a lock type of joint.

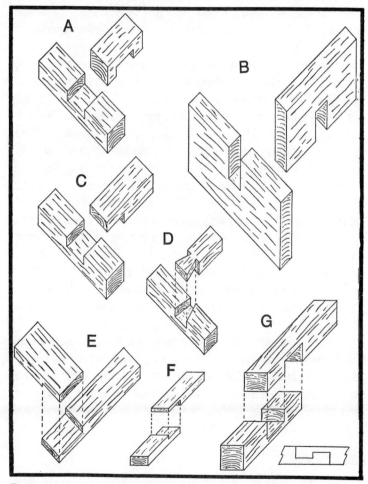

Fig. 7-6. Lap joints. (A) cross lap. (B) edge cross lap. (C) T lap. (D) dovetail lap. (E) end lap. (F) half lap. (G) squared splice.

MORTISE-AND-TENON JOINTS

Mortise-and-tenon joints require care and patience in the making, but produce exceptionally strong and rigid articles which can be subjected confidently to considerable weight and strain. These joints are widely used in furniture making of all kinds, and frequently in frame construction and casework as well. There are two general ways to make them: with all cuts square-edged or with all cuts rounded. The rounded variety is made with a router, while the squared types are most often made with special mortising tools. Either variety can be turned out with hand tools (drills, files, wood chisel, or similar shaping tools), but this takes a deal of skill and time. A high degree of craftsmanship is necessary if these joints are to come out right.

The two simplest mortise-and-tenon joints, however, can be made with a dado head, or even a standard blade, on a table or radial saw. Figure 7-7A shows the open mortise-and-tenon joint, which works fine if the exposed tenon end is not objectionable. The stub mortise-and-tenon joint (Fig. 7-7B) is somewhat the same. Note that the lower (inside angle) end of the mortise must be carefully squared to match the dimensions of the tenoned member. The blind mortise-and-tenon joint shown in Fig. 7-7C makes a completely concealed union of the two pieces. The joint shown is a square type, but it could be made round with no loss of strengh or effectiveness if the corners of the mortise were removed and the edges of the tenon shaped to fit. A full mortise-and-tenon joint (Fig. 7-7D) is nearly identical, except that the tenon runs entirely through the second workpiece. The barefaced mortise-and-tenon (Fig. 7-7E) is used where the show surfaces of one thin and one thick member present a flush face.

Most of the other mortise-and-tenon joints are more complex than those shown and wouldn't be of critical value to you in building cabinets and built-ins. For extra strength or for decorative effect, most mortise-and-tenon joints can be pinned or pegged; some even use external wood keys. Nails or screws, which may be concealed with filler or wood plugs, contribute additional strength and rigidity.

DOVETAIL JOINTS

Dovetail joints are difficult to build; furthermore, they require time, patience, and some special equipment. They are primarily

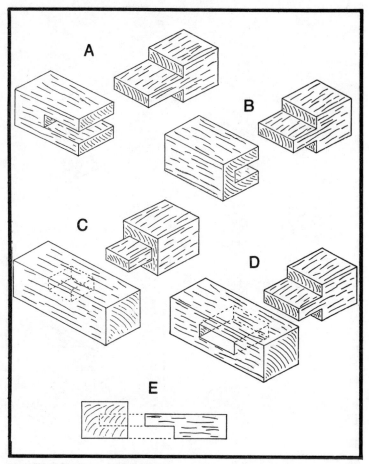

Fig. 7-7. Mortise-and-tenon joints. (A) open. (B) stub. (C) blind. (D) full. (E) barefaced.

used in the finest grades of furniture and cabinetry. Sometimes they are introduced merely for their decorative impact. Their holding power is dependent upon a tight fit, glue, and all-around good craftsmanship. Additional fasteners are seldom used. Dovetails are lock-type; they are robust and inflexible. They can provide you the finest joints possible for drawers and allied box structures, if you feel inclined to take the time and make the effort.

The half-blind or lap dovetail (Fig. 7-8A) is the most common variety of dovetail joint. This joint is visible only from one direction, and locks only for one direction. If you desire to hide the entire joint, use the stopped-lap dovetail joint (Fig. 7-8B). Locking action in both

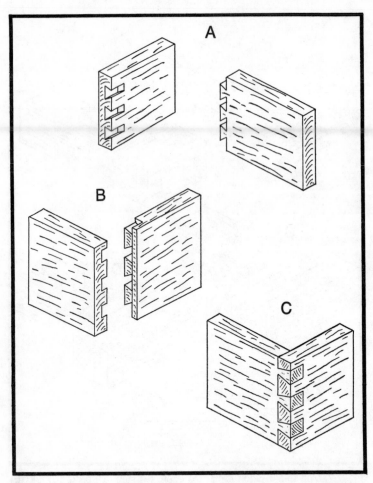

Fig. 7-8. Dovetail joints. (A) half blind or lap dovetail. (B) blind or stopped-lap dovetail. (C) through multiple dovetail.

directions requires the use of the through multiple dovetail joint shown in Fig. 7-8C. Dovetail joints may also be made with only one dovetail, in which case they are called singles rather than multiples.

BOX JOINT

Once upon a time the box joint (Fig. 7-9) was a feature of all manner of prosaic items, such as dynamite crates and salted fish boxes. Today it's seldom found anywhere except on items of furniture, where the joint is used primarily for its decorative appearance. Because it makes a strong and tight corner joint, it is valuable for constructing drawers. It is simple to form. Just cut a series of matching notches and fingers into the ends of the workpieces with a table or radial saw, and fit them together with glue. If the thickness and width of the workpieces are appropriate, a long slender pin can be set through the entire length of the joint.

LOCK JOINT

Five passes on a table or radial saw will give you the lock joint (Fig. 7-10), one of the most structurally solid joints attainable with so little work. The cuts must be accurate, of course, but the whole process is simpler than it looks.

Begin by making the wide cut into the end of piece A. Then make a second cut across the surface of piece A. The third cut is made on piece B, the cross-surface groove. The last two cuts on part B leave only the narrow tongue at the end of the workpiece. If your measurements are accurate, the joint will slip together easily. Allow sufficient clearance for a glue coating.

COPED JOINTS

Figure 7-11 shows two typical coped joints. Coped joints are used where there is a possibility that a miter joint will open up, or

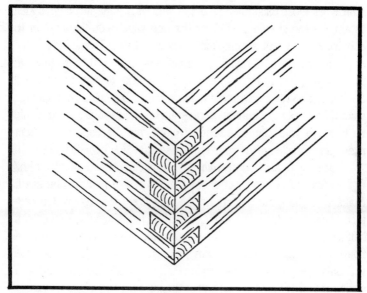

Fig. 7-9. Box or finger joint.

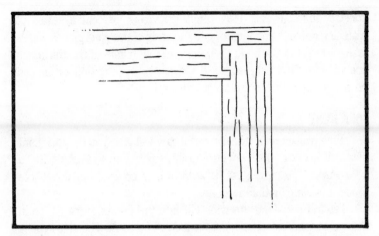

Fig. 7-10. Lock joint.

where one workpiece is already in place and another must be joined to it to form an inconspicuous joint. The process involves incising the profile of one workpiece into the end of another with a coping saw. A template former will help you make an accurate layout pattern.

TECHNIQUES

Joinery has a few simple principles to follow which will make your work more palatable. To begin with, it is generally a good idea to employ the simplest joint, or the one which you find easiest to construct, that will accomplish a specific task. There isn't much point, for instance, in building a small drawer entirely with through multiple or blind miter dovetail joints when the drawer corners will be hidden and the drawer will hold no more than a load of handkerchiefs. Probably the only good reasons for doing such a thing would be because you enjoy the kind of work, and because the project presents a challenge to your expertise that you cannot ignore.

After you have determined a particular level of strength/rigidity/durability, you can choose the types of joints to be used. Make sure that your selections are consistent throughout the project. Using two or three terrifically strong joints in combination with half a dozen simpler ones will probably add little, if anything, to the final product. Also, using as many joints as possible of the same type will make the project simpler to build. This means that you can use a series of tool setups to create all of the joint cuts on a mini-assembly line basis. Set up once for dado work. Do all the dados of one size and

202

then all the dados of another size. Then set up for rabbets. Cut all the necessary rabbets in a series of steps, then shift over to tenons, and so forth. Multiple identical cuts of whatever type can be accomplished in short order.

Measurement in making joints is critical. One way to avoid problems is to use a common starting point in laying out each joint. And instead of making separate measurements for each workpiece, use the first correctly cut workpiece as a template. For instance, if you want to cut a groove in one piece to accommodate the butt end of another, set that butt end against the surface to be grooved, line up the pieces exactly, and mark the guidelines directly. This process is superior to transferring measurements from one piece to another.

Tight fits are synonymous to good joints. But there is danger in making a fit too tight. Where both of the workpieces are solid wood and the joint is of considerable size, it does no harm to make the fit just a bit loose to compensate for expansion. If there is a possibility of substantial movement, as might be the case with long shelves set in dado joints, omit the glue and secure the pieces with screws only. Where glue is used with blind, pegged or doweled joints, allow enough extra space so that excess glue can escape without splitting the material under the extreme pressure buildup which occurs as the pieces are joined.

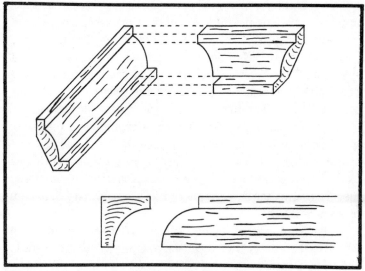

Fig. 7-11. Two examples of coped joints, both in cove moldings, where one section of the molding must be fitted (coped) to another.

Most cabinet and built-in construction need not depend solely upon the strength of glued joints. You can nearly always find some way to bestow additional strength to the joint, and consequently to the finished article, without undue difficulty. The simplest way, of course, is to use nails or screws in concert with glue. Of the two types of fasteners, screws are the better. Dowel pegs, wood or plastic pins, and long slender metal pins can be used as additional strengthening devices.

Dowels seem to work the best, especially when equipped with spiral grooves for free glue flow. Dowels should only be used when they are thoroughly dry. The moisture content of the dowel wood should be less than 5 percent if possible. The reason for this is that a dry dowel, when glued and fitted into a correctly sized hole, will swell from the moisture of the glue and lock firmly into place. Unfortunately, if the dowel is already high in moisture content, it will eventually shrink within the hole, and the result will be failure of the joint. Without special equipment, you can't measure the moisture content of a dowel. However, you can store dowel pins or pegs for a period of time in a warm, dry spot, such as near a heater. You could even bake them in an oven for a short while, or set them directly over a heater on a piece of screen shortly before using them. Always use dowels in pairs, about one-quarter of an inch shorter than the combined depth of both receiving holes, and in a diameter approximately one-third on the thickness of the workpiece.

Setting a spline is an excellent way to strengthen and align a joint. A narrow strip cut from ⅛-inch hardboard makes an excellent spline, and it need only be set into each adjoining workpiece about one-quarter of an inch, or a bit less. Allow enough clearance for the spline to slip readily into place, and to accept the glue coating.

Another and simple possibility for strengthening is the use of glue blocks. In most cabinetmaking projects, there will be some spot, particulary on the inside of right-angle joints, to hide a glue block. These blocks may be set with glue alone. In some instances they themselves can be strengthened with the addition of fasteners or even by joinery.

Common sense and a little ingenuity will enable you to decide where and how the individual joints in your projects should be made and strengthened.

Chapter 8
Doors

Doors, though not used on every project, are part and parcel of cabinetmaking and built-ins as a whole. Whether they are applied to cabinets, built-ins, cases, or furniture, they are properly, though not always, referred to as cupboard doors or case doors. They must be functional, and often they have to be decorative as well. Though considered a part of a cabinet, a cupboard door is actually a separate piece of work unto itself. Doors must be well made and sturdy to withstand the strains of constant opening and closing. They have to be well fitted, and they cannot rely upon any part of the cabinet except themselves for strength, rigidity and support.

PART I: TYPES

There must be a million and one variations on the theme of doors for cabinets and built-ins. Some variations are strictly plain and ordinary and simple to build, while others are astonishingly ornate and require lengthy and complex construction procedures. For the most part, however, the entire subject of doors can be reduced to a few simple categories and relatively straightforward building steps.

Hinged Doors

By far the most common type of door is the hinged door. This is taken to mean those doors which are mounted with hinges on one side or the other, and swing out to either the right or the left. In most cases, two hinges are used per door, with a third center hinge being added if the door is particularly heavy or exceptionally tall. Literally dozens of different types of hinges are available, so that you can effect just about any appearance you desire.

Hinged doors are denoted by the manner in which they cover the door opening. Figure 8-1A shows a flush door. The outer surface of the door is flush with the edges of the cabinet in box-style construction, or flush with the face-frame side rails in case construction. Clearances must be exact, and if any swelling or shrinkage takes place, or if the cabinet racks, the door may stick, catch, or appear to be out of true. The lip or offset door (Fig. 8-1B) has a narrow rabbet cut around the entire inside perimeter of the door. The resulting outer lip covers a portion of the cabinet edge or face-frame, hiding the entire opening. For this reason, the fit need not be as exact as with a flush door, and warping, sagging, or a bit of runout in the cabinet structure will go unnoticed. The overlay or overlapping cupboard door (Fig. 8-1C) rests entirely outside the cabinet edges or face-frame surfaces. The door may cover only a portion of each cabinet edge or face-frame member, or may cover the entire cabinet structure so that only one or a series of door faces, unbroken by any other lines, is presented to view. This type of door is easily fitted.

Drop doors are those which, instead of being hinged to swing sideways, are hinged to swing vertically. They are hinged along the bottom edge and have a latch at the top. When opened, the door swings down. A drop door may be arranged to swing 180 degrees and come to rest completely out of the way, or may swing only 90 degrees, like the tailgate of a pickup trick. In this latter case, light chains or elbow supports are used to position and hold the door. The inner surface of the door can then become a work surface, such as a writing top or auxiliary counter space. Depending upon the type of construction and the hinging methods used, these doors may also be made in flush, lip, or overlapping styles. A variation on this idea, sometimes used for storage areas located high on a wall, is to hinge the door at the top so that it swings upward for better access to the storage compartment. Special support hardware, of course, is needed to keep the door open.

Sliding Doors

Sliding doors are installed in pairs, two panels to any given cabinet opening. The panels may be perfectly plain, made from solid

206

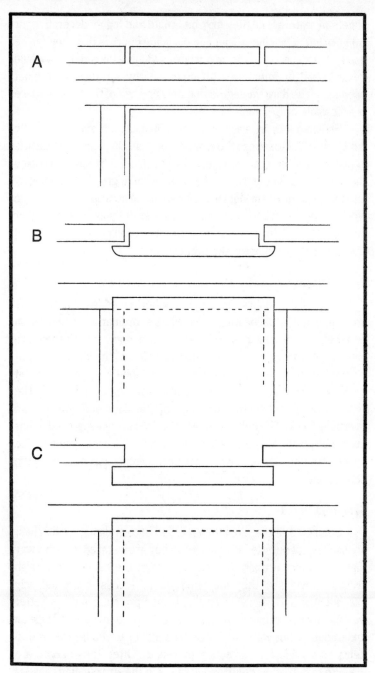

Fig. 8-1. The three types of cabinet door. (A) flush. (B) lipped. (C) overlap or overlay.

sheets of material, or they may be ornate and highly decorative, or transparent. The chief advantage of sliding doors is that they can be used where space is tight, and where swinging hinged doors would be awkward or interfere with other nearby furniture or cabinet openings. The disadvantage is that only one half of the cabinet space is accessible at a time.

Sliding doors are easy to fit, even in a cabinet which is slightly out of true. They are also the easiest to install, since once the track is in place, the doors can be installed and removed by simply slipping them in and out of the track. They can be set in grooves cut directly into the case, or run in slots made by securing appropriate mill-made wood molding strips to the cabinet surfaces. But you can get a higher quality job and better operating doors by installing plastic or metal tracks specially made for the purpose.

Rolling Doors

While sliding doors rest upon their bottom edges, rolling doors are supported by ballbearing roller wheels, ordinarily made of nylon or steel, which run in metal tracks. The doors themselves are usually substantial in size and weight, and are of the kind that might be used to cover a floor-to-ceiling pantry shelf section. The most common hardware system incorporates a suspended door. The rollers are affixed to the top edge of the door and travel in an overhead track. The bottom edge of the door is not supported, but is guided by plastic blocks or a spring-pin and track arrangement. The upper assembly does the work; the lower simply serves to keep the door in line.

Semifixed Doors

Semifixed doors, sometimes called access panels or hatches, are usually not outfitted with hinges. They are installed in such a way that they must actually be removed from the cabinet to furnish access. Obviously, they are used where access is needed only infrequently, and where space may be at a premium and it is better that the door be removed entirely. The purpose might be to hide an undercounter hot water tank, for instance, or to render mechanical items accessible for inspection or repair. Often these doors are made to match other doors and drawers in the surrounding cabinetry. They may be held in place by means of spring clips, cupboard door catches, a support groove and catch arrangement, or by concealed wood screws.

PART II: DOOR CONSTRUCTION

One of the ways to classify doors is according to the manner in which they are made. There are several possibilities, some widely used and some not, some practical in certain applications but not in others. Of the several general construction classifications, most can be handled in the home workshop. Three of them, however, are probably better obtained from commercial sources, both because of construction difficulties and because of the fact that there is a larger selection of sizes readily available at low cost. Remember, though, if you opt to buy your cupboard doors, choose appropriate sizes and actually have them in hand before designing and building the cabinetwork on which they will be installed.

Solid Wood Doors

The easiest solid wood door to make consists merely of a section cut from a board (Fig. 8-2). The limitations with this type of door are obvious; the door opening can be no wider than the plank width. This means that only narrow doors, whether horizontal or vertical, can be made in this fashion. Another disadvantage is that solid wood sections have a tendency to warp. Swelling and shrinking is not too much of a problem, depending upon how the door is fitted. Stock chosen for the job should be thoroughly seasoned and show no signs of warp after having been stored on the premises for at least six months. If the piece is perfectly flat to begin with, it probably will remain so. A slight warp, depending upon its type, can perhaps be smoothed out on a planer or surfacer. A hardwood is usually preferable to a softwood. Use either quartersawed or edge-grained stock, which are less susceptible to cupping and shrinking.

Glued-up doors are made from a series of small pieces of solid wood glued together edge to edge to make one large piece. The resulting piece is sturdy and solid, especially if made with reinforced edge joints. However, this type of door is also prone to warping, and the fit, even through carefully made, may shift about over a period of time and under varying atmospheric conditions. The larger the door, the greater will be the expansion and contraction problem. On the other hand, if used in a relatively stable environment, and made of

Fig. 8-2. Solid wood (mahogany) door, with semiconcealed pivot hinges. Duncan Photos.

prime materials and with good craftsmanship, glued-up doors can produce effective, interesting and handsome results.

Braced doors are also built up from several smaller pieces. This method is often used in building natural-finish doors of knotty pine. The usual procedure is to cut several pieces of paneling plank to identical lengths, then set them together edge to edge and face down. The edges may be smooth, but a tongue-and-groove joint is by far the better. The surface edges of the pieces frequently are beveled, or routed with some decorative shape.

With the pieces (they should be well seasoned) pulled tight together, a wide back-brace is fastened across the pieces, one back-brace near the top and another near the bottom. A third back-brace is run diagonally between the two to form a Z. The components are tied together with a few nails and then tightly secured with wood screws. Glue is not generally used, but can be. Once the door is completed to approximately the right size, the final trimming and fitting is done. The back-braces must be dimensioned and fitted in such a way that they do not interfere with the cabinet rails or shelf edges. Properly done, this type of construction produces doors of fine appearance, but they have the same disadvantages as other solid wood doors.

Batten doors can be used for large cupboard doors, but are usually confined to built-in projects which require heavy and sturdy doors. Continuous-batten doors are made by cutting a series of planks to the height of the door and another series to the width of the door. The vertical pieces are pushed tightly together and then the horizontal pieces are secured to them with wood screws in a continuous cover. The edge joints may be tongue-and-groove or simple rabbet. The result is a door that is two layers thick and tremendously strong. Warping, expansion, and contraction are less prevalent than with the other types of solid wood doors. However, batten doors are bulky, heavy, and expensive.

For an unusual, medieval castle effect, you can put these doors together with the old method of clinch-nailing. A clinch nail is a long tapered nail with a broad, rounded, hand-hammered head that looks much like a forged stud. Secure the components of the door from the back with ordinary nails to begin with, in order to hold them together while you work. Then, working from the face side, drive the clinch nails clear through the door in a predetermined pattern, and bend (clinch) them over on the reverse side. You could even go so far as to hang the door on old-style pintle hinges, and add draw bolts instead of latches. Make sure that the cabinet edges or face-frame stiles that hold the hinges are mightly solid; these doors weigh a ton and shut like a bank vault.

All of the solid wood doors can be made in flush, lip, or overlapping styles. They can be side-hinged, top-hinged, or bottom-hinged (to serve as drop drawers). In some instances they may be used as sliding doors, and the braced or batten styles can be affixed to roller tracks.

Panel Doors

Panel doors (Fig. 8-3) are easily made and widely used in all sorts of cabinet work. Plywood is perhaps the most commonly used material, since the doors can be quickly cut to size and readily fitted. No additional assembly work is necessary, though some sort of edge treatment and/or decorative work are often desirable. Softwood plywoods in cabinet grade most often get the nod if the finish is to be opaque. The reason is simply that the softwoods are less expensive, more readily available, and often a bit easier to work with. If desired, though, softwoods will take a fine semitransparent or transparent finish. Hardwood plywoods are used almost exclusively where the finish is to be transparent or natural. In this case, the decorative effect is provided by the characteristics of the wood veneer itself, rather than any applied finish. Either type of plywood has the great advantage of being relatively stable. Plywoods do not change dimensions readily, and are not particularly susceptible to warp. Plywood is also stiff, and even a large door will not feel limber or flimsy.

Hardboard is another stable material that is widely used for panel doors. Thin stock, such as ⅛ inch and ¼ inch, is not suitable for hinged doors, except in very small sizes, because it is not stiff enough. The greater thicknesses can be used with a reasonable degree of success, but here weight may become a problem, as hardboard is quite heavy. Also, thick hardboards are often not readily available. Hardboard is a most practical material for the construction of small sliding doors; for this purpose it works quite well. The perforated variety is an excellent choice where ventilation is a requirement.

Particle board is fairly good for panel doors, especially for panel doors on utility and storage cabinets. The material is stable, not likely to warp, and is solid and sturdy. It is a heavy material and must be supported well. With the proper edge treatment and finishing, it actually can be used under nearly all circumstances. Though usually covered with an opaque finish, it will accept stains and even clear finishes if its surfaces are properly treated. The minimum thickness which should be used is ⅝ inch, and the ¾-inch size gives the best results.

Fig. 8-3. Utility-type panel door of particle board, with plain wood knob and wraparound hinges. Duncan Photos.

Laminated panel doors can be used as either sliding or hinged doors, and can be made using either plywood, hardboard, or particle board as a core. A decorative laminated plastic is applied to the face of the core, followed by a suitable edge treatment. The best quality of construction uses a laminate on either side of the core for structural balance. In this arrangement, a standard grade of laminate, 1/16 inch thick, is applied to the face, and a backer grade of 1/16-inch laminate is bonded to the bottom face. Starting with a ⅝-inch core of particle board, for instance, you'll achieve a full ¾-inch-thick cupboard door. The specific edge treatment varies depending upon how the door is to be fitted, but frequently another band of matching laminate is added to each edge.

Glass panel doors are always made as sliding doors, running in tracks fitted with ballbearing rollers for the purpose. These doors can be made from several standard types of glass, as well as from a few stock sizes. These stock sizes can be bought over the counter, and the dimensions of the cabinet engineered to suit. In lieu of this, you can get special sizes cut to order at any competent glass shop and have the edges and corners ground and rounded for a good friction-free fit.

Sheets of clear, semiopaque, opaque, or patterned acrylic plastic may be used in the same manner as glass, though the special tracks are not necessary. You can buy acrylics in sheets and cut them to size in your own shop, and then bevel the edges and round the corners for easy sliding in standard routed, plastic, or metal tracks. With the proper hardware, plastic doors can also be hinged, but the door sizes should be kept small as the material is rather limber.

Frame-and-Panel Doors

As the name implies, this type of cupboard door is constructed by setting a panel into a frame (Fig. 8-4). There are many ways of going about the task. Many combinations of materials can be used and a wealth of decorative effects are possible. The frames are most often made from solid wood, with hardwood being preferred. Strips of plywood will do the job, but with more difficulty and less success. The panels which are set inside the frames may be made from either softwood or hardwood plywood, hardboard, or sometimes well-seasoned solid or glued-up wood. Glass is often used as a panel, and so is plastic, either plain or clear, or in any of a number of textures, patterns, and colors. Metal screening or decorative metal grillwork is also popular. Occasionally the panels themselves are combinations of two or more materials. Vertical grade plastic laminate can be applied to hardboard, either as a uniform sheet, or in a mosaic design consisting of numerous smaller multicolored and/or multishaped pieces. You can apply wallpaper, sheet vinyl, or fabrics to a hardboard backer by simply gluing. The possibilities are almost endless.

Frame-and-panel doors lend themselves nicely to almost any kind of installation. Though mostly set up as hinged doors, they can be used as drop doors as well, and in some instances as sliding doors. They work well as semifixed doors, made to match the surrounding drawer fronts and hinged doors. They can be easily fitted in flush, lip, and overlapping modes.

214

Fig. 8-4. Frame and panel door, panel beveled - raised one side, square sticker, with decorative surface hinges. Duncan Photos.

Louver Doors

The louver door (Fig. 8-5) is one type of door which is easier to buy than to build. Inletting all of those slats into the door paneling is a bit of a chore, and making the thin slats in the first place is no easy job. And since louver doors are such a popular type, they are widely available from commercial sources.

There are three different kinds of louver door. The full-louver door has a rank of louvers from top to bottom. On small doors the series is unbroken, but on larger sizes a cross rail is usually installed

Fig. 8-5. Louvered cabinet doors. Left, adjustable louvers. Right, fixed louvers. Duncan Photos.

somewhere near the midway point to provide additional rigidity. The half-louver style is generally found only in the larger sizes. Here, the upper section of the door is louvered, while the lower section has one or more panels inset into the frame. In adjustable louver doors, all of the louver slats are set on pivot pins at each end of each slat. A solid vertical bar is attached to the center of each slat, so that when the bar is moved up or down, all of the louvers open or close in unison.

Folding Doors

Folding doors (Fig. 8-6) take many forms. The simplest is the bifold, which consists of two doors tied together with special hinges to allow the door to fold in half. The individual door units may be solid wood, panel, frame-and-panel, or louver sections. With the correct hardware, the sections can be joined to form a trifold.

The accordion type of folding door can be made in a number of ways. Some accordion doors consist of a series of vertical sections of wood tied together with special plastic hinges. Another variation of the accordion door consists of vinyl or plastic sections attached to a folding frame. No matter the structural design or the composition of the material, every accordion door collapses upon itself and self-stores at the edge of the door opening or within a shallow pocket made for the purpose. All three varieties of accordion doors are commonly used as closures for cabinets and shelving openings, as well as for assorted special purposes.

Fig. 8-6. One type of folding door, a full-louver bi-fold, ready to be fitted to its opening. Duncan Photos.

The bifold and trifold doors can be made in the home shop in the usual fashion, then assembled with the proper hardware. Accordion doors, however, are almost invariably factory-made units. Openings must be sized to fit the available standard door sizes, rather than the other way around.

Tambour Doors

Tambour doors (Fig. 8-7) are another type best left to factory production. Though you can build them yourself, it's a whale of a job. Tambour doors look like the one on grandad's rolltop desk, and though they virtually disappeared for a time, they are now coming back into favor. Their great advantage is that they take up so little space and, when opened, simply disappear into the back of the cabinet. They can be used horizontally, vertically, or on a free-form track that curves in and around and about. All of the systems operate with equal ease.

Tambour doors are made in two ways. The visible portion consists of an appropriate number of narrow wood slats, usually hardwood with a natural or transparent finish. With one method, all of the slats are connected in a continuous strip by means of special plastic hinges inset into small slits which run the full length of each side of each slat. With the second method, the slats are firmly secured to a heavy canvas backer. Though manufactured in certain stock sizes, with care and patience they can be trimmed to other dimensions.

PART III: BUILDING DOORS

There are a few major steps to follow in building and fitting cupboard doors, as well as a few minor steps which are dependent upon the complexity of the door design. Some of those steps are interchangeable, and some vary slightly in detail depending upon door type and material used. The steps below will cover solid wood, panel and frame-and-panel doors. If you use commercially manufactured doors, regardless of the type, most of the following information, except Step 5, still applies. Remember to buy factory-made doors in sizes as close as possible to your proposed door opening sizes, and don't exceed the manufacturer's recommendations for trimming. Otherwise, the doors may disintegrate into a small pile of kindling.

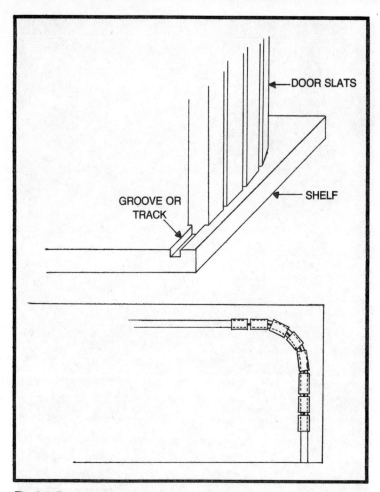

Fig. 8-7. Tambour door, shown here running in groove. Tracks work better, preferably at top and bottom.

Step 1

Regardless of the type of door or the manner in which it will be mounted and fitted, the first step is to see whether or not the door opening is square. To make a quick check, measure the two diagonals from top corners to bottom opposite corners. If the measurements are identical, the opening is square. Should the measurements not be identical, you will have to do some further checking to see which member is out of line. Use as large a square as you can fit into the opening, and check each corner separately (Fig. 8-8) to find out which edges are out of true. If the discrepancies are only slight,

Fig. 8-8. Checking wall cabinet door opening for squareness before making door. Duncan Photos.

on the order of one-sixteenth of an inch or less in total, you may be able to disregard the inaccuracy. With a flush door you can make some adjustments during the fitting process; with overlapping and lipped doors, the error can be compensated for and will go undetected. If the discrepancy is substantial, however, you should make a rough sketch of the opening and jot down the maximum out-of-square dimensions. At the same time, note on the sketch the exact positions of the faults. You will later have to shape the door to fit.

Step 2

The next step, again regardless of the door specifics, is to determine upon which side the hinges will be mounted. Then, check that rail or edge to see whether or not it is exactly plumb. For this purpose, use a level which reads in degrees of incline, or hang a plumb bob in place (Fig. 8-9). If the member is plumb, you are all set. If not, strike a light line (one which will not later interfere with the finishing process) on the edge or rail to give you a reference point.

Fig. 8-9. Checking the hinge stile of wall cabinet door opening for plumb prior to installing door. Duncan Photos.

The reason for all of this is that the door hinges must be aligned exactly above one another, with both pins in the same vertical line. If the hinges are aligned poorly, the door may swing of its own accord, and will not stay where you park it. Worse, the hinges may bind and throw excessive strain on either the cabinet or the door, or both, especially when three hinges (called a pair and a half) are used. If the mounting member is not plumb, you will have to adjust the hinged edge of the door to stand plumb, and shape the remaining three edges of the door out-of-square to line up with the rest of the cabinet. Unless the hinge mounting member is badly out of line, this will not be noticeable if the job is properly done.

Step 3

Make a dimension takeoff. Measure the height of the opening at several points, and do the same with the width (Fig. 8-10). If both dimensions remain the same, plus or minus one thirty-second of an inch, at every measuring point, all you need do is make a note of the maximum figures. If the dimensions vary, jot them down on a sketch so that you can program the variations, or clearances for the variations, into the door construction.

Step 4

Time now to lay out the door to rough size. Don't be misled by the term "rough," because in most cases this will be close to the finished, fitted size, and patience and care are needed right from the outset. Start with the base dimensions of the cabinet opening. We'll assume for the moment that the opening is plumb and square, and that there are no serious dimensional variations.

The outside dimensions of the door, relative to the door opening size, are taken from top to bottom and from side to side in accordance with the way in which the door will be mounted.

For flush doors, a clearance of one-sixteenth of an inch around the perimeter of the door is satisfactory for most cabinets. You may allow a bit more if you wish, but you might wish to reduce the clearance to about one-tenth of an inch if the project is fine casework. This means that for ordinary work the door will be one-eighth of an inch narrower and one-eighth of an inch shorter than the cabinet opening dimensions.

For lipped doors, first decide upon the width of the rabbet cut around the inner door perimeter. A ⅜-inch or ½-inch cut is usual.

222

Fig. 8-10. Measuring exact wall cabinet door opening to determine door size. Duncan Photos.

Again, a 1/16-inch clearance around the door edge (actually around the edge of the rabbet cut) is satisfactory. This means that the remainder of the lip will extend beyond the cabinet opening seven-sixteenths of an inch at each edge. This in turn makes the outside dimensions of the door seven-eighths of an inch taller and seven-eights of an inch wider than the cabinet opening.

With overlapped doors, the amount of the overlap can be any dimension which seems appropriate or which is allowable for the chosen hinges. You can use a modest ¾-inch extension (normal) beyond the cabinet opening in all directions, or a much wider overlap which entirely hides the cabinet edges or face-frame rails. The overlap can be greater at top and bottom than on the sides, or vice-versa. Clearance is of no consideration here, so all you need do is add double the side overlap to the width of the door opening (assuming the overlaps to be equal on both sides) and add the top and bottom overlaps to the door opening height. This will give you the outside dimensions of the door itself.

With the outside dimensions of the door in hand, you now have to look ahead. You may have to make some allowances, depending upon how you plan to construct the door. If the edges of the door will require no further treatment save for some light sanding, leave the dimensions as they are. If the door will be painted with a heavy enamel, it might be wise to reduce the overall size of flush or lip doors by one thirty-second of an inch on all sides to provide extra clearance for the paint thickness. Plywoods are often given some sort of edge treatment. If you plan on using a veneer tape, or any edge trim which will add width and height to the door, you will need to subtract the thickness of the edge-trimming material from the overall dimensions. This is particularly important with flush doors, but necessary with overlap doors only when the edge-trimming material is rather thick. For example, a 1-inch-wide solid wood band secured to the edges of a particle board door would doubtless increase the dimensions of the door too much. Cut the door one inch smaller on all sides, and then add the edge trim.

If the cabinet opening is out of square, or the dimensions do not run true from point to point, then you will have to allow for these problems when you trim the door stock to the final outside dimensions. This may involve cutting shy on one edge and full on another, making the edge cuts along slightly tapering angles rather than square angles, or leaving a bit of extra material all around that can be trimmed later to make a close fit. There really is no way to tell you how to go about this process, since the problem possibilities are practically infinite, and the solutions vary according to the specifics. If the dimensions are especially confusing, sometimes it is easier to make a pattern by covering the opening with a sheet of cardboard and tracing the outline from inside. Then you can use this as a template from which to work.

Step 5

Now comes the actual construction of the door. This step is divided into three sections: solid doors, panel doors, and frame-and-panel doors. If you plan to use commercial doors, skip these sections.

Solid Wood Doors. For single-piece doors, pick a suitable piece of stock. For glued-up doors, glue up and surface a sheet of material slightly larger than the overall dimensions which you will need. Once this is done, all that is left is to trim the workpieces accurately to size, with a hand saw or power saw and an appropriate blade (Fig. 8-11).

If you are building a braced door, cut the necessary pieces of board to the exact length required (or width if the pieces are to be stacked horizontally). Lay the pieces face down on a clean surface and line up all of the edges. Draw the pieces snugly together; bar clamps will work well for this. Then, cut two back-braces, one for the top edge and one for the bottom edge of the door. Usually the same type of material is used in a width of 3 to 4 inches, minimum. The length of the back-braces should be at least 2 inches shorter than the width of the door, but in any case short enough to clear any interior parts of the cabinet when the door is closed. Position the two back-braces 2 or 3 inches from the top and bottom edges and secure them with a few short nails. Then, measure and cut the diagonal back-brace, set it into place, and secure it with nails. If you wish, you can gain additional strength and rigidity by adding a second diagonal back-brace, fitting the two back-braces where they cross with a diagonal cross-lap joint. Check the surface pieces to make sure that none have moved out of line, then drill and countersink a series of screw holes. Drive the wood screws home, and the result should look something like the sketch in Fig. 8-12.

Fig. 8-11. Ripping stock to size for solid wood cabinet door. Duncan Photos.

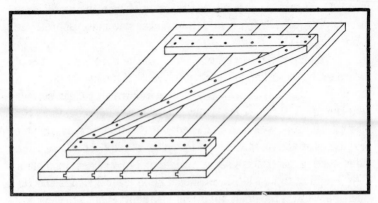

Fig. 8-12. Braced door made with tongue and groove stock.

Continuous-batten doors are put together in the same manner but with more pieces. The inside layer, or battens, may cover the entire inner surface of the outside layer, with all edges flush. If you prefer, you can make the battens somewhat smaller than the outside layer, leaving a lip around the perimeter. Much depends upon how the door will be fitted.

At this point, if the doors are to be plain and simple, your job is done for the moment. However, it may be that you dislike the appearance of the end grain portions of stock that are visible. If so, there are three ways to correct the situation (Fig. 8-13). One is to trim a ½-inch strip from the top and bottom of the door. Then fasten a ½-inch-thick piece of rectangular molding of the same material to the top and bottom edges. This will leave an obvious rail at each end of the door, and still present a small section of end grain at each corner. A second possibility is to make a 45-degree miter cut across top and bottom, with the cut angle facing inward. Then secure a fitted strip of wood, triangular in cross section, across each inside edge. The strips will not be visible from the front, the door dimensions not having changed, but there is still a small bit of end grain showing at each corner. If the door happens to be flush mounted, this is of little consequence. The third method is similar; it requires more work but is a bit sturdier. This involves routing or cutting a vee groove across the top and bottom edges. Then a triangular strip of wood is fitted into the vee groove and fastened in place. Again, the strip is invisible save for a small bit of end grain at each corner.

Panel Doors. To cut a panel door from plywood, hardboard, or particle board, all that you need do is transfer the proper measurements to the sheet of stock, and then make the necessary cuts. You can use a hand power saw, a table saw, a radial saw, or even a saber saw. With a saber saw, and also with a hand power saw, be sure to use a firmly clamped straightedge to guide the saw. A panel saw will also do the job, but it would be wise to allow a bit of extra material

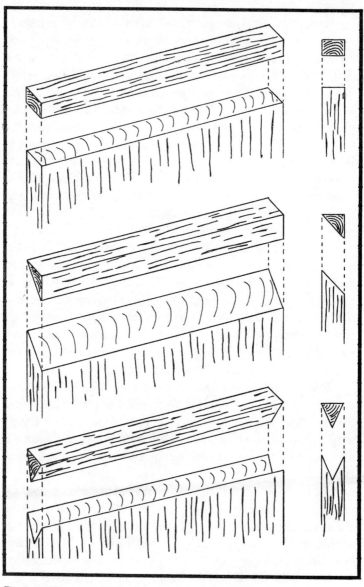

Fig. 8-13. Three possibilities for covering the end grain of a workpiece.

227

around each edge of the workpiece. This will compensate for any unevenness in the cut, and can be removed during the final fitting and finishing processes. Remember, too, to place the good side of the workpiece in proper relationship to the cutting action of the saw blade. In all cases, use a fine-toothed blade to achieve the smoothest possible cut.

Laminated panel doors are made in exactly the same fashion, except that in this instance there are two workpieces to be cut. First, cut the core piece to size. Plywood or particle board in a ⅝-inch thickness is usually used, although hardboard will also serve. Then, cut a piece of vertical grade laminate to a size just slightly larger than the overall dimensions of the core. This will allow for clean trimming of the edges. If the core edges are also to be covered with laminate, be sure to allow for the additional thicknesses of laminate along the door edges when calculating the size of the piece. Often a third piece is used as well. This is a backer laminate which is bonded to the inner face of the door. Cut this piece the same size as the outer laminate face, using a backing grade. Do not bond the pieces together until completing Step 6.

When making doors of acrylic sheet plastic, the initial cuts should be made as accurately as possible, and as close to the finished dimensions as you can make them. This will save time and labor in the fitting process. On the other hand, take great care not to remove too much stock, since there is no such thing as restitution in this cutting operation. Always cut sheet plastics with the protective paper covering in place. If there is no protective covering, handle the material carefully, as it can be scratched altogether too easily.

Frame-and-Panel Doors. Constructing frame-and-panel doors is considerably more difficult than building the other types. Some, in face, can be done only in an exceptionally well-equipped shop, and then only with a great deal of work. However, there are a few designs which go together nicely and present a fine finished appearance.

First, some terminology. A frame-and-panel door consists principally of two parts: a center panel, and an outside frame around the panel. The side pieces of the frame are called stiles, and the top and bottom pieces are called rails. The outer edges of the frame may be perfectly plain and square, or may incorporate some decorative molding. The inside edge of the frame, into which the panel is set, may also be square but is more often shaped in some fashion. This inside edge is called the sticking. A square sticking is perfectly flat, and contains only the groove into which the panel fits. There are a number of molded stickings (including the panel groove) which are cut directly into the rails and stiles on a shaper, and each has a separate name. In addition, the sticking may be formed by the application of thin strips of molding attached to the inner edges and forming the panel groove between them.

The center panel also has certain designations. If the panel is flat on each side, it is called a plane panel. Panels are often made with long bevels around each edge. If the bevel is on one side only of the panel, it is called beveled - raised one side. If the bevel is on both sides of the panel, it is called beveled - raised two sides. Similarly, a wide but shallow rabbet cut may be made around all edges of the panel. This is called either shoulder - raised one side, or if the cut is made on both sides of the panel, shoulder - raised two sides. A flush panel is set so that one surface of the panel is flush with the rails and stiles of the frame. An elevated panel is attached to the frame in such a way that its face protrudes beyond the frame surface. In many cases, the panel is set in a groove centered in the sticking, although there is no reason why the panel cannot be adjusted forward or backward as desired. Figure 8-14 shows some of the possible combinations used in frame-and-panel doors.

There are several steps in constructing a frame-and-panel door, and they are perhaps best illustrated by following through the process with a simple type like the square-edged frame with square sticker and plane panel.

First, select some appropriate stock for the door frame. Either hardwood or softwood may be used, in whatever width suits your fancy, and a minimum (normal) thickness of ¾ inch. Next, determine which sort of joint you prefer to use at the corners of the frame. Since the door will be subject to a certain amount of strain and racking, a strong joint should be used. Furniture makers often opt for the open mortise-and-tenon, a half-blind mortise-and-tenon, or a haunch mortise-and-tenon joint. Another possibility, though considerably less strong, is the end lap joint. You could also use a miter joint with a reinforcing spline, provided that the door is neither large nor heavy. A butt joint reinforced with dowels might also be used, but the result could be somewhat flimsy.

Next, cut the stiles and rails to length. With some joints, this means that the pieces will be full length or full width, while with joints

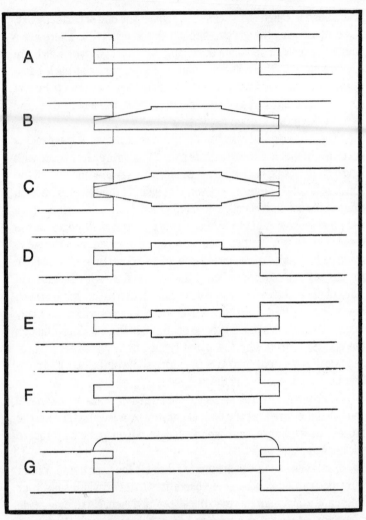

Fig. 8-14. Frame-and-panel door configurations in cross-seciton. (A) plane or straight. (B) beveled - raised one side. (C) beveled - raised two sides. (D) shoulder - raised one side. (E) shoulder - raised two sides. (F) flush. (G) raised or elevated.

like the half-blind mortise-and-tenon, the rails will be a bit shorter than the overall width of the door frame, while the stiles will remain at full height, or vice-versa. With the pieces cut to proper length, make the corner joints and check them for proper fit.

The next step is to choose the panel stock. Panels are usually made from hardboard or plywood but can also be made from glued-up solid wood stock. Measure the inside dimensions of the door frame.

Now check the thickness of the panel stock. The groove in which the panel will fit should be a bit deeper than the thickness of the stock. For a ¼-inch-thick panel, the groove should be three-eighths of an inch deep, for example. Cut the ¼-inch-wide and ⅜-inch-deep grooves down the centerline of each inside face of the door frame pieces to complete the sticking.

Now, add three-eighths of an inch to each side and to top and bottom of the door frame inside dimensions. The panel should actually be a tiny bit smaller than these dimensions. Taking about one-sixteenth of an inch from the height and one-sixteenth of an inch from the width of the panel should give you good results. Lay out these dimensions on the panel stock and cut the piece to size. Make sure that it is perfectly square, else there will be trouble later. Smooth off any rough edges on the panel for an easy fit into the frame.

The next step is a dry run for the final assembly. Snug all of the pieces together, as shown in Fig. 8-15, using clamps as necessary. Check all of the joints to make sure that they fit properly, and to verify that the panel is fully seated. Also, make certain that the door is in square. A frame-and-panel door simply will not go together properly unless all the components are accurately squared and matched. For this reason, you may have to allow a bit of extra material for later trimming and fitting if the cabinet opening is irregular or out of square itself. This could mean that the overall door dimensions need to be a tad larger then the door opening dimensions might indicate.

Disassemble the components, and make any further corrections or adjustments as necessary. If the door is to be lipped, you can make the rabbet cuts in the stile and rail outer edges before final assembly, or you can do it afterwards, whichever you prefer. The same holds true if the outer surface edges of the frame are to be beveled or otherwise molded. Once everything is set to your satisfaction, apply glue—not too much, please—and quickly put the pieces together. Apply firm pressure with clamps, but not so much that the assembly is crushed or skewed. Let the glue set up for the necessary time period, and the job is done.

A flush panel door is made in essentially the same way. However, instead of cutting a groove down the center of the square sticking on each interior edge of the door frame, the groove is

Fig. 8-15. Assembling frame-and-panel door, with square sticker, plane panel, and flat splined miter joints. Duncan Photos.

narrower and placed close to either the inner or outer face of the frame. Then a matching rabbet is cut in the edges of the panel, so that the two parts will lock together. A simpler method is to make a rabbet cut around the inside perimeter of the frame, and then drop the panel into the recess. This requires the help of small fasteners such as brads, driven through the edges of the panel and into the door frame, to hold the assembly together. Another possibility, one which is widely used if the center panel is a metal grill, plastic sheet, or glass, is to rabbet a deep groove around the inside perimeter of the frame edge, drop the panel into place, and then install thin retaining strips of wood, called stops, to hold the panel in place as shown in Fig. 8-16.

A simple frame-and-panel door with square sticking and plane panel can be made to look more ornate by the application of a molding around the panel perimeter, butting up to the inner edge of the frame. In this case, once the door is constructed as outlined above, choose an appropriate thin molding and cut two horizontal and two vertical pieces which will fit snugly within the frame. Make miter cuts at the corners and glue the molding into place.

Though in many cases the plane panel is made from hardwood plywood or solid stock which matches (or contrasts) the material of the door frame, hardboard makes an equally good center panel. The usual intent here is to later apply opaque finish. However, hardboard may also be used as a base for other applied materials of a decorative

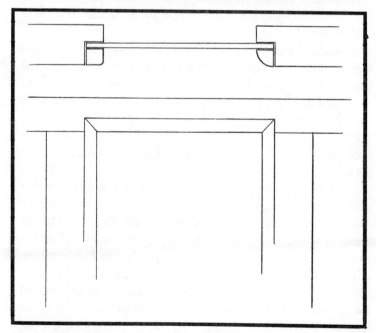

Fig. 8-16. Stop panel construction, shown here with a beveled stop on the left and a quarter-round stop on the right.

nature. Vertical grade plastic laminate is frequently added and this means a slight alteration in the steps listed above. The piece of laminate should be cut to approximately the same size as the panel, and then bonded to the panel before it is set in the frame. Since the edges of the combined center panel and laminate will be hidden, they need only be reasonably well finished. In cutting the grooves in the inside perimeter of the door frame, be sure to add the thickness of the laminate to that of the panel, to arrive at the proper groove width.

Hardboard also makes an excellent backer upon which a covering of fabric, wallpaper, or sheet vinyl can be glued. If you follow this course, you will probably find it easier to complete the door first, and then carefully cut the piece of decorative material to fit tightly into place on the center panel. After fitting the covering, make some sort of guide mark so that it will go back in the same position that it was fitted. Coat the panel with rubber cement or some other appropriate glue, and press the cover into place. A block of flat wood or a small roller gently run over the surface will squeeze out air bubbles. Use a light coating of glue so that it will not ooze from the edges. If a finish is to be applied to the door frame, install the decorative material as the last step.

Making a door with a shouldered panel, raised on one or both sides, is done in the same fashion as making a plane panel door. The panel stock used is solid glued-up wood, usually of the same type as the door frame, but often thinner. The only additional operation is the forming of the shoulder, which is merely a wide and shallow rabbet cut. The width of the groove in the inside perimeter of the door frame should be just a tiny bit more than the thickness of the perimeter of the panel.

Similarly, the process of making a beveled panel door, whether raised on one or both sides, is the same as for a plane panel door except for the cutting of the bevel. In the home shop, these bevels are generally cut on a table saw with the blade tilted to 16° and the workpiece stood on edge. On a radial saw, the saw head is swung down so that the blade is parallel with the table top, and then tilted slightly into a bevel position. The stock is laid flat on the table top and fed against the blade. In either case, cut the bevel on the end grain first, and then on the edge grain. The panel-holding groove in the door frame is not usually tapered to match the panel bevel, but

234

remains square. Measure the width of the groove carefully to make sure that it will accept the tapered panel edges.

Frame-and-panel doors with molded stickings are the most difficult to make. The process involves cutting the sticking and the panel retaining groove in one operation along the interior edges of the door frame members. The biggest problem comes in joining the rails to the stiles. The only applicable corner joint that can be readily made in most home shops is likely to be a miter joint, and this may not be sufficiently strong in a great many instances. With all of the other joints, the stiles and rails meet at right angles to one another, which means here that the adjoining edges of the joints must be coped so that the molded stickings will mate. This is done in the factory by special machinery, tools not normally available to the home craftsman. Unless you can successfully use miter joints, or are prepared for a considerable amount of arduous coping with carving chisels and other hand tools, or care to invest in an industrial shaper and assorted sets of matched sticking and coping cutters, all sized exactly to the thickness of the stock you plan to use, you had better forget about this type of frame-and-panel door.

Step 6

Once the door is built, irrespective of its type, the next step is the gross fitting of the door into the cabinet door opening. This applies to all doors, whether they have been commercially made or made by yourself, and includes the louver, folding, and tambour kinds of doors.

If the door is flush-fit, set it into place in the cabinet opening. If the fit is faulty, trim as necessary. Match any unevenness in the cabinet edges or face-frame with the door frame, or taper the door frame edges to match out-of-square openings. Judicious use of a plane, files, sander, or similar finishing tools will do the job. Use thin pieces of cardboard to wedge the door evenly in place in the opening, and shoot for the ideal uniform clearance of a 1/16-inch crack (or a bit less) at all meeting edges of door frame and cabinet frame.

If the door is of the lipped type, the task is a bit more difficult because you can't see what you are doing. First make sure that the rabbet cut is deep enough to allow the interior face of the door to sit freely within the opening. Then ascertain that the lines of the door edges are parallel with any visible lines of the cabinet face-frame. If those lines are obviously out of skew, you may have to make the rabbet cut a bit deeper and allow greater clearance so that the door edges will align properly with the cabinet lines.

With an overlapping or overlay door, the principal consideration is that the lines of the door match the lines of the cabinet. All the edges should at least appear to be plumb and level, and not out of true with one another.

Step 7

Once you are satisfied with the gross fit of the door, you can go ahead with any additional treatment that you may have planned. This usually takes the form of some sort of added decoration. For instance, edge treatment may be called for. This is particularly true of doors made from plywood or particle board. With plywood, a common practice is to add a thin strip of veneer tape over the banded edge of the plywood, for the sake of appearance. Or, you may wish to rout a vee groove with each edge and apply a filler strip of solid wood stock. Particle board cuts usually present a rough and pocked appearance. If a relatively thick band or frame of solid wood has not already been applied, you can fill the edges with a suitable wood filler and smooth them off. Self-sticking tapes will not adhere to particle board edges.

One popular trimming touch widely used on cabinet doors is the cutting of a curved edge around the outer door surface. This edge can be done with a router, a shaper, or a molding head in a table or radial saw. You can use a partial-depth arc, by which the curved edge covers only a portion of the total thickness of the door, or you can use a full-depth arc, by which the full thickness of the edge is rounded. This sort of trim is applicable to either lipped or overlapped doors. But you need not be confined to using only a curved edge. You could just as easily cut a narrow or a wide bevel or chamfer, or shape the edges with an ogee, rabbet, or beading cutter. Nor need such decorative cuts be restricted only to the edges of the door. If you wish, you can lay out a pattern on the face of the door and make shallow cuts with a router equipped with veining, vee-groove, or rabbeting bit. This process is not difficult, though it does require good guides and/or a steady hand, and can result in interesting decorative effects.

Another commonly used method of trimming out surfaces is to apply pieces of molding directly to the finished face. Choose a flat-bottomed type of stock molding, such as half-round, nose-and-cove, stop, or screen molding. Cut mitered joints at the corners, and glue the strips to the door as shown in Fig. 8-17. You can also purchase specialty moldings made in outside and inside curves, as well as various sorts of machine-carved wood blocks for similar

Fig. 8-17. Decorative molding being applied to a plain panel door. Duncan Photos.

application. The usual procedure in applying decorative moldings is to do all the necessary cutting and fitting at this state of the door construction, and then set the pieces aside until later. After the door surface has been sanded and is ready for the finish, the pieces are glued into place. This makes the sanding process much easier.

Where a single door is set flush in the frame, common practice is to allow the clearance crack around the perimeter of the door to remain visible, and this is not considered objectionable. However, where flush doors are set in pairs and are hinged opposite to meet in the center, the clearance crack between the meeting edges is sometimes objectionable. Or, there may be reason to mate the meeting edges in such a fashion that one door must be opened before the second one can be. Figure 8-18 shows a few ways of treating the meeting edges of double flush doors.

Step 8

The door is now almost in its final shape. Mount the hardware on the door and fix the door in place. Then take care of the final fitting. Exactly how this is done depends upon the type of door, and the type of hardware as well.

First, the hinges. If the door is smaller than 3 feet high and 2 feet wide, in a ¾-inch thickness, one pair of hinges should be sufficient. If either dimension is greater than this, you had better figure on a pair and a half, unless the door is particularly light. A 2-inch-hinge size is adequate for the smaller doors, but if they are larger, go to 2½-inch or even 3-inch hinges. Doors which are quite small can use smaller hinges, and small hinges may be used in multiples on large doors.

Next, install the hinges themselves. The exact procedure for doing so varies with the particular hinge. Usually you will find instructions on the package, and these should be followed to the letter. There are, however, some general steps to follow.

Measure a short distance down from the top of the door and a similar distance up from the bottom on the hinged side. The measurement you use is up to you—2 to 3 inches is common—and doesn't really matter so long as it remains the same for all doors in the same cabinet sections, and the spacings are proportionate to the door size. Mark the door edge and set the hinges in place. Line the hinges up so that they are square and in proper relationship with the

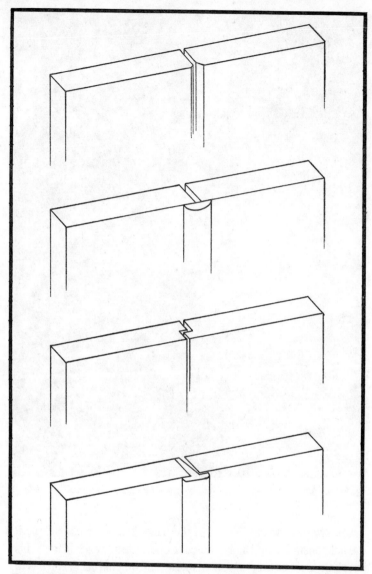

Fig. 8-18. Four possibilities for treating the meeting edges of double cabinet doors to hide or minimize the opening between them.

door edge, and so that the pins and barrels of the hinges are exactly in line with one another. If they are not, the door may bind or catch.

Hold each hinge firmly in place and mark the position of one screw hole. If a mortise must be made, as with a butt hinge, trace the position of the hinge leaf, measure the leaf thickness, and make the

Fig. 8-19. Mounting wraparound hinges on louvered cabinet door. Duncan Photos.

necessary mortise cut. Then set the hinge back in place, and mark the hole position. Drill a pilot hole for one screw at each hinge. This pilot hole must be properly sized to the screw being used, and has to be exactly straight and in the dead center of the screw hole in the hinge leaf. If it is not, the screw may drive at a slight angle or off center, which will draw the hinge out of line as the screw is tightened down.

Mount the hinges in place with one screw each (Fig. 8-19). Drive the screws slowly and carefully, checking frequently to make sure that they stay centered and straight. If the wood is grainy, the screw may try to cant off at an angle. If this happens, remove the screw and reset the hole, and try again until it drives true. Then, set the door in its proper position on or in the cabinet face-frame. Check the edge clearances all around, and make sure that the door is accurately placed. Mark the center of one hinge mount hole in each cabinet-frame leaf, and remove the door. Drill a single pilot hole for each hinge, reposition the door, and secure the assembly with one screw per hinge (Fig. 8-20). Swing the door carefully through its entire opening arc and check for any binding or racking, and for proper edge clearance and fit. If all is well, leave the door in place, drill the remaining pilot holes, and drive the rest of the screws.

If the fit is not just right, you may have to take any one of a number of corrective measures. If the swing seems all right and the door runs freely but has insufficient clearance when closed, you will have to remove a bit of material at the edges. Mark the spots that are bothersome, remove the door, and do a little sanding or planing. Take off only a tiny amount at a time, replacing the door and rechecking the problem as necessary. You may have to go through this operation several times, but that is better than removing too much stock and ruining the door. It may be that the door is out of line with the opening or with the cabinet frame edges. In this case, you

Fig. 8-20. Hanging cabinet door. Start with one screw in each hinge, then check for fit and alignment before going on. Duncan Photos.

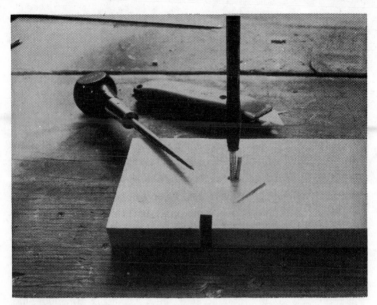

Fig. 8-21. Resetting misaligned screw by elongating hole and filling with wood splinters. Duncan Photos.

might have to place a thin cardboard slim beneath one hinge leaf, or perhaps mortise one leaf a bit deeper, to slightly change the position of the door. If the hinges are cockeyed, you will have to adjust the hinge position accordingly, perhaps by shifting the body of the hole to one side while stuffing the other with a splinter of wood (Fig. 8-21). Whatever the corrections that must be made, take care that the fit is accurate and just the way you want it before you install the remaining hinge screws.

As to the hinges themselves, those which do not require mortises are the easiest to work with, as a rule. For that reason, among others, butt hinges are not as widely used on cabinet doors as pivot or decorative surface hinges. When installing butt hinges, the mortise or gain cut can be done in two ways. You can make one cut, equal in depth to the thickness of one hinge leaf, in the cabinet face-frame edge and another in the cabinet door edge. Or, you can save a little work by making a double-depth gain cut in the door edge alone. The resulting fit will be the same.

Butt hinges should not be used on plywood or particle board door edges, as both materials have poor edge screw-holding capabilities. Instead, use decorative surface hinges which mount on the outside face, or concealed wraparound hinges which mount on the inside face. Note, too, that some types of hinges require a recess cut, often only on one leaf, to maintain proper door clearance.

Flush doors, and sometimes lipped doors as well, are often set with a tight clearance. This means that the inside corner of the door edge opposite the hinges may rub on the cabinet edge as the door closes. Yet when closed, the edge still presents a relatively wide clearance crack. Rather than trimming the entire edge of the door and creating an objectionably wide crack, just cut a slight bevel on the offending inside corner. The door will then clear the cabinet nicely as it closed (Fig. 8-22).

Once the door is anchored and swinging properly, the remainder of the hardware can be installed. Set the knobs or pulls in place and secure them, and then mount and adjust the catches inside the cabinet. Or, install latch assemblies according to the manufacturer's instructions.

Fitting a sliding door is a good deal simpler. If you are using commercially manufactured tracks, set them in place and attach them to the cabinet. The deeper track goes at the top of the cabinet, and the shallower one at the bottom. Then, put the door panels in place and check the fit. They should slide smoothly and freely, and the edges should line up with the cabinet sides with no gap. If the fit is incorrect, make whatever adjustments are necessary. Then, round and smooth the bottom running edges of the door panels, round the bottom corners so that they will not catch, and smooth the top edges as well. The last step is to mount the pulls or knobs.

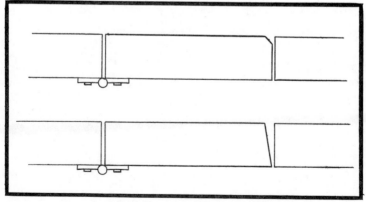

Fig. 8-22. Either the inside corner or the entire meeting edge of a tight-fitting cabinet door can be beveled for a smooth fit.

243

The procedure for hanging rolling doors is approximately the same. Mount the overhead track in place according to the instructions included with the kit, affix the rollers to the doors, and adjust them so that the doors hang straight and have the correct bottom clearance. Check the fit where the door edge butts against the cabinet edge and trim as necessary until you get a satisfactorily tight closure. Then mount the bottom guides if there are any, and add the knobs or pulls.

Step 9

The cabinet door is not complete, except for one last step. This involves the final sanding down and smoothing out, followed by the application of whatever finish is planned for the cabinet project as a whole. At this point, or whenever you are ready to go ahead with the finishing process, mark each cabinet door so that you know which door goes into which opening. Demount the doors from the cabinets and remove all the hardware from the doors. If you have some pieces of decorative molding or blocks which are to be applied later, be sure to set the proper collection of pieces with the right door. Skip ahead to the chapter on finishing for further details.

Chapter 9
Drawers

In the simplest possible form, a drawer is nothing but a box. The box, by one means or another, is made to slide in and out of an enclosed cabinet. But in cabinetmaking and built-ins, there are drawers, and there are drawers, and just any old drawer does not necessarily fill the bill. There are many levels of quality, durability, efficiency and usefulness, and there are a great many ways to build a drawer. On top of that, drawers are frequently fitted out to serve purposes other than just being an open container.

Of all the various parts and pieces of a cabinet assembly, drawers lead the toughest life. They are forever being yanked and pulled on, jerked sideways and out of line, and slammed back into place. They are frequently overloaded, and are subject to varying degrees of wear as they are used. Their several parts allow ample opportunity for expansion, contraction, and warping, not to mention easy susceptibility to physical damage. No other section of the cabinet is subject to such a high degree of stress, strain, and wear. And yet, if a drawer does not slide freely, close tightly, and otherwise function faultlessly at all times, we tend to curse mightily and question its ancestry vehemently.

The answer, then, especially if one wishes to avoid such frustrations, is to plan drawer construction well. Build drawers sturdily, design them to fit their intended uses, make them a bit more rugged than necessary, and lavish a bit of extra care and patience on them.

DRAWER CONSTRUCTION

There are four basic types of drawers, three of which are designed to match cupboard door types. With a flush drawer, the face of the drawer fits flush with the face-frame of the cabinet, and, like its cupboard door counterpart, it is the most difficult to fit with accuracy. A lipped drawer is made so that the drawer face sets partly within the drawer opening, while the lipped portion covers a part of any or all sides of the cabinet face-frame. The lip is formed by making a rabbet cut on one or more sides of the drawer's inside face, hiding the clearance crack around the drawer edge. The face of an overlay drawer lies entirely outside the drawer opening and usually covers only the sides of the face-frame. However, overlay drawers can also be made so that the drawer face covers the top and bottom rails of the face-frame as well. This type of drawer is often used where there are several drawers stacked and/or ranged alongside one another, in order to present a smooth, unbroken cabinet section face. Where both drawers and cupboard doors are present in the same cabinet section, matching types are generally used, although this is a matter of preference. A fourth type of drawer is sometimes used for decorative purposes. This is called an insert drawer, where the sides of the drawer protrude beyond the face, and sometimes below the bottom edge of the face as well. Figure 9-1 shows the basic drawer face concepts; design and construction details will vary considerably.

At a minimum, a drawer consists of five parts, and in some types of construction more are used. The five parts consist of the front or face, right and left sides, back, and bottom. Additional pieces may consist of a subface, or various types of runners and guides upon which the drawer slides in and out.

The drawer front is usually made either from solid wood or a plywood (either hardwood or softwood). The preferred stock thickness is ¾ inch, but this is not a hard-and-fast rule. You may use thicker stock if you wish, but don't go thinner except in tiny drawers. Side pieces are usually made from ½-inch stock, since this is less expensive but at the same time provides adequate strength and is easily workable. Here again, you may use thicker stock if you wish, either in solid wood or in plywood. For small drawers which will carry little weight, ⅜-inch stock is satisfactory, and allows a little extra usable space inside the drawer. The back is normally cut from

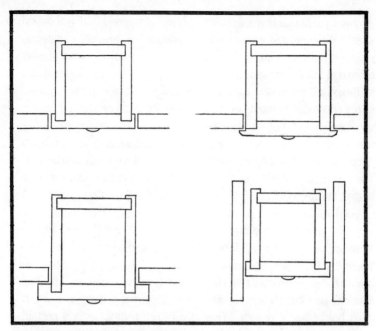

Fig. 9-1. The four common drawer face configurations. Top left, flush. Right, lipped. Bottom left, overlay or overlapped. Right, inset.

the same material as the sides. The most commonly used materials for drawer bottoms are plywood or hardwood of ¼-inch thickness. Both are tough and solid and not much subject to expansion and contraction. For small drawers, you could use 3/16-inch or even ⅛-inch hardboard, as long as there is little danger of any heavy weight being placed in the drawer.

Solid wood is a good choice for drawer fronts, sides, and backs because it is readily worked and usually requires no further edge treatment, as does plywood. White pine has long been a favorite, and edge-grained fir or similar softwoods could also be used. Of the hardwoods, mahogany is a good choice, and oak, maple, cherry, or any one of a number of others are equally usable. The chief disadvantage of using solid wood stock is the possibility of warping, and to a somewhat lesser degree, expansion and contraction. Another difficulty is that, if the drawers are large in size, the stock may have to be glued up from smaller pieces and then surfaced, a considerable amount of additional work.

The size of the drawer is no problem when you use plywood, unless you plan to build one larger than 4 feet high and 8 feet wide.

Any size piece that is needed can be handily chopped from a plywood sheet. Warping and expansion and contraction are not problems, since plywood is quite stable. On the other hand, plywood is a bit more difficult to handle and work with, joinery is more problematical, and exposed plywood edges require some sort of edge treatment. Often concessions must be made in one direction or another, when the drawer material, at least as regards the face, must match the remainder of the cabinet section. Incidentally, particle board is not a particularly good choice for home-shop drawer construction. Though most useful in many other phases of cabinetmaking, it is heavy, harder to work, and generally less serviceable than plywood or solid wood.

The strength, rigidity, and serviceability of a drawer, not to mention its appearance, depends entirely upon how well it is put together. Consider, for instance, that the drawer face takes the brunt of the punishment as the drawer is opened and closed. The abuse is particularly strong when the drawer is a large one which must hold a lot of weight. The back of the drawer gets a certain amount of stress as items slap back against it during the opening process. The sides must be sturdy enough to hold the drawer together, and perhaps to handle the guiding system as well. And the bottom obviously comes in for a lot of punishment. The better the joinery and the overall craftsmanship, then, the more durable and trouble free the drawer is likely to be.

The easiest way to build a drawer is to first construct a rectangle from four pieces of stock, using butt joints all around. Drive a few nails through the butt joints, and then tack a sheet of hardboard to the bottom. That's called a cheap and dirty drawer, and will fall apart faster than you could believe. Even substituting screws for nails and adding a liberal application of glue will not do much to help keep this type of drawer in one piece. There are better ways.

There a number of methods to securely affix the front of the drawer to the sides. Locking joints work the best, since this gives the drawer front little opportunity to separate from the sides under the strain of opening and closing. However, dado and rabbet joints can be used with equal success, especially if the drawer is of relatively small size. The simplest procedure is to cut a rabbet down the inside edge of each side of the drawer front. The depth of the rabbet cut is usually about half the thickness of the stock, or perhaps a bit more. The width of the cut may be equal to the thickness of the side pieces. This is called a simple rabbet or flush rabbet joint, and works nicely for flush-type drawers.

Better results are gained from a beveled rabbet joint, however, where the width of the rabbet cut is approximately one-sixteenth of an inch wider than the thickness of the side piece. Then the exposed edge of the rabbet cut on the drawer front is tapered inward slightly, allowing good clearance for the side pieces while at the same time showing only a small visible clearance crack between the drawer front edges and the cabinet face-frame. If the drawer is to be lipped, then the width of the rabbet cut should equal the thickness of the side piece plus the desired amount of lip, and the depth of the rabbet cut should equal the thickness of the drawer front minus the thickness of the lip.

The treatment is a bit different for overlap drawers. The easiest method is to use a dado overlap joint. Cut a dado groove down the inside surface of the drawer front a short distance from each end. The measurement from the drawer front ends in to the dado grooves should equal the desired amount of overlap plus about one-sixteenth of an inch for clearance. The width of the dado grooves should be equal to the thickness of the side pieces, and the depth is usually about half the thickness of the front piece. This type of joint, however, has no locking properties, and depends mostly upon glue and fasteners for its strength.

If more strength is needed, use a dovetail dado, which locks the two pieces firmly together. A half-dovetail dado also makes a good joint. There are several other strong locking joints which can be used for either flush or lipped drawers. The double dado makes an effective joint, is simple to cut, and lends itself equally well to either type of drawer. The lock joint is more difficult to cut, but is also stronger, and a milled shaper joint is also effective. The joint which is most commonly used in top-quality drawer construction is the multiple dovetail joint, either in half-blind or through mode. Note that in many cases, the front joints in a drawer can be made using a subface to which a surface drawer face is later attached. Though most commonly used with overlap or lipped types of drawers, it can also be applied to a flush drawer. Figure 9-2 shows some of the various possibilities of attaching drawer sides to front.

Fitting the back piece to the sides of a drawer can also be done in a number of ways. Here, the simple butt joint is often used,

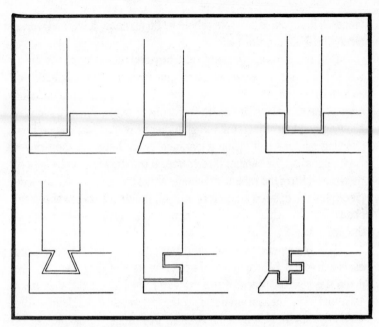

Fig. 9-2. Methods of attaching drawer sides to fronts. Sides are represented by the vertical members, fronts are horizontal.

especially in drawers of small size and lightweight construction. An ordinary dado joint is quite common, and, considering the amount of strength gained versus the simplicity of construction, this joint is a most effective one. The dado and rabbet joint is a slight variation on this, using a narrow dado groove on the side pieces and a matching a rabbet cut on the back. This too makes a good joint, though more operations are involved in its construction. For locking joints, the dovetail dado makes an excellent choice. Again, the joint found most often in high quality construction is the half-blind or through multiple dovetail. This type of joint requires skill and experience, along with some special equipment, to construct successfully, so you might wish to opt for a simpler kind. In any event, most home cabinetry and built-ins don't require this high level of construction, and there is little point in over-building. If you just can't bypass the challenge, or are building fine furniture, that's another matter. Some of the methods of joining drawer backs to side pieces are shown in Fig. 9-3.

The way not to attach a drawer bottom is to nail it to the bottom edges of the drawer frame; it will work loose in short order. In most cases, the drawer bottom is set into a groove cut close to the bottom edges of the inside surfaces of the drawer's front and side pieces. This gives the bottom good support around three of its edges. In high-quality drawer construction, the bottom is also fitted into a fourth groove in the back piece, but this can be a tricky bit of business and is usually not necessary. The groove procedure is used with ⅛-inch and ¼-inch plywood or hardboard bottoms. However, some heavy-duty or utility drawers are made with, or require, thicker bottom stock. Where ⅜-inch or ½-inch plywood is selected, for instance, a combination of dado and butt joints may be used. Picking the right combination of joints is important, because if the

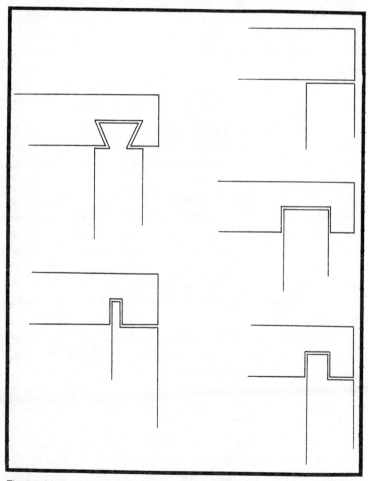

Fig. 9-3. Methods of attaching drawer backs to sides. Backs are represented by horizontal members, sides are vertical.

wrong series is used, there is no way to put the drawer together. For instance, if you use dovetail dados at all four corners, there would be no way to support the drawer bottom with a four-sided groove.

The fact that a joined drawer is considered best does not mean that you can't build one any other way. In fact, if you don't have the necessary equipment to cut joints, there really isn't much choice. One way around the problem is to build a double-box drawer. This consists of one box within another, both tightly joined together with interlocking butt joints. The bottom is held in place with support strips or cleats. Another possibility is to build a simple box frame with butt joints and to reinforce it with doweling and glue blocks at all joints. Install glued support strips for the bottom, with gusset blocks glued and screwed to each bottom corner to keep the drawer from racking.

DRAWER GUIDES

As was mentioned in an earlier chapter, a considerable assortment of hardware is being marketed these days which allows quick and simple drawer installation on premanufactured slides and glides. This equipment is advantageous in a number of ways. Chief among the advantages is a considerable savings in labor and consequently in overall cost, expecially to the professional cabinet builder and installer. Other advantages include durability and long life, as well as consistant and continued efficient operation of the drawer. This hardware also simplifies matters greatly for the home craftsman. All you need to do is purchase an appropriate number of installation kits of whatever type you choose, and then follow the directions. Some of the specific drawer construction procedures and dimensions are dependent upon exactly what sort of hardware you select, so have the equipment in hand before going ahead with the project. Then, just build to suit the hardware requirements.

On the other hand, there are a good many other ways to accomplish the same purpose with no out-of-pocket expenditures for hardware. Building corner runners is one of the simplest ways. With this system, the bottom side corners of the drawer are guided along the corners formed by the sides and bottom of the cabinet, or by the cabinet sides and face-frame edges. If the face-frame extends past the sides of the cabinet, leaving a gap between cabinet side and drawer side, an extra piece of wood is glued and nailed to the cabinet side to fill out the space and guide the drawer accurately. Where the drawer opening is bounded only by cabinet face-frame stiles and rails, an extra piece with a deep rabbet cut from it to form an ell must be secured on each side of the drawer between front and back of the cabinet (Fig. 9-4). In all cases, a kicker has to be secured from cabinet front to back and centered directly above the darwer. This device intercepts the back piece as the drawer is pulled out and begins to tilt, so that it will not tip too far and slide clear out.

Side guides and runners are quite commonly used in casework. All this amounts to is grooves in the drawer sides which run on cabinet rails, or, conversely, slots in the cabinet sides in which drawer rails run. In the former instance (Fig. 9-5A), a groove is cut lengthwise in each drawer side, about halfway (or a bit less) down from the top edge. The drawer side stock should be of minimum ¾-inch thickness, and the depth of the groove, or plough, about ⅜ inch. The absolute width of the cut is not critical. Then, a cleat or rail, preferably of hardwood, is secured to each cabinet side, or to front and back with rail or skeleton construction, properly positioned to

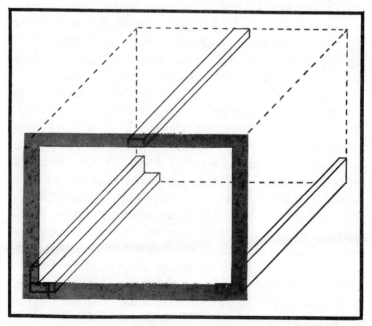

Fig. 9-4. Corner runners are mounted in bottom corners of drawer opening, secured front to back. Kicker is centered above, also secured front to back.

receive the drawer. The width of the cleats should be a bit less than the width of the grooves in the drawer sides, and the cleat thickness a bit less then the groove depth. Remember also to allow for sufficient operating clearance for smooth running. In the latter instance (Fig. 9-5B), the procedure is reversed, with the grooves cut into the sides of the cabinet and the cleats or runners secured to the drawer sides. In open cabinetwork which has no skeletal structure and there are no sides handy into which grooves can be cut, a substitute can be made by grooving thick pieces of stock and securing them from front to back on the cabinet. Or, use two pieces spaced apart to form each groove. Either general method of making side guides and runners works well.

Another way to guide a drawer is with a center guide and runner. This requires that there be a certain amount of space beneath the drawer, and between stacked drawers, and that the bottom of the drawer itself be set well above the bottom edges of the drawer frame. In simplest fashion, a strip of wood is secured to the cabinet front and back, centered at the bottom of the drawer opening, but higher than the bottom edge of the opening. Then, two more strips are attached from front to back on the drawer bottom, creating a wide groove or channel just slightly larger than the center runner (Fig. 9-6A). These two strips of wood comprise the center guide for aligning the drawer properly in the opening. In a more complex construction, the center runner in cross section looks like a fat T. The center guides are mounted upon the drawer bottoms in the same way, with the back piece of the drawer extending below them. Then a T-guide notch which corresponds in shape to the cross section of the center guide, but a bit larger for operating clearance, is cut in the skirt of the drawer back (Fig. 9-6B). This aligns the drawer better, and prevents it from tipping as it is opened. There are also a number of variations upon and additions to this scheme which are often used. For instance, stop blocks, bearing blocks, or plastic bearing pads can be added to aid in smooth operation. Or, two sets of guides and runners can be used, especially with larger drawers. This minimizes the possibility that the drawer will go crooked and stick in the opening. Another refinement is a hardwood T-guide attached to the rear of the drawer back in lieu of actually cutting a T-guide opening in the back piece itself. This allows the use of hardwood in a strong, solid block, which can readily be replaced when it becomes worn.

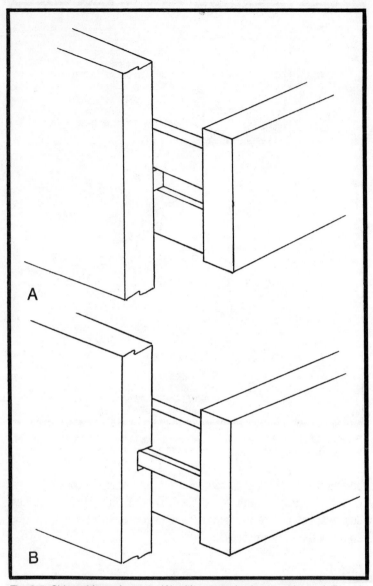

Fig. 9-5. Side guide and runner (A) with groove in drawer side, and (B) with groove in case side.

BUILDING DRAWERS

Though building drawers is not a difficult task, the process does require time and careful attention when it is properly done. For this reason, often it is advantageous to construct several drawers at once

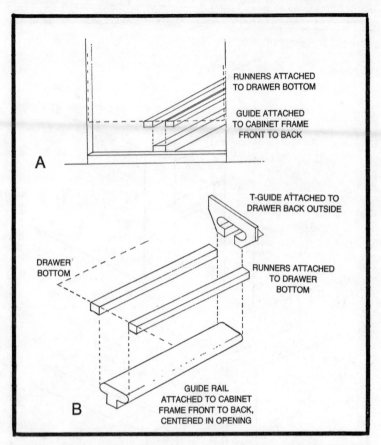

Fig. 9-6. Center guide and runner (A) using simple wood strips, and (B) with formed track, wood strip guides, and rear T-block.

so that you can curtail the amount of time ordinarily consumed by repetitive machine setups and such. By creating a mini-assembly line, you can do the job quicker and easier. There are only a few steps to the entire process.

Step 1

The first step is to make decisions and plans. First you need to decide how the drawer front will fit: flush, lip, or overlay. Then, determine what sort of material you want to use, and make sure that you have enough stock on hand to cut out all the necessary pieces. Decide exactly which drawer guide hardware you want to use, then purchase it. If you opt for making your own guides, determine the details of how you will go about the process. Lastly, decide upon the types of joints you want. Use the simplest of the joints which are adequate for the job. Remember that some joint combinations can be mutually exclusive, and if you pick the wrong ones you may not be able to assemble the drawer. Sort these details out ahead of time. Once you have chosen the joint types and the pieces are cut, you will not be able to change horses in midstream (except by a lot of extra work) because the dimensions of the pieces will vary according to the joint type.

Step 2

Check the drawer opening to make sure that the stiles and rails, or the cabinet edges, are level and plumb and that all the corners are square. Then, take accurate measurements of the height and width of the drawer opening, measuring at several points if the opening is large. If there are any serious dimensional problems with the opening, you may have to construct the drawer to suit, or make corrections and adjustments during the final fitting process. Next, determine the overall depth of the opening. This will translate into the length of the drawer. You may want to select some arbitrary drawer length—a 14-inch-long drawer will fit quite handily into an opening under a counter with a 20-inch depth, for instance. On the other hand, you might decide to make use of all the depth possible, and so accurate measurements become a necessity. Sometimes the drawer sides are extended so that the drawer stops with the face in exactly the right closed position as the sides contact the back of the cabinet or a rear cross rail. This too necessitates accurate depth measurements.

Now you must relate all of this dimensional information to the drawer size itself, the specific drawer guide system that you have planned for, and also to the types of joints that you will use. Allow 1/16-inch clearance at the most around the outer perimeter of the drawer front for a flush drawer. This can be somewhat less if the front joints are to be bevel rabbet. If the final finish will be a thick coating such as enamel, make clearance allowances for this. Check the guide hardware instructions, and work out any necessary dimensioning in clearances here. It is best to make sketches and note all of the figures as you go along. They can become confusing, and a mistake in the wrong place could be disastrous.

Step 3

This is a step which can be accomplished now or later; it is a matter of preference. There are occasions, however, when setting the cabinet-mounted portions of the guide system into place at this point can save some aggravation later. Also, working within the cabinet is more difficult than working on a drawer parked atop a workbench. Thus, any adjustments or alterations that must be made in the guide system are more easily done on the drawer in the early stages of construction than on the cabinet part of the system after the entire asssembly is complete.

If you are using commercial hardware for the guide system, follow the manufacturer's instructions and install the cabinet-mounted parts of the system. Depending upon the cabinet design, this may require the installation of some extra rails, support blocks, or wood shims to properly align the pieces. Make doubly sure that all tracks and rails are level and square to the opening and to each other, else you will later have problems with drawer fit. If you are making your own guiding system, cut and fit the parts which mount in the cabinet and install them in their proper positions. When everything is in place, take another series of measurements, remembering to allow for all necessary clearances, and then relate your findings to the figures you have jotted down on your rough sketch of drawer dimensions. You may find that the parts of the guide system you have just installed will actually require slightly different drawer dimensions than you had originally set down. Or, you may discover that for some reason you can not install the guide system in the cabinet in exactly the manner you had planned, and so the drawer construction must be slightly altered in compensation. If there are any problems, whatever they may be, make the necessary adjustments now.

Step 4

Select the material you plan to use to build the drawer. Lay out the dimensions on the stock and cut the five principal drawer parts: the front, back, two sides and bottom. Double check at this point to make sure that all corners are square, and that the stock is flat and true. Any problems of this sort will be magnified later when you start to cut joints and fit the pieces together.

Now comes the cutting of the joints and the actual assembly of the pieces. To give you a better idea of how this goes, we will run through the steps involved in two distinctly different types of drawers. The first makes use of simple joinery, resulting in a drawer which is perfectly adequate for just about any type of home cabinetry or built-ins. The construction process may be modified, however, with complex joints and ornamentation. The second type of drawer requires a bit more labor and material for any given size, but uses only the simplest joint of them all, the butt joint. This drawer can be made quite easily with no special equipment, and in fact without any power tools at all. It is perfectly satisfactory for utility use and with a little extra care and good craftsmanship can serve equally well in a fashionable living room or fancy kitchen.

The Joined Drawer. To establish the design characteristics of this drawer, we'll say that it is flush type, using double dado joints to join the front piece to the sides and simple dado joints to join the back piece to the sides. The four frame pieces of the drawer are made from solid ¾-inch mahogany, and the bottom is ¼-inch hardboard set in grooves on three sides. The drawer guide system consists of a bottom-mounted center guide and runners. The projected use of the drawer is in a built-in desk assembly. The joinery will be done on a table saw, using a dado head. The same operations could be performed with a molding head, or even by masking repeated cuts with an ordinary saw blade. Even a radial saw or router could be used instead of the table saw.

A. Set the height of the dado blade to just a tiny bit more than half the thickness of the side piece stock. In this case, a ⅜-inch-deep groove is needed. The dado head width should be set at ¼ inch. Determine which face of each side piece is to form the outer surface and which the inner, and mark them accordingly so that you won't get mixed up. Then, fix one side piece into a clamping miter gauge or a jig, or set the rip fence, so that the outside edge of the dado groove will be one-quarter of an inch from the end of the workpiece. With everything lined up and secured, make the dado cut in the side piece (Fig. 9-7). Repeat the process with the second side piece. Now set both pieces aside.

Fig. 9-7. Making first dado cut in drawer side piece. Duncan Photos.

B. Leave the dado blade set at a ¼-inch width, but jack up the
height to equal the thickness of the side piece stock plus
1/16-inch clearance. In this case, a 13/16-inch-deep
groove is required. Stand the drawer front piece upon end
and secure it in a jig or against the rip fence, lining it up so

that the centerline of the groove will fall exactly along the centerline of the workpiece. This will give you a transverse ¼-inch-wide groove in the edge center, with a ¼-inch-wide strip of stock left on each side. Doublecheck the setup, and cut the dado across the end of the front piece (Fig. 9-8). Turn the workpiece over and repeat the process on the opposite end.

C. Decide which surface of the front piece will become the outside or show face of the drawer. Now, at each end of the front piece you have two tongues, one on the inside

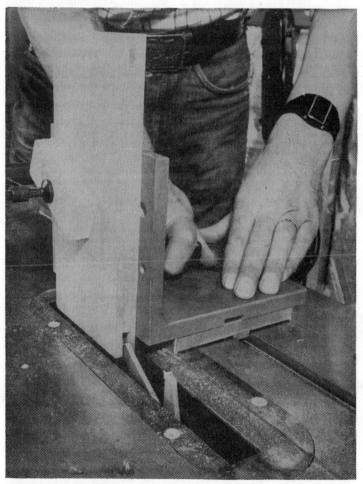

Fig. 9-8. Making dado cut in ends of drawer front piece. Duncan Photos.

and one on the outside. The tongues of stock which face the inside of the drawer are called tenons, since they will eventually fit inside the grooves you have just cut in the side pieces. Both tenons must now be cut to a shorter length, so that each will fit snugly within its dadoes. The outside tongues on the drawer front will remain as is, and completely hide the end grains of the side pieces. The length of the tenons, then, must be identical to the depth of the dadoes in the side pieces. In this case, you need a ⅜-inch tenon, so you must remove a 7/16-inch piece from each one. You can make these cuts with either the dado blade or an ordinary fine-toothed saw blade. Clamp the drawer front, face up, in a miter gauge or jig or set it against the rip fence, properly aligned to remove a 7/16-inch piece from the tenon, no more and no less. Take care that the dado or saw blade is not set too high, in this case, no more than half an inch. Make the trim cut (Fig. 9-9), then turn the front piece around and do the same at the other end. Now, check the joints for fit. If you have made the cuts correctly, the side pieces should slip onto the front piece easily and squarely, with each end of the front piece protruding beyond the side pieces one-sixteenth of an inch.

D. Back to the side pieces again, to cut the dadoes for the back piece. The cuts should be of the same width as the thickness of the back piece stock, and the depth of the groove should be equal to no more than half the thickness of the side piece stock. Here, the groove will be ¾ inch wide and ⅜ inch deep. Set the dado blade accordingly. Make the cuts so that the outer edge of each groove is half an inch from the back end of each side piece. Be sure to cut the grooves in the same face of the stock as the previous ones. Line up and dado just as you did in A.

E. Lay out the dimensions of the bottom piece on a sheet of ¼-inch hardboard. The usual practice is to allow at least a ¼-inch rim, but no more than ⅜ inch, to set into the retaining grooves in the front and side pieces. In this case, then, the width of the bottom piece should be equal to the inside width of the drawer plus half an inch, and the length

Fig. 9-9. Trimming tenon in drawer front. Duncan Photos.

(depth) equal to the inside depth of the drawer plus a quarter of an inch. Cut the bottom piece to size, check for square, and trim off any rough edges.

F. Lay out the front and side drawer pieces for the bottom piece retaining grooves. The depth of the groove should

Fig. 9-10. Cutting bottom grooves in the drawer sides to receive the drawer bottom piece. Duncan Photos.

allow a 1/16-inch clearance all around the edges of the bottom piece, and the width should be just slightly greater than the thickness of the bottom piece. In this case, then, the groove depth should be 5/16 inch. A 1/64 clearance in the groove width is sufficient; adjust the dado blade accordingly. Set the rip fence to allow a ⅜-inch clearance between the fence and the near edge of the blade. You could use a little less clearance on a small, light drawer, or you might need a bit more if a deep bottom guide system is to be used. After checking the measurements and the saw locking mechanisms, cut a groove at the bottom inside of each side piece and the front piece (Fig. 9-10).

G. All that remains now is the back piece. This may require some additional trimming. The width of the back piece should be equal to the distance from the top edge of each side down to the top edge of each bottom piece groove. This is because the bottom piece is first slid into its groove, and then the back piece slips down in its dadoes and comes to rest upon the bottom piece. Obviously, the bottom piece cannot be of the same width as the drawer sides and front. Often this piece is cut roughly to size at the outset, and then trimmed exactly to fit as the drawer is assembled. This is a worthwhile procedure, and may save installing an ill-fitting piece, or having to cut a new one which will fit properly.

H. Now is the moment of truth, when all of the pieces must be put together. Working on a flat, clean surface, set the sides on edge and join them to the front piece. Slip the drawer bottom into place, and then slide the back piece down into its groove (Fig. 9-11). Check each joint for a tight fit, and then check all the corners to make sure that they are square and flush. You may wish to hold the pieces tightly in place with a band clamp or bar clamp, or whatever other arrangement suits the purpose, to make sure that everything is just right. Make any adjustments that are necessary now. Then, disassemble the drawer and start over again, this time with glue and fasteners. Glue each side piece to the front piece, and secure them with nails or screws. Choose fasteners of adequate length, not too heavy for the job. Drill pilot holes and countersink as necessary, especially if the material is hardwood. If the drawer face will later have a natural or a transparent finish, omit any fasteners which might be visible, or counterbore for plugs. Next, slide the drawer bottom into place. No fasteners are used here, but you may wish to apply glue. Then insert the back piece into its grooves, again using glue, and secure it with fasteners. Remember that you are driving fasteners into an end grain where the holding power is relatively poor, so make the fasteners a bit longer than you ordinarily might. Turn the drawer over, and secure the bottom piece to the lower edge of the back piece, preferably with screws.

Double Box Drawer. This type of drawer is made without the use of any joinery beyond the simple butt joint. All parts of the

Fig. 9-11. Assembling the drawer. Duncan Photos.

drawer are fashioned from ½-inch softwood plywood. Since the projected use is merely to hold a collection of used plumbing parts and fixtures in a workshop storage compartment, the material is composed of scrap pieces of construction-grade plywood, with minimal regard for appearance. However, the use of higher quality stock would result in a prefectly presentable drawer that could be used anywhere. The guiding system consists merely of the corners formed by the storage cabinet sides and bottom, so no additional hardware or guide parts are necessary.

A. First establish the overall height, width, and length or depth of the drawer. For purposes of illustration we will assume the height to be 8 inches, the width 16 inches, and the length 20 inches.

B. Cut the pieces of stock for the inner box of the drawer. This inner box must be smaller than the overall dimensions of the drawer by the amount of the thickness of the stock on each side. In this case, the box is 15 inches wide and 19 inches long. The height is 1½ inches less than the overall height of the finished drawer, or 6½ inches. So, cut two side pieces 19 inches long and 6½ inches wide. Since butt joints will be used, the front and back pieces must be shorter than the overall inner box width by double the thickness of the side piece stock. Cut a front and a back piece 14 inches long and 6½ inches wide. Next, set all four pieces on edge on a smooth work surface and arrange them so that the front and back pieces stand between the side pieces, with all four corners flush and even. Apply glue to the butt joints and fasten all four pieces to form a box frame. Make sure that the box remains square.

C. Cut a rectangle of plywood 15 inches wide and 19 inches long. Set it in place on top of the box frame, and check that all edges of this bottom piece are flush with the sides of the box frame. Trim if necessary so that there is no overlapping. Slight undersizing will make no difference. Apply glue to the box frame edges, set the bottom piece in place, and secure it with fasteners.

D. Cut the pieces to form the outer box. This time the faces of the butt joints will be reversed. The drawer sides will fit between the front and back pieces, so they must be shorter than the overall length of the drawer by double the thickness of the stock. Cut two side pieces 19 inches long, and to the full width of 8 inches. Then cut the front and back pieces, each 16 inches long and 8 inches wide.

E. Set the inner box bottom-up on a smooth work surface. Stand the two outer box side pieces against the inner box side pieces, and check to make sure that the ends are flush. Apply glue down each end, and draw a wavy line of glue on the side meeting faces. Clamp 'the outer sides to the inner sides, keeping the ends lined up and flush. Fasten the outer sides into place along each end. Now, follow the same procedure with the front and back pieces, completing the outer box. Drive fasteners into both end-grain sections, front and rear. The resulting butt joint arrangement is shown in Fig. 9-12.

F. Cut two strips of wood, either the same ½-inch plywood stock or standard ¾-inch solid wood stock, 1 inch wide and 15 inches long. Fit one piece, on edge, across the back bottom of the drawer and the other across the front bottom to form cleats to help hold the drawer bottom in place. The upper edge of each cleat fits snug against the drawer bottom, and the lower edge is flush with the bottom edge of the drawer outer box. Glue and fasten the cleats in place. Then cut two more strips, this time 18 inches long and 1 inch wide, and fit them into place as side cleats. Glue and fasten them into place. One effective method of fastening is to drive a series of nails through the cleats and up into the drawer bottom, and then to set screws through the cleats and into the drawer sides.

G. A drawer of this sort, particularly one which will hold a great deal of weight, can be further strengthened by the manner in which the drawer pull is attached. For this particular drawer, a heavy pull with two points of attachment is in order. Rather than mounting the utility-type pull with the normal relatively short wood screws driven from the front, use sturdier fasteners. Position a stout handle on the front of the drawer, and drill a pair of holes entirely through the drawer face. Substitute long machine screws, flat washers, lock washers, and nuts for the usual wood screws, and bolt the handle firmly into place.

Now, back to the general construction sequence applicable to all drawers.

Step 6

Once the structure of the cabinet drawer is complete, you can install those portions of the guide system which mount upon the

Fig. 9-12. Butt joint arrangement used in making a double-box drawer.

drawer. Or, attach any remaining hardware, such as commercial slide tracks, following the manufacturer's instructions. (Understand that if you are using side guides and runners and if the guides are to be dadoes into the sides of the drawer, that operation would have been done prior to assembling the drawer.) Once the guide system is complete, install the drawer pull or knob. Then set the drawer in place in the cabinet, and check for good fit and smoothness of operation. If anything is amiss, make whatever corrections are necessary. Bevel the exposed end grains at each side of the drawer front piece for good clearance.

After you have finished the fitting work, apply any further decoration that you have in mind to the drawer face. As with cabinet doors, this may involve the routing of a design or the application of decorative molding. The bonding of laminated plastic to the drawer face can also be done now; additional clearance must be provided during the construction process if plastic laminate is to be applied to the drawer edges as well. Laminates can also be bonded to the inside drawer bottom, or to the entire inside of the drawer. This is the time, too, to install drawer dividers, drawer trays, or sliding tray sections.

Step 7

The very last step in constructing a drawer involves the final surface preparation, followed by application of a finish, with the exception of drawers which have been covered with plastic laminate. Remove the drawers from the cabinet and mark them so that you will know which drawer goes back into which opening. Then remove all of the hardware and set it aside. Refer to the chapter on finishing for further information.

Chapter 10
Shelving

A knowledge of the design and construction of shelves is an important aspect of building home cabinetry, built-ins, and storage units. After all, the chief function of a cabinet is to either store or display items, and the principal means for so doing is the shelf. Drawer space, although necessary in many instances, is usually of secondary importance. Certainly in terms of square footage of storage area, shelving is far and away the most prevalent. Storage units, except for a few types which are designed for special purposes, are next to useless without shelves. Even built-ins, which sometimes take the form of functional furniture, often are equipped with a certain amount of shelving. Furthermore, shelving is often its own *raison d'etre*. Whatever the purpose of the shelf or shelving section, whether for books or plants or china or fishing gear, it can stand alone as a complete piece of furniture, existing for its own purposes and unassociated with any additional cabinetwork or closeting.

Shelves can take many forms, serve a multitude of purposes, and be constructed in any number of different ways. They range from unappealing but functional utility types, through a tremendous gamut of possibilities, to ornate and highly imaginative furnishings. There is a lot of variation in detail, and as you might expect, there are right ways and wrong ways to build a shelf for any given purpose.

SHELF DESIGN

There are several materials from which you can choose that work well for shelving. Solid wood is a reasonable choice, especially where the shelves are not terribly wide. A soft wood like white pine is popular for both utility shelves and more decorative cabinet or furniture shelves. Hardwood is widely used, especially for the sake of appearance in open shelves and where a natural or transparent finish is desired. The problem with solid wood, especially when used to make adjustable shelves that are not securely fastened down, is warping. The stock has to be of excellent quality and properly dried. Whenever possible, use vertical-grained softwood or quartersawed hardwood stock. If the shelf width is greater than about 6 inches, the possibilities for objectionable warping are considerably increased.

Particle board also makes good shelving, provided that it has adequate end and edge support. Since this material has no grain, it does not have the rigidity of a plank of solid wood. However, it is inexpensive and can be worked with relative ease. Particle board does require some sort of edge treatment along the exposed shelf edges. Plywood is perhaps the most widely used shelving material, and for good reason. Plywood is stable, so that problems with warping, expansion, and contraction are not likely to arise. It has ample strength and sufficient stiffness to be used even in relatively long lengths. Shelving made from plywood should always be cut with the surface grain rather than across, as this in most cases confers maximum ridigity, makes the finishing process easier, and is more pleasing to the eye. Softwood plywoods of cabinet grade are most often used in enclosed cabinetwork, and either softwood or hardwood plywoods are used where appearance and decorative effect are a part of the design. As with particle board, some sort of edge treatment is needed. Both plywood and particle board can serve as a core upon which laminated plastics are bonded. Thin sheets of hardwood plywood primarily intended for wall coverings can be applied to particle board or to lower grades of softwood plywood.

Glass, usually of the ¼-inch plate variety, is sometimes used for shelving, especially in china cabinets, display cases, or etageres. Such shelves are much stronger then you might imagine; if properly arranged, they can be mounted with a minimum of edge support to form a most attractive shelving section. Acrylic plastics, by and large, do not make particularly satisfactory shelving. The major drawbacks are a relative lack of rigidity and a great susceptibility to scratching. They also have a marked tendency to collect great quantities of dust because of static electricity buildup. Acrylics can be used successfully, however, in certain types of display cabinetry, especially where the items shown are seldom moved about, and the shelving is enclosed in cabinets having glass or clear plastic panel doors. Also, translucent plastic display shelves can double as light diffusers for indirect lighting hidden beneath them.

Hardboard makes effective shelving if the thickness of the material is properly related to the shelf size and the load which must be carried. Tempered hardboard, which is quite stiff, can be used successfully as small compartment shelves, as in a multiple-shelf stationary cubby built into a writing desk section in a storage or divider wall. Thicker hardboard stock can be used for increasingly longer and deeper shelving for all manner of purposes. Edge treatment is usually not required for the thinner stock, and end and edge support arrangements depend upon the load to be carried.

Proper shelf sizing is an important factor if the shelving section is to be successful. Obviously, shelves that are designed for certain purposes, such as to store single rows of canned foods, to hold a collection of records or reel tapes, or for the sole purpose of supporting some particular appliance or piece of equipment, should be sized according to the items which will be shelved. The usual practice is to allow about an extra inch of width for clearance, plus additional spacing for a back support cleat for the shelf above if there is one, or for doors and door hardware if they exist.

Shelves which are set up for miscellaneous storage purposes, with no particular contents in mind, must be as utilitarian as possible. Shelves which are exceptionally narrow lack versatility and those which are too wide may be awkward to use. Shelves in overhead kitchen cabinets are normally about 12 inches wide, or deep, while those found in dining and living rooms run from as little as 6 inches deep to as much as 16 inches deep. Shelving in base cabinets is anywhere from about 10 inches wide to 24 inches wide, depending upon the construction of the cabinet and the placement of the shelves. Bookshelves should be a minimum of 8 inches wide, and 9 inches is preferable. The 9-inch shelves will handle about 90 percent of the books being marketed today, but the remaining 10 percent require shelving as wide as 12 inches. Utility shelving is often made in widths of up to 16 inches, but anything much deeper is likely to be a pain in the neck. There is one exception: shelves which are designed primarily for storing linens, towelling, and blankets are often 24 to 30 inches deep. Closet shelving is generally about 9 to 12 inches deep.

The spacing between shelves can also be critical. If the shelves are stationary, great care must be taken to make sure that all are accessible. In a closet, for instance, there may be two shelves above the clothes rod. The bottom shelf may be made narrower than the upper one, or vice-versa, depending upon the closet door arrangement, so that items on either shelf can be easily reached. In kitchen base cabinets, the floor of the cabinet serves as the first shelf, and is, of course, full depth. However, the second shelf may be approximately 15 inches wide, and the next one up only 10 or 12 inches wide, to allow easier access. Fixed bookshelves should be spaced no less than 9½ inches apart, and the maximum you are likely to need is 14 inches. In large bookshelf sections, a mix of 10-inch, 12-inch, and 14-inch spacings makes a good arrangement. A lesser amount of linear footage of the wide-spaced shelves is usually needed, and is generally placed in the lower portion of the section, with the narrower-spaced shelves above. Spacing for fixed shelves in kitchen overhead cabinets is difficult to determine ahead of time. There must be room enough for tall glasses, cereal packages, platters, and many other items of assorted and variable heights. One method is to space the shelves variously from about 8 inches to a maximum of about 14 inches, and then store whatever comes along in whatever fashion seems best. Space-saving subshelves, racks, and trays can be built and installed if, as, and when the need arises.

The best way to save space with any shelving arrangement is to make the shelves fully adjustable. There are a number of ways to go about this, and we will investigate them a bit later. The advantage of this type of shelving is obvious: the shelf can be placed at whatever height is best for the specific purpose at hand, and changed whenever necessary. Frequently, more shelves can be installed in a given space than would otherwise be possible. The disadvantage is that the shelves are loose, and may be wobbly if warped or not properly installed. Also, more labor is required if you make your own adjusting system, or additional expense if you decide to purchase special adjustable shelf hardware. Another possible disadvantage lies in the fact that open adjustable shelving, because of its appearance, may not conform with the decor of a given room. To many, this type of shelving simply does not have the appearance of fine furniture, even though it may fulfill its intended functions in superior fashion. The fact is, both kinds of shelving are commonly found in most homes, each serving its own purpose.

Shelving, no matter what its intended function, can be installed in the home in three different ways. Built-in shelving essentially becomes a part of the house structure, because it is attached permanently in place. The shelves themselves may be either fixed or adjustable, but remain a part of a stationary installation. On the other hand, shelving may be completely portable, either in the form of ordinary small bookcases, or as a part of cabinetry, casework, or furniture which can be moved about at will. Here, too, the shelf sections themselves may be either fixed or adjustable. The middle ground is occupied by shelving sections which are considered either semipermanent or semiportable. The shelves themselves are usually adjustable, although they may be nonadjustable as well provided that they are removable and not permanently fixed in place. The shelving section sides, dividers, or supports and standards, are either freestanding, or are held in place with easily removable fastening devices such as tensioners. This type of shelving is neither portable nor permanent, but must be disassembled to move it from one place to another.

SHELF SUPPORT

The key to building good shelving lies in providing adequate support in the proper places. This is dependent upon four things: the material from which the shelf is made, the width (depth) of the shelf, the length (width) of the shelf, and the maximum load that is likely to be placed upon the shelf. There is a continuous interaction of all four factors, and figuring out the details is not always easy. The best course is always to build a shelf sturdier then you think it has to be.

For most purposes, shelf stock of ¾-inch thickness is the normal choice. Thinner stock should only be used for shelves of short length which will never hold heavy loads. The maximum length of shelves constructed from solid wood or plywood should be 42 inches between supporting points. This remains true even when the rear edge of the shelf and each end are supported. If the stock is particle board, reduce that length to a maximum of 36 inches, and

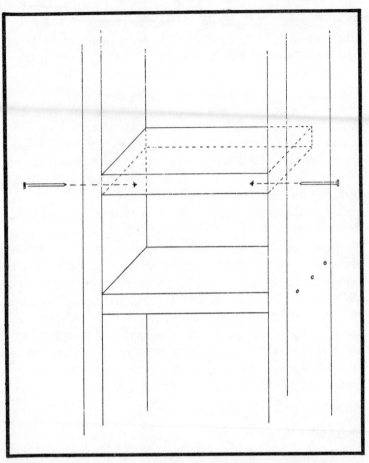

Fig. 10-1. Attaching shelves to standards or side pieces using butt joints and nails or screws.

preferably a bit less, even with shelf back support. If the shelf length must be greater than these figures, build the shelf from 1-inch-thick stock, or heavier. In most cases, the problem is not that the shelf will break, but that over a short period of time it will develop a noticeable sag which is difficult to correct after the cabinetry has been completed. This is particularly true of bookshelves, and can become a real problem if there happens to be a cabinet section beneath the shelf which has flush or sliding doors. Unless the top shelf remains perfectly flat, the doors can easily become inoperable.

There are a great many ways to support shelves. Where they are fitted between solid side pieces of at least the same depth (width) as the shelf, you have several options. The simplest method is to use a butt joint at each end of the shelf, apply glue to the shelf edges, and fasten them into place with screws or nails driven through the side pieces and into the shelf ends (Fig. 10-1). Screws will provide greater holding power than nails. Though simple, this method is also the weakest, and should be used only where the shelf loading is not likely to be especially heavy. One good way to provide an additional lift for this arrangement is to anchor a back cleat to the cabinet wall, giving the shelf full support along its entire back edge (Fig. 10-2). Better still, secure cleats on the side pieces to support each end of the shelf, and use the back edge cleat as well. This method is particularly helpful when there is no way to drive fasteners through the side pieces from the outside and into the shelf ends. However, if you are able to do so, as well as to use cleats all around, so much the better. A face-frame can be applied around the perimeter of the shelving sections and nailed in such a way as to give even more support to the shelf (Fig. 10-3).

Cleats can be easily made by ripping ¾-inch square strips from a solid wood plank, or by using a standard molding such as stop, screen, or quarter-round. Secure the cleats to the side pieces with glue and nails or screws, and to the back wall in the same manner, depending upon the wall material. If the cabinet or shelf frame is

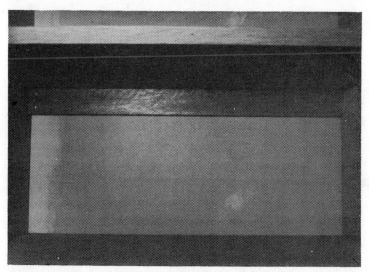

Fig. 10-2. Shelf installed using rear cleat with butt joints and nails at the ends. Duncan Photos.

Fig. 10-3. Shelf installed using a combination of rear cleat, end cleat, nailed end butt joint, and face-frame support. Duncan Photos.

open and backs up to a plaster or plasterboard wall, omit the glue and drive fasteners through the cleats and wall covering and into the wall studs.

Another simple and commonly used method of supporting shelves is to cut dadoes in the side pieces and fit the shelf ends into the grooves (Fig. 10-4). An alternate possibility is to use a stop or blind dado like the one shown in Fig. 7-3B. If the section of shelving depends upon the shelves themselves to provide part of the rigidity and solidity of the unit as a whole, then the shelves must be secured firmly with fasteners and glue. However, if the framework which holds the shelving is designed to be freestanding or depends upon being attached to the house structure for its main support, then the shelves may be left free in the dadoes.

Another possibility, one which makes a sturdy arrangement, is to use small steel right-angle brackets, two or perhaps three at each end of each shelf (Fig. 10-5). These brackets are relatively unobtrusive, particularly when they and the rest of the assembly are painted the same color. Small brackets using two screws in each arm are prefectly adequate. Mount them to the shelf side pieces first, then set the shelves in place and fasten them down with screws. For a more finished appearance, you can mortise each bracket into both side pieces and shelf ends.

Long shelves require additional support. One way of providing this support is to rest the rear edge of the shelf on a full-length cleat,

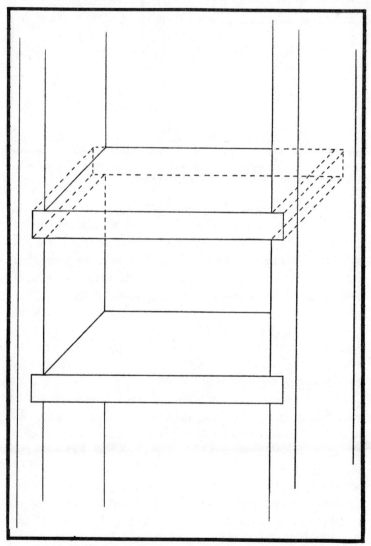

Fig. 10-4. One of the most effective ways to set shelves is in dadoes.

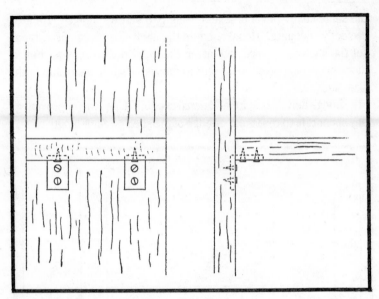

Fig. 10-5. Shelf supported and secured by angle brackets or braces, which may be either mortised (shown here) or surface-mounted.

and then tie each shelf to one or more strategically located vertical rails, as shown in Fig. 10-6. Where the shelf section has a face-frame around the perimeter, it is a simple matter to add a center stile which is nailed or screwed to each shelf edge it passes. However, shelf front edge support is then dependent upon a dab of glue and a pair of nails or screws driven into a relatively thin piece of material. That support may not be adequate, as in the case of bookshelves. Much greater strength can be obtained by gluing and nailing an additional support post behind the stile and between each shelf (Fig. 10-7). The posts are not noticeable at a casual glance, and do not interfere with items placed on the shelves.

Where a continuous cleat under the back edge of a long shelf is impractical or undesirable, you can use back standards. At appropriate distances along the length of the shelf, mount vertical boards against the cabinet back; two-inch-wide solid wood stock is a good choice. Notch the shelves to fit snugly over the standards, and secure each shelf at each standard with a small angle bracket beneath the shelf. You can use this same trick to support the front edges of long shelves by screwing more angle brackets to the support stiles.

Adjustable shelves are usually installed in one of three ways. They can be placed within cabinetry or casework which is self-supporting, or in an open framework assembly which is usually semipermanent but may be permanently affixed in some manner, or by means of shelf standards attached to the walls of the house. In simplest fashion, the shelving is simply laid across shelf brackets attached to the walls. The standards may either be mounted directly on the wall surfaces (Fig. 10-8) or mortised into wood strips for a more decorative appearance. Another type of standard can be mounted, either surface or flush, in pairs on the shelving side pieces to provide support at each end of each shelf (Fig. 10-9).

Another possibility is to cut dado grooves in the shelf side pieces in a continuous series about 2 inches apart. The grooves have to extend the full-depth of the side pieces, and be unobstructed by any face-frame or trim molding. Then the shelves can be slid in and out of the grooves at whatever levels are most appropriate. One way to accomplish this without making all of those dado cuts is to use a special type of plywood in which the grooves have already been cut

Fig. 10-6. This shelf is supported at the rear by a cleat, and in midspan at the front by a face-frame stile. Duncan Photos.

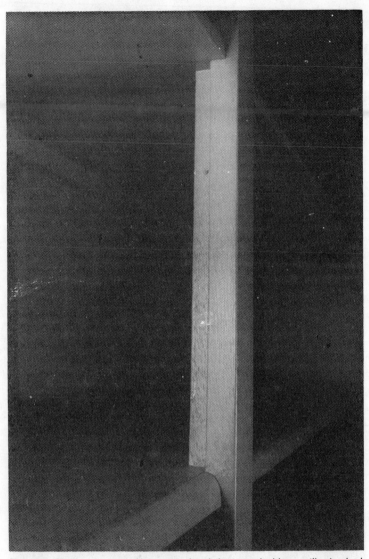

Fig. 10-7. Shelves supported by rear and end cleats, and midspan stiles backed by support posts. Duncan Photos.

at the factory. This is an exterior type of plywood principally used for finish siding on houses. One kind is called Texture 1-11, and it is available in several different groove spacings. You can match the thickness of the shelving stock to fit the grooves or you can cut a shallow rabbet at each end of the shelf to make it match up. The bottom side of this plywood is of low grade, and so must be covered with another material for the sake of appearance, or used in such a way that the back cannot be seen.

Shelving sections need not necessarily be housed cabinet-style, or built with solid end pieces. There are many designs where open end pieces serve the function of retaining the shelves and at the

Fig. 10-8. Either simple shelves or complex shelving systems can be mounted on brackets which look into rail-type tracks. Duncan Photos.

Fig. 10-9. Standards and clips supporting shelves in cabinet. This system can also be used for open or partly enclosed shelving. Duncan Photos.

same time enhance the decor. These open end pieces usually consist of a sturdy vertical rail located at each shelf corner, and either are attached to the building structure or constructed as a sturdy free-standing skeletal framework. Many of the same methods of attaching the shelves that are mentioned above may also be used with open-ended construction. Angle brackets work nicely, and so do cleats. The cleats may be short ones, extending only for the width of the individual corner supports, or they may run full depth of the shelves so that each end piece becomes in effect a ladder. Metal shelf standards can be surface- or flush-mounted on the end supports, and used in the normal fashion. A good choice for fixed shelving is the corner dado joint shown in Fig. 7-3C. This joint will also add to the overall strength of the shelf section.

Another way to support shelves, one that works with either open-end or closed-side shelf construction, is to use either dowels or shelf pins made especially for the purpose. Fixed shelves can be attached to side pieces or corner supports by setting dowels blind in both members and fitting them together (Fig. 10-10). This works particularly well where both shelf stock and side piece stock is 1½-inch-thick material. Here you can use ¾-inch hardwood dowel stock for a solid and sturdy shelf joint. An alternative method is to drill entirely through each side piece and into the shelf ends for an equal distance, and then drive hardwood pegs into the holes. Make the hole depth a bit greater than the peg length to allow space for glue. You can provide a much more flexible arrangement by drilling a series of holes, either through or deep-blind, in the side-pieces. Use short sections of dowel, two or three per shelf end, and merely rest the shelves upon these pegs at whatever heights are desired. The same thing can be accomplished by using shelf pins (Fig. 10-11). Or, in either case, the shelving can be made nonadjustable but remova-

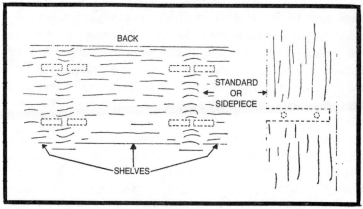

Fig. 10-10. Method of blind-doweling shelves to standards or side pieces.

ble by setting the pegs or pins only in predetermined locations, with no extra holes for additional adjustment.

There are literally dozens of ways to build shelves and shelving units, some of them most imaginative. For instance, you might cut a set of several shelves to the same dimensions and then bore through-holes slightly in from each corner of each shelf. Run a length of hemp or jute rope through each set of holes, tying single overhand knots identical distances apart in the rope for each shelf to rest upon. Then, tie the free ends of the four ropes to heavy screw eyes or eyebolts mounted securely in the ceiling.

Another design makes use of two or more 4-inch by 4-inch finished posts. Cut the bottoms perfectly flat and saw off the tops so that they will be within 1 or 2 inches of the ceiling. Secure tensioning devices to the tops and wedge the posts into place against the ceiling. Attach bracket standards to two opposite sides of each post and set the brackets and shelves into place. This will give you a two-sided, open-effect, movable or removable shelving section.

Another shelf arrangement that can be most interesting starts off not as shelving, but as a collection of boxes. Make a whole series of boxes, all of different heights, widths, and depths. They can have backs (or bottoms) or not, as you wish. Pick an appropriate spot in the house and start stacking them up on their sides. If the boxes have bottoms, you can arrange them so that they all are flush on one side, presenting a blank surface as a solid room divider. Or they can be backed up against a wall. Just keep stacking them up every which way, until you get a combination whose appearance pleases you. The box sides are now shelves, some deep, some shallow, some narrow, some wide. When you arrive at a final arrangement, you can bolt them all together at points where the hardware is relatively invisible, and end up with an extremely sturdy and stable semipermanent installation. If the boxes are merely frames with no bottoms, you can use them as a room divider and arrange them so that they are stacked unevenly on both sides and are equally usable from either side.

There are so many ways to put shelving together, and to install shelves in cabinets, built-ins, storage units, and furniture, that it would be totally impossible to cover them all. But by making use of some of the information and methodology just discussed, plus the exercise of some ingenuity and imagination, you can tackle about any shelving project that might crop up. The following chapters will

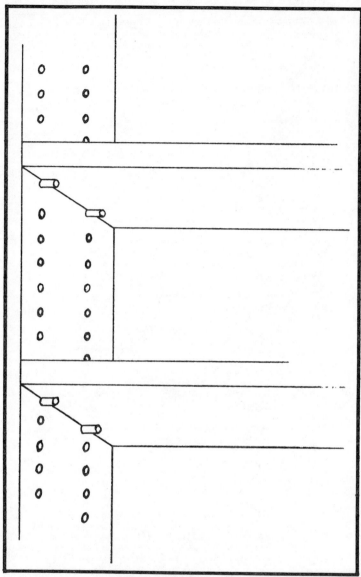

Fig. 10-11. Method of mounting fully adjustable shelves on pegs or pins set into the standards or side pieces.

give you some further information, as shelves are installed in both fixed and adjustable modes in multipurpose cabinet sections, and also in special purpose cabinetry and casework where shelving is an integral part of the assembly.

Chapter 11
Base Cabinets

Base cabinets, or base units as they are sometimes called, all have one thing in common: they stand upon the floor. Base cabinets are primarily thought of in connection with the kitchen cabinetry system. They comprise a large portion of the kitchen storage, serve to house some appliances, and also form the framework upon which the all-important countertops are placed. However, there are many other applications for base cabinets of various designs, and they may be used in virtually any part of the home. Some kinds of sideboards and servers used as dining area furnishings are base cabinets; vanities are base cabinets; built-in refreshment bars are base cabinets; even mobile food preparation centers and sewing centers are actually little more than base cabinets on castors.

The designs and functions of base cabinets are infinitely variable, and can easily be made to fit any particular set of circumstances. With the kitchen base cabinet, however, the design has been standardized to some degree. The depth of the cabinet at countertop level is usually 25 inches. Sometimes the cabinet is made with the front face flush with the countertop edge, in which case the overall depth of the cabinet is also 25 inches. More often, however, a lipped countertop is used and the face of the cabinet set back an inch or two, with a total depth of 22 or 23 inches. The width of a kitchen base cabinet assembly is usually determined by the size of the room and the layout of the cabinetry and appliances. Standard height is 36 inches.

Though the height and depth dimensions noted above are considered to be standard, there is no reason why they cannot be changed. This particularly true of the height. An even 3 feet might well be uncomfortable for many, and should be adjusted to suit the needs and comfort of those who habitually use the counter space. Note that just a slight change in the countertop height, even only half an inch, can make a pronounced difference in working comfort. Before designing and building a base cabinet whose top will be in constant use as a workspace, make a careful determination of exactly what height above finished floor level is optimum for the principal users.

Base cabinets may be designed and fitted out in combination of whatever storage facilities suit your needs the best. Shelving of various depths and heights, enclosed by cupboard doors, along with a series of drawers, is the most popular combination. However, all sorts of special designs can be implemented. These might include such things as slide-out vegetable and fruit bins, pop-up appliance shelves, swing-out wastebasket or garbage can shelves, special storage racks for pots, pans, mixing bowls, and small appliances, and any one of a thousand other items. Base cabinets which are used in other areas of the house, like the living room or rec room or the baths, are usually designed to fit the specific circumstances.

The materials and hardware used to build base cabinets are for the most part standard items commonly available anywhere. Softwood plywood or particle board is widely used for the larger pieces, with solid woods, either hard or soft, used for cleats, supports, and face-frames. Hardwood plywoods are frequently chosen when an attractive natural or transparent finish is desired. The wood itself provides the decorative effect, together with the trim and finish hardware. Countertopping may be a laminated plastic bonded to plywood or particle board, or may be ceramic tile, stone or pavers, sheet vinyl, or some other serviceable material. Where the base cabinet is designed more as a furnishing than as a utility unit, the top may be more akin to a tabletop than a countertop. In this case, a furniture finish or a paint may be applied to a wood surface.

There are two principal ways in which base cabinets can be constructed, regardless of their specific application. One way is by the built-in process, whereby the entire cabinet is built from scratch at its installation site. The second way is by casework construction, whereby the cabinet is built as a freestanding unit in the workshop, then transported to the installation site. There are advantages and disadvantages to both methods.

Built-in construction works particularly well where a cabinet must be fitted into an existing opening or niche. This is especially true where one or both sides of the space are bounded by walls, window or door casings, other cabinets, or existing structural or architectural features of some sort. Because each element of the cabinet is fitted into place as the job progresses, there are fewer chances for incorrect measurements or improper component fittings than if the same assembly were made in the workshop from a set of sketches and dimensions. This method is also easier where the various elements of the cabinet location are out of line with one another. A sloping floor which is out of square with a wall, a wall which is not plumb or is wavy, or a bounding wall or door casing which is neither plumb nor square to other nearby structural elements, makes little difference to built-in cabinet construction, except for the fact that extra work and care is involved. As the assembly is put together, each piece is cut and fitted to make allowances for any discrepancies found at the cabinet location. When the job is complete, and if done correctly, the door and drawer openings and the shelving will be plumb, level, and square unto themselves, irrespective of any surrounding problems.

Another advantage of built-in cabinet construction is the fact that in many (though not all) cases less material is required to complete the job. Often the floor, the wall against which the assembly will rest, and sometimes adjacent walls or other structural components of the home itself serve as anchoring and support points for the cabinet as well as a part of the cabinet itself, such as a back or side. The completed assembly will derive a large portion of its strength and rigidity from its attachment to an existing immovable structure. Furthermore, less material will probably be needed. Built-in cabinets are often easier than workshop cabinets to install merely because there is a stable existing starting point: the house itself.

The built-in construction method also lends itself quite nicely to large cabinet assemblies such as might be found in a kitchen. For instance, even though building a one-piece 16-foot kitchen base cabinet assembly in the workshop and then moving it into place would certainly be possible under the right circumstances, it would hardly be practical in most instances. Constructing the same assembly right at the installation site is not difficult, and is practical. An alternative method would be to construct several smaller sections in the shop, then join them into a single large assembly at the installation site. This is a common practice, and in fact is the method by which factory-made cabinet sections are assembled into a complete kitchen cabinet installation. For the home craftsman, however, the amount of labor and effort involved in that process is likely to exceed the task of building in an entire unit at the installation site. Trimming, shimming, and fitting a series of cabinets into place to make one unit can be quite a chore. Certainly a greater amount of material and a higher level of construction quality are required for the fabrication of a series of modules which must later be fitted to make up a complete installation.

There are some disadvantages to built-in construction, too. One is that the job site becomes your workshop, and you have to have sufficient room in which to operate. This means that furnishings may have to be shoved out of the way to gain more space, normal activities in the vicinity may have to be suspended, and tools, hardware, and lumber will be underfoot for the duration of the job. Sawhorses, power tools and extension cords, and an inevitable layer of shavings, sawdust and chips may spread even into the next room, much to the dismay of the rest of the family. Another problem is that while you are doing the job here, your tools and equipment and hardware are over there—in the workshop. The table saw, the shaper and other heavy power tools will also probably have to remain in the shop. This means a great deal of trailing back and forth from workshop to job site to trim a part or cut a dado or retrieve some forgotten tool or piece of hardware. This gets wearisome, and can easily lengthen the time span of a particular job, especially if it is a large and complex one.

Another potential problem lies in the level of cabinet quality which can be obtained through the built-in method. To digress a bit, there is general agreement that the highest quality of cabinetry is found in the top lines of commercially manufactured cabinet assemblies, which are delivered as complete units and then fitted into place. At the bottom of the quality level scale is the built-in type of cabinetry that we are discussing now. Generally, the least expensive commercially made cabinetry is considered to be on a par with the better, or even best, grades of built-in cabinetry. According to the consensus, then, the homeowner is better off to buy factory-made cabinets and then install them, or have them installed.

Now, this is all well and good, but is also an arguable situation from the standpoint of the home craftsman. Granted, the top-line factory-made cabinetry is indeed of excellent quality, on a par with the finest of furniture. But the point must be made that not all of us want, need, or can afford this sort of quality. Then, there is also some reasonable question as to whether the cheapest factory-made cabinets are indeed superior to top quality built-in cabinetry. Often, this simply is not so. Another point, high quality commercially made cabinetry is constructed with special equipment, processes, and techniques which are not normally available to the home craftsman. Complex joinery, superb finishes, a wide assortment of materials, expert gluing and other techniques do indeed make for fine finished products. But, again, the homeowner may not need all of this.

Another valid consideration is the fact that when using factory-made cabinetry, the cabinet installation must be designed around the specific products that a given manufacturer offers. What they make is what you choose from, and then live with. The only alternative is to have the factory build a complete custom-made installation, a horrendously expensive proposition and one that in many cases is not possible anyway. The home craftsman, however, can design and make his own custom cabinet installation, one which suits him and his requirements to a fine degree.

Economics also come into the picture. The fact that a particular line of factory-made cabinetry may be of higher quality than a similar built-in installation means little if the prospective owner thereof cannot afford the factory-made cabinetry in the first place. A contractor can purchase and install ready-made cabinetry for considerably less expense, at least in most installations, than he could custom-build the same installation. For the home craftsman, however, this is not true. The cost differential between buying the materials and doing the job himself and contracting the cabinet installation to a professional using either ready-made or custom-made cabinets is tremendous.

And lastly, there is the question of commensuration. The term "quality" is a nebulous one, dependent upon the criteria used to make the assessments, upon human judgment, and also to a degree upon personal preferences. Comparative level of quality may well be obscure to the user of the equipment, and an article of "high" quality may be of no more essential value to him then a similar article of "low" quality. The point is, the so-called quality of any particular piece of cabinetry should be proportionate to and commensurate with the function of the cabinetry, the surroundings in which the cabinetry will be installed, and the desires, needs, and finances of the user of the cabinetry. To boil this down even further, if you can build a kitchen base cabinet assembly, or any other type of cabinetry, which is sturdy and rugged, presents a fine and finished appearance in your judgment, is utilitarian, fulfills its functions, and will enjoy a long and useful lifespan without collapsing into a pile of kindling, then you have attained a level of quality well in line with your needs. Higher quality, however fine, probably will accrue no additional benefits directly to you. Unless, of course, you enjoy exercising your skills and expertise to the highest possible level, or you just need an ego boost. That's entirely another matter.

Time to terminate this digression on cabinet quality and to turn to an examination of the advantages and disadvantages of building cabinets by the casework method. Casework construction of cabinets is particularly suitable for medium-sized and small articles which are easy to handle and can be set into place without much trouble. The process involves first designing a layout for the cabinetry, and then cutting, joining, and assembling all the pieces into a complete unit in the workshop. This is a convenient method simply because all the tools, materials, and hardware are right at hand, and the whole job takes place in an area specifically designed for this kind of work, the shop. The noise, the sawdust, the tools and the shavings all stay out of the living quarters, much to the delight of the rest of the family. In some cases, the amount of time and effort expended on a particular project may be considerably less than if the same article were built into place. Sometimes the job is easier, too, since there is no need to crawl about on the floor in awkward positions, or endlessly tromp up and down a stepladder. Because of the nature of the construction process, you may be able to use more complex joinery and more intricate decorative details than would be practical with the built-in process.

On the other hand, some cabinet designs might require more time, effort and materials than would built-in construction. If the completed cabinet must be installed in a tight spot, or where abutting and adjoining elements are out of plumb or square, or where there are tricky architectural configurations, the installation process might be a difficult one, and perhaps even impossible. If the cabinet project is a substantial one, simple logistics may dictate against using casework construction. Manhandling a large cabinet section about and securing it into place can be a difficult proposition. Like the fellow who built the boat in his basement, you could end up with a few problems. This is not so say that casework construction cannot be used where a large section of cabinetry must be assembled, as in a full-length kitchen base cabinet installation. Usually it is necessary and more effective to build a series of small casework cabinets which can then be set into place, fitted, and secured. This process may well require more time and labor, as well as more material, than a built-in structure of identical capabilities.

The decision as to whether to build cabinets on-site or to construct casework in the shop and then install the complete assembly depends upon both circumstances and preferences. Obviously, the casework method is the one to use for freestanding pieces. On-site construction is called for when the cabinet design is complex or has to be installed in an existing niche bounded by other items. Compare the advantages and disadvantages noted above, relate them to your situation of cabinet design and location, as well as to your own skills and available equipment, and choose the easiest course.

On the following pages are two examples of base cabinets, one an on-site job and the other a casework project. The steps that are outlined represent the essential procedures in building any kind of base cabinet, regardless of its intended use. In some cases, the order of the steps may actually be somewhat different. Similarly, various kinds of materials and hardware could be used, the dimensions modified, the number and size of drawers and doors changed, or any one of a thousand other variations introduced. By following the broad outlines, however, you can adjust and rearrange and make changes to suit your circumstances. For the sake of illustration, both projects are constructed in simple fashion, yet with adequate strength to serve their purposes well and long. The complexity of the joinery, the overall strength and rigidity, and the "quality" level can be increased as much as you want by using locking joints, screws, glue, glue blocking, extra braces, heavier material, and extra-fine finishes.

BUILDING AN ON-SITE CABINET

The instructions for building an on-site cabinet are set down here in somewhat greater detail than the instructions for building a casework cabinet. Therefore, it would behoove the builder of a casework cabinet to study the procedural steps for building an on-site cabinet before turning to those directly related to his own project.

Step 1

The first step in building a base cabinet is to establish preliminary plans and to formulate a general cabinet design. Take some rough measurements of the space where the cabinet will be installed. Then, determine the various uses to which the cabinet will be put, and figure out what you will need in the way of drawers, doors, and shelves. Include any special items which will be housed in the cabinet section, like a pull-out pastry board, a chopping block, a built-in food preparation center, a range top or a sink.

Now, sketch out a rough elevation arrangement so that you can get some idea of what the finished cabinet will look like (Fig. 11-1). There is no need for this sketch to be anything fancy, and you may run through several drawings before you strike one that suits you. Once you have the generalities set down, it is a good idea to draw out a plan of the cabinet, as seen from directly in front, to rough scale, just to make sure that everything will fit in. This will allow you to balance out the numbers and sizes of drawer fronts and doors for a pleasing overall effect. You will quickly discover if some of the storage elements are going to be too large or too small, or if you have too much of one type and not enough of another. Chances are, you will need no further detailed plans for the construction of the cabinet, especially if you are able to visualize exactly how the cabinet will go together. Most of the dimensions can be taken directly from the job as it progresses.

Step 2

Now you must make a number of decisions. Decide what kind of materials you will use to build the cabinet, determine the decorative effects you would like, settle upon all of the hardware items, pick the countertopping, and choose a final finish. Then gather all the materials and hardware together before beginning actual construction. It

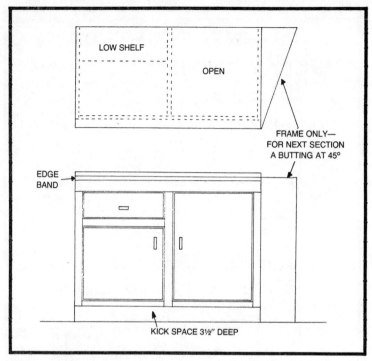

Fig. 11-1. Sketch of base cabinet project, drawn to rough scale. Dimensions and construction details, hardware and finish call-outs can be added as desirable to make a full set of working plans and specs.

is especially important to have everything on hand, so that you can build in accordance with whatever demands are made by hardware dimensions and types, and so that design, components, construction methods, and finish are compatible.

Step 3

The first step in construction is to mount the cabinet floor back support cleat. Begin by establishing whether or not the floor where it joins the wall is level. If it not, find the highest point and make a mark on the wall to indicate the spot. The top edge of the cleat must be high enough to provide an adequate kick space or toe strip at the front of the cabinet. Normal height for a kick space is about 2½ inches. For big feet that wear boots, however, 3½ inches is better and is also a stock lumber width, which helps make the construction easier. So, measure up 3½ inches from the high point on the floor line and make a mark on the wall. From this point run a level line in

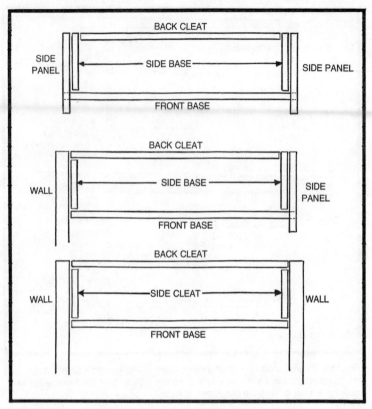

Fig. 11-2. Ways of fitting the base frame pieces together.

both directions at least as long as the overall width of the cabinet section. If the cabinet butts up against a wall at either end, continue the level line on either or both of those walls. Next, determine where the outside of each cabinet end piece will come, and mark the location. The next step depends upon the situation.

If a cleat will be installed only along a back wall, then a front base piece and a side piece at each end of the cabinet will be needed. Subtract the thickness of the base piece plus the thickness of the cabinet side piece from each end of the overall length of the back cleat. If the cabinet is bounded by one wall, then subtract only the thickness of one base piece and one cabinet end panel. If the cabinet is bounded by two walls, the back cleat will run full length, wall-to-wall. Where side cleats are used, subtract from the total length of the side cleat the thickness of the front base support, plus the depth of the toe strip (usually about 3 inches). The sketches in Fig. 11-2 will indicate how this is done. The important thing to remember is that you are working from the inside out, and have to make allowances for the thicknesses of those pieces which will be installed later. Once you have the dimensioning sorted out, go ahead and nail the cleats firmly to the wall studs and sole plate (Fig. 11-3). The cleat material can be almost anything of a minimum ¾-inch thickness, even a series of scraps.

Next comes the installation of the base sides and front. There are no base sides if cleats are used at each side, or only one base side where one side cleat is used opposite. Nail one end of each base side to the ends of the back cleat. Cut the base front piece to length, and nail it to the free ends of the base sides, or to the side cleat(s). In the case of cleats, they will be level. Base side pieces, however, may not be, since they will follow the floor. Both side pieces and front piece

Fig. 11-3. The back cleat, properly leveled and centered, being nailed to the wall studs and sole plate. Plastic film on floor is a part of the vapor barrier system which will eventually cover the whole subfloor. Duncan Photos.

Fig. 11-4. Attaching front base piece to extra cross support. Side base pieces are already in place. Duncan Photos.

may have to be notched, tapered, or shimmed up so that the top surface of the base frame will be level at all points and in all directions, and even with the back cleat. Once the proper position is established, secure the base frame to the floor by toenailing at hidden points, and/or with the use of nailing blocks at appropriate spots (Fig. 11-4). When the base frame is complete, it should be a solid part of the existing house structure, and perfectly level. Don't forget to make an allowance for base front piece overlap to cover the end grain of each cabinet side piece.

To arrive at the proper overall depth of the base frame from front to back, start with the overall depth of the countertop. If the countertop is exactly 25 inches deep, for instance, then the cabinet face beneath will probably be inset somewhat to allow for a counter overhang or lip. The bottom of the cabinet face further indents to form the toe strip or kick space. The base depth, then, must be equal to the width of the countertop minus the counter edge lip, minus the depth of the kick space. With a 3-inch kick space and a 1½-inch lip, the front to back depth of the base frame would then be 20½ inches (Fig. 11-5).

If the cabinet is a long one, more than about 3 feet, nail additional cabinet floor supports into place, running from front to back inside the base frame. Cut them to a reasonably close fit and toenail them to the floor of the house, or to nailing blocks, and to the base front piece. As you do so, make sure that the frame itself

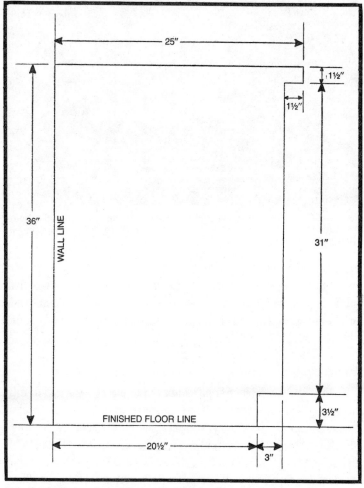

Fig. 11-5. Typical dimensions for base cabinet assembly.

Fig. 11-6. Cabinet floor being attached to base frame with glue and nails. Note the extended base front piece, which will later match up with the side panel. Duncan Photos.

remains level, and that the top edges of the added supports are perfectly in line with the base frame edges to present an entirely flat surface upon which the cabinet floor will rest. Humps and bumps and unevenness will just make matters more difficult as construction proceeds.

Step 4

Now cut the cabinet floor and fit it into place. Each end of the floor piece should be flush with the base sides or base end cleats, and fit snugly against the wall at the rear. The forward part of the floor should overhang the base front piece by an amount equal to the total depth of the kick space minus the thickness of the stock which will be used for the face-frame. When the floor is properly fitted, carefully mark the location of all of the base frame members, using a pencil or chalk line. Remove the floor, apply glue to all top edges of the base frame, and set the floor back into place (Fig. 11-6). Check to make sure of proper alignment, and then nail the floor down tight.

Step 5

Install the cleat which will support the back of the cabinet countertop, as well as side cleats to support the countertop ends where cabinet sides are not to be used. Note that you can set a full side piece or pieces even though the cabinet may be bounded by one or two side walls. This will give you a flat, solid structural component to which you can easily secure shelf cleats, the countertop, and the face-frame. In some instances, this is a much better situation than trying to fasten cabinet parts to a hollow wall covered with plasterboard or relatively weak plaster and lath.

First, determine the overall height of the cabinet, from finished floor level to finished countertop level. The normal height is 36

Fig. 11-7. Countertop back cleat being secured to the wall studs, properly leveled and lined up with the cabinet bottom below. Duncan Photos.

Fig. 11-8. Side panel fitted into place and being nailed to the countertop back cleat. Duncan Photos.

inches, but there is no reason this figure cannot be changed if you wish. The cook may request somewhat lower or higher counters; the object is to make the working conditions as comfortable as possible. A change in counter height of only an inch or even less can make a surprising difference. When you establish a proper figure for your counters, subtract the thickness of the countertop and run a level line at the appropriate point on the wall. Nail the back cleat into place (Fig. 11-7), and the side cleats if they are used. Follow much the same process as you did when installing the base cleats, remembering to allow room to fit the side pieces in. The length of the side cleats, or the width of the cabinet side pieces, should be figured with an allowance for the face-frame and for any back joints which might be used.

Step 6

If you are using side pieces, these can be put in next. Before cutting the pieces, check to see whether the cabinet floor is exactly at right angles to the back wall. If the wall runs in or out with respect to the cabinet floor, cut the back edges of the side pieces to match. If you do not, the side pieces will not sit properly, and you will have trouble later fitting the rest of the parts together. Once you are sure the pieces are correct, set them in place plumb and square and nail them to the base frame side along the bottom, and to the ends of the counter back support cleat (Fig. 11-8). Or, if the cabinet sides adjoin bounding walls, nail the side pieces securely to the wall studs.

If you are using countertop side support cleats instead of side pieces, secure a vertical face-frame support cleat between the bottom edge of each side cleat and the cabinet floor (Fig. 11-9). This will give you a solid mount to which the side stiles of the face-frame will later be nailed.

Fig. 11-9. Where side panels are not used, install a vertical cleat from countertop side cleat to cabinet floor to support the face-frame stile. Duncan Photos.

Fig. 11-10. Divider panel, notched around the countertop back cleat, being positioned and checked for proper fit. Duncan Photos.

Step 7

If there are any divider panels which separate the cabinet into sections, they can be installed now. Cut and fit the panels so that the front edges are flush with the cabinet floor front edge and are plumb, with the back edges fitting snugly against the wall and notched around the countertop support cleat. Use glue and toenails to secure them in place while the work continues (Fig. 11-10). At this point they will not be sturdy at all, but this problem will be corrected later.

Step 8

Establish the height of the shelving and draw in appropriate level lines to mark all shelf locations. Cut cleats to support the shelf back edges, and nail them in place to the wall studs (Fig. 11-11). If you can, stagger the shelf heights slightly in adjacent compartments, and then nail the side pieces or divider panels to the ends of the shelf cleats. You may wish also to put cleats in place on the side pieces or divider panels to support the shelf ends. Or, you can nail through the side pieces or divider panels directly into the shelf ends, and not bother with end cleats. As long as the loading factor is not too high, this will work fine.

Fig. 11-11. Setting back support cleat for shelf. Note angle drill, handy for working in tight or awkward spots. Duncan Photos.

Fig. 11-12. Installing shelf, using simple butt joints and ends with glue and nails. Duncan Photos.

Step 9

Now, cut and fit the shelving. Glue and nail the shelves to the support cleats, and also to the side pieces and/or divider panels if possible (Fig. 11-12).

Step 10

The next chore is to build the face-frame. Solid wood stock of ¾-inch thickness works well for this, especially since no added edge treatment is necessary. Start by installing the top rail, which runs full length from side to side. Set the top edge of the rail flush with the top edges of the side pieces or cleats and divider panels. The ends of the top rail should be flush with the outside surfaces of the side pieces, or butted snugly against the walls. Make sure that the rail is level and properly lined up, and that the lead edges of the divider panels are plumb and not cocked slightly to the left or right. Then glue and nail the rail in place (Fig. 11-13).

The side stiles are next. Fit them into place, butted tight against the bottom of the top rail with bottom ends flush with the bottom surface of the cabinet floor. The outside edges of the stiles should be flush with the outside surfaces of the side pieces, or butted tight against bounding walls. When properly fitted, glue and nail the stiles into place. Toenail at the inside angle of each upper flat butt joint, where the stile joins the top rail (Fig. 11-14). Then, follow the same procedures for installing the center stiles. These will cover the raw edges of the divider panels. You may be using other stiles as well to separate door and drawer openings.

Fig. 11-13. Top rail of face-frame being nailed into place. Side and divider panel top corners must be carefully aligned. Duncan Photos.

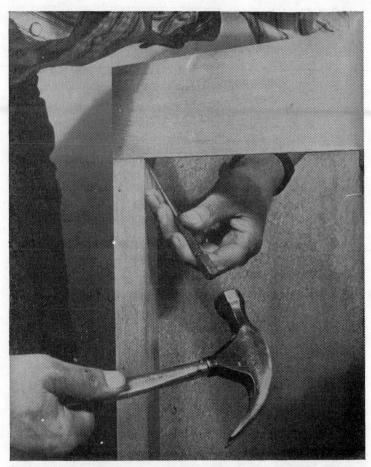
Fig. 11-14. Face-frame side stile is glued and nailed to side panel, then toenailed to top rail. Duncan Photos.

Fit the cross rails next. In some cases, these may be nailed directly across a shelf edge. If so, all that is necessary is to cut the rail to length and glue or nail it into place, toenailing at the flat butt joint angles. Where the cross rails are used as dividers between drawers, back supports must be added. First, cut and fit the cross rail. Then, cut a longer and narrower piece of stock which will fit crosswise inside the cabinet, in back of the cross rail and secured to the inside of the stiles. Glue and nail this piece to the back of the cross rail, and glue the assembly into place between the stiles. Clamp the assembly firmly in place (Fig. 11-15), nail the back support piece to the stile backs and then toenail the cross rail to the stiles at each butt joint angle.

All that remains now is to add the bottom rail. In this case, a piece of ¾-inch matching stock is applied to cover the raw edge of the bottom shelf. Cut the pieces to fit, and glue and nail them into place.

Step 11

If any raw edges still remain exposed on the shelving or other parts, apply an edge molding with glue and nails or a veneer tape. A thin strip of solid wood is used to cover the shelf edges in Fig. 11-16.

Step 12

This step is optional, but worthwhile. The addition of gussets to each corner formed by the side pieces, divider panels, back cleats, and front top rails will greatly strengthen the cabinet assembly. Cut some triangles of solid wood stock and fit them into place at each

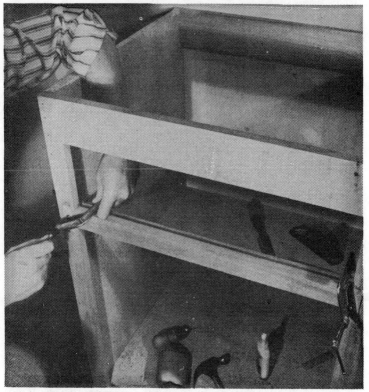

Fig. 11-15. Drawer divider cross rail with its back support being clamped into position prior to nailing. Duncan Photos.

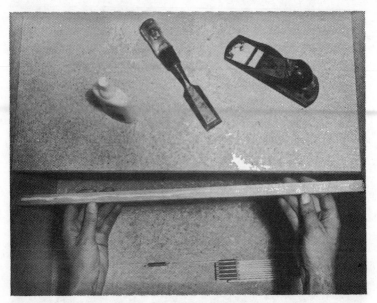

Fig. 11-16. Edging being applied to shelf edge. Duncan Photos.

corner, flush with the top edge of the cabinet, and secure them with glue and screws (Fig. 11-17).

Step 13

Cut the countertop to size and fit it into place. Check to make sure that it is level and even, and lies flat along the back cleat, side cleats or side pieces, and divider panel top edges. Make sure there are no gaps along the front top rail. Check the overhang or lip of the countertop at several spots to make sure that the distance between the countertop edges and the cabinet frame remains even. Find the exact location of all hidden members into which you will nail, and draw corresponding nailing guidelines on the counter surface so that you will not nail through into thin air. Remove the countertop and apply glue to all the nailing surfaces. Reset the top and nail it down tight (Fig. 11-18).

Step 14

The treatment of the countertop edge can be done in a number of ways. Which way often depends on the finished surface of the countertop. If that surface is to be a plastic laminate, you can apply the laminate first, and then put on a shaped wood edge, a plain and full-width wood edge, or various sorts of metal edges. Or, you can use a postformed edge where the laminate (post forming grade) follows a precut rounded counteredge. You can make a selfedge, where the laminate is first applied across a flat countertop edge, then to the top surface of the countertop, with another strip of laminate applied to the underside of the countertop lip.

In this particular project, a method known as edge banding is used. This involves attaching a strip of wood along the underside and flush with the countertop edge, doubling the thickness of the edge. Cut solid wood strips from ¾-inch stock in the same width as the depth of the countertop lip. Attach the strips with glue and nails or screws to form the edge band (Fig. 11-19). Trim and smooth the

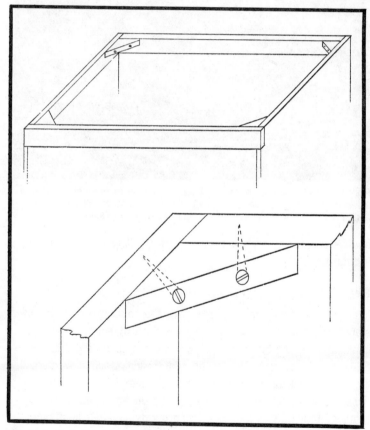

Fig. 11-17. Gussets can be glued and screwed into top corners of cabinet frame. This system for gaining added strength and rigidity can be used at any hidden corner point.

Fig. 11-18. Installing counter top. Left section is of laminated rock maple in a natural finish, secured from below with blocks and brackets. Right section is particle board, to be later covered with laminated plastic. Duncan Photos.

doubled countertop edge so that it is perfectly flat and the two pieces are flush.

Step 15

Now the finish can be applied to the countertop. In this instance, we will use a laminated plastic. Start by applying a strip of laminate along the edge band of the countertop. Position the strip flush with the bottom edge of the edge banding, and allow a small amount to stick up beyond the upper surface of the countertop. Spread contact cement on the strip and on the countertop edge banding. Allow the cement to set up properly, and then position the laminate strip. Remember, you only have one chance; so get the alignment right the first time. Roll the edge banding with a roller, or tap it gently with a hammer and block, to make sure that all the laminate is fully bonded. Then, trim off the protruding top rim of the edge banding so that it is square to and flush with the countertop surface. You can use a router or a special plastic laminate trimmer to do this.

Cut the plastic laminate pieces which will be applied to the countertop surface. The back edge can be set flush with the rear wall, or be inserted into a special molding made for the purpose. The same is true of the sides if the cabinet is fitted between two walls. Cut the laminate for an exact fit, but leave a small amount overhanging the front edge of the counter (side edges, too, if the cabinet sides are open to view). Spread on the contact cement, allow it to set up, and put the laminate in place. Roll or tap the surface gently, and then trim the exposed edges as you did with the edge banding, either squared or beveled.

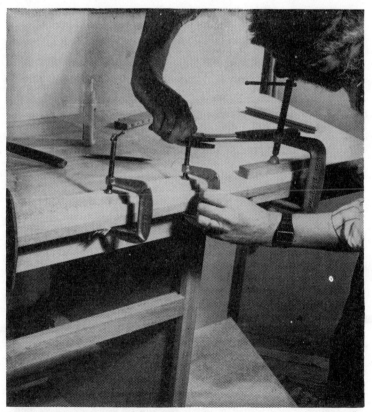

Fig. 11-19. Edge band being glued and clamped in place. Lip will be covered with laminated plastic edging later. Duncan Photos.

Step 16

Fit the cabinet drawers into place and check for fit and alignment. This may involve the mounting of guide system hardware, or the installation of rails or other devices upon which the drawer will slide. Depending upon the size of the cabinet, the complexity of the drawer guide system, and the amount of work involved in installing the drawers, you may wish to complete this phase of the construction before putting the countertop on. Sometimes this additional accessibility to the cabinet interior makes the task a good deal easier.

Fit the cupboard doors and make any necessary adjustments. Now, hang the doors. Install any special hardware, accessories, or specialty items, and check the assembly over to make sure that you haven't forgotten anything.

Step 17

The last item on the agenda is to prepare all the wood surfaces for whatever final finish you have chosen. Remove the doors and drawers and any hardware which might interfere, and proceed with the finishing process.

BUILDING A CASEWORK CABINET

As an example of the way in which a casework cabinet is put together, we will use the simple cabinet illustrated in Fig. 11-20. The general construction principles are the same, regardless of the design complexity of the cabinet or the materials used. Adjust the dimensions, materials, hardware, and drawer/door configurations to suit your needs.

Step 1

As with any cabinetry project, the first step is to make decisions and lay out the plans. Decide upon the overall dimensions for the cabinet, select the material and hardware and lay them in, and make up sketch plans as necessary for the cabinet.

Step 2

Cut all of the pieces which will be used in making up the face-frame. You can use either hardwood or softwood of ¾-inch thickness, and suit the width of the rails and stiles to your own taste.

316

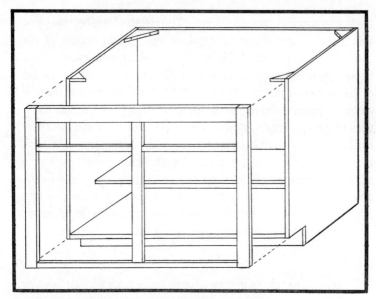

Fig. 11-20. Typical simple casework cabinet.

Mill stock of 1½-inch width is commonly used for this purpose, for both rails and stiles. Top rails are also often made from 3½-inch-wide stock. The dimensions of the pieces will be partially determined by the type of joints you plan to use, as well as by the design and overall dimensions of the cabinet.

Step 3

Lay out all of the face-frame pieces in their proper relationships on a flat, clean work surface. A sheet of hardboard or plywood atop sawhorses works well for this purpose. Mate all of the pieces together in their final positions, making sure that everything is square and all of the joints line up perfectly. If you are using other than butt joints, do the joinery work and assemble the pieces dry without fasteners. As you line up the parts, place them face down on the work surface.

When all is satisfactory, assemble the pieces permanently. Clamp as necessary, and allow the completed frame to cure.

Step 4

Cut out the bottom, side, and back pieces. The width of the bottom piece will equal the overall width of the cabinet, minus the thicknesses of the two side pieces. The depth of the bottom piece will be equal to the overall depth of the cabinet body (not the countertop), minus the thickness of the face-frame and the back panel. The height of the side pieces will be equal to the overall height of the cabinet, minus the thickness of the top. The width of the side pieces is equal to the overall width of the cabinet, minus the thickness of the face-frame. Don't forget to cut notches from the lower front corners of the side pieces to form the kick space. The back panel height is equal to the overall height of the cabinet minus the thickness of the top. The width of the back panel is equal to the overall width of the cabinet minus the thicknesses of the two side pieces. For joinery other than simple butt joints, make whatever dimensional adjustments are necessary as you cut the pieces.

Step 5

Glue and nail cleats along each side piece inner surface to act as end supports for the bottom piece. These cleats also make the assembly job a bit easier. Stand the side pieces up on their back edges, so that the edges to which the face-frame will later be mounted are facing you. Sandwich the bottom piece between the side pieces and snug against the cleats, and glue and nail the sides to the bottom. Clamping the parts together helps in the lining-up and fastening process.

Step 6

Set the completed face-frame into position on the front edges of the cabinet. Check for fit, make any adjustments that are necessary, and glue and nail the face-frame into place. Then cut and fit the toe strip, and glue and nail it to the side and bottom pieces.

Step 7

Stand the partially completed cabinet up on its base, taking care not to rack the still flimsy side pieces. Set the back piece into place, check for fit, and then secure it with glue and nails.

Step 8

Cut and fit a gusset to go at each corner of the cabinet, flush with the top edges. Glue blocks can also be put in at various advantageous spots for extra strength and rigidity, if you wish.

Step 9

Cut, fit, and install the shelves, using nails and glue. The shelves can be mounted on cleats, nailed to the sides and back of the cabinet case, or fitted into dadoes cut earlier.

Step 10

Install the drawer guide components, either hardware tracks or wooden guide and runner systems. Then put the drawers in place and check them for fit and ease of operation. Fit and hang the doors.

Step 11

Cut, fit, and install the top, using nails or screws and glue. Apply plastic laminate, tile, or other finish surface to the countertop.

Step 12

As always, the last step involves final surface preparation and the application of a finish. Remove the drawers, doors, and hardware, and go ahead with the finishing operation.

Step 13

This type of cabinet may be left freestanding and movable. However, you may wish to secure it to the building structure, as in the case of kitchen cabinetry. There are a number of ways to go about this. Usually, just a few long screws driven through the back of the cabinet and into the wall studs are sufficient to hold a cabinet in place. If you cannot locate the studs, you can use hollow wall fasteners run through the cabinet back and into the wall cavity. To further anchor the cabinet, you can nail a series of blocks to the floor along the front inside edge of the kick space, and then attach the cabinet to these blocks with wood screws. The same thing can be done along the sides of the cabinet. A certain amount of shimming, and perhaps some trimming, may be necessary. Check this before applying the final finish.

Chapter 12
Wall Cabinets

Wall cabinets, also called overhead cabinets, are most often thought of as being a part of the kitchen cabinetry installation. Indeed they are, but in various modifications and disguises, they are also found in many other parts of the home. A wall cabinet is essentially any cabinet which, not suprisingly, is mounted on a wall. Though usually the term implies cabinets attached to the upper portions of the wall, some may actually be only a few inches above floor level.

Kitchen wall cabinetry is almost invariably secured to the walls, or to the ceiling structure and against the walls, above the base cabinets or kitchen appliances. There are four distinctly different types. The full or standard wall cabinet extends from a point about 16 to 18 inches above the base cabinet countertops all the way to the ceiling level, or to a height of about 7 feet in open or cathedral ceiling home designs. Over-appliance cabinets are just that; the top of the cabinet lines up with the surrounding cabinetry, but the bottom is much higher than other cabinet bottoms. This type of cabinet is commonly used over refrigerators, freezers, and ranges. A combination wall cabinet includes both full and over-appliance cabinet sections in one module. Corner cabinets are designed to fit into corners, often with more cabinetry located immediately to one or both sides, and usually house triangular shelving or a multiple lazy susan.

In other areas of the home, wall cabinets may take on widely varying appearances. They may be full height, as over a sideboard or server, with cabinet sections to hold glassware and china, and possibly including some open display shelves as well. Small single- or double-shelf units, perhaps with glass doors, may be mounted at eye level to serve for display cases. A wall mounted gun cabinet is nothing more than a modified full wall cabinet. In a dining room of contemporary design, a casework wall cabinet may be mounted with the bottom a few inches above the floor and the top modified as a serving counter. This is not a base cabinet, because of the nature of its construction and the fact that it does not rest on the floor. Whatever the specific design, the finish or decoration, the size, or the intended use, if it hangs on the wall, it is a wall cabinet.

As with the base cabinets discussed earlier, there are two principal methods of building wall cabinets: (1) built-in construction and (2) casework construction. The built-in method works particularly well when you are constructing large sections of cabinetry with multiple storage compartments, as in a kitchen. It also is effective where ceiling and wall lines may not be level and plumb, or where the cabinets must be fitted between a pair of bounding walls, door or window casings, or other structural elements for furnishings of the home. Large sections of cabinets are not easy to mount high up on the wall as complete units, since they are so heavy and bulky. Nor can the installer be in several places at once to take care of all the checking, fitting, and leveling, plumbing and fastening that unavoidably must be done at the same time. Built-in cabinet construction takes care of that problem. In the main, the general advantages and disadvantages of built-in construction are the same as they were for base cabinets.

Casework construction can easily be applied to large pieces of wall cabinetry in the kitchen and elsewhere, but is especially good for smaller assemblies. Small cabinets are light, easy to handle, and conveniently built right in the workshop where a full array of tools and equipment is already on hand. This kind of cabinetry is most often hung on an open wall space, unbounded by other items. Practically no fitting is required and the process of mounting the cabinets on the wall is usually a simple one. There may actually be some savings in time and effort by using casework rather than built-in construction in these instances, and the difference in the quantity of material used is likely to be so small as to be inconsequential. Again, the general advantages and disadvantages noted earlier in the discussion of base cabinets also apply to wall cabinets.

In determining which type of construction to use, weigh the pros and cons in the light of your own skills and facilities. Then proceed with whichever method seems most suitable to the cabinet design and whatever installation problems there may be. Assuming that you do the job correctly and with good craftsmanship, the finished result will bear the same final appearance, and fulfill the same functions, with either method.

BUILT-IN WALL CABINET

The example that follows shows how a wall cabinet can be constructed using the built-in procedures. In this case, the illustrated cabinet is a three-section unit, full height, but deeper than a kitchen wall cabinet would be. Special dimensions are needed to provide room for electronics equipment in part of the cabinet. Materials used are ¾-inch particle board for the larger pieces, and solid mahogany for cleats and face-frame. Edging material is pine. The cabinet is bounded by walls on both sides. In this instance, the back wall slopes inward slightly towards the top, and has a slight double wave across its width. The left (facing) side wall is slightly out of square, and has a slight inward slant. This meant that as the job progressed, each piece had to be fitted exactly to its specific location.

Step 1

Establish the overall dimensions to the cabinet—height, width, and depth. Determine approximate shelf heights, location on the wall, and the general design and appearance of the cabinet. Choose joinery methods, if other than ordinary butt joints. Then, decide what kinds of stock to use, and what hardware, and lay in all the material. If necessary, make up rough sketches for later guidance. Continue these sketches throughout the course of the project, if you wish, to avoid running into problems such as improper joint fits, or incorrect piece dimensioning.

Step 2

With tape, ruler, straightedge, framing square, and any other helpful measuring devices, lay out the cabinet pattern on the wall

Fig. 12-1. Laying out wall cabinet directly on plasterboard wall. Duncan Photos.

surface (Fig. 12-1). Draw full pencil lines to show exactly where the side pieces will butt against the back wall and lie against the side walls, where the divider panels will fit, and where the shelves and shelf cleats will lie. Mark them in full dimensions, and place x's between the lines to indicate the areas where the edges of the material will rest. This will avoid the possibility of installing a piece in improper position above or below a line. Once the entire cabinet structure is outlined on the wall, double check to make sure that the cabinet is the proper height above the floor and below the ceiling, that the shelf spacings are to your liking, and so forth. Check to see whether the wall is plumb, and whether or not any bounding walls or other structural items are plumb and square. Also, verify that all of the horizontal lines you have drawn are level and square.

Step 3

Cut and fit the back side cleats to which the cabinet top will be nailed. Position them, making certain that they are level, and nail them to the wall studs (Fig. 12-2). For extra rigidity, two cross

Fig. 12-2. Nailing up top cleats to support cabinet top. Duncan Photos.

supports have been nailed to the ceiling joists to support the top piece at the one-third and two-thirds points. Cut the top piece to size and nail it to the cleats and cross supports (Fig. 12-3).

Fig. 12-3. Securing cabinet top piece to cleats, with shop broom wedging piece in place. Duncan Photos.

Fig. 12-4. Installing bottom shelf back support cleat. Duncan Photos.

Step 4

Cut and fit the back and side cleats which will support the full-length bottom shelf. Position them agains the level guidelines, and nail them to the wall studs (Fig. 12-4). (Note: Studs may not always be in the right places to afford good cleat nailing. Put in hollow wall fasteners wherever necessary to insure plenty of support.) Cut the bottom shelf to proper size, run a bead of glue along the top edges of the cleats, and set the shelf in place. Nail the shelf to the cleats, close to the points where the cleats are fastened to the wall structure (Fig. 12-5).

Step 5

Cut the two cabinet side pieces to proper width and height. Secure them into place (Fig. 12-6) by nailing to the wall studs. Shim as necessary to keep the pieces square. Apply glue to top and bottom edges, and carefully toenail the side-piece corners to the top piece and bottom shelf to keep everything lined up.

Fig. 12-5. Nailing bottom shelf into place. Duncan Photos.

Fig. 12-6. Installing right-hand side piece. Duncan Photos.

327

Fig. 12-7. Putting up shelf back support cleats in left-hand cabinet section. Duncan Photos.

Step 6

Cut the shelf cleats for the left-hand (facing) cabinet section to the proper size. The length should be accurate to one-sixtyfourth of an inch. Butt the cleats tight against the left side piece, using glue on the ends, and nail them to the wall studs (Fig. 12-7). Note: If one or both ends of this cabinet were show ends, open to view and unbounded by structural elements, this step and the previous one would be interchanged. The cleats would first be attached to the wall studs, and then the side pieces nailed to the cleat ends. The bottom shelf side cleats would not exist, and the bottom shelf would be installed later.

Step 7

Cut the divider panel which will separate the left-hand cabinet section from the center section. Here, the length and width of the divider panel is identical to that of the side pieces. Mark transverse guidelines on the top piece and bottom shelf, square to the leading edges and indicating the proper position for the panel. Set the panel in place, and mark the point where the cleat ends meet the panel in an edge butt joint. Take down the panel and drill a pair of nail holes at each butt joint location (Fig. 12-8). Apply glue to these points and the top and bottom edges. Set the panel back in place, and nail it to each shelf cleat end (Fig. 12-9). As you nail, make sure that the panel does not slip out of place, but remains snug against the wall and properly lines up with the cleats. Also, any runout in the plumb of the wall should be compensated for in the cut of the rear edge of the divider panel. If not, the front edge may tilt in or out, and be out of line with the end pieces (assuming that they are plumb). Nail up through the bottom shelf into the divider panel end, and toenail to top corner to the top piece. Or, if there is room enough to work, nail down through the top piece into the divider panel upper end.

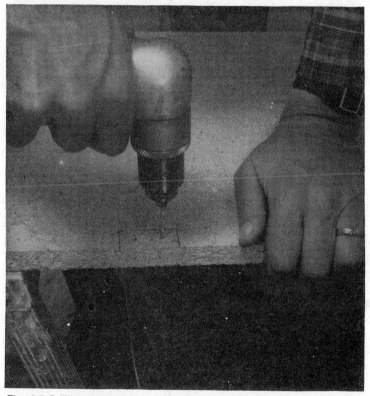

Fig. 12-8. Drilling pilot holes for nails where divider panel butts against shelf back cleat ends. Duncan Photos.

Fig. 12-9. Setting left-hand divider panel into place preparatory to nailing to shelf back cleat ends and to cabinet top and bottom pieces. Duncan Photos.

Step 8

Cut the shelf support cleats for the center section of the cabinet. Apply glue to the ends, and mount the cleats in place (Fig. 12-10). Nail the cleat to the wall studs. Nail through the left divider panel into the cleat ends. Then cut the right-hand divider panel and install it the same way you did the left-hand one.

Step 9

Mark level lines from each top corner of each shelf support cleat to the outer edges of the divider panels and the side pieces (Fig. 12-11). This will give you a visual guideline to follow in setting the shelves, and insure that they are level and correctly positioned. Cut the shelves to proper width and length—make sure that the fit is a snug one—and set each one in place in its turn to check for proper fit. Trim as necessary, and install the shelves.

Apply a bead of glue along the top of the shelf cleat, smooth a coating of glue on the shelf ends where they will butt with the side or

Fig. 12-10. Installing center section shelf back support cleats. Duncan Photos.

Fig. 12-11. Marking level guidelines on divider panel to align shelf. Duncan Photos.

331

Fig. 12-12. Putting in shelves. Duncan Photos.

divider panels and slide the shelf into place. Nail the back of the shelf to the cleats, preferably close to the points where the cleat is attached to the wall. Then, line up the front edge of the shelf with the guidelines and nail through the divider panels and into the shelf end (Fig. 12-12). Use three or four nails per shelf end, and pay careful attention as you do so. The nails must be driven straight, and about dead center of the thickness of the shelf stock. The nails closest to the outer edges of the shelves should be back at least 2 inches in order to avoid splitting the corners open. In this case, the far left-hand edges cannot be similarly nailed. Since additional strength will be gained when the face-frame is installed, one toenail set in a predrilled hole through the corners of the shelves and into the side piece is sufficient to hold them in place for the time being.

Step 10

Cut the top rail to length. Here, the rail drops down past the edge of the top piece to the ceiling. The ends should fit snugly against the walls. Apply a bead of glue where the top piece edge butts the rail, and at the ends where it joins the side pieces, and also where it lies against the divider panels. Nail the piece into place, taking care that it remains level and properly aligned (Fig. 12-13).

Step 11

Cut the vertical face-frame members for the cabinet sides. They should butt tight against the bottom edge of the top piece, and be flush with the bottom edges of the bottom shelf side support cleats. The width can be anything to your liking. Measure and cut the length of each piece individually. Though in theory the two should be identical, they may not be; make them fit the cabinet. Set each in place and carefully check the fit. Then trace a pencil line down the inside to indicate where the piece will meet with side and shelf edges. Apply a liberal coating of glue inside the pencil lines, set each piece in place, and nail them home (Fig. 12-14). Use a series of nails

Fig. 12-13. Installing face-frame top rail. Finish ceiling will later be fitted to the rail. Duncan Photos.

Fig. 12-14. Putting on face-frame side stile. Duncan Photos.

driven straight into the edges of the side pieces. Then, drill pilot holes at an angle and toenail into each shelf corner. Cut the stiles for the two divider panels and nail them into place in the same way, centering them on the divider panel edges. The top ends butt against the top rail lower edge, and the bottom ends extend beyond the lower surface of the bottom shelf by exactly the same amount as the side stiles (Fig. 12-15). Toenail all accessible stile upper corners to the top rail lower edge, to keep the butt joints lines up and add a bit of strength.

Fig. 12-15. Installing face-frame stiles on divider panels. Duncan Photos.

Fig. 12-16. Tapping bottom rail sections into place. Fit of rail width and butt joints is critical here. Duncan Photos.

Step 12

Cut the bottom rails and check them for fit. The top edge of each rail piece should be flush with the bottom shelf upper surface, and the bottom edge should be flush with the bottom edges of the side stiles and the divider panel stiles. Cut the length so that the rails must be perfectly clean and square to make tight butt joints. Apply glue to the back of the rails and to the ends, slip them into place and nail them down (Fig. 12-16). Use a series of nails driven through the rails and into the bottom shelf edges. Then, use small nails to toenail each bottom corner to the adjacent stiles. This will hold the lower edges of the butt joints in line.

Step 13

All that remains now to complete the cabinet structure is to cover the remaining raw shelf edges. Here, solid wood strips of ¾-inch height and ⅜-inch thickness where chosen. Cut the strips to length and check for proper fit. They should be snug, and flush with shelf top and bottom surfaces. Apply a liberal coating of glue to the backs of each edge strip (the porous edges of particle board soak up a great quantity of glue), set the strips in place and fasten them with small nails or brads (Fig. 12-17).

In this particular cabinet project, the right-hand empty section received special treatment, the details of which would be of little value to most readers. Wiring troughs and special support brackets were installed in the rear, and vertical side cleats near the front. Some odd-shaped shelves were fitted to adjustable tracks, and standard radio relay rack panels secured to the cleats. Hidden ventilating ports were cut in, fans mounted, and electronics gear installed and wired later. The cupboard door, however, matches the other two, and when closed there is no indication of what lies within.

In ordinary circumstances, additional shelves would be installed in the same manner as in the other two cabinet sections. Note too

Fig. 12-17. Covering the raw edges of shelves with edging strips. Duncan Photos.

that all of the shelving might have been placed on standards with adjustable clips, one pair at each shelf end. Many of the other construction specifics could have been different as well. This is especially true of the top piece, which in some designs might be lower and attached directly to the sides and dividers, or could be higher and secured directly to the ceiling. In some circumstances, the top piece might even be eliminated, with a finished ceiling serving instead.

Step 14

Build up the cabinet doors in whatever method you have chosen and fit them into place. Make any necessary corrections or adjustments, and mount the doors and hardware. As always, the last step is to finish the cabinet. Remove the cabinet doors and hardware, prepare all the surfaces, and proceed with the process of finish application.

BUILDING A CASEWORK WALL CABINET

This same cabinet could readily be built in the workshop using casework construction methods. The outward appearance and overall design would remain approximately the same. The cabinet could be built with a full back, or with combination shelf support and mounting cleats. The former would be a bit stronger and a little more expensive to build, while the latter would perhaps be a bit cheaper and easier. In brief, the construction steps would go something like as follows.

Step 1

The first step is about the same as Step 1 above. Make all the decisions as to materials, sizes, location, and hardware before you begin. Work out sketches and dimensions as necessary to help you along. Choose the type of joinery you want to use, and dimension and lay out the pieces of stock accordingly.

Step 2

Cut all the face-frame pieces. Perform any necessary joinery operations, place the parts on a smooth flat work surface, and check everything for proper fit and squareness. Put all of the pieces together to complete the face-frame, gluing, clamping, and fastening

338

as necessary. Set the face-frame aside to cure thoroughly before handling it.

Step 3

Being guided by the outside dimensions of the face-frame assembly, cut the two side pieces and the divider panels to proper dimensions. Make any necessary joinery cuts for the top piece, all shelf ends, and the back panel if there is to be one. If back cleats will be used, notch at the proper locations so that the cleat back surfaces will be flush with the back edges of the side pieces and divider panels. If the shelf ends are to be supported by cleats, these can be cut, fitted, and mounted now.

Step 4

Cut the top piece, make any necessary joinery cuts, and check for squareness and proper dimensions. Set the front edge of the top piece down on a flat work surface, stand the side pieces and divider panels in their proper positions and secure them to the top.

Step 5

Cut the bottom shelf. Check the fit, then glue and nail the piece to the bottom edges of the side pieces and divider panels. Keep all the parts aligned and square, checking often as you work.

Step 6

Cut the back panel and fit it to the cabinet frame. Or, if you are using shelf support and hanger cleats, cut these and set them into place. There should be a cleat below the bottom shelf, a cleat below each shelf in each cabinet section, and a full-length cleat across the upper back, flush with and nailed to the top piece as well as the side pieces and dividers. Note however, that the small shelf back support cleats could be eliminated where the shelves are relatively short, provided that the consequent loss of strength and rigidity is not objectionable. As you install the cleats, check continuously to make sure that the cabinet frame does not rack out of square. With a solid back panel, as long as the panel itself is square the cabinet will follow suit. Glue and nail the back panel or cleats into place only after you have double-checked to make sure that everything is correct. For additional strength, use screws.

Step 7

Cut the shelves and fit them into the cabinet sections. Check for squareness, and make sure that the shelves are not so long or so short that they cause the sides or dividers to blow. Glue and nail the shelves into position, or into dadoes. If a solid back panel is used, nail through the back panel and into the rear edges of the shelves for extra support.

Step 8

With the cabinet lying on its back, set the face-frame assembly into place and check for fit. If both face-frame and cabinet structure are in square, and if all of your dimensions are accurate, the face-frame should fit exactly into place with all edges flush with the cabinet frame. Incidentally, it does not harm to allow a bit of extra material around the outer edges of the face-frame. This will enable you to sand them perfectly flush with the cabinet sides during the finishing process. About a 1/64-inch overlap is good for hardwoods, and perhaps a bit more for softwoods. Anything much more than this could mean a lot of extra work.

When you are satisfied with the fit of the face-frame, apply a glue coating to the cabinet edges and nail the face-frame firmly in place.

Step 9

Set the cupboard doors in place and check for fit, making any necessary adjustments or corrections. Mount the hardware, and set the doors in place.

Step 10

Remove the doors and hardware, and go ahead with the surface preparation and finishing procedures.

Step 11

Locate all of the wall studs that lie behind the cabinet mounting locations. Transfer accurate measurements to the cabinet back panel or support cleats, and drill a series of holes for large wood screws. The mount holes should be located in as many spots as possible, within reason, along the top cleat or top edge of the back panel, and also along the bottom shelf support cleats. For extra support, you can also mount through the shelf back support cleats in the cabinet sections.

Boost the cabinet into place and make a check for rough fit. Get the cabinet in position, and then support it with props, or enlist a few more arms to help hold it in place. Drill starter holes in the walls through the cabinet mount holes and drive a few screws partway in, to help hold the cabinet in place. Check to see if and where shims will be necessary, and fit them into place. The cabinet must be supported so that it does not rack or pull out of shape when the mounting screws are driven down tight. This may require some fiddling around and shim shifting, and you may have to take the cabinet down two or three times before you get it right. Once everything is lined up, drive the mounting screws home and double-check to make sure that everything is still square.

There are many, many variations and minor differences that can be introduced in either the casework or the built-in method of cabinet construction. Obviously, cabinet sizes, functions, decor and trim, and construction materials and hardware will differ greatly from unit to unit. By following the general procedure that has just been outlined, however, you can change and adapt and redesign to suit your own requirements and wishes. The task of building any kind of wall cabinet is essentially a simple one, and with a little practice and experience, you will be able to put together anything your heart desires.

Chapter 13
Display Cases and Racks

Display cases, racks, shelves, and cabinets are in short supply in most homes. For the collector, this can be a dismaying situation. One of the great joys in having collections of antiques or memorabilia, whether of Kachina dolls, Dresden china, Indian arrowheads, Civil War items or whatever, is in arranging them in displays. Not only does the owner enjoy looking at his prize collectibles, but he also likes to show them off to others, as well as to use the collection as a decorative accent point in the home. About the only recourse for the homeowner-collector, then, is to construct his own cabinetry to suit the requirements of his collections.

Even though many of us do not have formal collections of specific artifacts, most of us do have a certain number of family heirlooms, souvenirs, knick-knacks, or just general personal possessions, with which we like to surround ourselves. Many of these items might well be put on display, or brought out of hiding where they can be enjoyed and used handily, or to serve as accent points for decorative motifs of the home. The usual problem is, where do you put the stuff? The answer: a suitable arrangement of cabinetry, either adapted to or designed for that particular purpose.

The range of possibilities for display cabinetry construction projects is truly staggering, because people make collections of everything from buttons to steam boilers, and accumulate possessions of amazing diversity and in endless array. The principal point to recognize is that constructing cabinetry of this type, either for displaying particular collections or simply to show off random and assorted pieces, is little different than constructing any other kind of cabinetry. The cabinets may be open or closed, of base or wall type. Joinery is accomplished in the same manner, shelving is mounted and supported in identical fashion, doors and drawers are similar, and the same material is used, as in any other kind of cabinetry. The essential differences lie only in dimensions, design particulars, and intended use. At one extreme, the display cabinetry may be engineered to exactly fit and most effectively house some particular item, or class of items. At the other extreme, the display cabinetry may be constructed in such a way that it is completely adaptable to showing off certain possessions, storing household goods, shelving books, or whatever other function happens to be most expedient at the moment.

The following brief examples are cited in order to show different approaches to the problems of displaying both particular collections and miscellaneous objects. Both built-in and casework types of construction are covered, and some of the units are adaptable to other or additional purposes and can be easily altered to suit somewhat different circumstances. These examples are not meant to be limiting, but only to point in a general direction and hopefully touch off some additional ideas for constructing display cabinetry of your own.

BUILT-IN LIGHTED DISPLAY CABINET

The space between two doorways is usually a complete waste, but in this case that space served as the starting point for a custom-designed, built-in, lighted display cabinet. This case and its displayed artifacts also serve as one focal point of several in a short, board hallway used as a gallery, and doubles as a night-light to boot. Though this particular cabinet was designed especially to house a large collection of sterling and coin silver napkin rings, it could be used without alternations for many other kinds of small and lightweight antiques, art objects, or knick-knacks. Also, the cabinet could be shaped somewhat differently, or built into or against a free wall section rather than between two doors.

To partially form the recess to house lighting fixtures, the plasterboard wall covering was omitted between the two doors. This left a floor-to-ceiling cavity about 3 inches deep between the door

Fig. 13-1. Fluorescent strips mounted in wall cavity where display case will stand. Duncan Photos.

casings, backed by a structural two-by-six. The first step in constructing the cabinet is to line up and temporarily install a pair of fluorescent lighting fixtures (Fig. 13-1). The wiring for the fixtures comes into the cavity from the rear, through a partition wall in the room beyond. Access could also have been gained from the ceiling area.

Fig. 13-2. Assembling base pedestal for cabinet—just a simple box. Duncan Photos.

With the wiring and the fixtures properly lined up, the next step is to plan the design and dimensional details of the cabinet itself. Because of the nature of the cabinet, the assembly is something of a Chinese puzzle. The problem is to make sure that the cabinet pieces can be put together, and once put together can be partially disassembled for access both to the interior of the cabinet and to the lighting fixtures behind. Once the essential characteristics of the cabinet are decided upon and the preliminary dimensions are in hand, the construction process can begin. Specific dimensions will not be noted here, because the chances are excellent that they would have neither meaning nor value to your own intended work.

The first bit of construction is the base pedestal (Fig. 13-2), which is nothing more than a box with its open side facing the wall. The pedestal is attached securely to the floor and to the door

346

casings. A series of small and unobtrusive holes is bored in the side of the pedestal to provide a cool air for the lighting fixtures.

Then, install an almost identical box directly overhead on the ceiling to form the cabinet head (Fig. 13-3). This part is likewise attached to the door casings and to the ceiling, and has a similar series of small holes drilled in its sides to allow venting of warm air from the lighting fixtures. The base and head must be exactly in line

Fig. 13-3. Cabinet head piece, another simple box with provision for lighting control switch, is secured to a piece of scrap mounted on the joists. Heavy cable passes through to electrical load center, small wire is for control switch. Duncan Photos.

Fig. 13-4. At the rear, side stile piece with diffuser panel stop attached. In the middle, side stile showing blind dado cuts which will hold case shelves. Foreground, diffuser panel stop to be attached to stile. Duncan Photos.

with one another. Here, the dimensions of both parts were worked out so that the distance between the base surface and the head surface is exactly 6 feet 3 inches. During the building process, an opening was cut in the face for a switchbox which will eventually contain the lighting control switch.

The next step is to cut the rear stile pieces. These will fit flush against the door casings at each cabinet rear corner, and serve three main functions. First, each stile is part of the frame which retains the clear ⅛-inch-thick Plexiglas side panels. Second, a small cleat is mounted on each stile, on the inside face toward the rear, to act as a stop for the translucent white acrylic panel which will act as a light diffuser across the rear of the cabinet. And third, each rear stile contains a series of horizontal grooves to hold the shelves in place (Fig. 13-4).

The two bottom rear stiles are installed first. Each must have a ⅛-inch by ¼-inch groove cut down the centerline of the forward edge to hold the acrylic side panel. A series of ⅛-inch by ¼-inch grooves are cut horizontally across the inside face of each back stile, located appropriate distances apart, to hold the shelves. The diffuser panel stops are cut from thin strips of solid wood and attached to the rear inside surfaces of the stiles, positioned so that the diffuser panel will be held in place by the pressure of the shelf rear edges and sit a satisfactory distance away from the lighting fixtures. Drill holes in the center lines of the stile side panel grooves, apply glue to the back edges of the stiles, and nail them into place along the jambs (Fig. 13-5).

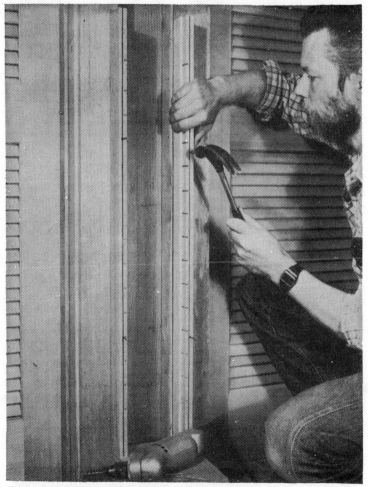

Fig. 13-5. Installing the finished lower back side stiles, using glue and nails set in predrilled holes. Duncan Photos.

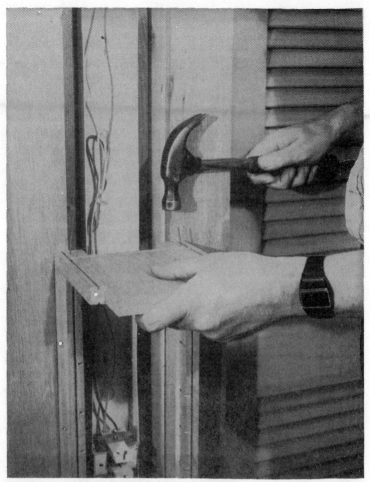

Fig. 13-6. Installing the partition shelf separating upper and lower case sections. Fluorescent fixtures have been reinstalled. Duncan Photos.

Now fashion a center dividing partition to go on the top ends of the rear lower stiles. Five grooves must be cut in this piece. A ⅛-inch-wide by ⅛-inch-deep groove is set on each side of the piece, and on both top and bottom faces, aligned with the groove in the leading edge of each stile. These grooves will hold the top of each lower acrylic side panel and the bottom of each upper acrylic side panel. An identical groove is cut across the rear of the partition piece, on the top surface only. The bottom of the upper acrylic diffuser panel will rest in this groove, which must be aligned with the diffuser stop cleats. In addition, a notch must be cut from each front corner of the partition piece. These notches are identical in size to the width and thickness of the front stiles, which will run full length from base to head of the cabinet. When all necessary cuts have been completed, position the partition piece atop the lower rear stiles, apply glue, and nail the piece in place (Fig. 13-6). Drilling slightly undersized pilot holes for the nails is a good idea, especially if you are using hardwood.

Cut the upper rear stiles, groove them and apply the diffuser panel stop cleats in exactly the same fashion as the lower rear stiles

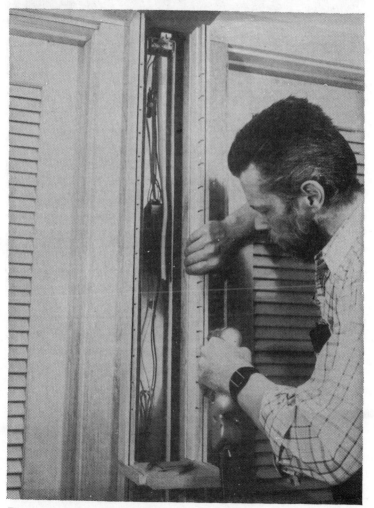

Fig. 13-7. Installing upper back side stiles between partition and head piece. Fit is critical here. Duncan Photos.

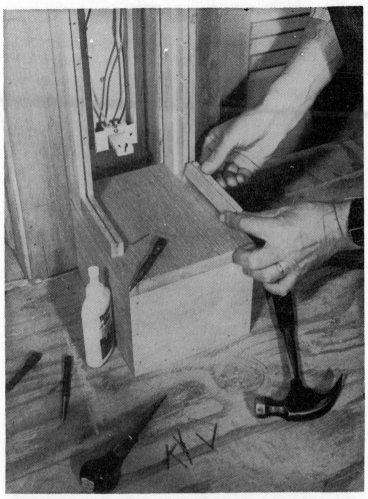

Fig. 13-8. Putting in the lower side panel retainers. Upper ones mount on head piece in same fashion. Duncan Photos.

were done. Fit them into place between the partition shelf and the cabinet head and nail them to the door jambs (Fig. 13-7).

Next come the upper and lower side panel end retaining pieces, one on each side of the base and a similar pair on the cabinet head. These are cut from ¾-inch by ¾-inch solid wood stock. The length of each piece is equal to the distance from the forward grooved edge of the rear stile to the front of the base or head assembly, minus the width of the front corner stiles and the door thickness. Each piece has a ⅛-inch-wide by ⅛-inch-deep groove cut in its upper surface.

The groove must line up exactly with the groove in the rear stile lead edge. Check the pieces for fit and nail and glue them into their respective positions (Fig. 13-8).

Cut and fit four clear acrylic plastic panels, two for the lower cabinet sides and two for the upper cabinet sides. Remember to allow an extra one-quarter inch in width to fit into the front corner stile grooves. Bevel all edges slightly with a sanding block or file, so that they will slide easily in the retaining grooves. Slip each panel into place, without using glues or adhesives (Fig. 13-9).

Fig. 13-9. Setting the plastic side panels into place. Duncan Photos.

Cut the front corner stiles to width and length. At the bottom they will sit flat on the base, in from the front edge by the thickness of the door, and butt tight against the lower side panel end retaining strips. At the center divider partition, each stile will fit flush into the notch made in the corners of the partition for the purpose. At the top, each stile will snug up against the face of the cabinet head and tight against the upper side panel end retaining strips, just as at the bottom. Each stile must have a ⅛-inch by ¼-inch groove cut the full length of the inside face to receive and retain the protruding edges of the acrylic side panels. Whichever stile will hold the full-length door hinge should be cut narrower than the other stile by the thickness of the folded hinge. Then, when the door is hung, no further gain cut will be necessary and the door will close tight all around. Fit the stiles carefully into place and secure them with long, thin wood screws at bottom, middle, and top (Fig. 13-10). Do not use glue. The front stiles must also be dadoed with ⅛-inch by ¼-inch horizontal grooves on the inside faces to hold the shelves. These grooves must line up exactly with those in the rear stiles.

Cut an appropriate number of shelves from ⅛-inch clear acrylic plastic. The depth of the shelves should be equal to the distance from the forward edge of the diffuser panel stop cleats to the front edge of the cabinet side, minus the thickness of the diffuser panel (here ⅛ inch). The width of the shelves should be equal to the distance between the shelf groove bottoms, side to side, minus a small amount of clearance. Polish all of the shelf edges until they are clear and smooth.

Cut two pieces of translucent white acrylic plastic to fit exactly in the back of the cabinet against the diffuser panel stop cleats. Trim the width to fit exactly, and the height of each panel to slip into the diffuser panel retaining groove at the rear and come flush with the underside of the divider partition or cabinet head. Remount the lighting fixtures, make the electrical connections, and put the tubes in. Set the diffuser panels in place and slip the shelves into their grooves to hold the panels in place (Fig. 13-11).

Now construct the cabinet door. This consists of two full-length side stiles, top rail and bottom rail, and a center rail. The three rails fit between the stiles. Cut all of the pieces to accurate length to make a door which is flush with the cabinet sides and flush with the cabinet base and head surfaces. Each stile must have a ⅛-inch by ¼-inch groove cut along one edge to form the sticking. The top and bottom

354

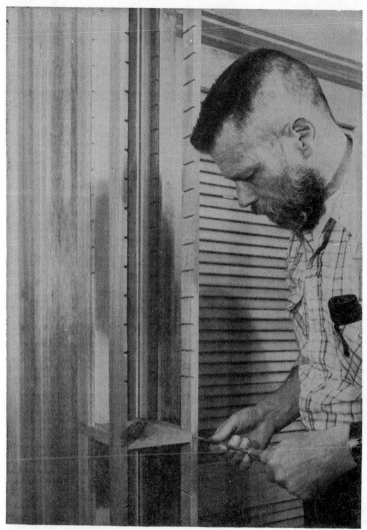

Fig. 13-10. Installing full-length front stiles. They are secured without glue and with screws to the notched partition shelf and the upper and lower side panel retainers, so that the cabinet can be partly disassembled for lamp removal. Duncan Photos.

rails must be similarly grooved. The center rail must have a matching groove on each edge. Glue and dowel the top, middle, and bottom rails to one stile. Make sure that the door panel retaining grooves all line up perfectly.

Cut two clear acrylic plastic panels to fit the upper and lower halves of the cabinet door. Bevel the edges slightly and slip them into

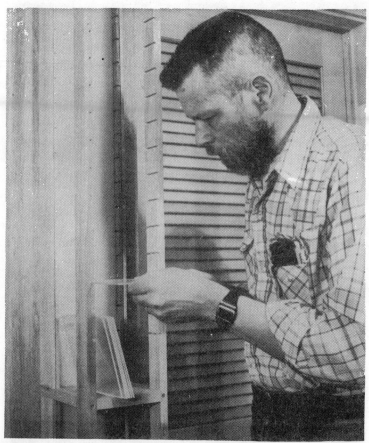

Fig. 13-11. Diffuser panels have been stood in place, and shelves are being put in. Duncan Photos.

place in the completed E of the door frame (Fig. 13-12). Then fit the remaining stile into place to complete the cabinet door. You can glue and dowel this piece as well, or attach it with long, thin wood screws.

Attach a full-length piano hinge, surface-mounted, to the inner side of the hinge-side stile. Set the door in place on the cabinet, and check thoroughly for proper fit. Then attach the second leaf of the piano hinge to the outer cabinet stile, again surface-mounted (Fig. 13-13). Attach or install cabinet locks, closure hooks, or some other appropriate latching mechanism to the opposite stile. Install the lighting control switch and activate the electrical system, add the small trim pieces around the edges of the cabinet base and head (Fig. 13-14), and the construction job is complete (Fig. 13-15).

All that remains now is the final surface preparation and application of a finish. In this case, a natural finish with wax coatings will be used, and the surfaces of the cabinet components are relatively smooth to begin with. This means that not much further work is needed. However, if a substantial amount of sanding is necessary, and/or if paint or some other finish is to be applied, the job is more

Fig. 13-12. Sliding the plastic panels into the partly completed door frame. Duncan Photos.

Fig. 13-13. Door being attached, using continuous strip of piano hinge for added strength and rigidity. Duncan Photos.

easily done with the acrylic panels removed. These panels scratch very easily, and there is not much working room in the cabinet. If you have used screws to hold the stiles in place, you can easily remove them and pull the panels out while the surface preparation is going on. The cabinet could also be painted piecemeal, and then fully assembled later. Or, much of the surface preparation, and even some of the painting, could be done during the construction process.

358

BUILT-IN WALL CASE

The built-in wall case is a handy item which can be used in practically any room in the house, wherever there is a free bit of wall space. In cold climates where heat loss is a consideration, this type of cabinet should be confined to inside walls only. If built into outside

Fig. 13-14. Adding final touches of trim to pedestal. Head piece was similarly treated. Duncan Photos.

Fig. 13-15. Completed but unfinished display case. Plastic panels can be kept free of dust accumulation by wiping on liquid used for static electricty control in carpets, available in spray cans. Duncan Photos.

walls, the nature of its design means that the insulation value of that portion of wall will be eliminated, and cold air transfer could be a problem. Also, this type of wall case is best constructed in partition walls rather than load-bearing walls, unless the size is kept relatively small, or the structure of the wall itself is engineered to include such cabinetry.

The built-in wall cabinet can be constructed during the house building process, or can be installed in an existing wall. The sketch in Fig. 13-16 shows the basic concept of the cabinet. To build the

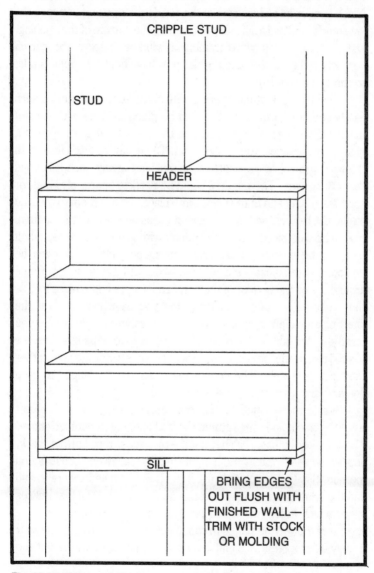

CRIPPLE STUD

STUD

HEADER

SILL

BRING EDGES
OUT FLUSH WITH
FINISHED WALL—
TRIM WITH STOCK
OR MOLDING

Fig. 13-16. One possibility for a shallow shelving or cabinet unit built into a standard stud wall.

cabinet, first locate the wall studs. These are usually, though not always, placed on 16-inch centers. Cut the wall covering away, leaving a hole in the wall approximately the size of the proposed wall cabinet. Saw out the sections of any studs which are in the way of the cabinet, leaving an intact stud at each side of the cabinet opening. Nail a header into place across the top of the opening between the side studs, and nail a sill into place across the bottom of the opening, just as though you were framing a window. Secure the cut-off portions of the full wall studs, which now have become cripple studs, to the header and sill.

Line the back of the opening with some suitable material, such as plywood or hardboard. This can be glued in place with dabs of mastic, or simply wedged in place by the cabinet side. Now cut pieces for the sides, top, and bottom. These can be fitted flush with the wall surface, or can protrude as much as several inches beyond the wall surface. The material could be particle board, plywood, or solid wood. Cut and fit the pieces into place and nail them to the side studs, the header, and the sill, shimming as necessary to keep them true. The side pieces could be dadoed with grooves to accept shelf ends, or be mounted with shelf end support cleats, or even be equipped with adjustable shelf standards. Cut and fit a trim frame around the outside edges of the case, and secure it into place to hide the rough edges of the wall opening you have just cut. Fit the shelving and apply a suitable finish to the cabinet. If desirable, you could also add doors with either solid or transparent panels. The use of solid panels means that the cabinet becomes a storage unit, rather than a display case. The door panel could also be hinged to drop down, making a writing desk or a bar top.

An alternative method of constructing this type of wall cabinet would be to cut and rough-frame the wall opening as outlined above. Then, make the basic cabinet itself—the sides, top, bottom, back, and shelves—in the workshop, using the casework construction method. Slip the completed case into place, shim and secure it, and add the trim frame around the outside. This sort of cabinet utilizes space which otherwise would probably be wasted, is unobtrusive and out of the way, is simple to construct, and yet provides excellent display or storage space and is an accent point to complement the decor.

There are some design variations which could be introduced into this assembly, too. For instance, instead of having the cabinet open only on one side, you could run it clear through the wall. The contents would be visible and accessible from both sides, and from two rooms. In a standard stud wall, the total depth of the cabinet could easily be a foot, and yet only project a short distance beyond each wall surface. Another possibility is to cut the cabinet all the way through the wall, but fit one side with a translucent acrylic plastic panel to form an indirect-lighting window effect. You might also hide lighting fixtures in the wall cavities, either above and below or to each side of the cabinet. Then, fit the corresponding cabinet sides with translucent plastic to diffuse light into the cabinet. Remember that the lighting fixtures must remain accessible. In warm climate areas, the indirect lighting and the translucent back panel ideas can be combined with a cabinet fitted into an outside wall, such as near an outside entrance. The back panel of the cabinet actually becomes part of the exterior siding of the building. In the daytime, natural light from outside illuminates the items displayed in the cabinet. At night, artificial light from within illuminates both the items on display and the back panel of the cabinet, and softly lights the exterior doorway area as well.

BUILT-IN GUN RACK

This built-in gun rack, shown in Fig. 13-17 at the point where the empty basic cabinet is complete, was made as an integral part of a large, floor-to-ceiling bookshelf section. The entire section was made by first building a platform base. The two end pieces were next put in place, then the right and left top pieces attached to the ceiling joists, followed by two vertical dividers which form the sides of the gun cabinet. Shelves were installed on either side of the gun cabinet section, fixed on end and back support cleats. The lower shelves are 12 inches deep, while the upper section sits back and is only 10 inches deep. After all of the shelves are installed, a face-frame was glued and nailed to all raw edges, and the shelves were edge-trimmed. The space below the gun cabinet in the center section was made into a cabinet containing one shelf and two hinged doors, with a full-width drawer above.

The gun cabinet is high enough to accept the longest rifles and shotguns currently being manufactured. There are some antique firearms, however, which would not fit in. The width of the cabinet allows about ten long firearms to be racked into place comfortably. The depth is sufficient that small arms could be mounted on the

Fig. 13-17. Opening for gun cabinet with drawer and cupboard below, built as part of a full-wall library shelving system. Duncan Photos.

sides. The full-width drawer beneath the gun cabinet is for various firearms accessories and equipment, but not ammunition. That should always be stored under lock and key at some point remote and hidden.

Once the basic gun cabinet is established, completion is not much of a chore. The interior surfaces of the cabinet could be painted or stained, covered with felt or other fabric, or treated in any of a number of different fashions. Here, pieces of plywood wall paneling were fitted into place on the back, sides, and top of the cabinet (Fig. 13-18). Then a slightly tilted subbase was fitted to the cabinet floor (Fig. 13-19). The subbase is canted inward, and fitted with a series of rails to form separate shallow compartments in which the gun butts rest. A cross rest was next fitted across the back of the cabinet

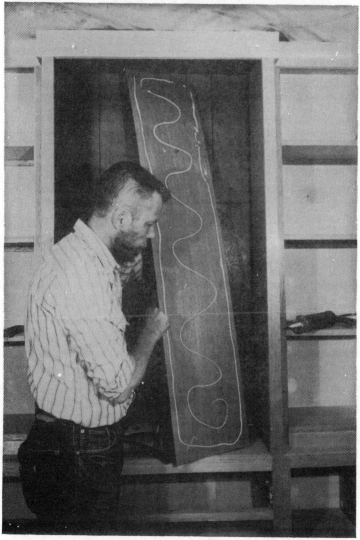

Fig. 13-18. Lining cabinet opening with wall paneling. Duncan Photos.

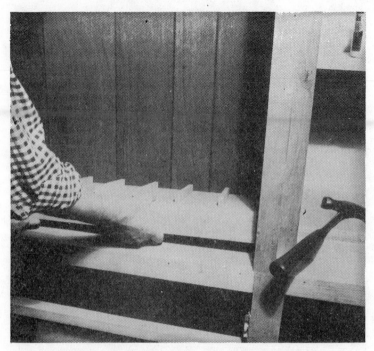

Fig. 13-19. Installing slightly tilted base upon which gun butts will rest. Duncan Photos.

and about halfway up (Fig. 13-20). This was made by cutting a piece of solid wood stock to twice the width needed and half the length. A series of 1¼-inch holes was bored along the centerline of the piece, which was then ripped down the middle, leaving two pieces with rounded notches cut in one edge. The two pieces were mounted in line with one another, and later will be covered from end to end with a strip of soft felt to protect the gun barrels which will lie in the notches. Incidentally, double-barrel shotguns and some antique pieces would require holes larger than the 1¼-inch size used here.

The last step was to install the doors. Heavy roller tracks were fitted to the cabinet roof behind the face-frame, and another track in a corresponding position was attached to the cabinet floor in front of the subbase. A piece of trim molding was fitted between the face-frame side rails and directly in front of the track, partly hiding it. Then, two sliding panels were cut from high impact clear acrylic plastic and set into place. The last act was to attach the locking hardware, completing the project (Fig. 13-21).

CASEWORK CARTRIDGE CABINET

Not all display cases need be constructed using the built-in method, and in fact more are probably put together as simple cases with certain modifications to fit specific needs. Small cases can be easily designed so that they may be stacked or fitted into spare shelf openings. They are simply made, and have the advantage of being completely portable. They are, in effect, part of the household

Fig. 13-20. Putting in the gun barrel rest strip. Duncan Photos.

Fig. 13-21. Completed gun cabinet, with plate glass rolling doors set in recessed tracks. Duncan Photos.

furniture. This particular case (Fig. 13-22) was built specifically to protect and effectively display part of a collection of firearms cartridges. The design is such that the bullet, full case, and head stamp of each cartridge is visible, with the help of the back-mounted mirror.

The case is a simple box of ½-inch-thick white pine, with a forward portion of one side piece cut and hinged to form a tiny door.

This allows the plate glass front panel, which is a stock size medicine chest shelf, to be withdrawn from its retaining grooves and allow access to the inside of the case. The cartridges rest in round-bottomed shallow grooves cut into a tilted platform, also made from pine. The angle of the platform, 25 degrees, is just sufficient to allow good viewing in the mirror. The front of the platform is wide enough to permit labels to be pasted on. The design was figured to allow the use of stacked pairs of cabinets in an existing bookshelf section.

CASEWORK MARBLE CASE

Another example of highly specialized display cabinetry is shown in Fig. 13-23. This case was designed solely for the purpose of showing off a collection of antique marbles. Since many of the marbles are either transparent or translucent, the decision was made to indirectly light them from below. The case is wall-mounted, with the electrical wiring brought in through the hollow wall behind, and completely hidden. The lighting fixture used inside the cabinet is a small fluorescent one with a remote switch.

The case is nothing more than a long box set upon its side and fastened to the wall through the back. The lower front of the case is

Fig. 13-22. Small case with sliding glass front designed especially for firearms cartridge collection. Mirrored back shows displayed pieces from all angles. Duncan Photos.

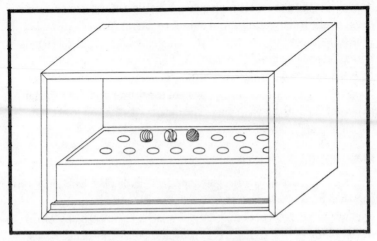

Fig. 13-23. Special case designed to house collection of antique marbles. Hidden light source beams up through holes to illuminate the displayed pieces.

enclosed, with the platform holding the marbles attached to it. The fluorescent light is hidden within this cavity. A series of carefully sized holes was bored in the platform, each with a slightly chamfered edge. The marbles rest snugly in the holes, and the light from below is transmitted through the glass of the marbles themselves so that they glow in colorful fashion. Access to the cabinet is gained by moving the simple clear acrylic plastic sliding doors.

This type of display case can easily be revamped, rearranged, and redimensioned to suit any number of purposes. The overall size, of course, can be adjusted to suit the specific requirements. The lighting fixture could be fitted with a cord and plug, rather than being wired directly, and thus the cabinet becomes completely portable. The platform upon which the marbles rest in this case, could be exchanged for a sheet of translucent white acrylic plastic. Objects resting upon this shelf would be indirectly illuminated from below, a particularly pleasing method of displaying many types of antiques and art objects. Or, the entire case could be turned upside down, so that the light shines down upon objects arranged along the case floor. To further heighten the effect, a mirror could be mounted at the rear of the case, either flat or at an advantageous angle.

SHADOW BOXES

Among the simplest kind of casework display cabinets to build are shadow boxes. A shadow box really is nothing more than a shallow tray which can be hung or mounted upon a wall. The dimensions are infinitely variable to suit whatever objects are to be displayed, and the box may be left open or equipped with a door fitted with a transparent panel. The one shown in Fig. 13-24 was designed to hold a solitary antique pistol. The interior is finished with a dark semitransparent stain to show off the pistol, but could just as well be painted or covered with felt or velveteen. The case door is framed plate glass, hinged at the top and held closed by gravity. A latch or cabinet lock could easily be fitted, however. To suit different purposes, a shadow box might be fitted with shelves, display pegs or pins or special stands, or divided up into compartments of assorted sizes and shapes.

COMBINED STORAGE AND DISPLAY

The combination of display space and storage space in the same cabinet assembly is a common one. For example, a piece of furniture called a hutch consists of a deep lower section arranged into cupboards and drawers, while the shallower upper section contains open shelves. The shelves are usually grooved near the rear edge so that plates can be propped up against the back panel, while other china and glassware can be set on the forward portions of the shelves. Many hutches also are fitted out with special little display racks which hold spoons or forks. In similar fashion, a modern

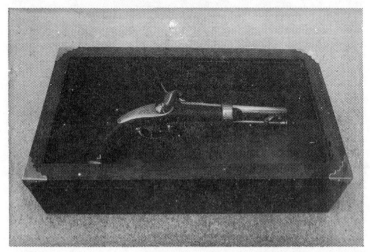

Fig. 13-24. Simple casework mahogany shadow box with brass hardware. Duncan Photos.

371

Fig. 13-25. Pair of casework sliding door cabinets designed to hold reel-type recording tapes. Enclosed display area in between is made by sliding glass or plastic panels into dadoes. Duncan Photos.

built-in server or buffet may consist of a deep cabinet section below with shallow flanking cabinets above, separated by open shelving for china or glass display.

The arrangement shown in Fig. 13-25 is an example of a contemporary style of combined storage and display cabinetry. The upper and lower cases were designed especially to hold and protect a collection of reel-to-reel music tapes. Each is merely a long box mounted back to the wall and secured to the wall studs. The cases are sized to exactly fit the tape boxes, with thin sliding panel doors set in tracks to protect the tapes from dust. Each cabinet is split in the middle by a divider partition which adds strength, reduces the possibility of warping (the cabinets are made from solid wood stock), and renders the door panel size easily manageable.

Fig. 13-26. Detail of panel mounting arrangement. Duncan Photos.

To provide the enclosed display space, the cabinets were first mounted on the wall and accurate measurements were taken of the spacing between the two cabinets. Then the cabinets were removed and a ⅛-inch-wide by ⅛-inch-deep groove was cut in the top surface of the lower cabinet, just in from the edges across both ends and across the front. Matching grooves were cut in the bottom surface of the upper cabinet, and the cabinets were remounted on the wall. Then, two pieces of clear acrylic plastic were cut and fitted to slide into the side grooves, flush against the wall at the rear and flush with the back edge of the groove across the front. A third piece of clear acrylic plastic was fitted to slide into the front groove, completely enclosing the space. Access is gained simply by sliding the front panel aside. The panel mounting arrangement is shown in Fig. 13-26.

Chapter 14
Storage Units

Storage units is a collective term which covers a tremendous amount of ground, because obviously you can store items in or on practically any kind of cabinetry or built-in, and a good many pieces of furniture as well. In the strict sense of the word, all cabinets and shelving, as well as many built-ins, are storage units. But in a general way, the term is loosely taken to mean all of those hundreds of miscellaneous assemblies which provide places to tuck away innumerable household items. Sometimes these units are quite plain and simple, and at other times they are complex and unique.

SHELF STORAGE

For instance, one of the simplest of all storage units is a single shelf tacked up on the wall at some handy spot. The one shown in Fig. 14-1 is just a piece of unfinished edge-grain fir, laid upon a pair of cheap commercial brackets. The purpose was merely to provide out-of-the-way storage space for some collateral that was in the way at another spot. The window shelf shown in Fig. 14-2 is another example of a simple storage unit. This shelf is built in, and takes the place of a window sill. The existing sill was removed, the shelf fitted and edge-trimmed and secured to the bottom edges of the window casing. Then a bottom trim cleat was installed, along with two solid wood brackets for support. Located above a desk, this shelf gives extra space for a couple of plants, a few books, and miscellaneous items that were previously sitting around on the desk top.

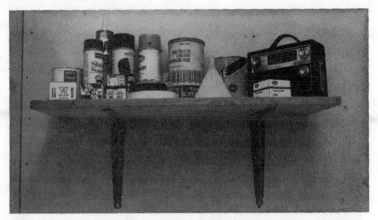

Fig. 14-1. Elementary shelf on brackets, such as might be used in a garage or utility room. Duncan Photos.

AN INDOOR WOODBIN

Often the key to, or the reason for, a storage unit is need. When a particular storage need arises, something is designed and built to fit that need. Such was the case with the woodbin shown in Fig. 14-3. A place was needed to store firewood for a nearby freestanding fireplace unit, but there seemed to be no suitable spot. The old-fashioned open woodbox would have been incongruous in that particular room. The alternative, then, was to construct a built-in woodbin in a convenient spot, and yet in such a way that it would not interfere with the room decor or living pattern. The final solution was to make a simple plywood box out of construction-grade plywood and cut the whole assembly into a partition wall behind the fireplace. A large base cabinet was built as a server on the opposite side of the wall, with the woodbin protruding into the cabinet space (Fig. 14-4). Some storage space was sacrificed in the server to gain storage space for the wood, accessible from the opposite side. Both cabinet functions were thereby served in a practical and pleasing manner.

PHONOGRAPH RECORD STORAGE

Much the same situation is obtained with the stereo record storage unit shown in Fig. 14-5. Space was needed to store recordings in a relatively dust- and light-free enclosure, convenient to a music wall. The problem was that there was insufficient space in the music wall itself to accommodate the entire record collection. How-

Fig. 14-2. Built-in window shelf replaces sill, is supported by wood brackets. Built-in valance assembly above hides shade, serves as knick-knack shelf. Duncan Photos.

Fig. 14-3. Built-in woodbin, shown here untrimmed, extends through wall and into cabinet on the other side. Duncan Photos.

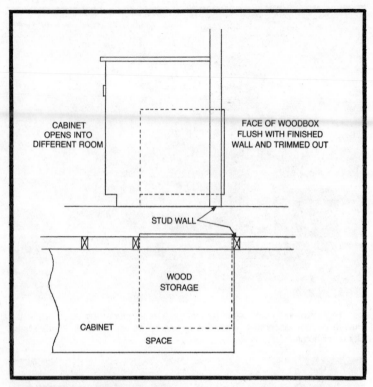

Fig. 14-4. Sketch of built-in woodbin.

ever, a large kitchen base cabinet assembly was due to be built on the opposite side of an adjacent wall. There are already plenty of base cabinet storage in the kitchen, so some of this new added space could be sacrificed. An opening for the record storage cabinet was cut through the wall, and the cabinet was constructed as an integral part of the kitchen base cabinet (Fig. 14-6). Since the record cabinet did not require the full depth of the kitchen cabinet, there was still some storage space available in the forward part. Once again, two storage needs serving two entirely different areas and purposes were suitably combined.

Both the woodbox and the record cabinet were constructed with the simplest kinds of joinery and fastening, and there was nothing particularly complex about either job. The trick, and also the touchiest part of the job, was to effectively combine two designs into one, and then get the dimensions and the interacting component fits to work out properly.

STORAGE WALLS

The music wall mentioned above is one example of a loose category of cabinetry and/or built-ins which are called storage walls. A music wall actually is a wall-mounted or floor-to-ceiling cabinet and shelf section designed to house a number of stereo sound system components and accessory items. The particular unit noted is totally enclosed and from all outward appearances is just another cabinetry furnishing which could be used for almost anything. There are a great many variations on the theme, both in construction and design possibilities, as well as in usages.

HALLWAY STORAGE

One of the simplest types of storage wall is shown in Fig. 14-7. The purpose of this wall is for miscellaneous storage. The entire structure is simply constructed with wide particle board shelves supported by cleats secured to the rear wall. The end pieces and the face-frame are made from inexpensive resawn fir. The whole structure is mounted on a base frame made of two-by-fours, and is

Fig. 14-5. Record storage case, shown here without trim or doors, extends through wall into cabinet behind. Duncan Photos.

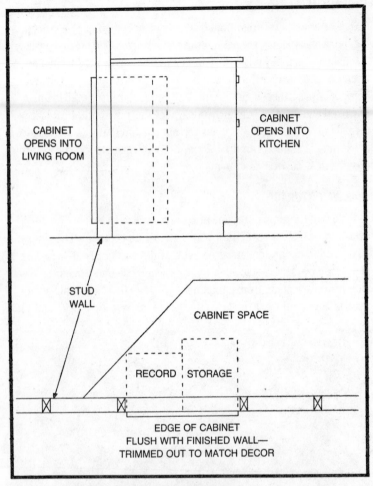

Fig. 14-6. Sketch of built-in record storage case.

attached securely at the ceiling as well. The lead edges of the shelves are supported by metal shelf brackets mounted to the inside faces of the divider stiles. This storage wall was built in a little-used hall, thereby gaining some 70 cubic feet of storage space where none existed before. Though this particular unit does not have doors, they could be installed easily enough.

Many hallways contain a certain amount of useless space which can easily be converted to some worthwhile purpose, even if the hallway is narrow. Consider, for instance, a blank-walled hall leading from a kitchen to a utility room or some other area of the house. This situation is ideal for the installation of a floor-to-ceiling mini-pantry along one wall (Fig. 14-8).

The first step in construction, after making rough sketches and taking dimensions, is to make a sturdy base frame and attach it

Fig. 14-7. Deep storage shelving section occupying entire wall of utility room. Doors could easily be added if desired. Shelves are supported at front edges by shelf brackets secured to middle stiles. Duncan Photos.

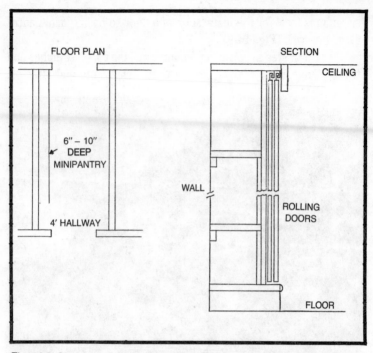

Fig. 14-8. Sketch of shallow shelving section or minipantry built into hallway.

solidly to the floor and back wall. The ceiling piece comes next, unless an existing ceiling is to be used, followed by side pieces if necessary (when the cabinet is not bounded at one or both ends by walls). Then the back support cleats for the shelves can be put up, and shelf end support cleats attached to the side pieces of the existing walls. The cleats should be rugged to bear the weight of a quantity of canned goods and such. If the unit is long, then one or more vertical divider panels might well be installed for greater strength.

The shelves go in next, glued and nailed (or screwed) to the cleats. Add a face-frame consisting of top rail, side stiles, divider panel or midspan stiles if needed, and bottom trim rail. The front edges of the shelves should have plenty of support, which means adding post supports or shelf brackets behind the midspan stiles and inserting extra stiles as needed.

Doors can be of the usual hinged variety, or large rolling doors in pairs. The latter are easier to install and to use, but be sure to allow for the extra door thickness and the tracks.

OPEN DIVIDER WALL STORAGE

One of the most popular concepts for storage walls is the open divider wall. This type of unit lends itself nicely to homes of contemporary design and furnishing motifs, but can just as well be used in many other circumstances. There are so many different ways to build this type of unit, and so many variations in specific design, finish, and arrangement, that partically any set of requirements can be met. Basically, the open divider wall consists of a series of standards or supports upon which open shelving is placed. There are no sides or doors and the unit only partially blocks sight lines from one part of the room to another. The unit is accessible with equal ease from both sides.

One of the simplest open divider walls to build is shown in Fig. 14-9. Pick out a suitable number of high quality two-by-fours, preferably edge-grained if you can find them. Lay out a longitudinal centerline on the wide face of each one, after cutting the length to fit between floor and ceiling. You may allow clearance to install tensioning devices to hold the two-by-fours in place, or cut them to fit tightly and secure them with nails, screws, or other fasteners. Line all of the two-by-fours up edge to edge, with the centerlines facing upward. With a square, mark transverse lines across them every 6

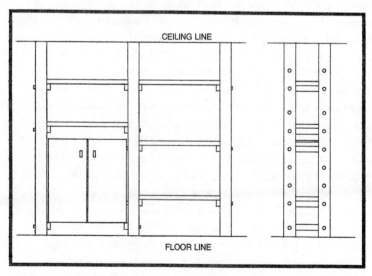

Fig. 14-9. Sketch of open-type room divider or divider wall, including both shelving and cabinet space.

inches, or 8 inches, or whatever distance appeals. At each point where a transverse line crosses a centerline, drill a 1 1/32-inch hole.

Next, select some shelf stock. Edge-treated plywood is fine, particle board is a possibility, and wide solid wood stock such as birch, mahogany, and pine, provided that the wood is well cured, will also work nicely. You can even purchase commercially-made shelf sections of particle board covered with a layer of simulated wood grain laminated plastic. A shelf length of from 24 inches to 36 inches is about right. The shelf width (depth) may be whatever is most appropriate, from perhaps 8 inches to as much as 16 inches. Cut and trim a suitable number of shelves, taking care that all edges are square.

From 2-inch by 2-inch solid wood stock, but a number of short pieces the same length as the width of the shelving stock, one pair for each shelf. Lay out each piece to drill a 1 1/32-inch hole in each end. These measurements are critical. All of the pieces should be identical, and the center of each hole must be set so that the edges of the two-by-four standards, the edges of the shelves on both sides, and the ends of the short support pieces are all flush when the parts are assembled. The distance between the two holes in each support piece must be exactly the same in all pieces.

Now cut a number of pieces from 1-inch dowel stock, two for each support bar, four for each shelf. Here you have two possibilities. One is to cut each dowel just long enough to go through the two-by-four standard and through the support bar, with the dowel ends flush at the faces. Or, you can cut each dowel pin so that it extends about an inch beyond the face of the standard in one direction and a similar amount beyond the face of the support bar in the opposite direction. Then, drill ¼-inch holes through each end of each dowel pin, about ½-inch back from the ends. Cut another series of smaller dowel pins which will fit through these holes to serve as locking pins. An alternative is to fit tapered pegs into each dowel pin end hole. These added pins will insure that the large support dowels do not slide out of their holes. Where two sections of shelves adjoin, as they do at the center standards in the illustration, make the large dowel pins long enough to pass through the standard and a pair of shelf support bars wherever you want side-by-side shelving.

Set the standards in place and secure them. Then place the shelf support bars in position, run the large dowel pins through the holes, and insert the locking dowel pins if you are using them. The shelves can be set at whatever levels you desire on the support bars. You can also construct one or more small casework cabinets which will just fit between the standards and rest upon the shelf support bars in the same manner as the shelves do.

BOOK WALL STORAGE

One common storage need in many households is for a place to put books and magazines, particularly the former. For those who love to read and collect books at a great rate, adequate book shelving seems to be a constant problem. One answer to that problem is to build a book wall. There are any number of ways to go about this task, some simple and some complex. A series of open shelves set on standards and brackets will do the job. Floor-to-ceiling book walls can be built in with a modest amount of work, filling up existing inches and spaces which might otherwise be of little value. Even a narrow space between a pair of windows is sufficient to shelve a great many volumes.

Or, a book wall can be made as a room divider, starting from an existing wall and extending into the room. Such a divider wall can be made accessible from one or both sides, and can be combined to include bookshelving, a writing desk, display cabinetry, and music and television equipment. It might be made to house books on a living room side of the divider, and china and tableware on a dining area side. The possibilities are limitless.

The book wall shown in Fig. 14-10 is a permanent built-in of four sections, covering an entire wall. Though rather time-consuming, this type of book wall is not difficult to construct. The entire assembly is tied to the existing partition wall behind the shelving, and to the floor and ceiling. In this particular project, ¾-inch particle board was used for shelving, side pieces, and the divider panels between sections. The face-frame, cleats, and shelf edging was made from mahogany. All shelves are fully cleated at back and ends, and their heights were staggered to that they could be further secured by nails driven through the side and divider panels.

The same project could have been constructed using plywood for all components, or solid wood, or a combination of solid wood and plywood. By providing heavier and stiffer side panels and divider panels, the shelves could have been made fully adjustable with track standards and clips mounted at the shelf ends, or with rows of dowel pegs or shelf pins. Or, the shelves could have been set in dados, thus

Fig. 14-10. Full book-wall section undergoing final sanding prior to finish application. Duncan Photos.

doing away with the support cleats. In that case, the shelf length would have been shortened and/or a thicker and stiffer shelf material chosen. In fact, there are many more ways in which this same book wall could have been constructed, and there are any number of specific design points and finished appearances which might have resulted.

To build a book wall of this sort, start by making a base frame, solidly attached to both floor and back wall. Here, the height of the base was made to match existing mopboards in the remainder of the room. Then, stand up one side panel, making sure that it is perfectly plumb, and fasten it to the base side. Determine the width and exact location of the first section, secure the top piece of that section to the ceiling, and then nail and glue the top end of the first side piece to the top piece. Cut the bottom shelf of the first section, and nail and glue it into place atop the base and butted against the first side piece. Then cut and fit the first divider panel, stand it in place on the base frame, and secure it to the free end of the bottom shelf and to the top piece. Repeat this process (Fig. 14-11) for the total number of sections, until you come to the second side panel. In this project both side panels extend from floor to ceiling, while the divider panels run only from the top of the base to the ceiling.

Lay out all of the shelf back support cleat locations on the wall between the side and divider panels. Cut a suitable number of cleats to accurate length—¾-inch by ¾-inch solid wood stock was used in this project—and nail them to the wall studs. Make sure that all of them are perfectly level. Then nail each side or divider panel to the cleat ends, using a single nail and taking care not to split the wood. Drilling slightly undersized pilot holes is a good idea.

Lay out the guidelines for the shelf end support cleats on the side and divider panels. The cleats should be set square to the lead edge of the case, lined up exactly with the shelf back support cleats, and level front-to-back. In addition, each shelf end support cleat should line up exactly with its opposite number so that each shelf will be level side-to-side. Cut the cleats from the same stock as the shelf back support cleats. To install, first apply glue to one cleat face, and

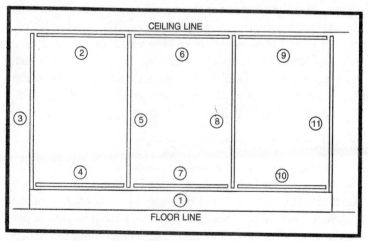

Fig. 14-11. Assembly pattern for shelving sections. After #11 come the shelf cleats, shelves and faceframe.

387

then clamp the piece into position, keeping an eye on the guideline to make sure that the cleat does not slip out of line. Nail the cleat to the panel with small finish nails.

Cut and fit all of the shelves. In this project, the shelf edges were left raw and aligned to be flush with the lead edge of the panels. To install the shelves, run a bead of glue around the top edges of the support cleats, set the shelf into position, and nail to the back support cleat with small finish nails. Clamp the leading edges of the shelf to the forward portion of the end support cleats, and then nail through the side or divider panels into the shelf edges. Remove the clamps and nail the ends of the shelves to the end support cleats.

Cut and fit the top face-frame rail. Using glue and finish nails, secure it to the top pieces and to each side and divider panel. Cut the stiles to fit between the bottom edge of the top rail and the bottom surface of the bottom shelf. The stiles used on the side panels are set with the outside edge flush with the outer surface of the side panels, and here were cut from standard 1-inch by 2-inch solid wood stock (actually ¾-inch by 1 ¾-inch). The stiles placed over the divider panel edges were ripped from 1-inch stock to a 2 ¾-inch width. These stiles are centered on the divider panel edges. Apply glue at all meeting points on the reverse sides of the stiles, set them in place, and nail them to the side and divider panel edges. Then, nail into the end of each shelf end support cleat as well.

The final step is to cover all of the visible raw edges. In this project, all of the shelf edges are capped with standard ½-inch by ¾-inch base shoe molding. Each piece was individually cut and fitted, and then glued and nailed into place. The rough edge of the bottom shelf was covered in a similar manner, but using ¾-inch by ¾-inch stock quarter-round molding. As the book wall is shown in the illustration, construction has been completed and the nail holes have been filled; sanding preparatory to applying a finish is under way.

COMBINATION OFFICE AND BOOK WALL

Storage walls can upon occasion become considerably more complex than the book wall described above. The assembly sketched in Fig. 14-12 shows a front view of a combination office and book wall. This unit was designed to act as a room divider. It can stand alone, reaching from floor to ceiling, or be anchored to a wall on either or both ends. This is a double-sided unit, with the reverse side

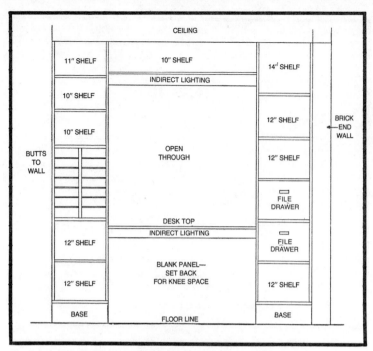

Fig. 14-12. Front elevation of combination office/book-wall.

designed to house books (Fig. 14-13). As Fig. 14-14 shows, the unit has greater depth from the front than from the rear. The space above the desk top is open all the way through. Below the desk top, however, a partition is designed to be installed toward the rear, allowing the construction on the reverse side of a series of shallow shelves made especially to hold small paperback books.

The indirect lighting section above the desk is set back slightly so that there is no danger of bumping one's head when rising from the desk. The lighting itself consists of both fluorescent and incandescent lamps hidden above a translucent acrylic plastic diffuser panel. The two types of lights are separately controlled, so that they may be used individually or together (the combination makes excellent lighting for drafting, artwork, layout work, and the like). The indirect lighting concealed beneath the desk top is fluorescent alone, and diffuses upward through a translucent white acrylic panel. This arrangement was designed primarily for use in photographic slide sorting and negative inspection, but could also be used for various types of artwork. The drawers are constructed in the usual manner

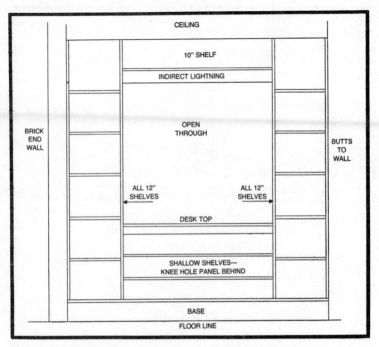

Fig. 14-13. Rear elevation of combination office/book-wall.

but sized to file folders, and are installed on heavy-duty full-suspension drawer slides. The multishelf rack section on the left uses hardboard panels slid into dadoes, for holding stationery, papers, magazines, and the like.

Though a complex unit, the construction procedures remain much the same as for the simpler projects discussed earlier. Start by building a base frame for the entire unit. Assuming that the unit will be freestanding, and not attached to a wall at either or both ends, next install a full-width end piece. Secure it top and bottom, and then install the divider panel which separates the front half of the section from the back half. Glue and nail it into place at top and bottom and along the edge which butts against the surface of the end piece. Then put up the next panel, to form a tall double-sided box. Follow the same procedure on the opposite end section. Then fit the divider panel which separates the forward portion of the upper shelf between the two sections from the rear part. Install the top shelf above the desk, next.

Arrange the lighting fixtures on the undersurface of that shelf, build an enclosure around them, and mount the translucent diffuser panel, in a frame, to the bottom edge of the lamp enclosure. Set into place the panel which divides the desk kneehole from the paperback book shelves at the rear. Then construct the lamp enclosure and desk-top frame, which is little more than a deep tray set between the shelf sections. Install the lighting fixture in this compartment and then put the desk top on. Here, a large sheet of plywood was used, with a 16-inch by 36-inch rectangle cut from the sheet. A ¼-inch rabbet cut was made around the perimeter of the rectangle, and a closely-fitted sheet of ¼-inch translucent acrylic plastic dropped into the opening. Two small and almost unnoticeable semicircular thumbnail slots were fashioned, one at each side of the plastic panel. Inserting a pen knife or a nail file into the slots pops the panel up for access to the lamps.

With the basic structure of the storage wall completed, all of the various shelves can be cut, fitted, and mounted. The stationery rack section can be built on the workbench as a unit and then slid into place. The last step is to construct the file drawers and install them. Other drawers could be substituted for some of the shelf space, or cupboard doors hung to enclose some or all of the space.

If the storage unit is to be secured against a wall at one or both ends, then the construction might well be a bit different, though the overall results would be the same. For instance, the end panel or side piece butting against a wall might better be made from two pieces instead of one. Cut a side piece to full height, but only to the depth of the front section. Secure this panel to the wall. Then cut and fit the divider panel which separates the front from the rear sections,

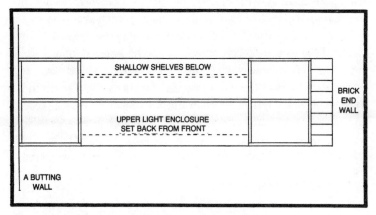

Fig. 14-14. Top view of combination office/book-wall.

butt it against the wall and against the rear edge of the side panel, and nail it to the side panel edge. Cut and fit the second side panel piece to the depth of the rear section, place it flat against the wall and butted against the divider panel, and fasten it to the wall. Then proceed with the remainder of the construction in the same fashion discussed above. This is a little more work, since more pieces must be cut, handled, and fitted, but the process allows more nailing points and a stronger, more easily assembled unit.

OTHER COMBINATION STORAGE UNITS

Storage units or walls of this type, whether single-sided or double-sided, can be built for any number of purposes, and designed and trimmed to fit practically any decor, so that they can be used successfully in most areas of the home. For instance, this same basic structure could be used for combined cabinets, shelves, and pass-through counter unit between a kitchen and a dining area. It could be used as a combination bar, bookcase, music wall, and china and tableware storage unit between a dining area and a living room. Placed against a wall of a bedroom, it could become a child's storage wall. Just convert one shelf section to a series of bureau-type drawers, place open shelves above, make the opposite shelf section into a closet or wardrobe with perhaps two or three adjustable shelves in the upper portion, raise the desk-top section somewhat to become a dressing table top, and mount a large mirror at the back of the opening. In a family room or game room, this structure could be converted to use as a hobby center, a model-making workshop, a hand-loading or fly-tying center, merely by changing, adding, or deleting drawers, shelves, and doors as the functions demand.

The height of any given storage wall may be established by virtue of the existing ceiling height, or can be lowered for an open-top effect. The overall width is simply suited to the space available, or to the dictates of the unit's intended functions. Overall depth is dependent primarily upon whether the assembly will be single-sided and backed up to a wall or double-sided with both faces accessible. This must then be related to the space available where the unit will stand, and also to the uses that the storage compartments will serve.

IDLE SPACE STORAGE

Most homes, whether old or new, contain a good deal of unused space in odd spots, while at the same time convenient storage space may be at a premium. With a little bit of ingenuity and imagination, you can convert some of this idle or otherwise wasted space into handy storage compartments. Some spots lend themselves quite nicely to workaday storage cabinetry and built-ins which enjoy constant use on a daily basis. Others are best employed for dead storage, where access is needed only infrequently.

BEDSTEAD STORAGE

Consider, for instance, that many bedrooms are furnished with high-posted beds. Those same bedrooms may well be short of closet storage space, and the home might also lack adequate facilities for storing seasonal clothing, extra pillows and bedding, or just miscellaneous personal possessions and such. Now, the underside of a high-posted bed may clear the floor by as much as 2 feet, and usually by at least a foot. This means that there could be as much as 50 cubic feet of space under that bed which normally does nothing but gather dust pussies. Get rid of the dust and provide yourself with some useful storage space.

Make an accurate set of measurements of the space available under the bed. Then construct a box like the one shown in Fig. 14-15, and mount it on low castors. The box rolls easily under the bed, where it is both out of sight and out of the way, and yet can be easily reached when needed. An alternative is to set a series of drawers in the outer face of the box. These can run full depth so that the case itself need never be rolled out from under the bed, or the drawers can be made short, with dead storage compartments behind

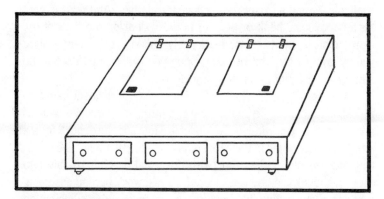

Fig. 14-15. One possibility for an under-bed storage box. Storage compartments can be changed and rearranged to suit demands, while keeping the same basic concept.

the drawers. If the bed is large, and open on three sides, you can construct a set of three boxes. One rolls out from the end of the bed while the other two roll out to each side. Or, move the bed, build one large stationary box with drawers which slide out on both sides and at the end, then replace the bed over the box. There are all kinds of combinations.

Another possibility is to do away with the bed and start from scratch. Build a large cabinet section of appropriate width, length, and height, with the top platform sized to a standard mattress. Build drawers, shelves, racks and storage compartments into the structure as you go along. You could include a deep headboard complete with bookshelf, magazine rack, and built-in lighting. A thick footboard might be set up with shelving or drawers facing outward and a built-in television set facing the headboard. Controls for lights, television, and radio can be built right into the headboard assembly. The whole unit could be made freestanding, positioned in midroom away from any walls, or could be anchored directly to a wall at the head, foot, or side. Again, the possibilities are endless.

BETTER STORAGE FROM CLOSETS

Every home has at least a few closets, and this is where there are usually ample amounts of wasted or unusable space. This applies not only to bedroom closets, but to hall, entryway, utility, and other general-purpose closets as well. Typically, a closet consists of a shallow and all too often narrow cubicle containing one dinky shelf approximately at eye level, with perhaps another nearly inaccessible shelf above, and a closet rod for hanging clothes. And that, except for an occasional hook or peg set in the wall or on the back of the closet door, is about all. Unquestionably, this is an inefficient design, and by doing a little bit of rearranging you can at least double the storage capacity of practically any closet.

The sketch in Fig. 14-16 shows how a typical closet might be redesigned to provide more efficient storage space, as well as greater utility. The width of the closet is 8 feet and the depth 2 feet, a size commonly found in the bedrooms of modern houses. The single long and wobbly clothes rod (with the usual one or possibly two shelves above) has been eliminated. A casework bureau assembly containing four or five full drawers, or whatever other combination appeals, is installed in the center of the closet opening. Shallow, slanted shoe racks are attached to each side of the bureau. Divider

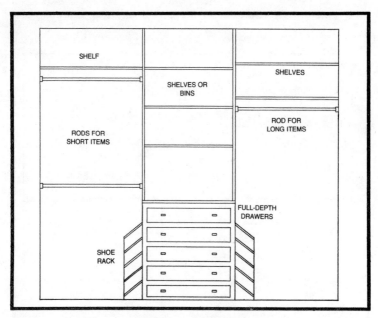

Fig. 14-16. Space-saving design for built-in clothes closet.

panels rise from the bureau top to the ceiling. A series of shelves or bins, or both, can be installed above the bureau top, or a large mirror and lighting fixtures installed on the rear wall to convert the space to a dressing table arrangement. Two clothes rods are mounted, one above the other, at one side of the closet for hanging up short items such as shirts and blouses. On the opposite side of the closet another clothes rod is mounted well above the floor for hanging up long items like pants and dresses. Above this rod are deep shelves for storage. Additional fixtures and accessories might be added as well, either to the closet door backs if they are hinged rather than sliding doors, or to appropriate points within the closet enclosure. Such fixtures might include additional lighting, necktie rack, belt rack, built-in jewelry case, hat rack or built-in hat compartments, small multiple storage trays racked on one of the shelves, or any of a considerable array of similar items.

CLOSET WALLS

Where two adjacent bedrooms are separated by a nonload-bearing partition wall, space can be saved and convenience gained by removing the partition wall and substituting a two-section closet wall

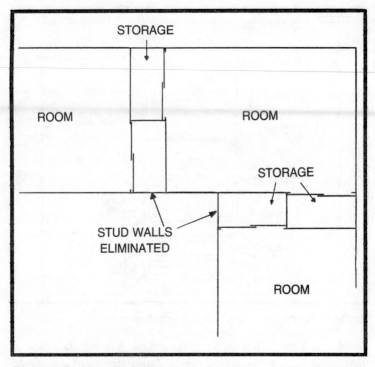

Fig. 14-17. Double built-in closets or storage walls can substitute for ordinary stud walls between rooms.

as shown in Fig. 14-17. The panel separating the two closets, one facing into one bedroom and one into the other, can be made from a sheet of plywood or particle board. Though the particle board would be less expensive, plywood would be the better choice because of its strength and rigidity. The end pieces, which presumably would lie flat against opposite bedroom walls, could also be made from either material. Rolling panel doors could be used, but bifold, accordion, or standard hinged doors allow better access and are more convenient. The drawer sections, which can be built either by the casework method or built-in procedures, can be of whatever size and shape you desire. The back panels of the closet should be made from plywood, which can then be painted or papered to suit the remainder of the room.

UNDER-STAIRWAY STORAGE

Many older homes, and a few newer ones as well, have stairways which lead to a second floor and are open underneath. This leaves an awkward area of odd proportions which seems not to lend itself easily to any use, and so is usually ignored. This spot, however, is an excellent one for a multipurpose storage unit.

The sketch in Fig. 14-18 shows one possible arrangement for such a storage unit. In that part of the area where there is sufficient headroom, a narrow coat or utility closet can easily be constructed. The remaining wedge of space formed between the floor and the stairway is framed up and panelled in as necessary to provide an appropriate arrangement of cupboards and drawers. In most cases, some space will inevitably be lost or unusable because the width of the staircase is considerably greater than the useful depth of the cupboards or drawers would be. Probably you would have to install a back panel or backframe at a depth of about 2 feet, and leave the rest of the space empty. Unless, of course, your fertile imagination can dream up some specialized use for that space.

BATHROOM STORAGE

Another part of most homes which can well stand the addition of some convenient storage space is the bathroom. This statement is especially true of half baths, which always seem to get left out when the cabinetry is passed around. Even though the bath may be small, there are usually at least a couple of possibilities for adding storage

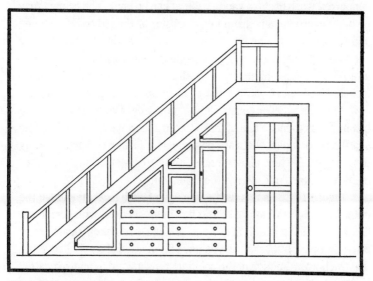

Fig. 14-18. Wasted space under single stairwell can be converted to multipurpose storage.

Fig. 14-19. Top cleats, top piece, and side pieces in place in above-stool bathroom cabinet. Duncan Photos.

units. For instance, wherever there is a wall-mounted or leg-supported wash basin, a vanity cabinet can be built. The cabinet may be built up around an existing wash basin, or the old basin removed and replaced with a new one flush-mounted in the vanity top. The vanity can be built in, or made as a simple casework project and then moved into place. Shelving, as well as a drawer or two, could be installed within the vanity cabinet to provide extra storage space.

Another excellent possibility, a most effective one especially in half baths, is to make use of that wasted space above the toilet. The seat-backs of most toilets are positioned at least 8 or 9 inches away from the wall, which allows ample space to install cabinetry, either built-in or casework, above the toilet tank.

Figure 14-19 shows the beginnings of such a cabinet above the toilet in a tiny half bath. The top has been secured with cleats just below the ceiling joists, and the side pieces and shelf cleats are in place. In Fig. 14-20, the shelves have been fitted and installed. Note that the bottom section of the cabinet steps inward to approximately half the depth of the upper section to allow plenty of clearance above the toilet tank. Because of the small size of the lower cabinet section, sliding doors made from hardboard will be set in tracks. Figure 14-21 shows the cabinet with the face-frame installed. The face-frame dimensions were chosen to allow the use of a pair of stock factory made louver doors in the top section. In Fig. 14-22, the cabinet is complete. The doors are fitted and hung, the sliding panels set and

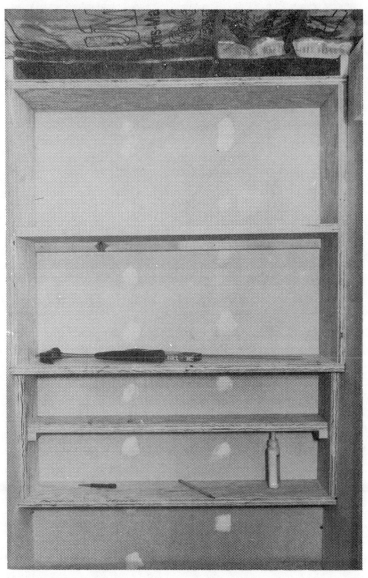

Fig. 14-20. Cleats, shelves and bottom section added to above-stool bathroom cabinet. Duncan Photos.

properly adjusted, and a small towel rack has been attached to the underside of the bottom shelf. All that remains is surface preparation and painting.

These are only a smattering of the possibilities open to you in the way of storage cabinets and built-ins. The chances are that these

Fig. 14-21. Above-stool bathroom cabinet with face-frame installed. Duncan Photos.

Fig. 14-22. Completed above-stool bathroom cabinet, utilizing space usually wasted in small half baths. Duncan Photos.

particular projects will not fit into your scheme of things at all, especially in a specific manner. The point is, once you determine that there is a particular need for some kind of storage spaces, you can probably discover some place to put such a unit. Then, you can go ahead and design and build the unit by using the general procedures and information we have discussed.

Chapter 15
Built-In Furnishings

The step from cabinetry to built-in furnishings is a small one. In fact, if you consider the definition of furnishings as objects which increase and enhance utility, comfort, and livability, them some items of built-in furnishings have already been mentioned. But, there are a great many more items which might be discussed, and the following ideas may serve to evoke a few of your own projects, similar or perhaps totally dissimilar.

The techniques and procedures used in constructing built-in furnishings are approximately the same as those discussed for cabinetmaking, and for general woodworking as well. Hand tool skills, power tool operation, joinery and gluing, hardware and materials are all pretty much the same. The chief differences lie primarily in specific designs of the assemblies. As an adjunct to the construction of built-in furnishings and depending upon the specific project, you may need to investigate some additional skills such as tile setting, upholstery, methods of fiberglassing, and maybe even masonry work. None of these activities, however, should present any great difficulties to the home craftsman of at least modest skills.

On the following pages are a few brief examples of projects in the built-in furnishings line. Some are very simple, and some are not. And though none of them may appeal to you, they are at least indicative of the tremendous range of possibilities, and may start some further ideas.

WINDOWSEATS

The windowseat has enjoyed great popularity for many years and is found in a great many older homes. Though seemingly forgotten in the construction of newer homes in the past few decades, now windowseats are beginning to appear once again. If you have a suitable spot in your home, you can easily build such an arrangement, either as a separate entity, or in conjunction with other storage elements (Fig. 15-1). If you are laying plans to build a new home, you might consider including one or a series of windowseats right in the drawings.

Basically, the requirements involve only a suitable amount of window space 20 to 24 inches above floor level and at least 3 feet wide with sufficient available floor space to build a comfortable windowseat. A bay window arrangement is also ideal. In any case, the window area ideally should be on a sunny side where it will receive plenty of light and warmth. The height of the windowseat itself can be anywhere from 16 to 24 inches above the floor, and should be at least 18 inches wide and preferably 24 inches or more.

Essentially, all the assembly consists of is a sturdy box built against the wall and directly below the window area. The top, or a part of it, can be hinged to lift up, providing a considerable amount of storage space. Alternatively, the front face may be fitted out with drawers and/or cupboard doors to achieve the same purpose in a somewhat different fashion. The latter arrangement is usually more utilitarian and convenient. The top of the windowseat can be permanently upholstered with foam rubber cushions covered with a suitable material or fitted out with a series of removable cushions. Another trick is to cover the top, and possibly front as well, of the windowseat with the same carpeting material as is used on the floor of the room. Indirect soft lighting may be included above the windowseat or lighting fixtures installed at the sides. Bookshelves, display shelves, magazine racks, cupboards, and other cabinetry can be built flanking the windowseat on one or both sides.

SOFAS

If you don't happen to have a good spot for a windowseat, consider making a sofa. This too can be built directly against a wall, or into a corner formed by two walls, in much the same fashion as a

Fig. 15-1. One possibility for window seat and storage unit combination.

windowseat. The basic structure is again merely a box, with the top of the box (sofa seat) slanted down slightly toward the rear for comfort. A slanted back piece can then be built against the rear wall. The sofa can be designed with arms or not, as you choose, and a considerable amount of storage space can be built into the sofa frame just as with the windowseat. Upholstery may be permanent or take the form of removable cushions.

Another possibility is to cantilever the sofa assembly out from the wall, leaving the space beneath completely open (Fig. 15-2). The trick to successful construction of this type of built-in sofa is to anchor the bottom frame to the wall so that the basic sofa platform framework is exceptionally strong and rigid. When a 200-pound body perches on the outer edge of the sofa, the unit force exerted upon the frame and the fasteners is tremendous, so a great deal of strength is needed.

A concept which lends an unusual effect to a large room is the suspended sofa. Using the strongest joinery and the best craftsmanship you can muster, build a freestanding sofa minus legs and with a primary framework of exceptional rigidity and strength. The material used must in itself be strong and rugged. Attach heavy chains to

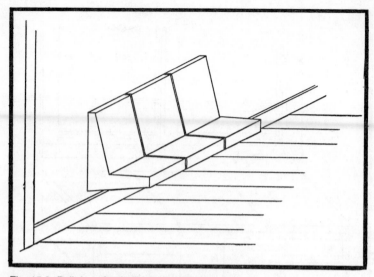

Fig. 15-2. Built-in sofa cantilevered from wall. A similar built-in unit could be supported by a storage section mounted on the floor.

all four corners of the sofa, and anchor the other ends of the chains solidly to the structural framework of the ceiling so that the sofa swings free. Heavy dimension stock may have to be added above the ceiling to take the extra weight and strain. When finished, the sofa should be suspended so that the tops of the seat cushions are about 18 to 20 inches above the floor. Obviously, a goodly amount of free floor space is necessary around this type of sofa.

INGLENOOKS AND FIREPLACE SEATING

Another place where it is nice to have ample seating is around the fireplace. Many years ago, homes which could boast a large central fireplace also had a place called an inglenook. This was a snug little corner built right into the fireplace structure, where the masonry always remained warm and cozy from the heat of the fire. Complete with cushions and pillows and a bit of reading material, this was a marvelous spot to while away a wintery evening. These huge fireplaces are seldom built any more, though they certainly could be, and an inglenook designed and built right into the structure in the process. Much the same effect can be created with today's fireplaces, either built-in masonry or freestanding steel, simply by making a compatible arrangement of fireplace and built-in seats, settle benches, or even short sofas like love seats. If the fireplace is installed in a sunken pit, built-in and upholstered seating can be arranged around the perimeter of the pit, facing the fireplace. As with the windowseat or the sofa, this is primarily a matter of constructing a suitable solid framework and then adding something comfortable to sit upon.

BEDS AND BUNKS

Since sleeping is the way that we spend a large part of our lives, and probably the greater proportion of our time at home, beds form an important part of the complement of furnishings in any house. The possibilities of constructing built-in or freestanding beds including storage compartments of various sorts was mentioned in an earlier chapter. Another item worthy of consideration, particularly for children's bedrooms, is a built-in bunkbed arrangement (Fig. 15-3). There are many effective designs, which can be suited exactly to individual requirements. For instance, you might build a simple rectangular double bunk for two children, with the upper bunk reached by the traditional ladder. This basic concept can be further amplified by building storage compartments beneath the lower bunk

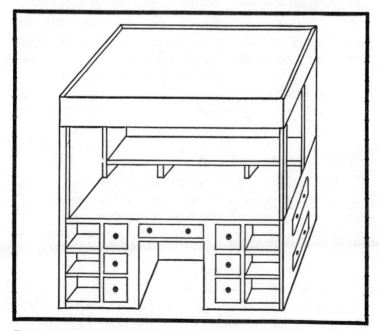

Fig. 15-3. Combined bunk, storage, and work area unit. Specific details could be changed around in any number of ways.

Fig. 15-4. Simple cedar window box or planter with framed top. Duncan Photos.

and by adding cupboards, bureau drawer sections, a wardrobe, or a desk and shelf combination at the end of the bunk. The lower section of a double bunk set might be rearranged to comprise a desk area for school work, one or two drawer sections, and cupboards or shelves for storing toys, collections, and hobby equipment, with indirect lighting built right into the structure. The upper level would remain as a bunk. Similar projects might be built for adult use, especially for guest quarters in a summer cottage or ski lodge. With thoughtful designing, it is possible to arrange an averaged-sized room to hold bunks and adequate closet, cupboard, and drawer storage space for four or more vacationers and all their gear.

WINDOWBOXES AND PLANTERS

Over the past few years in particular, the raising of assorted house plants has become a popular pastime. The first requisite for house plants is to have a suitable place to put them, and this gives rise to numerous built-in projects. The simplest project, of course, is a sturdy shelf or series of shelves upon which potted plants can be set. Another simple project is the windowbox (Fig. 15-4). Window-boxes are quite easy to make, though they must be solidly put together to hold the weight of soil, drainage gravel, and plants. They must also be ruggedly attached to the house structure. Cedar or redwood are both good choices for materials, and, though plain butt joints are most often used, more complex joinery would be better.

Windowboxes made from other materials are best lined with a metal insert—copper is often used—or coated with fiberglass resin to prevent rot and decay. Though usually designed to mount directly below an exterior window ledge, there is no reason at all why similar boxes, pehaps with a bit fancier design and better finish, cannot be mounted on the inside of a window.

Another possibility is to choose an appropriate window in your home and outfit it with a series of permanent built-in shelves. This can be accomplished in a number of ways, and the specifics are largely dependent upon the size, design, and shape of the window

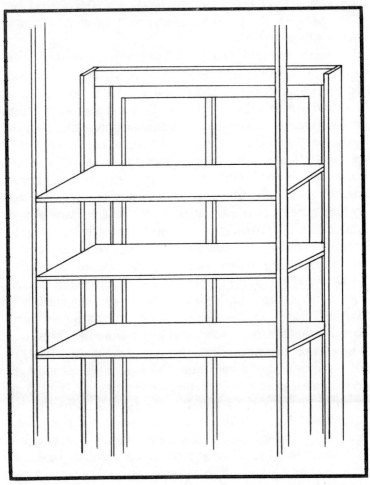

Fig. 15-5. Simple planter or display shelves built in as a unit against an existing window.

and the surrounding trim. One way is to remove the existing window casings and any additional trim, and then erect the shelving, tied directly to the window jambs and adjacent wall studding. The window opening can be retrimmed as you go along (Fig. 15-5). Provide plenty of support for each shelf by means of side pieces or standards and stiles as necessary. The shelves should be fitted with a slight lip at each edge to lessen the danger of a heavy pot being scooted off the shelf and through the window or onto the floor. Either solid wood or plywood makes good shelf material for this purpose, together with solid wood for standards and trim. With the proper arrangement, heavy plate glass could also be used for shelves. This material has the advantage of allowing light to reach all of the plants; it also does away with shadowing.

Another interesting way to construct a window planter is to do away with the window entirely. Remove the window assembly and all of the trim, leaving an empty rough opening in the wall. Then construct a skeletal framework (Fig. 15-6), anchored firmly to the rough opening side studs, header, and sill, and protruding 12 to 18 inches or so beyond the exterior of the building. The top, or "roof," should slant downward for drainage of snow and rainwater, while the sides, bottom, and front can be rectangular or slanted in whatever manner you choose. Glaze the entire framework (except for the bottom, which can be solid material) with glass or heavy acrylic plastic sheets. Make sure the entire assembly is sturdy and weatherproof. In cold-weather climates, double glazing either with plastic or with glass is a good idea. If the double glazing is not hermetically sealed, make one layer or the other of the glazing removable so that the interior surfaces can be cleaned; otherwise a film of dirt will inevitably find its way between the panes. Once the framework is complete, install a series of shelves at appropriate points. These can be made from solid stock or from plate glass, and either fixed in place or set upon adjustable standards. The finished result makes an excellent minigreenhouse of an attractive nature and yet takes up no space within the living quarters. Note that either this project or the interior shelf project above could also be used for display purposes, showing off a collection of cut glass or antique bottles, for instance.

House plants need not be grown right in a window space, nor need they remain in pots. Indoor planters, especially when provided with artificial lighting designed to aid plant growth, are very successful as focal points of decorative attraction in a room or as room

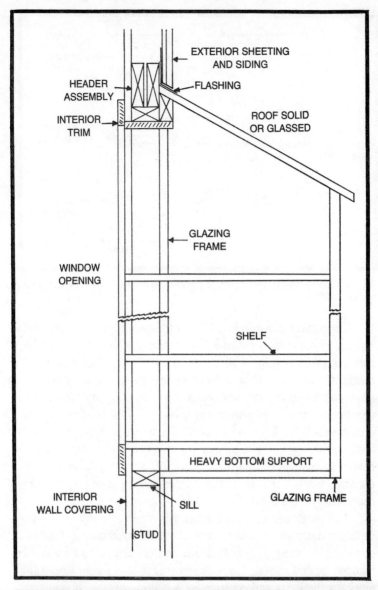

EXTERIOR SHEETING
AND SIDING

HEADER
ASSEMBLY

FLASHING

INTERIOR
TRIM

ROOF SOLID
OR GLASSED

GLAZING
FRAME

WINDOW
OPENING

SHELF

HEAVY BOTTOM SUPPORT

INTERIOR
WALL COVERING

SILL

GLAZING FRAME

STUD

Fig. 15-6. Section view of minigreenhouse built into an existing window frame or rough opening.

dividers. Such planters can be built in an endless array of sizes, shapes, and general designs. Large ones work particularly well, provided that there is ample space in the room and that the floor structure is rugged enough to take the weight.

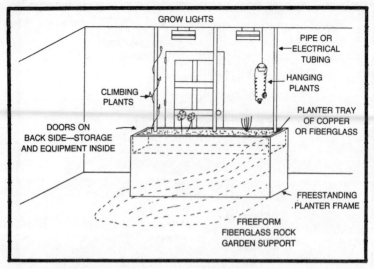

Fig. 15-7. Room divider type of planter screens the exterior door from room and creates an entryway.

The planter shown in Fig. 15-7 forms the basis for a screen wall dividing a front entry door from the remainder of the room. It can be constructed by building a simple skeleton of dimension stock, anchored firmly to the floor but otherwise freestanding. Cover the skeleton with plasterboard or paneling to match (or contrast) to the decor of the room. Set a deep tray in the top of the resulting box to accommodate a collection of plants. Mount grow lights at ceiling level and arrange a row of hanging plants which will grow (hopefully) downward to meet those growing upward. Four lengths of pipe are anchored betwen the top of the planter and the ceiling to provide support for vining plants.

The lower section of the planter is made accessible through cupboard doors to provide storage space for equipment and accessories and to house a water tank and recirculating pump for a small fountain located above. There is also room here for an automatic timer for the lights and controls for a built-in spray-mist watering system. The room side of the planter can be extended in a free-form fiberglass shell, making a series of troughs spreading to the floor in spiral staircase fashion. The fiberglass can be laid over a random steel mesh framework, and the troughs filled with more dirt for additional plants. The structure could also be made sturdy enough to support a number of large mineral specimens—clumps of amethyst and other quartz crystals, pyrites, and such—around which the plants can be positioned, forming an indoor combination rock garden and mineral display as part of the planter. One of the troughs could form a watercourse, complete with tiny falls, for the overflow from the fountain to follow in returning to the water tank.

Indoor planters or even complete gardens of this sort can easily be constructed in any home where there is a suitable spot and sufficient space. The larger projects usually combine the skills needed in rough framing, general woodworking, cabinetwork, and often bits and pieces of the electrical, sheetmetal, and plumbing trades as well. A lively imagination is perhaps the greatest assest in designing indoor planters and gardens, and there is no end to what can be done, in practically any area of the home from kitchen to bathroom.

DESK AND OFFICE CENTERS

Another area of home furnishings which lends itself nicely to built-in projects is in the work department. A built-in desk, for instance, can be handy to have around, and can take many forms. One such is shown in Fig. 15-8. Here, the basic structure of the desk

Fig. 15-8. Built-in desk assembly, shown prior to final finish and as laminated plastic top is being installed. Duncan Photos.

has been completed, and the Formica laminated plastic top is being fitted. The assembly was built into a corner spot, using the two walls for support. The first step was to construct a small cabinet containing a single drawer with storage space below, made accessible by one cupboard door in the front and another on the side at the rear. Once the cabinet was built into place, a back support cleat was attached to the rear wall and the narrow left end support leg installed. A front support rail runs from the end support leg to the cabinet, with a pair of cross supports running between the rear cleat and the front support. This forms a solid framework upon which the particle board top was placed. After the laminated plastic has been bonded and trimmed, the remainder of the desk will be painted to match the room decor. The same basic concept could be executed in a number of different ways and sizes and could include additional cupboard or drawer storage beneath and shelving or cupboard space above or to the sides.

One good way to go about building a substantial office work-center is to build a large but lower than normal base cabinet designed to accommodate whatever office functions are necessary, such as file drawers, typewriter space, storage for bills and stationery, and so forth. Then build a matching set of wall cabinets above, making them somewhat lower than those that would be found in a kitchen. An appropriate desk top height is from 27 to 30 inches, with the wall cabinets starting 16 to 20 inches above the desk top. The bottom of the wall cabinet is a good place to mount indirect lighting for the work area.

SEWING CENTERS

A built-in sewing center is another good project. Here again, base cabinets and wall cabinets combine. Accommodation for plenty of specialized storage space for sewing equipment in the way of cupboards, drawers, and racks will get the job done nicely. A complete sewing center should include a full-length mirror and plenty of good lighting. One of the best combinations includes a sewing table with an extension apron, a cutting table or counter, and an ironing counter or table. Additional flip-up counter extensions mounted upon piano hinges are often helpful. Special drawers or racks can be made to hold spools of thread, sewing accessories, packets of patterns, and the like.

LAUNDRY CENTERS

The laundry is another spot where built-in furnishings of a utilitarian nature can be most helpful. These might include such items as a work center with large countertops, perhaps with some flip-up sections, for sorting and folding clothing. An ironing station is needed, and a broad adjacent counter or worktop upon which large items such as table cloths or sheets can be spread during the ironing process is handy. Tilt-out bins or laundry baskets on sliding trays are useful for storing dirty laundry. Large compartmented drawers can also be used for dirty laundry, or for separating work clothes, whites, permanent press fabrics, and so forth. Storage compartments or racks might be installed to hold freshly washed and folded clothing and linens, while separate bins can be made for damp laundry awaiting ironing. Along with all of this, there is a definite need for storage space to house laundry supplies, and perhaps additional built-in tubs or sinks as well. With some of these utilitarian furnishings, it is sometimes difficult to determine where ordinary cabinetry leaves off and the furnishings begin. The two are very close and they are often considered as one.

REFRESHMENT BARS

A built-in item likely to be a good deal more popular than laundry cabinetry is the refreshment bar. This is a handy piece of furniture for the family that does a considerable amount of entertaining. It can be adapted to practically any room decor and established in a living room, family room, or recreation room, and is relatively easy to construct (Fig. 15-9). The assembly is essentially a large box set upon its side, with the bottom facing the "patrons" and the open top facing the bartender. The bar may be anchored to an adjoining wall or tucked in between two adjacent walls. Access is from the back to a series of shelves containing glassware, refreshments, and accessory items. The rear opening may be enclosed with cupboard doors or not, as you choose.

The assembly can be constructed from plywood or particle board, along with pieces of solid wood stock for trim as necessary. Laminated plastic, plastic resin, and copper are good choices for the countertop. The front and sides may be given an applied finish; i.e., covered with laminated plastic, or padded and covered with upholstery material such as a vinyl fabric. In a relatively large assembly, provisions can be made for a bar sink, an ice chest or small refrigerator, a beer keg cooler rack and tapping head, or whatever other accessories are desirable. The unit may also be built to include an overhead cabinet section, with storage space for additional glassware and supplies, and built-in lighting as well. Note that this basic structure, at least in the smaller sizes, can be mounted upon casters to serve as a completely portable unit. In this case, it could be used as either a refreshment bar or a server and is a piece of casework rather than a built-in furnishing.

STORAGE SPECIALTIES IN THE BATHOOM

As mentioned earlier, bathrooms are often apt to be short of storage space, particularly the older bathrooms. One of the easiest built-in furnishings to provide in a bathroom is a vanity cabinet containing a wash basin. A further variation is to convert a single wash basin situation by installing a large vanity with two wash basins tapped from the same water supply. Such an installation can be further modified by providing built-in makeup or dressing tables, large mirrors, built-in indirect lighting, and maybe even a planter or two.

If the bathroom is a large one, you can let your imagination run wild. For instance, you might be able to build in a king-sized shower stall. This sort of a project can be accomplished by several methods, the most common being to build a structural framing arrangement and cover it with wallboard and finish it out with laminated plastic or ceramic tile. There is another possibility, too, which is a woodworker's delight. The entire shower cabinet, which actually can be as large as a big closet or even a small room, can be constructed entirely from edge-joined and matched cedar planking applied to a sturdy framework in whatever interesting patterns the builder chooses. All sorts of decorative fillips and architectural niceties can be introduced without much trouble. Edge joining is done entirely with waterproof glue. After the wood is smoothed to a satin finish, a transparent protective finish which is totally waterproof is applied as the last step. The completed installation can be remarkably handsome.

To carry this idea one step further, instead of installing just a shower cabinet, you might opt to include a sauna in the program. Sauna building is a rather specialized area of contruction, insofar as

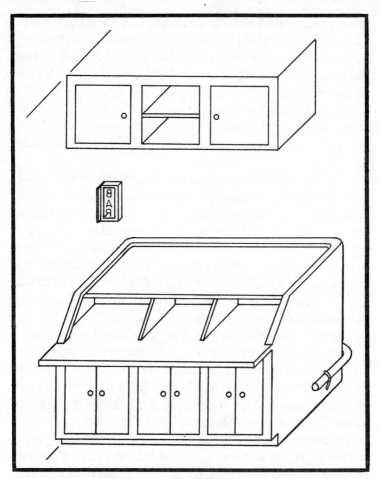

Fig. 15-9. One possibility for a bar or refreshment center with overhead storage.

specific details are concerned. However, the woodworking involved is of the usual variety. There are several kits on the market, as well as plans and specifications, which deserve investigation before proceeding with a sauna project. Suffice it to say, however, that the job can be done by a competent home craftsman at not unreasonable cost.

Another interesting built-in is the bathtub, and this can be done in a number of ways. One commonly used method is to start with an ordinary tub which sits upon the floor and against a wall in the usual fashion. Surround the existing tub with multilevel decking, done in stairstep fashion so that the top level is butted against, and at the

417

same level as, the tub rim. The vaious platforms should be wide and sturdy and may be finished in a waterproof transparent material for a natural look or with an applied opaque finish. Any applied finish should be of the nonskid variety in the interest of safety. A small portion of the platforming can be built above tub level at some out-of-the-way position to serve as a planter (ferns will grow wondrously here). Extra storage can be included beneath the platforms in the way of cupboard and/or drawer space, depending upon their design.

Another method is to recess the tub partway, or even all the way, into the floor so that a sunken tub effect is achieved. Then decking, perhaps combined with a low safety wall around the edge of the tub which can also double as a seat, is installed to surround the tub. The tub can be placed against a wall, but the whole arrangement is more effective in a relatively large bathroom where the tub installation can be made away from any wall space. Again, additional storage places for toweling and bath accessories, planter sections, and even lighting may be included in the design.

Another possibility, a good deal more complicated but also having greater design flexibility, is to start from scratch, building tub and surroundings as an integral assembly. The assembly can be floor-mounted or partly or wholly sunken. The tub unit itself can be made in any size or shape that is convenient or interesting, and the surrounding area can take the form of the designs mentioned above, or be arranged otherwise to suit your wishes. The tub itself can be shaped of fiberglass against a skeletal framework of appropriate shape, and with complete flexibility of form. You can also use mosaic tile set in concrete. In effect, it could easily become a tiny swimming pool, even one with underwater lights. Or, the tub can be made of cedar strips backed against a ribbed frame, much in the manner of a canoe with the ribs on the outside instead of the inside. The tub is then sealed and finished with a waterproof coating similar to that used in the cedar wood shower cabinet. As mentioned before, all finishes should be nonskid. One point to remember in constructing a scratch-built tub is that a large one filled with water is extremely heavy, so the assembly must be given plenty of rugged support. For those who enjoy sumptuous and luxurious bathrooms, these projects are worthy of investigation. Using imaginative design and your cabinetmaking and woodworking skills, you can construct a bathroom which is more than just another bathroom.

Chapter 16
Finishes and Finishing

The last step in any cabinetwork, casework, or built-in project is to prepare the surfaces of the assembly and then apply a finish. This is the frosting on the cake, a final process that can make or break the completed project. A poorly done finishing job can completely ruin the appearance of an otherwise excellent piece of cabinetry, so great care should be taken to use the correct combinations of materials and procedures to produce the finest possible finish. Conversely, no amount of expert finishing can salvage a poorly made cabinet. In most instances, it is well to know before even starting the project what kind of final finish will be applied.

A great deal of information is available from various sources regarding specific finishes and finishing procedures, and the field is an extensive and involved one. Many craftsmen spend the better part of their lives perfecting their finishing techniques to a high degree of excellence and in learning exactly what procedures to use under varying circumstances and with different materials and types of finishes. Obviously, we can do little more than scratch the surface here. The following information is general in nature but should see you through almost any kind of average finishing job. For special or unusual circumstances, or for some of the more exotic treatments such as pickling, antiquing, and distressing, or difficult techniques such as simulated wood graining, additional research is suggested.

REPAIR WORK

There are usually some imperfections on the workpiece surfaces which must be taken care of before the finish can be applied. These may consist of slight dents, cracks or fissures, pinholes, nail or screw holes, and the like. Often the patchwork is taken care of before the sanding begins, and at other times it is easier to do the job between the rough sanding and the preparatory sanding stages. Slight imperfections may be taken care of even between the preparatory and the finish sanding. Frequently there is no "best" procedure, and exactly what to do depends upon circumstances and preference.

Small dents in the wood can sometimes be removed by steaming. This is usually successful only if the dent is shallow and the wood is not torn or abraded. Place a damp cloth over the dent and bring a hot iron in contact for a second or two. Repeat the process several times until the dent disappears. If this does not work, then you must use a filler. Nail holes, cracks, rough spots, and the like can also be plugged with a filler. The material that you use depends upon the type of finish which will be applied.

Where the surface will be covered with an opaque finish, practically any kind of filler will do the job. Plastic wood or wood dough works fine, and glazing putty may be used under some circumstances. The putty, however, will remain soft for a long time, and may be attacked by solvents in the finish. Spackle works particularly well, and comes ready-to-use in cans and tubes or in a powder form which must be mixed with water. Follow the directions which come with the product that you choose, and fill all imperfections with a putty knife or palette knife. Usually it is necessary to overfill the imperfection to compensate for any shrinkage of the filler as it dries, and so that it can be sanded perfectly flush with the workpiece surface after it does dry.

If the finish is to be natural, transparent, or semitransparent, then the filler situation changes remarkably, and may be a bit frustrating as well. Some fillers, for instance, will not take a stain, and so leave an obvious different-colored patch. Other fillers will absorb stain at a greater rate than the workpiece, also leaving an obvious patch. If the finish is to be natural, then the filler must exactly match the color of the workpiece. With semitransparent finishes, the filler must match the combined coloration of the workpiece and the finish in such a way that the patches are invisible. All of this can cause problems if the process is not approached with caution. Usually a certain amount of experimentation must be done on scrap pieces to arrive at the desired results.

Wood dough is often a good choice in this situation. It will take stain to a certain extent, although not necessarily in the same degree that the workpiece does. However, the material itself can sometimes be stained before use and made to match the workpiece. Afterwards it will absorb the finish to the same extent as the workpiece. Shellac sticks are widely used, and are available in colors which match most of the common woods. The solid shellac is buttered into the crack or hole with a hot burn-in knife blade, heated over an alcohol lamp or a torch. Wax or putty sticks are also available in a great many colors to match various woods. These soft fillers are rubbed into the imperfections directly from the stick. They are generally applied after the surface preparation has been completed. Where stains are involved, often the best course is to fill imperfections after the staining is completed, and match the filler to the stain color.

Another widely used filler consists of fine sawdust saved from the cutting and sanding processes. The sawdust is mixed with glue and patched into place. If the sawdust, application tools, and mixing tools are all clean, the resulting patch will exactly match the workpiece except in the matter of grain. It is a quite effective method for most finishes, but may not work well with stain. The wood particles, being coated with glue, will not absorb the stain in the same way that the rest of the workpiece does, and may becomes obvious. On the other hand, they may not; much depends upon the specific finishes, and you will have to experiment.

Filling holes and imperfections in resawn or rough-cut wood can be done with any suitable filler. Use a small flexible-bladed knife to apply the filler. Before the filler dries, brush it lightly with a coarse-bristled brush. When properly roughened, the surface of the filler will be patterned much like the surface of the workpiece. When the finish is applied, the filled spots will be indistinguishable. Knots also require some special treatment. Wherever knots appear on a show surface of a cabinet, they should be sealed with one or two coats of shellac after the surface has been finish sanded. When the shellac dries, lightly finish-sand the area again, feathering the shellac edges to the workpiece surface, taking care not to cut completely through the shellac coating over the knots. This is especially important with resionous woods, to prevent sap from bleeding through the finish coats.

Covering screw holes can be done with fillers, but is best accomplished by gluing and inserting either flush or button plugs into the holes. For transparent or semitransparent finishes, the plug material should either sharply contrast with the workpiece material, or be exactly the same, with the grains matched up as closely as possible. With opaque finishes, of course, this is immaterial.

SURFACE PREPARATION (SANDING)

The preparation of cabinetry surfaces for the final application of a finish is done by sanding. This presumes that all forming—the removal of any great quantities of wood—has already been accomplished during the construction process, and that the cabinet components are well lined up and closely fitted. The sanding process is broken down into three distinct stages: rough sanding, preparatory sanding, and final sanding. In some finishing procedures, additional sanding is needed between applications of finish, but that comes later.

Sandpaper comes in several grades, ranging from coarse to very fine. The cheaper and lower-quality types are simply designated as sandpaper. For longer life and better cutting action, however, use garnet paper or aluminum oxide paper. Another type of paper, common to auto-body finishing but also used in some cabinetry finishing procedures, is called waterproof or wet-or-dry paper. This is a soft-backed paper coated with particles of silicon carbide. All papers are designated or graded by the size of the grit particles. The larger the number, the smaller the grit. Thus, 60-grit and 80-grit papers are very coarse, while 320-grit and 400-grit are extremely fine. Any of these papers works nicely on wood surfaces and can also be used on metal. However, emery cloth, which has a fabric backing, does a better job in some respects on metal surfaces, and is commonly marketed in grades of coarse, medium, and fine. For a final polish on metal surfaces, use crocus cloth, which is so fine as to appear smooth. You may also see sandpapers graded by another numbering system, such as 3% or 5%. Again, the smaller the number, the coarser the paper.

The purpose of rough sanding is to remove a relatively large amount of unwanted material, partly smoothing high or rough spots.

In some intances, especially with well-built cabinets or casework, rough sanding may be unnecessary. The paper grades most commonly used for this process are 60-grit, 80-grit, and 100-grit. These coarse papers cut rapidly and leave obvious scratches, so proceed with caution. Always sand with the grain of the wood (exceptions noted later) and try never to move the sandpaper in a crossgrain direction at all. The resulting scratches are most difficult to erase. Also, the softer the wood, the faster the paper will cut and the easier it is to leave deep scratches. As you work, check the surface frequently, clear the dust away often, and clean dust from the sandpaper by slapping the back of the sheet against some solid surface. The tendency is to oversand; this creates all sorts of problems in later stages. Remain aware of this fact and let up a little earlier than at first seems reasonable.

The preparatory sanding stage is done with medium-grit paper, usually 120-grit or 150-grit, or thereabouts. This will leave a much smoother surface than the coarser papers, and eliminate many of the fine scratches. Preparatory sanding is used to slightly round component edges and to produce a uniformly flat, relatively smooth surface. Again, keep the surfaces and the paper free from sawdust, and always sand with the grain of the wood.

The finish sanding is done with 180-grit, 220-grit or an even finer grade paper. The purpose is to render the surface satin smooth in all directions. Experienced craftsmen determine the relative smoothness of the workpiece by a combination of two methods. Most often, the message is carried through the fingertips. By running his fingertips lightly over the surface, the experienced craftsman can tell just when his sanding job is finished, and just which spots need a bit more attention. Another method is to shine a strong light across the surface so that even slight imperfections or unevenness are either highlighted or shadowed. The problem areas are easily spotted and can be treated further. This state of surface preparation is critical because, unless you have a completely smooth and satiny surface, the applied finishes may turn out to be somewhat less perfect than you had hoped for and to require a good deal of additional work between finish coats. Granted that the job is tiring and tedious, and sometimes seems as though it will never end. Nonetheless, have patience and keep on sanding, until you are absolutely certain that the surface is as smooth and free from imperfections as you can hope to make it. Your reward will come in the form of a flawless finished product.

All three stages of sanding can be done by hand with a sanding block or a sanding plane, but the job is considerably easier with a machine. Where substantial amounts of material must be removed, rough sanding can be done with a belt sander. Because of its rapid cutting action, however, the belt sander must be used with great caution. An orbital sander will also work for rough sanding, and can with care and practice be used for preparatory sanding too, though the practice is not recommended. Never use an orbital sander for finish sanding, though, because the action of the pad will leave little whirligig scratches all over the workpiece surface. Instead, use an inline sander for all final sanding operations. This same type is best used for preparatory sanding as well. At least the last few passes in the finish sanding stage are usually done by hand, since this seems to produce the best finish. Veteran craftsmen will often hand-sand without block, using only their fingers against the paper. This is a most effective procedure when properly done, but requires a definite feel for the work. In the hands of an inexperienced sander, the usual result is a series of shallow ripples or waves from uneven finger pressure. Use this method sparingly and with great caution until you develop experience and a feel.

Though machines and blocks are generally best and safest for flat surfaces, hand-held sandpaper does do a better job on rounded or convoluted surfaces, and in fact may be the only possible way. Using fingernails, fingertips, curled fingers, or the sides of your fingers, you can match most of the surfaces which need to be sanded. Refrain from using heavy pressure and let the sandpaper do the work. You may find that emery boards such as normally used for manicuring fingernails are quite useful in tricky cabinet sanding situations.

PREFINISHING PROCESSES

There are other processes which may be considered either a part of the surface preparation or an early phase of the final finishing procedure. Included among the processes are bleaching, sizing, surfacing, sealing, and filling.

Bleaching

The purpose of bleaching, as you might expect, is to render a dark wood lighter or a light wood nearly white. It is used where an extremely light-colored finish is desired or as a base for honey-colored finishes. Bleaching can also be used to lighten certain darker portions of a workpiece to make them blend in better with the remaining surfaces. Working with bleaches is a tricky business, and, since the solutions are so dangerous, great caution and strict safety rules must be observed.

There are three principal chemicals which are used for bleaching wood. The weakest, and the simplest to use, is a solution of oxalic acid crystals in hot water. Another consists of a solution of hydrogen peroxide, which is applied in combination with a liquid caustic soda. The components can be put on one immediately after the other, or both at once. The strength of the bleach can be altered by varying the proportions of the two solutions, and by dilution of one or the other, or both.

Bleaches can be injurious immediately upon contact, and may be inflammable as well. When using them, no matter how small the job, outfit yourself with rubber gloves, full-length rubber apron, sleeve protectors, and a full face shield, or at least goggles. You will need plenty of ventilation, and must work well away from any open flames or spark-producing equipment. Mixing and application procedures should be done strictly according to the manufacturer's directions.

Surfaces to be bleached must be properly dried and cured before the process begins. After the bleach has been applied, the residue must be washed off and the workpiece allowed to dry thoroughly at a minimum temperature of 70° for 24 hours. Then a final finish sanding must be done before any finish coating is applied. Great care must be taken when bleaching glued-up stock so that the glue does not begin to dissolve or separate. If it is known ahead of time that a bleaching process will be used, glued-up stock can be assembled with waterproof glue to avoid this problem. Another potential problem is that excessive moisture may lift the grain badly, or cause the sheet to warp. Never let any moisture stand on the surface, and, when washing off the bleached surface, wash the opposite side as well to equalize the moisture content on both surfaces. This hopefully will help to minimize any warping problem.

Sizing

This is often recommended where a particularly smooth surface and consequently smooth finish coating is desired. The sizing is made by mixing animal glue and warm water in a ratio of ¼ pound to 1 gallon. The solution is applied with a brush in a thin coating to the entire surface of the workpiece and allowed to dry for a full day. Then the final finish sanding is done. This requires a bit of judgment, since just the right amount of sizing must be sanded away. If the entire coating is sanded off, then the value of the sizing will be completely negated. On the other hand, if not enough sizing is sanded away, it may interfere with the finish coating. The object of the process is to bind the tiny wood fibers tight to the body of the workpiece in order to allow a smoother finish. This works particularly well with fibrous wood which tends to develop a feathery surface when sanded.

Filling

This is a process whereby open grain lines and pores in open-grained woods are filled to present a uniformly smooth surface. Many woods, such as white pine and cherry, do not need this treatment. Others which are only moderately porous, such as some maples or birches, can be smoothed out with the application of a relatively thin liquid filler especially made for the purpose. The very porous woods like mahogany and oak require a liberal application of heavy paste filler to plug the large cavities.

Various commercial fillers can be bought for different filling processes, and they may be lightly colored to match the color of the wood. White lead or white zinc pastes may also be used, and these can be tinted to suit if necessary. Other fillers are available in natural tones. Where the finish will be opaque, Spackle can be effectively used, especially on broad, pocked surfaces like particle board.

Colored paste fillers should always be tried first on scrap stock to make sure that the effect is the desired one. The colored fillers are made by adding turpentine or mineral spirits to the filler base and then mixing in a bit of color until the proper shade and tone is reached. The resulting mixture is scrubbed onto the workpiece surface with a stiff-bristled brush, both with and across the grain, and then rubbed hard with heavy cloth or the heel of your hand to force the material well into the pores. The trick is to rub hard enough to pack the pores and open grains, but not so hard that some of the filler is sucked back out of the cavities, leaving air pockets. A little practice will show you just how the process goes.

Fillers are usually applied after the finish sanding has been completed. The surface must be absolutely clean and dry for best results. All sawdust should be vacuumed from the surface. Vacuuming will effectively pick small particles of dust out of the pores as well. Then, go over the entire surface with a tack rag to pick up any specks that are left. A tack rag, incidentally, is a pad of cheesecloth which has been dipped in a sticky substance, and will pick up the tiniest particles without itself sticking to the workpiece surface. Tack rags are available at most hardware or paint supply stores.

Sealing

Seal coating and wash coating are two identical processes which serve the same purposes. A wash coating has two principal functions, both of which may be obtained on the same workpiece. A coating is spread on the raw finish surface of porous woods prior to the application of fillers. The thin coating provides a hard surface to which the filler can bond readily, and yet does not itself fill the wood pores. A wash coat is also applied over a stained surface to prevent color from seeping into the topcoat finish. Where both filler and stain are used, two separate wash coats may also be applied.

One of the best materials for wash coating, and probably the one most commonly used, is shellac. To make a wash coating solution, mix "orange" shellac (actually it is white in the bottle and goes on clear) with denatured alcohol in a ratio of seven parts of alcohol to one part of four-pound-cut shellac. This mixture can be used in combination with all other finishes except those which are lacquers or are lacquer-based. Whenever the final finish is to be a lacquer, or if any materials containing lacquer thinners are to be used, then the wash coating must be a special lacquer sealer.

Surfacing

This is a process of applying a relatively heavy coating to a raw wood surface which contains slight imperfections, pocks, or wavy grain lines which cannot be readily sanded out. The surfacer builds up in a layer on the wood, and is then sanded off the high spots and remains intact in the low spots, evening out the surface of the workpiece. Where the unevenness of the surface is relatively slight, you can use a surfacer of one part of orange shellac to one part of denatured alcohol. Brush on two or three successive layers and then sand for the final finish.

Where a greater amount of filling is necessary, you can use a material called sander-surface, which is available more often from auto-body repair supply houses than from hardware stores. This is a thick primer-like material which can be either sprayed or brushed on and then easily sanded. Properly applied, even to a rough surface, this material can lead to a fine, smooth finish. Unlike shellac, though, it can only be used with opaque finishes.

FINISHES

When the surface of the wood has been brought to a satisfactory state by the prefinishing processes, it is time to select one or more of the materials designed for a final finish. To help you decide, the following section discusses each of these materials in turn.

Waxes

There are many waxes available for wood finishing, some in liquid form, others in paste form. Most are made from a combination of paraffin, carnauba, and beeswax, with a turpentine thinner. Waxes may be applied directly upon a raw wood surface and will act to some degree as a filler. They may also be applied over some fillers, some sealers, and most topcoat finishes, though in the latter case their use may be redundant. Wax provides a good finish on most surfaces which are carefully prepared, is relatively water resistant, and makes an easily renewable finish. Most waxes will darken the wood color by a small amount; they also emphasize the grain and figure characteristics of the wood.

Stain waxes can be used in the same manner as plain waxes, but the resulting finish will be different in color. Stain waxes have a small amount of pigment added to them, and come in a variety of wood-tone colors. The color and tone which finally results when the stain wax is applied depends upon both the color of the wax and the color of the wood. You should experiment with stain wax to be sure of the color and tone before you apply it to a cabinet project. Maple stain wax applied to white pine, for instance, will look entirely different than if applied to birch or red oak. Remember, too, that the wood surface itself will darken with age, so take this into account. Stain waxes are applied to raw surfaces in one or more coats to gain the desired color effects, and then rewaxing is done with a plain wax.

Oils

Oil finishes are popular today on modern furniture, and look especially nice on certain hardwoods, such as walnut and teak. This

428

finish is not accomplished with the assorted furniture oils and polishes which you find on your grocery store shelves, but with a special mixture which you can easily make up yourself.

A straight oil finish is made by mixing one part of turpentine with two parts of boiled linseed oil. A combination oil-varnish finish is made by mixing one part of turpentine, one part of boiled linseed oil, and one part of spar varnish. The finish is applied to the raw wood surfaces in several initial applications, each rubbed thoroughly and hard. The original wood color will darken somewhat, and will continue to darken and richen slightly as time passes and further applications are made over the years. The finish can easily be renewed, and this is usually done about twice a year. It is a water-resistant coating, but affords no mechanical surface protection.

The Watco oil finish is a somewhat different type. This is a commercial product, ready to use from the can. The finish consists of a combination of oils and resins which are put on in a single application, and it seals, primes, finishes, and protects the surface all in one operation. Unlike the oil treatments mentioned above, the Watco oils penetrate deeply into the wood and then solidify, hardening the wood surface and affording mechanical protection. The finish is also resistant to water and stains. Taken all around, the Watco oil finishes are about the easiest and fastest to apply, and the most easily repaired later on if necessary. They are especially effective with the darker hardwoods such as walnut and teak, but work nicely on all natural wood surfaces.

Shellac

Shellac is not used as a finish as much as it once was, but nonetheless remains a good one. Though shellac will bring out the grain and figure characteristics in a wood surface, it is colorless and adds no tone to the wood. For this reason, it works particularly well where a natural finish is desired on light-colored woods such as white pine or maple. The major drawbacks are a susceptibility to water-spotting and a minimal amount of mechanical surface protection. Four-pound-cut shellac is used in a one-to-one mix with denatured alcohol and several coats are needed to provide a good finish.

Sealer Finish

There are several brands marketed of a special sealer finish which penetrates the wood surface and provides a complete finishing system with only one or two quick and easy applications. It is designed to be used on raw wood surfaces and may be tinted to various shades to achieve the desired final color. The sealer finish works well with all natural woods, is water resistant, and affords a small amount of mechanical surface protection. A final topcoat of the same material, clear instead of tinted, can be added for further protection.

Stains

Stains are widely used to provide both color and a richness of undertone unobtainable with other finishes. Different stains react to different woods in various ways, and should always be experimented with before being used on a staining project. The general characteristics as well as the color of woods can be entirely changed by the use of stains. No other finish will do as much to enhance and accent the natural beauty of wood grain and figure.

Stains consist of two components, the vehicle and the coloring agent. This gives rise to the two basic types of stains, water stains and oil stains, depending upon which vehicle is used. The coloring agents are either dyes or pigments. Water stains are made with dyes, while oil stains may use either dyes or pigments. Pigment-oil stains are made with a mixture of pigment, linseed oil, and turpentine. Penetrating-oil stains are made by mixing soluble dyes with the vehicle oils. There are two other types as well, neither of which is as readily available or useful to the home craftsman. One is spirit stain, which is made by dissolving dye in alcohol. The other is a non-grain-raising stain, made by mixing glycol and alcohol with soluble dyes. Though each has its advantages, particularly in color fastness, working with them is a bit difficult.

You will also run into some additional terms with regard to stains. Transparent stains add a certain amount of color to the wood and bring out the grain pattern, and are thin and not at all obscurative. Semitransparent stains add a much greater amount of coloration and may obscure some of the finer grain patterns. Opaque stains are much like paints, in that they hide everything beneath them. These stains may also be called solid-bodied.

Water stains are inexpensive and easy to apply. The powder is mixed thoroughly with water and the resulting solution applied with a brush. Colors and tones can be mixed to suit, and should be tried on scrap wood first. Remember that, because of the water vehicle, the stain will appear darker when wet but will lighten as it dries. Water stains are relatively quick-drying and fairly resistant to fading when exposed to the light, and the color effects can be deepened by adding more coats of stain as necessary. However, water stains can also raise the grain of the wood and can cause problems with glue joints.

Pigment-oil stains are widely available in a good range of colors. Though fairly expensive, they are ready to use from the can and are easily applied. By following the instructions on the label, you will find no difficulty in obtaining an even, unstreaked finish. These stains can be easily applied with a brush, a roller, or even a rag or sponge. Penetration of the color is not especially good, so the surface can easily be sanded down to plain wood. By the same token, scratches or dents show up rapidly. Grain raising or swelling of the wood surface is not a problem, and this type of stain can be mixed with a filler for combined application. They do fade somewhat, and heavily pigmented types may also chalk upon exposure to the weather.

The penetrating-oil stains are also readily available at most paint stores, and are used for much the same effects and applied in much the same way as pigment-oil stains. They are, however, more subject to fading, and are not used under a lacquer topcoat because they tend to bleed through, even with a sealer.

Lacquer

Lacquer has been a premier finish for many years. Wherever high standards of excellence were required in the way of a finish, lacquer most often was the choice. Today, various synthetic materials are slowly replacing lacquers in many instances. Lacquer finishing is not a usual choice for the home craftsman because of one major double-barreled stumbling block. Lacquer dries very rapidly, and for this reason is best applied with a spraying outfit, in a spray booth with all of the necessary safety equipment, ventilating means, and dustproofing. Few home shops are so equipped. The other barrel of the problem is that because of the fast-drying qualities, lacquer seldom can be successfully brushed on, which is the method most adaptable to home shop work.

Lacquer is a tricky substance to work with, and has a number of distinct advantages and disadvantages. Even though most lacquers today are made from a nitrocellulose base, there are literally dozens of additives which can be mixed in. This means that there is a good deal of incompatibility between the various brand names of lacquers. So much so, in fact, that different brands should never be mixed together, and should be thinned only with thinners made by the same manufacturer.

Nor is lacquer compatible with other types of finishes. For instance, lacquer may be applied over a special lacquer primer, but never over an enamel primer. Lacquer cannot be applied over an old finish coat which is not lacquer, and often cannot be applied over another lacquer coat of a different manufacture. On the other hand, paints, varnishes, and similar finishes can be successfully applied over a lacquer coat. This business of compatibility is one which must constantly be watched, and if you are unsure as to whether there will be any reactions, experiment before going ahead. If there is an incompatibility, the finish will be ruined and the piece will have to be completely stripped and refinished.

Once the technique is mastered, lacquer sprays onto a finished surface beautifully. The fast-drying qualities mean that several applications can be made in a short period of time, and numerous coats built up in short order. This multiple coating—each one is very thin—results in finishes which have a depth and beauty seldom equalled by other finishes, especially when as many as 20 or 30 hand-rubbed coats are used. The resulting finish is durable and has high resistance to water, stains, and dust scratching. Mechanical protection is good and damaged surfaces can be easily repaired, though exact color matching may be difficult. Some of the newer finishes are tougher, though, and more readily applied. Lacquers will not hold up under excessive moisture conditions and will dissolve when touched by any liquid similar in character to its own base, such as nail polish, nail polish remover, and perfume.

Lacquers come in clear and a full range of colors, and are ready to use from the can. Thinning is seldom required and usually is not a good idea. Follow the manufacturer's instructions explicitly. Nearly all lacquer products are intended for spraying use. Lacquers which have been formulated for brush application are so named.

Varnish

Varnish is a tried and true finish which has been around for many decades. Though it is seldom used any longer in commercial cabinetry finishing applications, it still remains a highly effective finish and one which is well suited to home cabinetry applications.

Where lacquer is extremely light, and consists of about 80 percent thinners and additives which rapidly evaporate to leave only a thin coating of solid finish behind, varnish is much heavier. Nearly half of the bulk of liquid varnish remains after the slow drying process is complete, leaving a relatively thick coating of solid material. Varnishes are available in gloss, semigloss, and satin finishes, and may be brushed or sprayed on. When properly done, the brushing application works out nicely, leaving an excellent finish. The resulting surface is tough, has a high water resistance, and is not particularly susceptible to food stains or similar household problems. Coverage is good and the cost is low.

Clear varnish, which actually looks yellow-brown in the can, imparts little additional color to the wood surface and emphasizes grain and figure characteristics while adding depth. Stain varnishes do the same but add a bit of color at the same time. Various shades are available, usually designated as wood colors, such as red maple, mahogany, red oak, and so forth. As with all other stains, some experimenting should be done in order to arrive at exactly the right color. Stain varnishes are applied to raw wood and successive coats will darken the finish a bit. Clear varnish may be applied to raw wood, sealed and/or filled wood, or over stains. Varnish will take over a well-dried oil finish, but not over a wax.

Synthetics

Today, nearly all finishes can be considered as synthetic, since in large measure the use of natural materials was discontinued long ago. However, the general term "synthetics" is for the most part reserved to indicate a new group of finishes which has come into the marketplace only in the past few years. These finishes are entirely manmade and include such items as the urethanes, polyurethanes, epoxies, and polyesters. To the public at large, they are generally known simply as plastic coatings.

Synthetic finishes have a great many advantages. Chief among them is their toughness and durability. Most synthetics are completely impervious to damage by water, alcohol, food stains, thinners and oils, and are highly resistant to dirt and abrasion. They clean quickly and easily, require only a minimum of care and maintenance, and afford a great deal of mechanical surface protection.

Though often expensive, the synthetics are generally easy to apply and can be used almost anywhere for almost any purpose. Both clear and colored synthetics are available, and some of them are compounded for particular uses, such as floor coverings, deck finishes, and furniture finishing. Synthetics may be applied to almost any kind of surface, and over any other kind of finish, including primers, sealers, stains, or lacquers.

Paint and Enamel

Probably the most familiar finishes of all to most of us are the paints and enamels. There are a great many different kinds and various formulations made by numerous manufacturers for assorted specific purposes. Sometimes the names and terminology associated with paints and enamels can be confusing because they vary so widely across the country. There is also a certain amount of incompatibility between the different types of paint. The trick is to settle with a brand name or two that you like and are easily available to you, and then stick with those lines, choosing the most appropiate types of paints or enamels for your intended use. Paints can be bought in an endless array of colors, which you can have custom-mixed to any shade or tone you desire. They are available in high-gloss, semigloss, satin, and flat finishes, all of which may go under slightly different terms. You can also choose between an oil-based paint, latex paints, alkyds, and various other kinds. Some use turpentine or mineral spirits for thinning and cleanup, while others use water for the same purposes. The two types do not mix, though either can be applied as a topcoat over the other.

Paints and enamels are opaque and completely hide the surface. They brush on and level well, and if properly applied have good adhesion. Durability varies with the type of paint. Some require little maintenance and wash easily, while others are more susceptible to marking and harder to keep clean. Your best bet is to consult with a reputable paint dealer, and ask his advice and recommendations for the proper specific paint or enamel to fill your needs. Then use the products strictly according to the manufacturer's directions. Note that drying times, coverage in terms of square footage per gallon, covering and hiding power, and necessary undercoats, all vary considerably with the particular paint or enamel.

FINISHING PROCEDURES

There are dozens and dozens of possible finishing procedures. There is no one method (or finish, for that matter) which is "best" for

434

any given project. Indeed, there is considerable argument among experts as to exactly what the best way might be to produce a given final result. One of the best teachers of finishing procedures is practical experience, and after a time each craftsman will evolve a system with which he is comfortable and which produces the desired results for him.

There is no possible way to go into all of the various finising procedures and techniques here. Numerous volumes have been devoted to the subject, and you can doubtless find more information at your library. However, the following methods are basic and will at least give you some starting points from which you can evolve your own processes through experience, experimentation, and further research.

Shellacking

This is an easy finishing procedure which lends itself well to close-grained woods where a natural effect is desired. The surfaces to be covered should be sanded as smooth as you can possibly get them, until they feel silky to the touch. Use a solution of four-pound-cut shellac mixed with an equal amount of denatured alcohol. With a quality, full-bristled brush, apply an even and smooth coating of shellac to the entire project. Back-brush as little as possible, and do not try to go back over spots which have just been shellacked.

Depending upon humidity conditions, the first coat should be allowed to dry thoroughly, at least for four hours. Then smooth the surface carefully with fine steel wool—number 4/0 is about right—and then put on another coat of shellac. Make sure that all of the tiny broken bits of steel wool have been removed from the surface. Do your work in as dustfree an environment as possible, and allow for plenty of ventilation. After the second coat is dry, steel-wool again and repeat the shellac application. Do the same a third time, and more if you wish. After the last coat has been applied, steel-wool again, still using the 4/0 grade, but rub lightly and carefully. Always go with the direction of the grain. Then apply a coat of high-quality paste wax, well rubbed, and the job is done.

French Polish

This is an old-time method of treating woods which can produce a natural finish of great depth and extremely high gloss when properly applied. Though primarily intended to be put on round work-pieces as they revolve slowly in a wood lathe, French polish can also be applied on small nonmoving projects. The process is less success-ful on large surfaces. Though simple to put on, this finish requires a great amount of elbow grease and not a little sweat, as the ultimate gloss is dependent upon the pressure put on the polishing pad and the consequent heat developed by friction.

The first step is to mix a solution of shellac and boiled linseed oil. The ratio is approximately 1 cup of shellac to 1 tablespoonful of linseed, but this can be varied to suit your liking. Again, a little experimenting is a good idea. Apply a small amount of the solution to a folded pad of fine cotton cloth or cheesecloth and rub the workpiece surface with firm, even strokes. The trick is to keep the pressure as even as possible, and avoid streaking. Replenish the solution from time to time to keep the pad fairly well saturated. Allow the coating time to dry, then start all over again. Usually at least four or five applications, and perhaps more, are necessary to bring up a fine finish. The oil-shellac solution can be tinted or toned slightly with oil pigments such as raw umber.

Waxing

A wax finish is about the easiest to apply in terms of expertise and requires no equipment save for a few rags, but can be tedious and tough on the arm. A power buffer can be a help, though. The workpiece surfaces should be perfectly smooth and satiny to the touch, with all imperfections completely disguised with burnt-in shellac from a stick or some other suitable filler. If stain wax is to be used, make up some samples on scrap pieces of the same type of wood to determine exactly what effects you want to get. Use high-quality liquid or paste waxes made for the purpose. Apply a liberal first coat to the entire workpiece surface in even, firm strokes, and allow the coating to set up for a bit. Polish the surface vigorously and apply a second coat. Continue this process until you have a finish that is to your satisfaction. Note that, once a wax finish is applied, subsequent coatings of other materials are difficult if not impossible to apply.

Oiling

Oiling is a particularly effective way to provide a natural finish on hardwoods and works better with close-grain wood than with open-grain. This is one of the best finishes to use to emphasize grain and figure. It also affords a measure of protection for the wood surface.

Mix one part of turpentine and two parts of boiled linseed oil. Place a pan about one-third full of water on the stove and bring the water to a rolling boil. Place the container of oil and turp into the boiling water and let it remain for about 15 minutes, to heat and thin the oil. Keep an eye on the mixture at all times. Saturate a rag with the mixture, and wipe the entire surface of the workpiece until the coloration is uniform and consistent. Then grit your teeth and commence the hard part.

Choose a small section of the workpiece and rub, rub, rub. Apply plenty of pressure and rub this one section for at least 10 minutes. To get excellent results, you may have to rub for as long as half an hour. Continue the process, always on small sections, until you have covered the entire workpiece surface. If there is any excess oil still standing upon the surface, wipe it off with a clean, lint-free cloth. Then wait at least 24 hours and go through the whole procedure again. Two applications should be considered a minimum and you may well want to apply four or more. The second and subsequent applications will go a bit faster and require a bit less oil as the wood surface finally reaches the point where it can absorb little more. After a month or two has passed, make another application to catch all those spots on the surface where the absorbtion rate or capacity was greater than the remainder. After that, periodic applications can be made to keep the finish looking nice, perhaps on the order of once a year.

Staining

Staining is a popular method of finishing cabinetry because of its ease of application and good flexibility in coloration. Wood grain and figure can be either enhanced or subdued, or even covered completely, and there is a considerable range of colors from which to choose, although most are relatively dark. Usually stains are applied in conjunction with a topcoat for added protection. This topcoat may consist of wax coatings, varnish or synthetic finishes, or oils.

The heavily pigmented opaque or solid-body stains are applied in much the same manner as a paint, using a brush or roller. The surface should be smooth and free from defects. A long drying period, often as much as one or two weeks, should be allowed before applying a topcoat. Transparent or semitransparent oil-pigment stains are handled a bit differently. For maximum coloration and penetration, these stains should be applied to the raw wood surface. If the coloration and penetration is to remain relatively light, brush the surface first with a coating of raw linseed oil, and then wipe off the excess immediately.

Apply the stain with a long, soft-bristled brush, stroking in the direction of the grain. Keep the brush reasonably full of liquid, so that the flow of stain onto the work surface is neither dry nor excessively wet. Let the stain set up for just a few moments, and then go over the surface with a clean, dry, lint-free cloth, rubbing lightly in the direction of the grain in order to blend and even out the coloration, and to pick up any excess stain from the surface. The longer you let the stain set up before wiping, the darker it will become, and thus you have a certain measure of control over the coloration. Additional coats will darken the surface even further. Allow the stain to dry for at least 24 hours, and preferably for 2 or 3 days, before applying a topcoat.

Penetrating-oil stains are applied in much the same way. They do not streak and will lay on quite evenly, so that the mopping-up step is primarily to remove any excess material. If the topcoat is to be lacquer, do not use this type of stain, as it will bleed into the topcoat, even through a sealer. Other kinds of topcoats, however, work nicely.

Water stains are first mixed and then tested on scrap pieces of wood to attain the proper color and tone. Sponge the entire surface of the workpiece to dampen it slightly before applying the stain. Wherever end grain appears, moisten this an additional amount so that it will not absorb a greater amount of stain than the remainder of the surface and thus become too dark. The stain should be applied in long, even strokes with either a long-bristled brush or a clean, fine sponge. Allow the surface to dry for at least 24 hours and then sand very gently, using a fine grade of paper and light pressure. Let the piece dry further for another day or two, clean the surfaces thoroughly with a tack rag, and apply a topcoat.

Varnishing

Varnish can be used alone and directly upon a raw wood surface, or can be used in conjunction with other finishes. It can be applied over sealers, fillers, stains, or even over paint to change the gloss. When starting with raw wood, first thin the varnish in a ratio of

438

one pint of turpentine to one gallon of varnish. Stir the mix thoroughly, but never shake. Make the first application across the grain of the wood, and immediately follow up by brushing the varnish out with the grain. Work in small segments, and always from a dryer area into a wetter one. Work quickly so that the edges of the finish don't have time to dry or begin to get tacky, in this way you will avoid brush marks and laps. Let the finish flow out of its own accord and never go back in an attempt to touch up a spot which looks dry or skipped. This will only make matters worse.

If the application is to be made on a surface which has already had some sort of treatment such as sealer or stain, do not thin the varnish, but use it just as it comes from the can. Choose a good-quality, long-bristled brush suitable for varnish work and proceed as above.

After the first coat is thoroughly dry, usually a matter of 6 to 12 hours under normal circumstances, sand the surfaces lightly with a fine grade of paper and apply a second coat uncut. Continue this process until you have achieved a satisfactory finish.

Lacquering

Although lacquer is usually put on with a spraygun, certain types can be brushed on. In most cases, lacquer is not left as is after the last coat has been applied, but receives further treatment such as rubbing out and polishing. More about that later.

Brushing lacquer should be put on with a brush of about 2- or 3-inch width, depending upon the size of the workpiece. The bristles, such as camel's hair, should be long, fine and extremely soft. Most ordinary paint brushes, especially cheap ones, will not do a creditable job. The workpiece surface should be sealed with shellac or a special sealer before the job begins and the surface should be as smooth as possible. To apply the lacquer, dip the brush to about half the bristle length. Let some of the excess drip away but do not scrape any off on the side of the can, as you normally would with paint or other finishes. Keep the brush well loaded with liquid. Stroke the lacquer onto the workpiece surface in long even paths, with the grain of the wood, and in one direction only. Work from the wet area out onto the dry surface, as rapidly as you can and with as little overlapping as possible. Speed and accuracy of brush placement is important because the lacquer dries so quickly.

Always use lacquer in a well-ventilated area. Often it is possible to work outdoors on a calm day, provided that you stay in the shade.

This is especially advantageous if you are spraying. Dust is a problem only if there is a considerable amount of air motion, because of the fast drying times. Nonetheless, work in as dust-free an area as you can. Humidity will have some effect on the drying time of the lacquer, but usually a wait of about 2 hours is about all that is necessary. Then sand the surface lightly and evenly with a very fine grade of sandpaper and apply a second coat. Again, speed, accuracy and avoidance of backbrushing and touch-up are most important. The second coat of lacquer will partially soften the first coat, so any attempt at doctoring up is likely to prove disastrous. You will probably need a third coat, and might like to have as many as five to complete the job. Once the last coat has dried completely, then the rubbing-out process can begin.

Painting

Paint is widely used on all sorts of home cabinetry and built-ins and provides an excellent finish when properly done. It is one of the easiest and least expensive finishes and has the greatest number of available color variations and tones and decorative possibilities.

Start with as smooth a workpiece surface as you can achieve and make sure that all defects are well filled and sanded. Though paint hides the wood, it will not hide defects, but instead will follow their contours. The color and gloss of the paint also have a bearing, as do the prevailing lighting conditions at the side of the cabinetry. For instance, light-colored surfaces will show defects more readily than dark-colored surfaces. Similarly, glossy surfaces will show every ripple and pit, while flat or matte surfaces tend to hide such defects. The brighter the lighting conditions, the more any imperfections are likely to be visible, while dimness and gloom will hide them. A flat black cabinet located in a dark corner, then, is the best combination for hiding defects. A high-gloss, pure white cabinet directly under fluorescent lighting fixtures will quickly show every bump and pit and line.

A paint job starts with a sealer, a primer, an undercoat, or a sander-surfacer. Some products combine two or more of these functions, such as an undercoat-sealer. On porous, open-grain woods, use a filler as well. When the primary coating is dry, check the surface over thoroughly for pits, pockmarks, blemishes, and other defects. Fill them all with Spackle and then sand the surface thoroughly with a medium-fine grit of sandpaper to smooth out the repair work and to remove any nibs of dust which might have gotten caught up in this primer coat. Then apply the first coat of the final finish material, following the manufacturer's directions and using a clean, high-quality paint brush. Always brush with the direction of the grain and try to avoid scrubbing and back brushing and touch-up as much as possible. Flow the material on evenly and smoothly.

After the first coat has dried completely, check the surface once again for any obvious defects or bits of dust or lint which may have settled onto the paint. Spackle any defects and knock off dust nibs with very find sandpaper in a gentle cut. Steel wool of a fine grade can also be used for this purpose. Then apply a second coat, and the job is finished. As the last coat dries, keep the doors and windows of the room closed, and if possible eliminate all traffic through the area. This will minimize the amount of dust stirred up and will allow a cleaner, smoother finish. A third coat is seldom necessary, but if deemed so, follow the same procedure.

Finishing Softwood Plywood

Finishing softwood plywood, most of which is made from Douglas fir, can be something of a core when either a particularly smooth or an evenly stained appearance is desired. This is because of the nature of the wood grain. The often large and extensive swirls of dark-colored wood are composed of hard fibers and a certain amount of resin. The light-colored areas are made up of much softer fibers and a good deal less resin. The problem arises because of the fact that the absorption rate of the two different hardnesses of fibers is considerably different. The soft areas will absorb more stain, giving the surface a mottled appearance which may be unwelcome. The grain pattern may also be altogether too emphatic for some purposes. This difference in hardness also leads to difficulties in sanding the surface smooth. No matter how hard you try, the sandpaper will remove more soft material than hard, resulting in a ripply effect where the dark hard-grain portions stand slightly above the softer areas. Even an opaque finish does not hide the difficulty, and the grain pattern is quite obvious, especially when viewed in strong side light.

The way to get around the staining problem is to first seal the surface with a half-and-half mixture of denatured alcohol and four-pound-cut shellac. Apply a couple of coats of this mixture, and let it dry thoroughly. Then sand the entire surface of the workpiece, using as large a pad of sandpaper as you can, but with only light pressure. The object is to sand the shellac off the raised hard-grain areas, while at the same time leaving the shellac to coat and fill the lower soft-grain spots. Inspect the surface carefully and frequently to make sure that you don't remove shellac from the low points.

One difficulty with this system is that the shellac is colorless, and sometimes it is difficult to judge exactly what is happening as you sand. Once the hard-grain portions have been sanded clear of shellac, apply the stain. The absorption rates of the two dissimilar areas should now be approximately equal and the stain will go on evenly and yet at the same time present a grain and figure pattern which is not overpronounced. Once the staining is to your satisfaction, you can apply a clear topcoat of wax or varnish for further protection.

If the finish is to be opaque and smooth, you can follow the same procedure of applying shellac. Very likely, more than two coats will be necessary, perhaps as many as five or six. Sanding should be done between coats, again taking care not to remove any of the shellac from the low areas. After sufficient coats have been applied and the excess sanded away from the higher hard-grain areas, the two surfaces will come level. Here again, it is difficult to judge at what point the surface becomes completely level because of the clearness of the shellac. You can get around this difficulty by using a sander-surfacer, which you can buy at auto-body repair supply shops, instead of the shellac. Sander-surfacers are thick and opaque, and are especially compounded for easy sanding. They are best applied with a spraygun, but can be brushed if necessary. Make liberal applications, sanding between coats. Sand the high spots off until the dark, hard-grain areas show through, then apply more sander-surfacer and repeat the process. Eventually, you will find yourself sanding a smooth and level surface with both hard and soft areas completely obscured. Then the finish topcoat can be applied in the usual fashion.

Topcoat Finishing

Topcoat finishing is often done to achieve what is called a furniture finish. In cabinetwork the topcoat material is usually lacquer or varnish, either clear or semitransparent. Though the same process can be applied to some paints, there would be little purpose, except perhaps to somewhat dull an over-glossy surface. This process would add nothing to a painted finish, so the extra work would be rather pointless.

The purpose of topcoat finishing is twofold. The first is to provide a satiny-smooth surface. The second is to achieve certain visual effects in the way of surface appearance, aided and abetted by the manner in which light reflects from the piece. There are several such finishes, but among the most popular are the deep luster finish, the high-sheen satin finish, and the dull satin finish.

Any of these three finishes are led up to by applying two or more topcoats, wih careful sanding between each coat to insure as smooth a surface as possible. A fair amount of sanding must be done during the topcoat finishing process, so the total thickness of the previously applied topcoats should be reasonably substantial to avoid sanding down through them.

A deep luster finish is achieved by first sanding the last topcoat with successively finer grades of wet-or-dry sandpaper and a small amount of water for a lubricant. Start the process with about a 280-grit, then go to a 300-grit, and then a 400-grit. Clean the surface of the workpiece well as you go along. The last sanding should be done with 500-grit paper, followed by a thorough cleaning and drying. Then use a lambswool buffing pad with a deep pile on a rotary polisher to remove the last vestiges of tiny scratches and bring the surface to a high polish. Finish the job by polishing the entire surface with a high-grade furniture cleaner.

The high-sheen satin appearance is reached in much the same way as the deep luster. In this instance, however, the last two steps are different. After the last sanding with 500-grit paper, apply a mixture of rubbing oil and FFF pumice to the surface. Use a block of wood with a felt pad attached to hand-rub the entire surface, always with the grain. Continue this process until the surface is as smooth as you think you can make it. Then clean the surface and do the same thing all over again with a mixture of rottenstone and rubbing oil. As you proceed with this step, check your progress by inspecting the surface frequently after cleaning off a small patch. When the smoothness and sheen are to your liking, quit.

The dull satin finish is probably the easiest of all to achieve. Stop the sanding process when you reach the 400-grit level. Clean the surface thoroughly with a high-grade furniture cleaner and apply a liberal coat of either liquid or paste wax.

A rubbed finish can be achieved on either a lacquer or varnish topcoat with less difficulty than on any of the above finishes. The finish will not be a high gloss, but will be smooth and satiny, with whatever sheen you choose. Basically, there are four steps involved: rubbing out, polishing, cleaning, and protecting. The rubbing out is done with a very fine grit of wet-or-dry sandpaper and a water or oil lubricant. The process need not be extensive, since the object is simply to remove any small traces of dust or surface irregularities left in the final topcoat. Then the polishing is done with very fine pumice or rottenstone, much as outlined above. The job can be done by hand with a felt-covered wood block or with a pad attached to an in-line power sander. Do the cleaning with a soft cloth, warm water, and a small amount of ordinary detergent soap. Follow this up with a thorough drying with a clean, dry cloth. Nooks and crannies and small crevices should be completely cleaned out with the aid of a nail file or some similar instrument and a cloth, so that there will be no buildup of foreign material as time passes. The final protective coat consists of any high-quality furniture polish or wax, thoroughly wiped on and polished off. Those products which contain silicones are especially effective because of their water-repellent properties and relatively hard finish.

Index

447